JESSE LIBERTY'S
from scratch
PROGRAMMING SERIES

Active Server Pages 3.0

from scratch

Nicholas Chase

201 West 103rd Street,
Indianapolis, Indiana 46290

Active Server Pages 3.0 from Scratch

Copyright © 2000 by Que

International Standard Book Number: 0-7897-2261-5

Library of Congress Catalog Card Number: 99-65937

Printed in the United States of America

First Printing: December 1999

01 00 99   4 3 2 1

Trademarks

Warning and Disclaimer

Publisher
Dean Miller

Acquisitions Editor
Michelle Newcomb

Development Editor
Bryan Morgan

Managing Editor
Lisa Wilson

Project Editor
Natalie Harris

Copy Editor
Sydney Jones

Indexer
Larry Sweazy

Proofreader
Juli Cook

Technical Editor
Vince Mayfield

Novice Reviewer
Dallas Releford

Team Coordinator
Cindy Teeters

Software Development Specialist
Andrea Duvall

Interior Design
Anne Jones

Cover Design
Maureen McCarty

Layout Technician
Steve Geiselman
Brad Lenser

Overview

		Introduction	1
Chapter	1	Planning and Designing a Professional Web Site	11
	2	Getting Started with Active Server Pages	41
	3	Creating Interactive Web Content	65
	4	Database Access Using ASP	97
	5	Personalizing the Site Using Cookies and Database Information	133
	6	Adding Person-to-Person Auction Capabilities	179
	7	Creating Electronic Storefronts and Implementing Shopping Carts	231
	8	System Administration via ASP	291
	9	Adding Professional Site Features	363
		Index	381

Contents

Introduction   **1**

Chapter 1   **Planning and Designing a Professional Web Site**   **11**

Why Plan? 11
Defining the Project 12
    The Project Goals 13
    Your Target Audience...14
    User Goals 15
    Content and Functionality...15
    Information Architecture 16
How the Web Works...19
    Windows 2000 20
    Windows 95/98/NT...23
    Other Systems and Options 23
Working With the Personal Web Manager 24
    Creating Directories...27
Building a Shell 29
    Basic HTML 29
    Getting Ready...30
    Formatting Text 30
    Links 32
    Images 33
    Putting it All Together 34
Interface Design...36
Summary 39
Next Steps 39

Chapter 2   **Getting Started With Active Server Pages**   **41**

Using Visual InterDev...41
Using an FTP Client..44
Starting Our Interface 45
What You're Shooting For 50
ASP Basics 57
    Setting a language...57
    Objects 59
    Debugging Your Code 62
    Working Without a Debugger..62
    Where You Go From Here 63
Summary 64

Chapter 3 Creating Interactive Web Content   **65**

The User Interface 65
Typical Content 69
Server Side Includes 75
The Importance of Being Consistent 77
Digging a Little Deeper 80
The Content Linking Component 83
    Creating the List 84
    Creating an Object 84
    Moving Among the Files 87
Content Rotator 89
Banner Ads and AdRotator 90
    Using AdRotator 91
The Page Counter Component 95
Next Steps 95

Chapter 4 Database Access Using ASP   **97**

Creating The Database and ODBC DSN 98
Inserting Records into the Database..100
Creating a Connection to the Database 102
SQL Basics: Insert 104
Adding Interactivity with Forms..106
Data Modeling..115
    Determining Entities 116
    The Actual Tables...118
    Inserting the data 119
Error Handling 120
Completing the Form 123
    Multi-purpose Forms 125
Tidying Up—HTML Tables 127
Summary 130

Chapter 5 Personalizing the Site Using Cookies and Database Information   **133**

Why Personalize? 133
Introduction to Cookies 134
    Cookies and Privacy Concerns 135
    Cookies and Collections...136
Querying the Database 139
Cookie Expiration Dates..149
    Other Cookie Properties 152
Customizing mySpace 154
Putting It All Together 170
Summary 178

Chapter 6 Adding Person-To-Person Auction Capabilities   **179**

Auction Data Model 179

More on RecordSets 197

    Source 197

    ActiveConnection 198

    CursorType 198

    LockType 199

    Options 200

    Constants 201

Moving On..201

Seeing Our Auctions 204

Personalizing Our Site Through myAuctions 216

One More Step: Third Party Components and Emailing Users 225

    You've Been Outbid 227

Next Steps 230

Chapter 7 Creating Electronic Storefronts and Implementing Shopping Carts   **231**

Category Listings..234

Searching For Products..241

Taking Orders 255

    Adding a Product to Your Cart 255

    Counters 268

    Security in an Insecure World (Wide Web) 271

    Reviewing the Order 273

Chapter 8 System Adminstration via ASP   **291**

Security 292

Displaying a Table 296

Storing myLinks Information in the Database...298

Uploading myNews Files: From the Browser to the Server 309

Creating Files on the Server: Formatting the News 319

Reading a File: Importing Product Data 326

    Folders and Subfolders: Moving around in the Filesystem 327

    Reading a File from the Filesystem 331

The Next Big Thing: eXtensible Markup Language...................................340

    Creating XML 344

    Importing XML 345

Transactions and Errors 347

Handling Errors in ASP 359

Summary 361

Next Steps 361

Chapter 9 Adding Professional Site Features   **363**

Know Your Audience 363
    Discussion Groups 366
    Chat Rooms 368
    Upsizing the Database 368
Bells and Whistles 369
    Browser Capabilities 370
    Dynamic HTML (DHTML) 372
    Java Applets 373
Letting the World Know You're Out There 373
Search Engines 374
    The Basics of Search Engines 374
    Stealth Advertising 377
    Link Exchanges and Partnerships 377
    Paid Banners, Sponsorships, and Affiliate Programs 378
    Press Releases and Testimonials 378
    The Real World 378
Where Do We Go From Here? 379
    Keeping in Touch 379

About the Author

Nicholas Chase has worked on websites for companies such as Lucent Technologies, Sun Microsystems, Oracle Corporation, and the Tampa Bay Buccaneers. He got his first email account in 1989, and before immersing himself in the web, he was a physicist, a high school teacher, a low level radioactive waste facility manager, an online science fiction magazine editor, a multimedia engineer, and an Oracle instructor. These days he is an independent consultant, helping companies make the most of the internet. He gets through life with the help of his beautiful wife Sarah, who may never know how important she is to him. They live in Florida with their teenage son Sean.

Dedication

To my father, who knew I could do it long before I did.

Acknowledgments

First and foremost, I'd like to thank my wife for a faith so strong it even convinced me. Thank you also for all those nights you kept me awake so I could make deadlines and especially all those times the words just wouldn't come and you forced me to sit back down and work anyway. There are so many more things to thank you for that I couldn't hope to mention them all here.

I'd also like to thank Seli Groves for all of her encouragement, and for pointing me in the right direction all those years ago.

I'd like to thank my son Sean for putting up with me when I'm overworked and don't have as much time for him as I would like.

Finally, thanks to Michelle Newcomb for getting the ball rolling.

Foreword

Welcome to *Jesse Liberty's Programming from scratch series*. I created this series because I believe that traditional primers do not meet the needs of every student. A typical introductory computer programming book teaches a series of skills in logical order and then, when you have mastered a topic, the book endeavors to show how the skills might be applied. This approach works very well for many people, but not for everyone.

I've taught programming to over 10,000 students: in small groups, large groups, and through the Internet. Many students have told me that they wish they could just sit down at the computer with an expert and work on a program together. Rather than being taught each skill step by step in a vacuum, they'd like to create a product and learn the necessary skills as they go.

From this idea was born the *Programming from scratch* series. In each of these books, an industry expert will guide you through the design and implementation of a complex program, starting from scratch and teaching you the necessary skills as you go.

You might want to make a *from scratch* book the first book you read on a subject, or you might prefer to read a more traditional primer first and then use one of these books as supplemental reading. Either approach can work; which is better depends on your personal learning style.

All of the *from scratch* series books share a common commitment to showing you the entire development process, from the initial concept through implementation. We do not assume that you know anything about programming: *from scratch* means from the very beginning, with no prior assumptions.

While I didn't write every book in the series, as Series Editor I have a powerful sense of personal responsibility for each one. I provide supporting material and a discussion group on my Web site (www.libertyassociates.com), and I encourage you to write to me at jliberty@libertyassociates.com if you have questions or concerns.

Thank you for considering this book.

Jesse Liberty

Jesse Liberty

from scratch Series Editor

Tell Us What You Think!

As the reader of this book, you are our most important critic and commentator. We value your opinion and want to know what we're doing right, what we could do better, what areas you'd like to see us publish in, and any other words of wisdom you're willing to pass our way.

As an Executive Editor for Que Publishing, I welcome your comments. You can fax, email, or write me directly to let me know what you did or didn't like about this book—as well as what we can do to make our books stronger.

Please note that I cannot help you with technical problems related to the topic of this book, and that due to the high volume of mail I receive, I might not be able to reply to every message.

When you write, please be sure to include this book's title and author as well as your name and phone or fax number. I will carefully review your comments and share them with the author and editors who worked on the book.

Fax: 317.581.4666

E-mail: programming@mcp.com

Mail: Tracy Dunkelberger
          Executive Editor
          Que Publishing
          201 West 103rd Street
          Indianapolis, IN 46290 USA

Introduction

In this chapter

- *A Short History of the World Wide Web*
- *Dynamic Content and Active Server Pages*
- *What You're Going To Do*
- *What Aren't You Going To Do*
- *System Requirements*
- *Next Steps*

People decide to learn a new computing technology for one of only two reasons: they want to or they have to. In the world of computers today—especially when it comes to the Internet—no one person can know everything. The best you can hope for is to be able to catch up when you need to. I don't know a single programmer who hasn't had to learn one or more languages or computing technology on the fly, with a project in front of them and a deadline in sight.

Personally, it's happened to me at least three or four times.

Most recently, it happened to me when I was presented with an Active Server Pages project. Not that I hadn't tried to learn ASP before that. I'd checked out resources on the Web, and even started an online class, but while I'd gotten the gist of it—it's not complicated—I knew deep down inside that as busy as I was, the only way I was really going to learn it was to actually build something. That's exactly what you do in this book. Rather than learn a mass of concepts in a vacuum, you build a project from start to finish. There will be plenty of time later to learn all the nuances.

Of course, if you've ever learned a tool or technology by doing this, you know that you spend a great deal of time trying to find the answers to the inevitable questions of syntax and technique that come up as you build. You've very likely—unless you were blessed with one—wished you had someone you could simply ask. Now you do. You and I are going to build this project together, and hopefully I'll be answering all of your questions as they come up.

A Short History of the World Wide Web

Whenever you see a diagram of something that has to do with the Internet, the World Wide Web is most often represented as a cloud—an undefined mass where things go in and come out, but nobody really knows just how. I suppose it's understandable in a way. The Web is a part of the Internet, which is made up of literally millions of computers all attached to one another like the tunnels in a giant anthill.

The Internet is a descendent of ARPAnet, created by the Defense Advanced Research Project Agency (DARPA) in the 1960's. ARPAnet (and subsequently the Internet) was structured so that each computer was connected to two other computers. Messages could be passed along from anywhere on the network to anywhere on the network along different paths, so that a single break in the system would cause a limited number of problems (see Figure Intro.1).

how too pro nouns' it	ARPAnet is one of those acronyms you read aloud instead of spelling out, so it's pronounced are-pa-net.

Figure Intro.1

By connecting each server to two other servers, the designers of ARPAnet limited the capacity for damage. Even if line 1 were cut, messages could still get from A to B by traveling A-D-C-B.

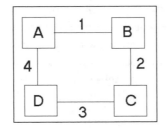

ARPAnet eventually developed into the Internet, a global network that was initially used mostly by scientists and universities. At first, most access was text-based. People sent text-only email. Users logged on to text-based systems. The most graphically-oriented access to the Internet a consumer ever saw was logging into an online service, such as CompuServe, to get text-based Internet mail.

Those were the ancient times—the late 1980s.

Meanwhile, the idea of "linked" documents had been around for decades, starting with Vannevar Bush's seminal article "As We May Think" in the July 1945 issue of The Atlantic Monthly describing the "memex", a machine that would allow users to follow "trails" of information. In the 1950's Ted Nelson discussed the "Xanadu", a system where users could leave annotations on existing linked data, or "hypertext."

Then in 1980, Timothy Berners-Lee, a consultant for the Eurpoean Laboratory for Particle Physics (CERN) created a program called "Enquire" which used "hot spots" to keep track of people and information. In 1989, he wrote a paper proposing that CERN create a hypertext based system to keep track of the multitudes of information it gathered.

It was this system that became the World Wide Web. The first Hypertext Markup Language, or HTML, was published in August of 1991, but most users were able to experience it only as text in a browser such as Lynx, which could handle basic text formatting such as bold and italic and allowed users to "jump" between links. In 1993 a software program out of the National Center for Supercomputing Applications, or NCSA, at the University of Illinois-Urbana/Champaign added something to the mix. Mosaic did everything that Lynx did. It ran on Windows and the Macintosh, as well as UNIX, and it had one very important improvement: it displayed images. Suddenly there was a creative element to this new World Wide Web.

By this same time, the Internet was growing in popularity. Long before the Web, the Internet had email, chat (in the form of Internet Relay Chat, or IRC), and discussion groups (in the form of Usenet).

IRC is short for Internet Relay Chat. It's a system of interconnected servers that enables users to chat with each other in real-time without having to be connected to the same computer.

A *Newsgroup* is a type of electronic discussion forum, or bulletin board. Users leave messages that are forwarded from server to server like email messages. Unlike email messages, which are addressed to a specific person and delivered without intervention, newsgroup messages are stored for general access. A user has to specifically go to a newsgroup to get the messages.

Usenet is a system of interconnected servers that forward messages, maintaining the system of general public newsgroups.

how tōō prō nouns′ it	IRC is one you spell out, so it's eye-are-see.

This new method of displaying information, with its associated images and new-found creativity, captured the public imagination, and the firestorm started.

Dynamic Content and Active Server Pages

When the World Wide Web burst on to the already-established Internet scene in the early 1990s, it was a static medium. A Web page was nothing but a file of text, albeit text specially formatted in HTML. It couldn't change or adapt to user input or current conditions.

HTML, or *Hypertext Markup Language* is a way of using text tags, such as <B> for bold or <I> for italics to mark up, or describe, information so a browser knows how to display it. For instance, a simple page giving information may look like Listing Intro.1:

Listing I.1 A simple HTML page

```
<HTML>
<HEAD>
    <TITLE>Our Home Page</TITLE>
</HEAD>
<BODY>
    <H1 align="center">Welcome!</H1>
    We're so glad you found us here on the World Wide Web.  We've got lots of
    <a href="info.html">information</a> for you!
</BODY>
</HTML>
```

A browser takes this text and formats it into something much more friendly (see figure Intro.2).

Figure Intro.2

Our listing, as viewed in a browser.

Eventually, CGI emerged. The *C*ommon *G*ateway *I*nterface (or *C*ollege project *G*one *I*nsane) gave developers the ability to set things up, so that instead of simply retrieving a static text file, the Web server executes a script and returns the results.

Most CGI scripts were (and still are) written in C or Perl. A Perl CGI script might look like Listing Intro.2:

Listing I.2 A simple Perl CGI script

```
#!/user/bin/perl
use CGI qw(param)

$the_section = param("section")
if ($the_section eq "A" {
    $sitting_with = "with Bob Jones."
} else {
    $sitting_with = "by yourself, for now."
}

print <<TOP_OF_PAGE
Content-type: text/html

<HTML>
<HEAD><TITLE>Seating Arrangements</TITLE></HEAD>
```

```
<BODY>
TOP_OF_PAGE

print "You will be seated $sitting_with"

Print <<BOTTOM_OF_PAGE
</BODY>
</HTML>
BOTTOM_OF_PAGE
```

Static content doesn't change. Most HTML pages are static. Every time you open one with your browser, they say exactly the same thing.

Dynamic content changes and adapts to the situation at hand. When you go to your bank's Web site and pull up your bank balance, that's dynamic content. It changes depending on how much money the bank's mainframe says is in your account at that instant.

This ability to provide up-to-the-minute information gives Web page authors a tremendously powerful tool. Instead of just blindly providing information to the mass of users, they could now accept information from individual people. Searches had been a part of the Web since its inception, but now authors could collect information from their users and provide customized content generated on the fly.

This opened up a whole new world of possibilities, from simple information retrieval to the current boom in electronic commerce.

CGI remains popular today even though there are better solutions for larger projects. This is largely because of its portability, with scripts written in languages that can run on many different platforms.

But CGI still has some issues with scalability and ease-of-use. In most cases, every time a script is called, the CGI needs to start a new process on the web server, execute the script, then clean everything up. In many cases this is sufficient, but when usage grows, it can easily overwhelm a server.

In addition, while the traditional CGI languages, C and Perl, aren't overly difficult to learn, they can be a little intimidating for new programmers, effectively keeping many people out of the dynamic content business.

Scalability is the ability to handle large amounts of activity. Some systems work fine whether there is a small number of users or a deluge, as long as they have enough hardware to back them up. Some, however, consume so many resources that beyond a certain usage level, supporting them becomes extremely difficult, or even impossible.

Active Server Pages, or ASP, changes all that. Instead of running a program that happens to spit out an HTML page, an Active Server Page is an HTML page that happens to have programming commands in it. The reduction in complexity is enormous. What's more, the language generally used for ASPs, VBScript, is a lot simpler than most; it's much easier for a novice to pick up.

> **Note** This isn't to say that simpler is always better. There may be times when you have a complicated task to accomplish and a CGI script written in C will actually be faster and simpler than ASP. "The right tool for the right job" doesn't only apply to hardware!

All of this has the effect of making it easier for potential Web programmers to get started.

What You're Going To Do

In this book you are going to build a Web site for a (fictional) science fiction magazine, Primary Outpost. The magazine contains news and interviews, of course, but also archives, a small memorabilia store, person-to-person auctions, and personalized start pages. (You're going to try and make this site as "sticky" as possible.)

 A Web site is considered *sticky* if it keeps people coming back.

In doing this, you'll cover the following topics:

- HTML: This isn't an HTML book, so I don't cover it too deeply, but I provide the basics for those of you who haven't seen it before.
- The basics of objects: what they are and how to use them.
- Built-In ASP objects: ASP provides a set of objects with which you can do just about everything you need to in a basic, and even not-so-basic Web application.
- Using ActiveX Components: Occasionally you'll bump up against something you can't do with the built-in objects. Fortunately, there are plenty of third-party objects you can use.
- Database Access: ASP makes it easy for you to bring your database to the Web, and vice versa. I also cover some very basic Structured Query Language, or SQL.
- VBScript: When in Rome, it's best to speak Italian. You'll learn the language most commonly used to build ASPs.

- Cookies: For those times when you need to recognize your users.
- Credit Card transactions: The foundation of e-commerce and issues to consider when using them.

What You Aren't Going To Do

ASP has the ability to do some extremely complicated things, but that doesn't mean that you need to learn them all in this book. Since that first project was thrust upon me, I have written or participated in the writing of several commercial ASP-based sites, including one that took several programmers more than a year to complete. Every concept we needed on those projects is covered in this book. Some things that I will not cover are as follows:

- Detailed tuning and maintenance of Internet Information Server. (Unless you're a system administrator, you won't need to do this, and if you are, you'll need to know a lot more than I could ever fit into this book.)
- CORBA
- COM
- Building ActiveX Components

System Requirements

In the course of this book, you need to do two very different things: write ASPs, and read ASPs. Each has its own requirements.

Authoring pages

As with HTML, all you really need to write Active Server Pages is a text editor, such as Notepad or Simpletext. If you have a development tool, such as Visual InterDev or Microsoft FrontPage, great! That will make your life (and debugging!) a little bit easier, but it's by no means necessary. We can't visually debug an ASP script without Visual InterDev and IIS4.0 or IIS5.0, but there are other ways to find out what's going on in our pages.

Serving Pages

After you write an Active Server Page, all you have is a text file. It still needs to be served, or executed by a Web server. Here's where things get a little complicated. Serving the pages can be accomplished in diverse ways and not all of them involve running software on your own machine. Briefly, and grouped by operating system and situation you can serve pages as follows:

Windows 2000: Both Windows 2000 Server and Windows 2000 Professional ship with Internet Information Services (IIS) 5.0, but it is not installed automatically unless you are upgrading a system that had a previous version installed. Instead you will have to add the component to the system using "Add/Remove Windows Components."

Windows NT: Windows NT 4.0 ships with Internet Information Server (IIS) 3.0, which enables you to run ASPs. To get IIS4.0, you will need to first download and install Service Pack 4 or Service Pack 5, then dowload and install NT Option Pack 4. Microsoft may also make IIS5.0 available as a standalone product, but as of this writing, plans had not yet been finalized.

Windows 95/98: You do not need a Big Honking Box to run ASPs. You can run them instead in Microsoft Personal Web Server (PWS) on your desktop Windows 95 or Windows 98 machine. PWS is free, and at the time of this writing can be downloaded as part of the Windows NT Option Pack, available on the Microsoft Web site at `http://www.microsoft.com/Windows/ie/pws/default.htm`. Hardware and software requirements for PWS are:

- 33 MHz or faster processor; Pentium 90 MHz recommended
- 16 MB of memory (RAM); 32 MB or greater recommended
- 40 MB of available hard-disk

Unix/Linux: You can now run Active Server Pages on non-Windows platforms by taking advantage of third-party products that have hit the market. The most prevalent is ChiliASP!, by Chilisoft, which enables you to add ASP support to a variety of operating systems and Web servers. Typically you run a Web server, such as Netscape Enterprise Server or Apache and add ChiliASP for ASP support. For more information on ChiliASP, see `http://www.chilisoft.com`.

Macintosh G4 or other Platforms: Another entry into the ASP market is InstantASP, which will add ASP functionality to any Java-enabled web server. For more information, see `http://www.instantASP.com`.

Older or less powerful PC's, (or if you can't/don't want to run a server on your computer): You can choose to use an external Web host to serve your pages. If you use a Macintosh, this may be your best bet. In this case all you need is a browser and an FTP client.

Web Host: Because of the need for a 24x7 very fast connection to the Internet, few people can host their own Web sites. In most cases, they rent space on someone else's machine, paying a monthly fee in exchange for the ability to publish their content to the Web by placing it on the host machine. These hosts are also referred to as Internet Service Providers, or ISPs, although that's really the company you use to get yourself on the Internet, not your Web site.

An *FTP client* is a program that enables you to transfer a file to another machine on the Internet via the standard File Transfer Protocol. Examples include WS FTP (Windows), and Fetch (Macintosh).

So now that you know where you're going and what you need to get there, let's be on our way!

Next Steps

In Chapter 1, we'll be getting ready to publish our Web site. We'll need to plan and design the site itself, then install our web server software. We'll also look at some very basic HTML and create a shell for our site.

Chapter 1

In this chapter

- *Why Plan?*
- *Defining the Project*
- *How the Web Works*
- *Working With the Personal Web Manager*
- *Building a Shell*
- *Interface Design*

Planning and Designing a Professional Web Site

Why Plan?

I know that you're anxious to start building something. I also know that some of you are already thinking about skipping to Chapter 2, "Getting Started with Active Server Pages." It's only natural. In many (or even most!) programming projects, planning is savagely short-changed. Programmers are eager to dive in and build something, or deadlines are so tight that they think they don't have time to plan. Management needs something by next week! Get out the coffee and start coding!

All of this pressure leads to situations in which the project is started, and then halfway through the project, management decides not to track activity by product, but by customer, or the programmers realize that there's no way to save the reports they've had the application build. Pieces get added on like mismatched additions to a house. One of my favorite sayings is, "If architects built buildings the way that programmers build programs, the first woodpecker to come along would annihilate civilization." This problem is especially bad when you are building something for others. When they get their first look at it, they inevitably decide that they need major changes, and you've wasted a good deal of your time. It's better to agree on a clear definition before you start! The problem might be as simple as changing the look of a few navigational elements. However, if you have dozens or even hundreds of pages and you haven't planned for it, something as simple as changing a button, can take hours, or even days!

Of course, if a project only takes you a few days to put together and you have to scrap it and start over, it isn't that big of a deal, so detailed planning beforehand isn't nearly as crucial as it is on a large project. The project you build in this book isn't very large, and most of the pieces of it could probably be built organically, but I'm going to take you through the steps to plan it anyway.

Organically built programs are started with little or no advanced planning, and the programmer adds each feature as the need for it is discovered.

I introduce planning here for two reasons. The first, and simplest, is the fact that after you get going with the actual project, you're going to have enough to keep track of without wondering what it is that you're trying to build. By putting together a blueprint, you make your life a lot easier.

The second reason is that while I wouldn't want to give the impression that the entire process can be taught in one chapter, it's important to have at least a familiarity with the planning process. Even if you've built sites before, you might find some helpful hints here. The Web evolves so fast that even professionals get left behind in the area of planning and design. The majority of sites on the Web today—and that includes many of the high profile sites!—have grown so organically or were so poorly designed in the first place that they border on unusable, and that doesn't help anybody.

Now, when I say design, I don't necessarily mean the artwork. Artwork is an important—even crucial—element, but it's by no means the only aspect that you need to consider.

Defining the Project

On a typical Web project, you need input from people doing many different jobs. The actual number of people and their functions varies. On this job, you're going to be everybody, but on a typical Web project, you need the following:

- A designer to produce the interface, layout, and art design.
- A writer to produce the copy.
- A programmer if there's any dynamic content—and there almost always is these days, lucky you!
- A producer to keep things together.

Again, that doesn't necessarily mean a minimum of four people, just four jobs. On a corporate project, you might also want to get some input from people in sales, marketing, and even finance.

Fortunately, in this project, you can be everybody and make all the decisions your-self. But you still have things to consider.

The Project Goals

You can't build an effective site until you know what it is you want to accomplish.

In a personal site, the goal might be to have a homestead on the virtual frontier. Maybe you want to provide information about a social cause close to your heart, or a television show that you love, or maybe you, like millions of others, want a place to post those pictures of your cat you need to share with the world. (What is it with cats and the Web, anyway?)

In the business world, however, the goal almost always boils down to one thing: mak-ing money. Businesses are finally learning that making money on the Web doesn't necessarily mean selling millions of books, computers, or whatever. A company Web site can bring in money directly, in the form of e-commerce or advertising revenues, or it can bring it in indirectly, in the form of brand recognition, better customer rela-tions, cutting supply chain expenses, better interactions with suppliers, or decreasing other costs.

E-commerce has meant many things over the past couple of years, but it seems to be settling down to mean selling products or services over the Web. In the past it was also used to refer to business-to-business electronic activities and other areas that are now known as e-business.

I was once involved in building a site for a large telecommunications company that wanted to put its telephone equipment into an online catalog. Management wasn't particularly worried about how many sales came through the site. It already made back the money the site cost by not having to mail a 400 page catalog to the entire list of customers. Instead the company sent out smaller supplements and referred its customers back to the Web site. As an added bonus, it saved around $12 in costs every time a nonpurchasing customer got information off the site instead of tying up phone personnel.

In this case, you are going to build a fictional magazine, *Primary Outpost*. Your goals are as follows, in order of importance:

- To build an audience sufficient for advertising revenue.
- To sell memorabilia and other science fiction-related products.

The order here is important. Because you want to build a large and loyal audience, most of your content and functionality is going to center around providing your users with reasons to stick around for long periods of time, and to come back on a regular basis. You're going to provide constantly changing content and try and build a sense of community into the site.

If you were concentrating on e-commerce, you might focus more on streamlining the purchasing process and making those areas of the site more prominent.

Content includes static and dynamic information that is contained on the site, such as news and product specifications.

Functionality refers to what the user can do on a site, such as bid on auction items or check a bank balance.

Your Target Audience

The target audience determines a lot about how you build and promote your site. It's fairly obvious that a children's gaming site should look and act differently than the online presence of an investment firm, but what may not be so obvious is how your target audience can determine things such as whether you can use newer technologies like Dynamic HTML (DHTML) on your site.

Dynamic HTML is a combination of layout and scripting capabilities that allow someone creating a web page to do things like moving items on the page or changing their appearance when the user rolls the mouse over them. DHTML applies to more than just animations, and can be an extremely powerful tool if handled properly.

For example, in this project, you are aiming for science fiction fans, including professionals who surf from work (on their own time, one would hope!), but mostly students and other consumers surfing from home.

What does this mean for you? I'll discuss the implications in more detail later in this chapter, but here it is in brief:

- Users are likely to be surfing from a relatively slow connection, so you want to keep graphics to a minimum.
- Users have a diverse set of browsers and operating systems, so you can't depend on the latest technology for the site.
- Users may not have the same level of experience and sophistication as those who use the Web every day as part of their job, so you need to keep things simple and user friendly.

Now, this doesn't mean that you can't do an ultra-hip, graphics-heavy site. It just means that if you do, you also need to provide a low-bandwidth alternative, such as a text-only version of the site.

Bandwidth means the amount of information that can be transferred over the Internet connection. For example, a 56Kbps modem is faster than a 28.8Kbps modem, so it is said to have higher bandwidth. An ISDN connection, at 128kbps, has even higher bandwidth. A cable modem can reach speeds up to 27Mbps but in practice it is more like 1.5Mbps (or 1500Kbps).

Kbps and *Mbps* are units of speed for network connections, kilobits per second and megabits per second respectively.

A *T1* is a permanent connection to the Internet, usually found in offices. This has very high bandwidth when compared to traditional analog modems.

Double-publishing means creating two versions of a Web site, usually high-bandwidth and low-bandwidth. This way the user can choose which one to view.

User Goals

For their part, users have goals in mind when they visit the site, and it is beneficial to you to have some idea what those goals are, so that you know whether your design is going to help them or hinder them. In an actual site, users might want to contact the company, order products, check on existing orders, get offline information, or any number of other activities that you can only imagine at this point. Assume that your users have the following goals, in order of importance:

- To get the latest information about their favorite science fiction television series and movies.
- To get together with online friends.
- To obtain science fiction memorabilia.

Now, you're just making educated guesses here. In practice, you could spend money on market research to find out exactly what your audience wants, but in any case, after the site is up you can track what users do to see whether you need to alter these priorities.

Content and Functionality

Now that you know what you're going to try to accomplish, you can define the content and functionality that your site contains. Looking at your audience's goals, you know that at the very least you're going to need the following:

- News
- Interviews
- Spoilers (plot giveaways about upcoming TV shows or movies)
- Archived Information
- Chat and/or discussion forums
- Memorabilia store

Because they're very hot as I write this, this project also includes

- Person-to-person auctions

And to get users to come back, offer them

- A personalized start page

Chat is a window where users can type comments that are seen by everyone else who is in the same virtual room at the time, and see comments made by everyone else.

Discussion forums are similar to electronic bulletin boards, where users can see and respond to comments left in the past, and leave comments of their own.

Information Architecture

After you decide what information you want to put on your Web site, the next (sometimes overwhelming) task is to group things together in a coherent way. This can be especially tough if you have a lot of existing content to knit together. Fortunately, you don't, but you still have to organize what you do have, and the process is pretty much the same.

What you want to do is group different kinds of information together in such a way that visitors can easily find what they're seeking. (Therefore, you wouldn't put Check your order status in the same category as News.) Take your different types of content and write the name of each on an index card. Do the same for your functionalities. In this case, you have the following types of content:

- Current TV news
- Current movie news
- Current book news
- Archived TV news
- Archived movie news
- Archived book news
- Current TV interviews
- Current movie interviews
- Current book interviews
- Archived TV interviews
- Archived movie interviews
- Archived book interviews
- Current columnists
- Archived columnists
- Spoilers
- Chat and/or discussion forums

- Look at catalog
- Order items
- See what's up for auction
- Bid on an auction
- Place an item up for auction

Some things are obvious. The auction and store items should clearly have their own groups. Other things are less obvious. Should you have separate groups for TV items, movie items, and book items? Or should you lump them all under News?

You have the perplexing question: Just how many groups should you have? I'm afraid there is no established answer. Traditional design and psychology say that you should never have more than seven options on your home page. (This is for reasons similar to those that established seven digit phone numbers in the United States.) So that should answer the question, right?

Wrong. Perhaps while surfing you've seen those sites with literally dozens of choices on the home page. They're so crammed full of information that it seems the designers forgot that white space is an essential design element. Why do they do that? They do it because conventional Web wisdom says that the user should never have to click more than three times to get to what they're looking for. This means that your site shouldn't be more than three, or maybe four levels deep.

To put it into web-speak, you must decide whether your site should be deep (with many levels) or wide (with just a few levels, but lots of stuff in each of them). In all likelihood, the ideal arrangement is somewhere in the middle.

The *interface* is the skin on a Web site, which includes buttons, graphics, layout, and so on—the pieces that you see and interact with.

Usability testing means objective testing of an interface to determine how easy or difficult it is for users to find what they're seeking.

You could agonize over these decisions, but because you can always change them later, just press forward. You're going to go with the following groups:

News

- Current TV news
- Current movie news
- Current book news
- Current TV interviews
- Current movie interviews

- Current book interviews
- Current columnists
- Spoilers

News Archives

- Current TV news
- Current movie news
- Current book news
- Archived TV news
- Archived movie news
- Archived book news
- Current TV interviews
- Current movie interviews
- Current book interviews
- Archived TV interviews
- Archived movie interviews
- Archived book interviews
- Current columnists
- Archived columnists
- Spoilers

Personalized Start Page (mySpace)

- Chat and/or discussion forums
- News
- Check on my bids
- Check on my items
- (Selected) current TV news
- (Selected) current movie news
- (Selected) current book news
- (Selected) current TV interviews
- (Selected) current movie interviews
- (Selected) current book interviews

Memorabilia Store (The Bazaar)

- Look at catalog
- Order items
- See what's up for auction

Auctions

- See what's up for auction
- Bid on an auction
- Check on my bids
- Place an item up for auction
- Check on my items

Notice that some items are in more than one place. This is quite all right and is in keeping with the way the Web works. Surfers should never be faced with the old saying, "you can't get there from here." Of course, that doesn't mean we'll have more than one copy, just that you can get to it in different ways, like finding a phone number for the same business in different categories of the telephone directory.

How the Web Works

Now that we know what we're building, we need to look at what we'll need to make it available once it's done. Let's take a look at what a web server actually does.

When you access a Web page with your browser, you are communicating with another computer, possibly halfway across the world. Here's what happens:

1. Your computer looks up the IP address of the computer you're calling. Every computer on the Internet—including yours, while you're connected—has a unique IP address that identifies it to the rest of the Internet. For example, the IP address for `http://www.yahoo.com` is (as of this writing) 204.71.200.67. The IP address is like the computer's phone number.

2. Your computer sends out a message, or request, to that address. To continue the analogy, this is like making a phone call. If nobody is home to answer the phone, it keeps ringing until the browser decides it's not going to get an answer and hangs up.

3. The someone who normally answers the phone, so to speak, is the Web server program. It acts, in many ways, as a switchboard operator, receiving requests and taking the appropriate action.

4. The first thing the Web server needs to do is to determine what is being requested. In most cases, the request is for a static Web page, so the server gets

the appropriate information and sends it back to the browser. Sometimes, however, the request is for dynamic information, such as an Active Server Page. In this case, the Web server has to actually do something, such as execute commands or run a program, to retrieve the information. It does and assembles the information into a page, which it then sends back to the browser.

5. The browser receives the information. It has absolutely no idea, nor does it need to know, whether the page was generated out of 14 databases scattered around the world, or whether it was a plain old text file. All it knows is that it's receiving information. It decides what to do with this stream of information based on the headers—information that comes just before the page and describes what it is. For example, an HTML page is identified as "`text/html`", so the browser knows it needs to look for tags and display the text. An image file might be identified as "`image/gif`", which tells the browser it needs to take that information and reassemble a picture out of it.

The process is actually more complicated than this, but we don't need to deal with the nuances just now.

 An *IP address* is a computer's Internet Protocol address, a four-part number that uniquely identifies it on the Internet. It's like a computer's phone number.

Figure 1.1

In order for a browser to see data over the Internet, it must talk to a web server. This process consists of several steps.

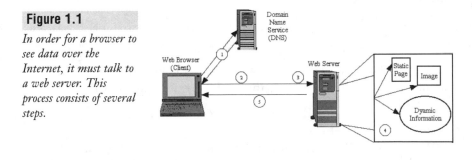

In order to be able to execute any dynamic content on your own personal machine, you'll need to have a web server at your disposal. How you accomplish this will depend on your operating system, but in every case the ASP and HTML will be the same. The important thing is to decide on a set of tools and install it so we can move on.

Windows 2000

Windows 2000 ships with Internet Information Services 5.0 (IIS5.0), which is all we need for serving Active Server Pages. IIS5.0 isn't installed automatically unless you are upgrading a system that had Personal Web Server installed, but adding it isn't difficult. Follow these steps to install and start IIS5.0

1. From the Start menu, choose Settings, then Control Panels. Double click Add/Remove Items.

Figure 1.2

To add a windows component such as IIS, choose Settings/Control Panels from the Start menu, then Add/Remove Items.

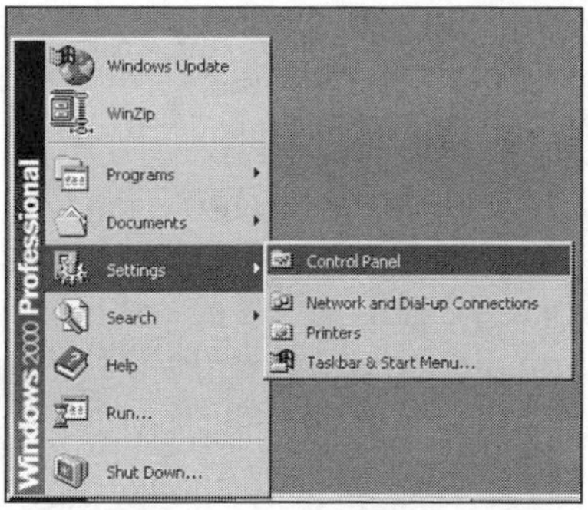

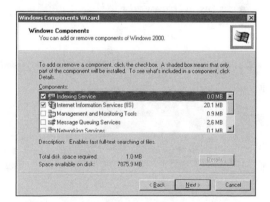

2. Choose Add/Remove Windows Components.

Figure 1.3

Tell the setup wizard to install a new component. You may need your Windows 2000 CD.

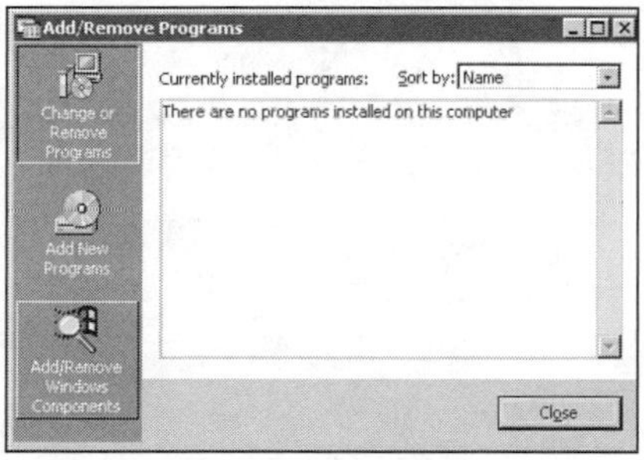

3. At a minium, make sure that the Internet Information Services (IIS) and Script Debugger checkboxes are selected. Click Next. You may need to insert your installation CD.

Figure 1.4

Not all components are necessary for this book's project.

4. The software installs all on its own. When it's finished, click Finish.

From here it depends on your version of Windows 2000. If you are running Windows 2000 Server, you will see an entry under Programs for Administration Tools/Internet Services Manager.

If you are running Windows 2000 Professional, however, you actually have two choices. Go back to Control Panels, as in step 1, but this time double click Administrative Tools. From there we can choose either Internet Services Manager or Personal Web Manager. Both of these tools administer IIS5.0, and neither of them are really new.

The Internet Service Manager is very similar to the interface for IIS4.0. It allows you to start, stop, and manage multiple web sites and other services, such as FTP and email. It looks similar to the Windows Explorer (see Figure 1.5).

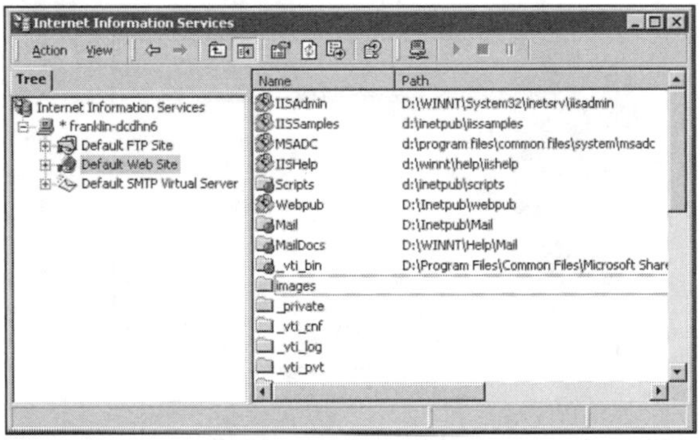

Figure 1.5

The Internet Service Manager gives a webmaster complete control over all web sites hosted on a particular machine.

The Personal Web Manager (PWM) is virtually identical to the interface for Personal Web Server 4.0, which was designed to run on Windows 9x machines. Personal Web Manager is just a front end for IIS5.0, but it's much simpler than the Internet Service Manager.

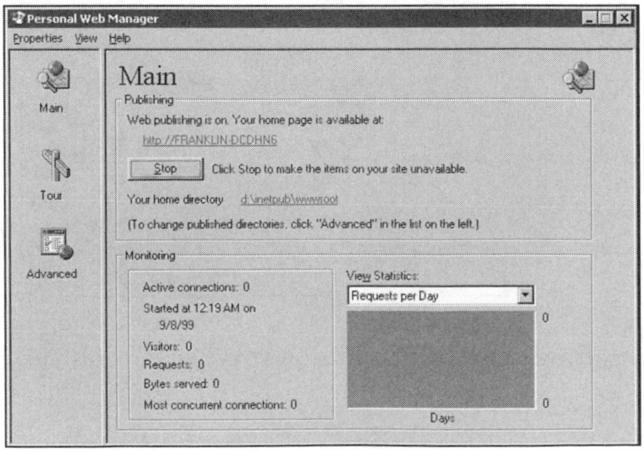

Figure 1.6

The Personal Web Manager allows you to start, stop, and do very basic management of the Default Web Site.

While the Internet Service Manager allows us to do anything we need to on any web site on the machine, PWM allows us to do just a few things, and only to the Default Web Site. The main tasks are to start, stop, make new directories, remove existing directories, and decide whether scripts will run in a particular directory. We won't need to do much more than that in this book, so it's up to you which you choose to use. For simplicity's sake, we'll try to use PWM as much as possible.

Windows 95/98/NT

At the time of this writing, it is unclear whether IIS5.0 will be made available as a stand-alone product for non-Windows 2000 systems.

Fortunately, you don't need IIS5.0 to run Active Server Pages on a Windows system. All you need is Windows 95 or higher and Windows NT Option Pack 4. This is a bundle of software that includes IIS4.0 for Windows NT systems and Personal Web Server for Windows 95/98.

You can download it at:

```
http://www.microsoft.com/msdownload/ntoptionpack/askwiz.asp
```

> The Microsoft site contains a lot of Dynamic HTML that only works in Internet Explorer. If you get only part of the page, you may need to download the Option Pack with Internet Explorer.

In this case, you're actually installing the Download Wizard, which will take care of downloading the rest of the software for you. If you're running Windows NT, it will download IIS4.0, and if you're running Windows 95/98 it will automatically download Personal Web Server instead.

Instructions for installing Personal Web Server can be found in Appendix A.

A *Wizard* is software designed to walk you through the process of doing something, such creating a database or downloading an application.

Other Systems and Options

If you're not running a Unix or other non-Windows system, or if you already have another web server installed and you don't want to install another one, you can use third party products like ChiliASP! (`http://www.chilisoft.com`) or InstantASP (`http://www.instantasp.com`), which run on any Java-enabled web server. These programs will work with your web server to handle ASP files.

Finally, if you're running a Macintosh or a lower-capability Windows machine, these options are probably not appropriate for you, but there is still something you can do. One industry that has exploded in the last several years is Web hosting, where a company takes your pages and puts them on its server, where they become available to the Internet at large. Some of these companies also host Active Server Pages. After you establish an account with one of these providers, the instructions you'll see as we go along are pretty much the same, except that instead of saving your files directly to the Web directory, you need to save a local copy and then upload them to your Web host's machine.

Download means to take a file that is currently on a computer elsewhere on the Internet and put a copy of it on your machine.

Upload means to take a file that is currently on your computer and put a copy on a computer elsewhere on the Internet. This is normally accomplished with the help of an FTP client.

An *FTP Client* is a program used to transfer files over the Internet using the standard File Transfer Protocol.

Working With the Personal Web Manager

As far as serving our Active Server Pages, it makes no difference what server we use. The pages themselves and the HTML they produce will work exactly the same way as far as the browser is concerned. We just need to choose a tool and use it. For the sake of simplicity, we're going to use the Personal Web Manager.

EXCURSION
Using Other Web Servers

No matter what web server you choose to use, the tasks are the same. It's just the way we accomplish them that's different.

If you're using Personal Web Server for Windows 95/98, you'll find that it's virtually identical to the Personal Web Manager. If you're using another web server, check the documentation for instructions.

Start the Personal Web Manager by choosing Start/Control Panels and double clicking Administration Tools and the Personal Web Manager. Every time you open PWM you see a tip, but you can stop this by unchecking the box in the lower-left corner (see Figure 1.7). This will take you to the main management page.

Figure 1.7

You can stop tips from appearing when you start up the Personal Web Manager by unchecking the box on the lower left.

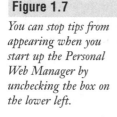

You have the following three options at this point:

- **Main**: This is where you stop and start PWM, and where you can get general information.
- **Tour**: Gives you a basic explanation of the capabilities of PWM.
- **Advanced**: Enables you to create and remove web directories.

You're going to concern yourself only with Main for now. Make sure that the web server is running by clicking Main. If the message in the right hand window tells you that "Web publishing is off" click the Start button. You are now ready to serve your Web pages.

Two important pieces of information reside in the top half of this screen. The first is the name of your machine. The Manager reads, Your home page is available at: and gives you an address (see Figure 1.6).

In my case, my pages are at `http://nick`. This is because when I was setting up my machine, Nick is what I called it. Your machine probably says something different (unless your name happens to be Nick). Whatever name you used, you can use it to see your pages. Click that link to open your browser and display the page that is there. Because you haven't actually published anything yet, this is just the default page for IIS.

 Note

You can change the name of your computer by going to Start/Settings/Control Panel and double clicking the System icon. Click on the Network Identification tab, then click Properties. From there you can enter a new computer name.

In addition to the name you see in your Manager, every Windows machine recognizes the name localhost as referring to the IP address 127.0.0.1. This is a special loopback address, so the machine knows to make the call back to itself. This means you can also use the following URLs to refer to your pages:

http://localhost

or

http://127.0.0.1

Because we all have different names for our machines, I'm going to use localhost to refer our sites throughout this project.

EXCURSION

DNS and Working Offline

When your browser tries to reach another server on the Internet, it first needs to look up the IP address by making a call to a Domain Name Server, or DNS, which is usually at your Internet Server Provider.

Unfortunately, this can be a problem if you're not connected to the Internet, because Windows tries to find the DNS before even trying to make a connection. This happens even if it's a connection to the local machine. In this case, every time you try to access a local page, Windows tells you it's not available while you're offline.

You can keep Windows 2000 from doing this, however.

First start Internet Explorer and choose Tools/Internet Options. Click the Connections tab. Make sure that your Dial-up Settings are set to Never dial a connection, and click LAN Settings. Uncheck all checkboxes except for Bypass proxy server for local addresses. (If it's not checked but it's grayed out, check Use a proxy server, then check Bypass proxy server for local addresses and uncheck Use a proxy server.)

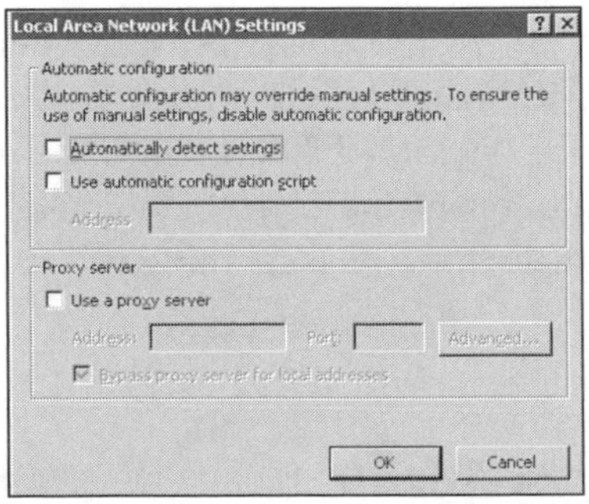

Figure 1.8

Internet Explorer settings for working offline.

Next right click **My Network Places**, then right click Local Area Connection and choose Properties. **Click Use The Following IP Address** and set the IP address to 10.10.1.1, then set the **Subnet Mask** to 255.0.0.0 (see Figure 1.8).

Click **Use the following DNS server addresses** and set the **Preferred DNS server** to 10.10.1.1. This tells the machine to use itself as the DNS server.

> **Warning**
>
> Make a note of your original settings so you can change them back when you want to go back online.

Figure 1.9

DNS settings for working offline.

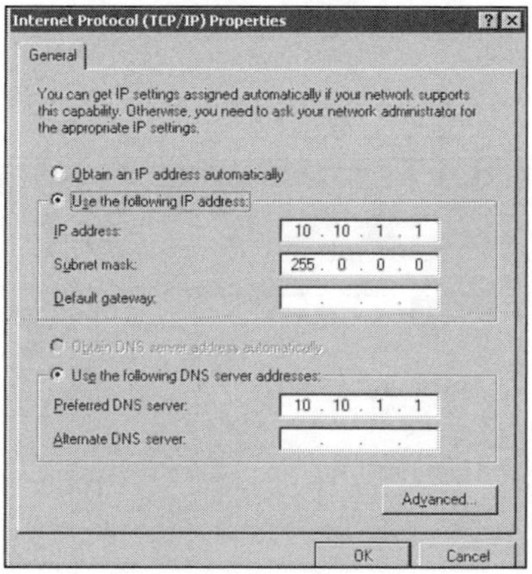

Creating Directories

Now that you've installed the web server, you need to put the files into a directory where it can see them. You certainly wouldn't want to publish your entire hard drive to the Internet. IIS serves only files in directories you specifically designate as available.

We do this by creating a *virtual path*. This is a name that is part of the URL, and tells the server where to look for the real files. For instance, the main directory is called the document root, or home directory. This is the directory the server looks at when you ask for http://localhost/, so we say that it has a virtual path of /.

This virtual path corresponds to a physical path. For the default site in IIS5.0, this physical path is normally C:\inetpub\wwwroot, so that's where the server will look for the files in our home directory.

If we create a directory called images in that directory, the physical path is C:\inetpub\wwwroot\images, and the virtual path is /images. In this way, anything in any directory under C:\inetpub\wwwroot can be made available to the Internet.

This is a double-edged sword. Make sure sensitive files are never placed in a directory that may be made available to your web server.

But what if we wanted a location that wasn't under our home directory? We can also set up virtual directories with different locations, and even different names. Let's say that our images where in the directory c:\work\outpostimages. We can create a virtual directory called /images and map it back to c:\work\outpostimages directly from Personal Web Manager.

In PWM, click Advanced. From here you will see a listing of all current virtual directories (see Figure 1.10).

Figure 1.10

The Advanced option of Personal Web Server allows you to manage virtual directories and their properties.

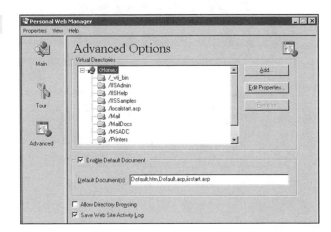

To create a new virtual directory, click Add. You can use the Browse option to navigate to the directory you want to serve, then enter the virtual path as the Alias (see Figure 1.11). Click OK to save your changes.

For this project, we will need to create the following directories.

Physical Path	Virtual Path
C:\inetpub\wwwroot	/
C:\inetpub\wwwroot\images	/images
C:\inetpub\wwwroot\news	/news
C:\inetpub\wwwroot\bazaar	/bazaar
C:\inetpub\wwwroot\auction	/auction
C:\inetpub\wwwroot\mySpace	/mySpace

Figure 1.11

Specify the physical and virtual path for your files.

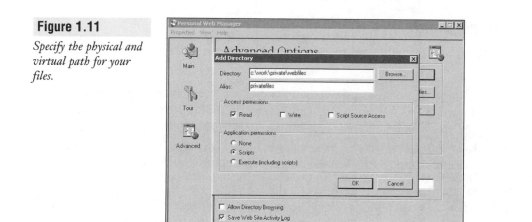

Note

Since the directories are under the home directory and have the same names as their virtual equivalents, you do not need to specify the virtual paths; the server will know where to look for them. If you want to put them in different places or call them by different names, you can do that, just create the virtual directories in the Advanced section of PWM and keep the differences in mind when we talk about file placement.

If you have a different home directory, adjust the physical paths accordingly.

Building a Shell

Now that you've decided on your overall architecture, you're finally ready to build something! What you want to build is a shell—placeholder pages that you can put content into later. You're not going to worry about content or appearance; just link the important pages together. This is a good time for the artist (if you're not wearing that hat as well!) to start working on a design to integrate into the pages later.

Basic HTML

HTML, or HyperText Markup Language, is a way to format a page, so that a browser knows how to display the information. I could devote an entire book to HTML, but for our purposes, you really only need the basics. For a more in-depth treatment of the subject, you can pick up any number of books available.

HTML is a standardized markup language. The current version is HTML 4.0, but everything we do in this book will conform to the previous standard, HTML 3.2. For more information on the HTML standard, see http://www.w3.org.

Take a look at three important concepts: text formatting, links, and images.

Getting Ready

The first thing that you need to do is to go to your computer and create an HTML file.

If you are a professional web developer, you will likely use an authoring tool, such as Visual InterDev. HTML authoring and generating tools have come a long way since their primitive beginnings, and there can be considerable time savings from using them. Even a tool that simply color-codes HTML tags or the ASP sections of a page can drastically reduce errors and the time spent looking for errors.

You don't need anything fancy to create these files, however. If you don't have one, simply start up a text editor, such as Notepad or SimpleText. Almost any program you use to type will do, as long as you can save a file as plain text. You might not want to use Microsoft Word, though because it tries to be a little *too* helpful and interprets HTML like a browser instead of letting you see it. The first HTML pages, housed on UNIX machines, all ended in .html. Because at that time Windows could only handle three letter file extensions, however, .htm also became common-place. Either one will tell the server and the browser that this is an HTML page.

Open a new document and save it as index.htm. Because this is our temporary home page, save it to the home directory.

Formatting Text

HTML is made up of tags, which are enclosed in greater than and less than signs. For example, to tell the browser to start printing in bold, use the bold tag, which is `<B>`. To tell the browser to stop printing in bold, use the tag `</B>`. The slash tells the browser that this is a close tag. In your index.htm file, type the following:

```
This <I>is</I> going to be the <B>main</B> page for our
website, <I><B>Primary Outpost</B></I>.
```

Save the file. Next, look at the file in a browser, such as Netscape Navigator or Microsoft Internet Explorer. Start your browser and send it to `http://localhost/index.htm`.

Note If you do not yet have your web server installed, you can access the page using `File/Open`. This won't work for an ASP page, but it's fine for plain HTML.

You should see the following (see Figure 1.12):

Figure 1.12

A basic HTML page.

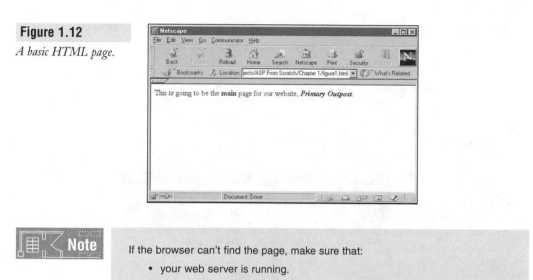

Note

If the browser can't find the page, make sure that:

- your web server is running.
- the file is in the root directory.
- you've typed the URL correctly, with no spaces.

Many other formatting tags exist. I cover them as you use them, but the important thing to understand here is what tags are and how you can use them.

Another important thing to understand is that HTML ignores white space. In your `index.htm` file, add some blank lines and additional text, so that the file reads as follows:

```
This <I>is</I> going to be the <B>main</B> page for our
website, <I><B>Primary Outpost</B></I>.
```

Users will come here first when they come to the site.

Now that you made changes to the file, you want to see them. You do that by getting the browser to take a new look at the file. Click the Reload or the Refresh button and you should see the window change to read as shown in Figure 1.13.

Figure 1.13

HTML ignores white space.

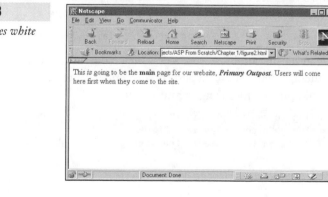

HTML ignores the blank lines you entered, so you have complete control over things, such as line breaks. To insert line breaks and spaces between lines, you use two special tags, the line break tag, `<BR>` and the paragraph tag, `<P>`. So you use

```
This <I>is</I> going to be the <B>main</B> page for our
website, <I><B>Primary Outpost</B></I>. <BR>Users
will come here first when they come to the site.
```

...to give you the output shown in Figure 1.14.

Figure 1.14

The <BR> tag inserts a line break into the page.

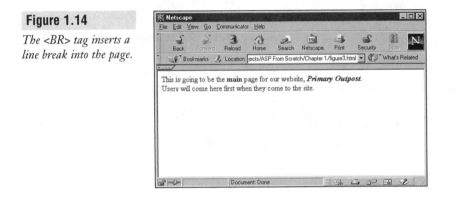

You say you don't see the difference? Remember to reload the page, like you did the last time you made a change. The browser only looks at the file when you tell it to.

The paragraph tag is like the break tag, except that it inserts a blank line between paragraphs, whereas the break tag inserts a line break. (Hence the name.) Try replacing the break tag with a paragraph tag. Save the file and reload it to see the difference.

Links

This is all well and good for formatting text, but you need to do two very important things before you can build your site. You need to put images on the page, and you need to put in links the user can click to go to another page. You designate text as a link with the anchor tag, as follows:

```
The latest information on Active Server Pages is available <A>here</A>.
```

That's fine, but you haven't told it where you want it to go. You do that using an attribute of the anchor tag, `HREF`, or hypertext reference. To tell the browser you want to make a link, put the following tag into `index.htm`:

```
This <I>is</I> going to be the <B>main</B> page for our
website, <I><B>Primary Outpost</B></I>. <BR>Users
will come here first when they come to the site.

<P>
```

1

```
The latest information on Active Server Pages is available
<A HREF="http://www.activeserverpages.com">here</A>.
```

This gives you the output shown in Figure 1.15.

Figure 1.15

Making text into a hypertext link.

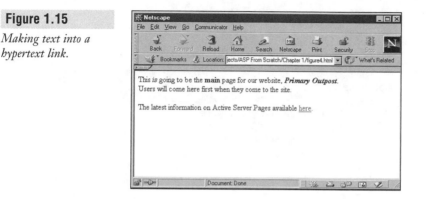

In this case, you have a link you can click for more information. If you're connected to the Internet, go ahead and try it.

Congratulations, you've made a Web page!

Images

OK, so it's not a very attractive Web page right now, but you'll soon take care of that. The first thing to do is to decide on an image to put on the page. On the CD that comes with this book, you will find a small collection of them in the Chapter 1 folder. Back in your operating system, open that folder and the images folder within it. Now drag one of the images to the `home` directory we created earlier. For my examples, I'm going to use `logo.gif`.

Now you need to reference that image in `index.htm`. You do this with the image tag, `<IMG>`. Add the following text to your file:

```
<IMG src="logo.gif">
```

This text tells the browser two things. First, it tells it that you want to display an image, and second, it tells it what the source of that image is. Note that you don't have all that http:// stuff you're used to seeing because this image is in the same directory as your file, so you can use a relative reference.

An *absolute reference* is a complete address, such as `http://www.nicholaschase.com/images/logo.gif`, that doesn't change depending on where it's being called from.

A *relative reference* is a partial address, such as `logo.gif`, that is measured from the place from which it's being called. For example, if the page `http://www.nicholaschase.com/info/main.html` contains the reference `moreinfo.html`, it would point to `http://www.nicholaschase.com/info/moreinfo.html`.

Your `index.htm` file should now look like this:

```
<IMG src="logo.gif">
<P>
This <I>is</I> going to be the <B>main</B> page for our
website, <I><B>Primary Outpost</B></I>.   <BR>Users
will come here first when they come to the site.
<P>
The latest information on Active Server Pages is available <A
HREF="http://www.activeserverpages.com">here</A>.
```

Save the file and reload it (see Figure 1.16). If you don't see the image, or if you get a broken image, check to make sure that you have put the image in the same directory as `index.htm`, and that you spelled it correctly. Also, on most home systems it doesn't matter, but most servers are case sensitive; upper and lower case matter.

Figure 1.16

Adding an image to the page.

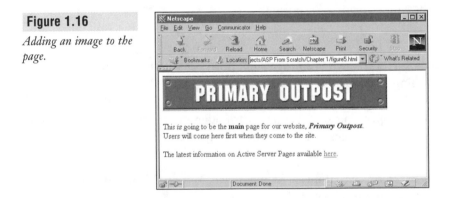

That's all there is to it! Sure, you produced only a very simple page, but you now have all the building blocks that you need. As you go along, you'll learn more about HTML.

Putting it All Together

Now that you have the basics, you're ready to put together the shell of your Web site. You already created the home page, `index.htm`. Now you're going to create the rest of your pages. You could go ahead and create all the subpages under each category, but you can take care of that as you go along. For now, just take care of the main subpages.

1. In your text editor, create a new file.

2. Put a name in your file, so you know what it is when you call it up. For this, use the header tag, `<H1>`. Headers come in six sizes, but `<H1>` is the biggest. Type the following into your file:

   ```
   <H1>Archives</H1>
   ```

3. Save your file in the news directory and call it `archives.asp`. We've changed the file extension because we will eventually be putting ASP commands into the page, so we want to be prepared.

4. Open `archives.asp` in your browser by entering `http://localhost/news/archives.asp` in the location box.

5. Repeat steps 1-4 for the files `news.asp`, `bazaar.asp`, `mySpace.asp`, and `auctions.asp`, saving each in the proper directory. Do the same for `register.asp`, which belongs in the home directory. Feel free to experiment with the text you put into each file. Remember, you can't hurt anything! The worst thing that can happen is that it will look funny, and that never hurt anybody.

Now that you have all the pieces, it's time to put them together. Create a new file called `index.asp` and save it in your home directory. You're going to create a home page for your site. You need to create a header and links to the other pages, and you want it to at least be readable, if not attractive. (You worry about attractive in the next section.) Type the following text on the page:

```
<H1>Primary Outpost</H1>
Your source for science fiction news.
<P>
We will put current news here.
<P>
News
Archives
<P>
The Bazaar
<BR>
mySpace
<BR>
Auctions
```

Now you have your basic page, but you still need to add the links to your other pages. When you're finished, it should look like this:

Listing 1.1— index.asp: Our Home Page

```
<H1>Primary Outpost</H1>
Your source for science fiction news.
<P>
We will put current news here.
<P>
<A href="news/news.asp">News</A>
<BR><A href="news/archives.asp">Archives</A>
<P>
<A href="bazaar/bazaar.asp">The Bazaar</A>
<BR>
<A href="auction/auctions.asp">Auctions</A>
<BR>
<A href="mySpace/mySpace.asp">mySpace</A>
<BR>
<A href="register.asp">Register</A>
```

You've done it! You created a Web site!

Interface Design

Of course, if you try to use the Web site you created, you might notice that it's not very usable. After you go from the home page to one of the subpages, there's no way to get back to the home page short of clicking the Back button. This isn't a big deal when you're only one click away, but it's certainly not a long-term solution if you want people to stick around. After you get an interface design, test it for usability. You made assumptions about what your visitors are likely to want to do. Does your design make it easy for them to do it?

But before you can worry about that, you have to have a design, of course.

If you have any artistic talent, you can certainly do this design yourself. As it happens, I have no artistic talent whatsoever, so I've enlisted the help of my friend Jay to give me a hand in designing the interface for *Primary Outpost*.

Whether you design the interface yourself or recruit someone to do it for you, you should keep some things in mind.

First of all, Web design is not print design. It's becoming less common to find an artist who has absolutely no understanding of Web design, but it still happens. Here are some things you need to remember.

Although the bandwidth situation is certainly improving, the vast majority of Web users still surf by modems—and slow modems at that. This is especially true if you are targeting users outside the United States. This means that you need to be careful when adding graphics to your pages. Every new image is a new connection to the server and takes time. What's more, each of your images must be as small as possible. Now, by small, I don't necessarily mean height or width. Instead, I mean file size. Check to see how big your image files are, and add them all up. The actual numbers vary, but in general, a page shouldn't be more than 60K, including all images.

In certain circumstances, you can relax this restriction a little bit. You don't need to worry about this as much when you're certain your audience has a faster connection. For example, if you are designing for users on your corporate intranet, all (or at least most) of your users are on your local network, so you can build larger pages.

Analyzing our audience can give us information about their likely connection speed and browser. For instance, unlike a business-to-business application, where most users will be on a fast network connection, our audience will be made up of mostly consumers, who access the Internet by modem.

The browser issue is just as important as the speed issue in designing your interface. The first browsers were very simple, and didn't provide developers very much flexibility. In the last few years, things have progressed significantly. Now you can display images and complex animations as well as actually program in the browser. HTML is quickly giving way to Dynamic HTML, or DHTML, giving programmers more control than they ever got from earlier versions of HTML.

The trouble is, most users don't have the latest browser. In fact, a small contingent of users still use Lynx, that text-only browser I mentioned in the Introduction. If your interface requires DHTML, those users won't be able to use it. So what's an enterprising Web designer to do?

Well, one option is to double publish. This means that when visitors come to your site, they automatically access a page appropriate for their browser. Double-publishing almost always requires programming of some sort, and might seem like a lot of work, but it's worth considering. Using this method, you can have your high-octane interface and users who can use it get to use it, but users who can't are still able to use your site.

A simpler interface is also useful for people who use text-only browsers out of necessity. These browsers allow disabled users to access the Internet, and if your site is unusable without the latest technology, these visitors will be deprived of your content, and you will be deprived of their attention.

Note   There are numerous guides to good design availabe in the bookstores and online. Microsoft has a series of articles on various topics at

`http://msdn.microsoft.com/workshop/c-frame.htm#/workshop/design/`

This book is about Active Server Pages and not Web site design, so I'm going to keep things simple. Jay has designed an interface for me that is usable, but not complicated, either for you or for the user (see Figure 1.17).

Figure 1.17

The complete interface concept.

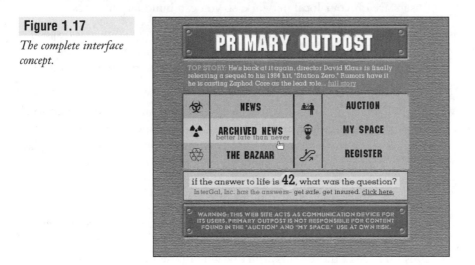

It's got everything you need: menu items, a place for news highlights, and advertising. It's even got rollovers. It is a little more than you can handle right now, though, so I'm going to scale it back, and start with a variation on one of Jay's earlier designs, shown in Figure 1.18.

When you pass your mouse over a *rollover* something changes. The most common use of rollovers is to display more information about the item you're pointing to.

In the next chapter you start to build your Web site. You still need to design the subpages, so that users can get around after they leave the home page, but you get that later.

Figure 1.18

A scaled back version of the interface concept.

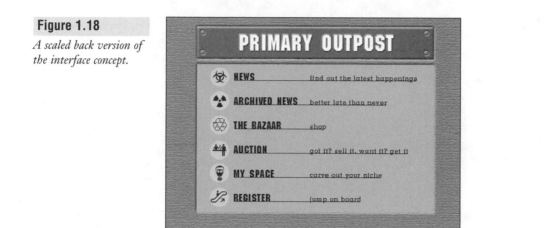

Summary

In this chapter we have planned our site, analyzing our audience and our content. Then, once we knew what we wanted to build, we've prepared the way by installing Internet Information Services 5.0 and creating our directories. We've also built a small skeleton of a site and discussed design issues such as speed and usability.

Next Steps

In the next chapter, we'll be delving more deeply into the structure and details of HTML. We'll also put together a basic Active Server Page and discuss some basic concepts of VBScript, the language we'll be using to build the site.

Chapter 2

In this chapter

- *Using Visual InterDev*
- *Using An FTP Client*
- *Starting Our Interface*
- *What Your're Shooting For*
- *ASP Basics*

Getting Started With Active Server Pages

In the last chapter, we set up a web server and built some basic pages using a text editor such as Notepad or Simpletext. Now let's look at some tools that can make our coding more accurate and faster, or simply allow us to work under less than ideal conditions.

Using Visual InterDev

Like HTML, you can create ASPs with nothing but a text editor, such as Notepad on Windows or vi on Unix, but Microsoft has a tool that can make your life easier. Called Visual InterDev, it's part of the Visual Studio suite of products, and the current version, 6.0, introduces Design Time Controls (DTCs), which are designed to automate the process of building pages. Because you want to learn the actual workings of ASPs, we're not using any of those DTCs. However, InterDev can still make your life easier by color-coding your pages and offering a few other features.

If you have Visual InterDev, install it, and restart your machine if prompted. When your machine has restarted, make sure that the Web server is running. You're now ready to create a new project to contain references to your files.

Choose File, New Project, and choose the New tab. This presents you with wizards designed to help you create different types of projects.

Click New Web Project and type a name for your project, such as Outpost, in the Name text box. The Location text box tells InterDev where to store a working copy of your files. Click Open.

Now you need to let InterDev know where to look for this site on the Internet. InterDev enables you to work remotely on any site, as long as you have the proper security access. If you're using the Web server on your local machine, enter `localhost` (see Figure 2.1). If you're working on a site hosted elsewhere, you need to get the proper information from your hosting company, but it's usually the same as your URL. For example, if I were working on `http://www.primaryoutpost.com`, I would enter `www.primaryoutposte.com` in this text box. Make sure Master mode is selected and click Next.

Figure 2.1

Let Visual InterDev know what machine is hosting your pages.

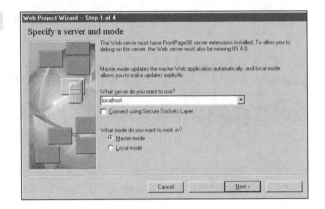

Because you are just starting to work, the logical thing would be to choose Create a new Web application, but if you do, InterDev will put all of your files in a subdirectory instead of in the home directory, where we'll be placing them. If you want to use the same URLs that we will reference in the book, choose Connect to an existing Web application on localhost and make sure that <Root Web> is selected (see Figure 2.2). If you do choose to create a new Web, InterDev will ask if you want to install the Visual InterDev Script Library. This library is required for using Design Time Controls, but is not required for any of the work we will do in this book.

> **Note**
>
> Visual InterDev will install several directories of files in a new application directory. If you have been instructed to connect to a Web that was already set up, click Connect to an existing Web application on localhost and choose the appropriate menu item.

Figure 2.2

In most cases we would have Visual InterDev create a new web for us, but for this book we will use the root web.

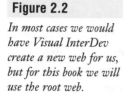

When you create an empty project, you need to add files to it. (Since we're pointing at the server's home directory, you don't need to add those files again.) From the menu, choose Project, Add Web Item, Active Server Page then click the Existing tab and find the files that you want to add. You can highlight multiple files by holding down the Ctrl key and clicking the files that you want to add. Click Open to add these files to your project. InterDev copies them to the Web server.

Once you understand the basics of ASP development, Visual InterDev can speed up your work by prompting you with appropriate code snippets provided in the Toolbox. Before you've reached that point, however, one way that InterDev assists in Web development is by simplifying the process of changing documents on the Web server. Close the Document Outline, Task List, and Properties windows, leaving you with the Project Explorer. In this window you see all the files and folders within your project. (If all you see is the name of the project, try clicking the plus sign (+) to expand that menu.)

To edit a file, double-click it in the Project Explorer. It opens in the right side of the window. When you make changes and save them, Visual InterDev automatically copies the new file to the Web server, saving you the trouble of moving it manually.

 Note

If this is the first time you have worked with the file, InterDev will ask if you want a Working Copy, which will allow you to make changes, or a Read Only copy. You can prevent this window from appearing by clicking Use as default response and making a choice. Even if you choose Read Only, you have the option to overwrite the live copy when you save the file.

Using an FTP Client

If your site is externally hosted, you need to have a way to get your files over to the live machine. If you are not running Visual InterDev, you probably need an FTP program, such as WS_FTP or Fetch. FTP is short for File Transfer Protocol, and it is a way to move files from one machine to another over the Internet.

Different FTP programs, or clients, are available on the Internet, many of which are free. For this example, we use WS_FTP, a Windows 95/98 application, but the concepts are similar, no matter what client you use.

To use an FTP client

- First connect to your Web host. You should have received connection information, such as your hostname, username, and password, when you signed up for service. If you don't have this information, contact your system administrator or help desk.

- When you connect, you see two windows with files or folders (see Figure 2.3). The one on the left (in this case—it could just as easily be on the right, or even on top) is your local directory. That's the directory on your own computer that the program's looking at. The other window is the remote directory, and it probably points to the directory where you will be putting your files. If not, you need to go there, probably by double-clicking your way down through the chain. For example, if you need to put your files in /pub/outgoing/public, double-click the pub directory, outgoing, and then public.

Figure 2.3

Most FTP clients present you with two windows: one for your machine, and one for the destination machine.

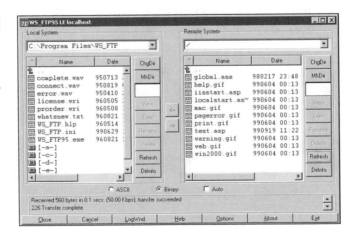

- If your local window isn't pointing to the directory with the files you want to move, change it now, the same way you changed the remote window. You may need to move up the hierarchy. You can do this most easily by double-clicking the two periods (..). Two periods always means to move up one level.

- After both windows point to the proper directories, it's a simple matter to move files from one to the other. In some programs you can drag the file from one window to the other. In others, you need to highlight the file you want to move, and click the arrow pointing in the correct direction. Move the shell files you created in Chapter 1 to your home directory on the server and try to call them up with your browser. For instance, if my hostname were `www.primaryoutpost.com`, I would point my browser to `http://www. primaryoutpost.com/index.htm`.

Just to make sure things are working properly, open up the `index.asp` file and make a change to it. It doesn't matter what you put into it, as long as it's visible. Save the file and click Reload or Refresh on your browser. Even though you saved the file, you won't see the changes because the Web server is still looking at the old file. Move the saved file to the Web server and click Reload again. Now you should see the changes. This is what you need to do as you build your Web site.

EXCURSION

FTP and Windows

Windows 95/98/NT comes with a command-line FTP client. Open a DOS Prompt window and type `ftp <servername>`. This will connect you to the server, where you use:

cd: change directory (same as Windows)

ls: list files (similar to dir)

get <filename>: transfers the file from the remote machine to your machine

put <filename>: transfers the file from your machine to the remote machine

A *live* Web site is a site that is available to the general public. Normally you make changes to a development machine, and the general public doesn't see the changes until you take them live.

Now that you know how to put your pages where you need them, you're ready to build.

Starting Our Interface

In the last chapter, you created the simple home page, shown in Listing 2.1.

Listing 2.1—index.asp: Our simple home page

```
<H1>Primary Outpost</H1>
Your source for science fiction news.
<P>
We will put current news here.
<P>
<A href="news/news.asp">News</A>
<BR><A href="news/archives.asp">Archives</A>
<P>
<A href="bazaar/bazaar.asp">The Bazaar</A>
<BR>
<A href="auction/auctions.asp">Auctions</A>
<BR>
<A href="mySpace/mySpace.asp">mySpace</A>
<BR>
<A href="register.asp">Register</A>

http://localhost/index.asp
```

This is the file you're going to start changing.

 **Note**

If you are not building this project on your local machine, you'll need to adjust the URL's we discuss accordingly. For instance, if you build the project in a web directory called `outpost`, the above URL changes to `http://localhost/outpost/index.asp`.

If you build it on an external machine, it takes the form `http://www.mypersonaldomain.com/index.asp`. Contact your web hosting provider for more details.

In either case, adjust all URL's we discuss accordingly.

Figure 2.4

In the last chapter you created a very basic home page.

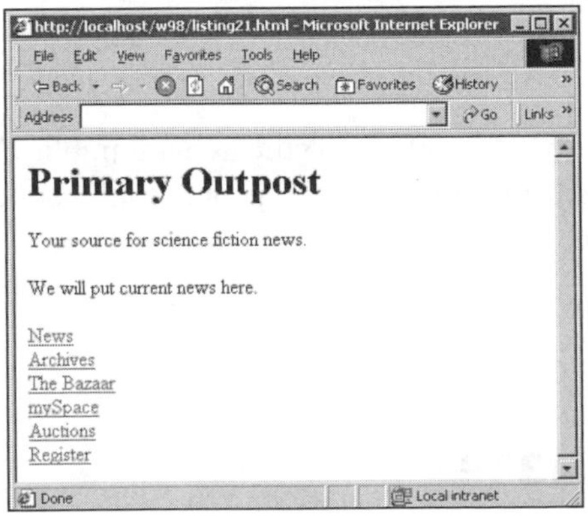

Primary Outpost

Your source for science fiction news.

We will put current news here.

News
Archives
The Bazaar
mySpace
Auctions
Register

First you need to look at the structure of an HTML document. Rather than just a mass of text, an HTML document actually has two sections: the head, where you can put client-side scripting and similar information, and the body, where you put the actual content. You let the browser know where these sections end with their own special tags, shown in Listing 2.2 in bold.

Note Even if you've just been reading along until this point, I recommend actually typing in the HTML and VBScript code you see in the listings. There's no substitute for doing it yourself. If you really, really don't want to do it, however, the listing files are provided on the CD.

Listing 2.2—index.asp: Adding HTML structure tags

```
1: <HTML>
2: <HEAD>
3: <TITLE>Primary Outpost</TITLE>
4: </HEAD>
5:
6: <BODY>
7:
8: <H1>Primary Outpost</H1>
9: Your source for science fiction news.
10:<P>
11:We will put current news here.
12:<P>
13:<A href="news/news.asp">News</A>
14:<BR>15:<A href="news/archives.asp">Archives</A>
16:<BR>
17:<A href="bazaar/bazaar.asp">The Bazaar</A>
18:<BR>
19:<A href="auction/auction.asp">Auctions</A>
20:<BR>
21:<A href="mySpace/mySpace.asp">mySpace</A>
22:<BR>
23:<A href="register.asp">Register</A>
24:
25:</BODY>
26:</HTML>
```

Note The line numbers are not part of the page. They're only there to make it easier to draw attention to specific lines, so don't type them into your code.

The `<HTML>` tag surrounds the entire document, separating it out as a unit in and of itself. Within that unit, the head section is empty, and the body contains your original content. Make these changes to your `index.asp` file, save it, and pull it up in your browser. See anything special on the page? No? That's because everything you added was in an HTML tag, and your browser knows not to display it directly.

EXCURSION

What Happens if My Browser Doesn't Understand a Tag?

Your browser is designed to treat absolutely anything between the less than (<) and greater than (>) symbols as a tag. But not all browsers are created equal; a browser can only understand tags that were in existence when it was made, so as time goes on, new tags are introduced that the browser doesn't understand. For example, tables are useful for formatting information, and we'll talk about them in Chapter 3, "Creating Interactive Web Content." However, when they were first introduced, a whole bevy of browsers didn't know what they were or what to do with them.

Fortunately, the inventors of HTML understood that this was going to happen, and therefore all browsers (in theory, at least) ignore tags they don't understand. So if you were to put together a page that said:

```
This is my <reallynewneatstuff>very own tag</reallynewneatstuff>.
```

it would simply be displayed as:

```
This is my very own tag.
```

It didn't have any effect, but it didn't break the page, either. This also means that you have to be careful when you use these two characters. For example, if you typed

```
Making sure that things are clean is <very, very important>!
```
you would see

```
Making sure that things are clean is!
```

The browser looked at that text as a new tag it didn't understand and simply ignored it.

Since we use HTML 3.2 for this project—considered the lowest common denominator in modern browsers—it seems strange to worry about unsupported tags. The current trend, however, is toward using HTML in many new devices, most of which don't use a traditional browser, instead interpreting the HTML on their own. As developers, it's our responsibility to know what happens to our content when it's accessed in this way.

So if your browser isn't going to display those tags, why bother putting them in?

I can answer that question in one word: standards. Although it seems at times as though HTML is an anarchist's dream, there is actually a standard. Although you may not care about whether you follow the standards, the people who build browsers do. True, at times, browsers display information properly even if the pages don't follow the standard—we just proved that. But it isn't a good idea to count on that because you never know when a user's browser won't cooperate.

For example, one thing you never want to do is overlap tags. Take, for example, a line from your page:

```
We will put current news here.
```

You could format it like this:

```
We <I><B>will</B> put current news here</I>.
```

This formats most of the line in italics, and the word "will" in italics and bold (see Figure 2.5). If you overlap the tags in this manner:

```
We <B><I>will</B> put current news here</I>.
```

you get unpredictable results. Back when Netscape 3.0 was the standard, I was teaching Web development, and I pointed out to students that if they tried that, they might have trouble with older browsers. After all, the current browser would display this just fine. Now the major browsers have moved on to version 4 and 5, and the previous line of code gives you something different (see Figure 2.6).

Figure 2.5

Properly formatted tags.

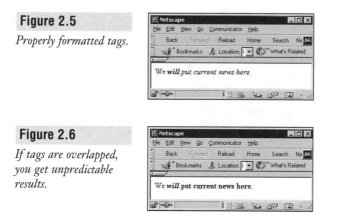

Figure 2.6

If tags are overlapped, you get unpredictable results.

So just because something nonstandard works today doesn't mean it's always going to work. If it's not in the standard, browsers don't have to support it, particularly with the proliferation of HTML in devices such as cell phones.

One thing that did get added to your page is the title. You don't see it on the page, but if you look way up at the top of the window at the menu bar, you see that the title, "Primary Outpost," is added. This is because you placed that text between title tags in the head section. Any text you put between that open and close tag displays in the menu bar.

What You're Shooting For

Now that you're ready to start adding content, take another look at where you're going. You're going to get as close as possible to Jay's simpler design with your currently limited skills. (As you go along, you get a lot closer.)

First you need to get your graphics together. Open the Chapter 2 directory, and drag the images folder to the home directory for your Web server, or, if you already have an images folder, copy the contents into it.

Next you start adding images to your page, starting with the logo at the top of the page. Replace the text header with the image of your logo (see Listing 2.3).

Listing 2.3—index.asp: Adding the logo

```
 1: <HTML>
 2: <HEAD>
 3: <TITLE>Primary Outpost</TITLE>
 4: </HEAD>
 5: <BODY>
 6:
 7: <IMG SRC="images/logo.gif">
 8: <P>
 9: We will put current news here.
10:<P>
11:<A href="news/news.asp">News</A>
12:<BR>
13:<A href="news/archives.asp">Archived News</A>
14:<BR>
15:<A href="bazaar/bazaar.asp">The Bazaar</A>
16:<BR>
17:<A href="auction/auctions.asp">Auctions</A>
18:<BR>
19:<A href="mySpace/mySpace.asp">mySpace</A>
20:<BR>
21:<A href="register.asp">Register</A>
22:
23:</BODY>
24:</HTML>
```

Save the changes and reload the page. That was easy! If you don't see the image on the page, make sure that you

- Copied the file to the Web server, if necessary.
- Spelled the name of the file correctly.
- Put the file in the images directory.
- Made sure that the case matches the file, in case you are hosting on a case-sensitive system, such as UNIX.
- Made sure there aren't any double quotes missing, or any smart quotes left over from the text editor.

You've put the image on the page, but the only people who can see it are the ones who have image-capable browsers and who have images turned on. Web designers often forget that most of the world is still surfing on slow modem connections, and because images take the most time, users frequently set their browsers so that images download only on request. So those people, and people using text-only browsers, such as Lynx, know only that there's an image there, and not what it is. You can fix that by giving the browser text to display. You do that using an attribute of the image tag:

```
<IMG SRC="images/logo.gif" ALT="Primary Outpost Logo">
```

This tag also shows up in many browsers as a notation when the user holds their mouse over the image. Go ahead and add the other images to this page, as shown in Listing 2.4.

Listing 2.4—index.asp: Adding icons

```
1: <HTML>
2: <HEAD>
3: <TITLE>Primary Outpost</TITLE>
4: </HEAD>
5: <BODY>
6:
7: <IMG SRC="images/logo.gif" ALT="Primary Outpost Logo">
8: <P>
9: We will put current news here.
10:<P>
11:<IMG SRC="images/news.gif" ALT="News">
➥<A href="news/news.asp">News</A>
12:<BR>
13:<IMG SRC="images/archives.gif" ALT="Archived News">
➥<A href="news/archives.asp">Archived News</A>
14:<BR>
15:<IMG SRC="images/bazaar.gif" ALT="The Bazaar">
➥<A href="bazaar/bazaar.asp">The Bazaar</A>
16:<BR>
17:<IMG SRC="images/auction.gif" ALT="Auctions">
➥<A href="auction/auctions.asp">Auctions</A>
18:<BR>
19:<IMG SRC="images/myspace.gif" ALT="mySpace">
➥<A href="mySpace/mySpace.asp">mySpace</A>
20:<BR>
21:<IMG SRC="images/register.gif" ALT="Register">
➥<A href="register.asp">Register</A>
```

continues

Listing 2.4—continued

```
22:
23:</BODY>
24:</HTML>
```

You can do couple of things to tweak this page. First, line up the text. Instead of it hanging off the bottom of the image, center it vertically and add a space between the image and the text, like this:

```
<IMG SRC="images/auction.gif" ALT="Auctions" ALIGN="middle">
<A href="auctions.asp">Auctions</A>
```

This code places the text, but the browser won't be able to display it until it knows where the text goes. You could wait for each of the images to download, but then you leave your users staring at nothing, and that's bad. Let me tell you one of the secrets of Web design:

It doesn't matter how fast your pages download. What matters is how fast they *seem* to download.

That means that you can put whatever you want on a page—within reason, of course—as long as the user isn't sitting there waiting for it for more than a few seconds. So to help the browser along, tell it how high and how wide your images are. This way the browser can lay out the text and users can read it while the images are downloading.

If you're creating the images yourself, you probably know the dimensions, but if you're not, there are a couple of ways to find out. You could open them up in an image-editing program, but it's much faster and easier to use your browser. (This trick doesn't work in Internet Explorer, but I use it so often that all by itself it's reason enough to keep Netscape on my machine.)

Position your mouse over the image and right-click. (On a Macintosh, hold down the mouse button.) On the menu that pops up, choose View Image. This shows you the image all by itself, and if you look in the window's title bar, it also gives you the dimensions of the image. (This is also a good way to see where the browser is looking for an image if it doesn't come up, because it displays the address in the location box.)

 Note

Windows 2000 will give you the dimensions of an image from Windows Explorer. Right click on an image, then choose properties. Click the Summary tab, then Advanced.

Add the dimensions of our images and the alignment, as in Listing 2.5:

Listing 2.5—index.asp: Adding dimensions and alignment

```
1: <HTML>
2: <HEAD>
3: <TITLE>Primary Outpost</TITLE>
4: </HEAD>
5: <BODY>
6:
7: <IMG SRC="images/logo.gif" ALT="Primary Outpost Logo"
➥HEIGHT="67" WIDTH="496">
8: <P>
9: We will put current news here.
10:<P>
11:<IMG SRC="images/news.gif" ALIGN="middle" ALT="News"
➥HEIGHT="39" WIDTH="39">
12:<A href="news/news.asp">News</A>
13:<BR>
14:<IMG SRC="images/archives.gif" ALIGN="middle" ALT="Archived News"
➥HEIGHT="39" WIDTH="39">
15:<A href="news/archives.asp">Archived News</A>
16:<BR>
17:<IMG SRC="images/bazaar.gif" ALIGN="middle" ALT="The Bazaar"
➥HEIGHT="39" WIDTH="39">
18:<A href="bazaar/bazaar.asp">The Bazaar</A>
19:<BR>
20:<IMG SRC="images/auction.gif" ALIGN="middle" ALT="Auctions"
➥HEIGHT="39" WIDTH="39">
21:<A href="auction/auctions.asp">Auctions</A>
22:<BR>
23:<IMG SRC="images/myspace.gif" ALIGN="middle" ALT="mySpace"
➥HEIGHT="39" WIDTH="39">
24:<A href="mySpace/mySpace.asp">mySpace</A>
25:<BR>
26:<IMG SRC="images/register.gif" ALIGN="middle" ALT="Register"
➥HEIGHT="39" WIDTH="39">
27:<A href="register.asp">Register</A>
28:
29:</BODY>
30:</HTML>
```

Save and reload the page. One more tweak on the menu items and you'll be almost done with the menu. You know if you click link text, you go to one of the subsections, but you want to make the images into links too. You can do that by including the image tag within the link tag. While you're at it, add the description text for your menu items, as shown in Listing 2.6.

Listing 2.6—index.asp: Turning the icons into links

```
1: <HTML>
2: <HEAD>
3: <TITLE>Primary Outpost</TITLE>
4: </HEAD>
5: <BODY>
6:
7: <IMG SRC="images/logo.gif" ALT="Primary Outpost Logo"
➥HEIGHT="67" WIDTH="496">
8: <P>
9: We will put current news here.
10:<P>
11:<A href="news/news.asp">
12:<IMG SRC="images/news.gif" ALIGN="middle" ALT="News"
➥HEIGHT="39" WIDTH="39">
13:News</A> -- find out the latest happenings
14:<BR>
15:<A href="news/archives.asp">
16:<IMG SRC="images/archives.gif" ALIGN="middle" ALT="Archived News"
➥HEIGHT="39" WIDTH="39">
17:Archived News</A> -- better late than never
18:<BR>
19:<A href="bazaar/bazaar.asp">
20:<IMG SRC="images/bazaar.gif" ALIGN="middle" ALT="The Bazaar"
➥HEIGHT="39" WIDTH="39">
21:The Bazaar</A> -- shop
22:<BR>
23:<A href="auction/auctions.asp">
24:<IMG SRC="images/auction.gif" ALIGN="middle" ALT="Auctions"
➥HEIGHT="39" WIDTH="39">
25:Auctions</A> -- got it?  sell it.  want it?  buy it.
26:<BR>
27:<A href="mySpace/mySpace.asp">
28:<IMG SRC="images/myspace.gif" ALIGN="middle" ALT="mySpace"
➥HEIGHT="39" WIDTH="39">
29:mySpace</A> -- carve out your niche
30:<BR>
31:<A href="register.asp">
32:<IMG SRC="images/register.gif" ALIGN="middle" ALT="Register"
➥HEIGHT="39" WIDTH="39">
33:Register</A> -- jump on board
34:
35:</BODY>
36:</HTML>
```

Now if you click the image, it takes you to the subsections, but you still have that ugly blue line to deal with (see Figure 2.7). Your final tweak is to take out the blue line and make the images blend in with the background. You can do that by setting the background color of the page to match the background color of the images (see Listing 2.7).

Figure 2.7

Your images are links now, but that gives them a blue border unless you do something about it.

Listing 2.7—index.asp: Hiding image borders and setting a background color

```
 1: <HTML>
 2: <HEAD>
 3: <TITLE>Primary Outpost</TITLE>
 4: </HEAD>
 5: <BODY bgcolor="#32C800">
 6:
 7: <IMG SRC="images/logo.gif" ALT="Primary Outpost Logo"
➥HEIGHT="67" WIDTH="496">
 8: <P>
 9: We will put current news here.
10:<P>
11:<A href="news/news.asp">
12:<IMG SRC="images/news.gif" BORDER=0 ALIGN="middle" ALT="News"
➥HEIGHT="39" WIDTH="39">
13:News</A> -- find out the latest happenings
14:<BR>
15:<A href="news/archives.asp">
16:<IMG SRC="images/archives.gif" BORDER=0 ALIGN="middle"
➥ALT="Archived News" HEIGHT="39" WIDTH="39">
17:Archived News</A> -- better late than never
18:<BR>
19:<A href="bazaar/bazaar.asp">
20:<IMG SRC="images/bazaar.gif" BORDER=0 ALIGN="middle" ALT="The Bazaar"
➥HEIGHT="39" WIDTH="39">
21:The Bazaar</A> -- shop
22:<BR>
23:<A href="auction/auctions.asp">
```

continues

Listing 2.7—continued

```
24:<IMG SRC="images/auction.gif" BORDER=0 ALIGN="middle"
➥ALT="Auctions" HEIGHT="39" WIDTH="39">
25:Auctions</A> -- got it?  sell it.  want it?  buy it.
26:<BR>
27:<A href="mySpace/mySpace.asp">
28:<IMG SRC="images/myspace.gif" BORDER=0 ALIGN="middle"
➥ALT="mySpace" HEIGHT="39" WIDTH="39">
29:mySpace</A> -- carve out your niche
30:<BR>
31:<A href="register.asp">
32:<IMG SRC="images/register.gif" BORDER=0 ALIGN="middle"
➥ALT="Register" HEIGHT="39" WIDTH="39">
33:Register</A> -- jump on board
34:
35:</BODY>
36:</HTML>
```

Right about now you're probably looking at that body tag on line 5 and asking yourself what that crazy code is. If I wanted green, why didn't I just say green? I could have, but the color would have been too dark, and you wouldn't be able to see the text on it. Fortunately, in addition to a few dozen pre-set colors, such as blue, pink, and yellow, you can set exactly the color you want by specifying the red, green, and blue, or RGB values. They look a little funny, though, because it's a hexadecimal value. This means that instead of the normal base 10 numbers we deal with every day, where the first digit is 0 to 9 and the second digit is 10, 20, 30, and so on, it's a base 16 number, where the first digit is 0 to 15, using 0-F, and the second digit is 16, 32, 48, and so on. In this case, the red value is 32, or 50 ((3x16) + 2), the green value is C8, or 250 ((12x16) + 8), and the blue value is 00, which means there's no blue at all.

Finally, on lines 12, 16, 20, 24, 28 and 32 you tell the browser that you don't want the border around the images by setting it to zero, so the images blend in with the background (see Figure 2.8).

Figure 2.8

Your home page is complete for now.

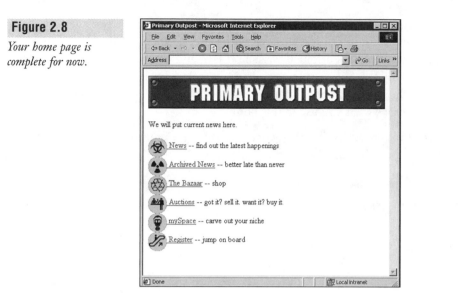

ASP Basics

Now that you have the basics of HTML, it's time to move on to actual Active Server Pages. First you need to tell the Web server that you want an Active Server Page so it knows to look for ASP commands.

A Web server knows what to do with a file based on the file extension, or the letters after the period in the name. For example, the file extension for index.htm is htm. This extension tells the server that the file is just a plan HTML file, so it should serve it as is, and let the browser know to look out for tags.

When we created our second file, index.asp, we told the web server that there may be ASP commands in it, so look for them before serving the page. In past versions of IIS, this caused the server to process the page as though it had commands even if it didn't, which slowed things down. In version 5, however, Microsoft added scriptless processing, where pages can have the asp file extension but the server won't process them as ASP unless they have any commands. This enables you to name your pages with the asp file extension if they might have commands in the future, saving you the trouble of fixing links later.

Open it in your browser and your text editor.

Setting a language

A common misconception among some Web developers is that Active Server Pages is a programming language. It's not. Instead, it's a programming platform of sorts— an environment in which your programs live. As such, you can use any language that your Web server understands to build your Active Server Pages. The two most popular languages are VBScript (a subset of Visual Basic) and JScript (slightly different from JavaScript, which was originally based on Java and is now more of a language of its own). Personal Web Server supports them both. Perhaps logically, since Microsoft created ASPs, the most common language used for putting together ASPs is VBScript, and that's what you use in this book.

First you need to tell the Web server what language you're using for this page. You do this at the top of the page (see Listing 2.8).

Listing 2.8—index.asp: Setting a language

```
0: <%@ LANGUAGE="VBSCRIPT" %>
1: <HTML>
2: <HEAD>
3: <TITLE>Primary Outpost</TITLE>
4: </HEAD>
...
```

 Note   The ellipsis (...) is not part of the code. When you see that, it means that that part of the page doesn't change, so you should leave it alone.

Take a close look at line 0. It almost looks like a tag, but those percentage signs (%) are significant. They tell the server that it needs to take a look at what's between them. The @ sign tells the server that this is the language declaration. You can make only one language declaration per page.

Another special version of this tag requires some explanation. Have you ever seen pages that show you the current date and sometimes even the time? You're going to include them right now. Add the following line to your page (see Listing 2.9).

Listing 2.9—index.asp: Adding text using ASP

```
...
4: </HEAD>
5: <BODY bgcolor="32C800">
6:
7: <IMG SRC="images/logo.gif" ALT="Primary Outpost Logo"
➥HEIGHT="67" WIDTH="496">
8: <P>
9: <%= "Today is Monday." %><P>
10:We will put current news here.
...
```

On line 9, with the text <%=, you told the server that you want it to print something to the page. Of course, it's kind of silly to use this to print out something you could just put on the page. The code in Listing 2.10 makes more sense.

Listing 2.10—index.asp: Printing the current date on the page

```
...
7: <IMG SRC="images/logo.gif" ALT="Primary Outpost Logo"
➥HEIGHT="67" WIDTH="496">
8: <P>
9: Today is <%= Now %>.<P>
10:We will put current news here.
...
```

In VBScript Now is a predefined function that automatically gives the current date and time. Of course, if that were all you could do with Active Server Pages, it wouldn't be terribly useful! Normally you have a block of commands, or code. Let's take a look at how you would print information from within one of those code blocks.

Objects

The first thing you need to look at is the idea of objects. You know what an object is in real life: a chair, a telephone, a computer. These objects have properties, such as upholstery type, color, or model number. They can also do several things. The phone on my desk will ring when a call comes in, place a call when I dial the number, or put the caller on hold when I press a button. In object-oriented terminology, these are methods of the telephone; they are things it can do. These methods and properties are fairly set for each object. Talking about the upholstery type of my computer doesn't make much sense, and my chair doesn't ring when a call comes in. (I can sit on my phone, but that's not good for either one of us.)

In computer programming, objects are similar. They have properties and methods. For example, I might create an object called myHat. It might have properties, such as size, color, and amount currently in stock. It might also have methods, such as the ability to decrease the amount in stock when somebody orders a hat.

You get six built-in objects with Active Server Pages:

- Server
- ObjectContext
- Application
- Session
- Request
- Response

It's the last one, `Response`, that I'm going to discuss right now. `Response` is, as you might imagine, the object that's responsible for returning the page to the browser. It literally responds to the `Request` object. The `Response` object has a number of properties, such as whether the output should be sent to the browser as it's created, or held and sent when processing is complete, and a number of methods, such as the very useful `write` method. It's this last one that you're going to use (see Listing 2.11).

Listing 2.11—index.asp: Using Response.Write

```
...
7: <IMG SRC="images/logo.gif" ALT="Primary Outpost Logo" HEIGHT="67"
➥WIDTH="496">
8: <P>
9: Today is <% Response.Write Now %>.<P>
10:We will put current news here.
...
```

That's the format, or syntax for using a method of an object: `objectname.methodname`. You use this over and over again as you continue.

Notice also that you changed the first part of this tag to <% from <%=. That's because you don't want it to just print something, you want it to look at the code inside. Of course the code inside doesn't do anything you couldn't do more simply, so let's shake things up a little bit. Let's customize your greeting depending on the day of the week, as shown in Listing 2.12.

Listing 2.12—index.asp: Using an if-then-else statement

```
...
7: <IMG SRC="images/logo.gif" ALT="Primary Outpost Logo"
➥HEIGHT="67" WIDTH="496">
8: <P>
9: Today is <%= Now %>.
10:
11:<%
12:if Weekday(Now) = vbSaturday then
13:    response.write "Have a good weekend!"
14:else
15:    Response.Write "Hang in there, the week will get better!"
16:end if
17:%>
18:<P>
19:We will put current news here.
...
```

First off, on line 12 you check to see if it's Saturday.

Unfortunately, there's no easy way to get the day of the week out of a date. (It'd be simple to write something, but for now stick with what you already have.) The

Weekday function takes a date and returns an integer from 1 to 7. Because that's not very convenient, VBScript defines several variables for you to make your code more readable. After all, you could have written the following:

```
if Weekday(Now) = 7 then
```

but that's not very obvious months later when you go back to figure out what's going on. So instead, you can use the VBScript variables. You'll look more at functions later, but for now it will do to have a general understanding of what you're doing.

What you're doing is asking the server to check something for you. If it's true, you want it to do one thing, if it's not, you want it to do something else. This if-then-else statement is one of the most important things you will use later on, so look at it a bit more closely. If the condition is true—if today is Saturday—then the server executes all the following statements until it reaches something telling it to stop. In most cases this is either the keyword else, which tells it what to do if the statement is false, or the keywords end if, which does just what it says: it tells the if statement where to end.

An if-then statement won't just do what's in the code block, in fact. You could rewrite the if-then statement as shown in Listing 2.13.

Listing 2.13—index.asp: Using an if-then-else statement with HTML

```
...
7: <IMG SRC="images/logo.gif" ALT="Primary Outpost Logo"
➥HEIGHT="67" WIDTH="496">
8: <P>
9: Today is <%= Now %>.
10:
11:<% if Weekday(Now) = vbSaturday then %>
12:
13:    Have a good weekend!
14:
15:<% else %>
16:
17:    Hang in there, the week will get better!
18:
19:<% end if %>
20:
21:<P>
22:We will put current news here.
...
```

A quick note about formatting: Very few real requirements for formatting in VBScript or ASPs exist, but your eyes (and co-workers!) will thank you if your code is as readable as possible.

Debugging Your Code

No matter how carefully you plan, you will always encounter errors in you code, whether they're typos, such as leaving out a quotation mark or other required punctuation, or logic errors, such as specifying "greater than" when you really mean "less than." Finding them can be difficult, depending on the type of error.

If you are working directly on the server and you're using IIS, you can take advantage of the Microsoft Script Debugger. This program allows you to set breakpoints in your script, to step through your script one line at a time, and to view the values of your variables and how they change while the script is running.

To use the Microsoft Script Debugger to analyze your pages, you first need to enable Server Side Debugging on the server. In the Internet Services Manager, right click the default web site and choose `Properties`. Click the `Home Directory` tab, then `Configuration`. Select the `App Debugging` tab, then the `Enable ASP server-side debugging` checkbox. When an error or intentional stopping point is reached, the Debugger will start, open the file in question, and point out the likely source of the error.

> **Warning**
>
> Never enable server side debugging on a production server. At best it will slow down processing. At worst it has been known to take down not only the site being debugged, but also other sites on the machine.

A good debugger can save you hours of work looking for errors. I encourage you to investigate what using a debugger can do for you.

Working Without a Debugger

If we're not working on the actual server, or if we are using Personal Web Server or another non-IIS solution, we don't have the option of using Debugger. That doesn't mean we're out of luck, however. We can still get your scripts to tell us what's going on. We just have to ask.

Let's consider our existing home page. If it were Saturday, and we didn't see the Saturday message, we'd want to know why. We could add debugging statements that give us more information about what's going on. I'm going to introduce an intentional typo into the code, and add some statements to help us find it in Listing 2.14.

Listing 2.14—index.asp: Debugging without a Debugger

```
...
7: <IMG SRC="images/logo.gif" ALT="Primary Outpost Logo" HEIGHT="67"
➥WIDTH="496">
8: <P>
9: Today is <%= Now %>.
10:The value of Weekday(Now) is <%= Weekday(Now) %>, and vbSaturday is
➥<%= vbSaturday %>.<P>
11:<% if Weekday(Now) = vbSatrday then
12:    Response.Write "It's TRUE"%>
13:    Have a good weekend!
14:
15:<% else
16:    Response.Write "It's FALSE" %>
17:    Hang in there, the week will get better!
18:
19:<% end if %>
20:
21:<P>
22:We will put current news here.
...
```

I'm being a little more formal here then we probably need to be, but the important thing is that we're checking two things: value and flow.

On line 10, we're printing the value that we're looking at to the page. We're also making sure that there's text immediately before and after it so we can see if any extra spaces or other unexpected characters are getting added.

On lines 12 and 16 we're checking to see whether the if or the then is being executed. In this case it's obvious, but many times instead of displaying information we'll be doing calculations, and this can help isolate logic errors.

What we find out here is that Weekday(Now) and vbSaturday are returning what we expect, but that the if-then-else statement is still going to the wrong place. That means there can be only one culprit: the if-then-else condition. A careful look points out the typo. In some cases it's helpful to copy and paste text from the area in question to the debugging print statement. The human brain often sees things differently from how they really are, especially on a computer screen.

Don't forget to remove your debugging statements before the application goes live!

Where You Go From Here

If you've been following along, you've created a fully functional Active Server Page. Granted, it doesn't do much, but that's all right, it will grow as you go along. In doing this, you should have a good handle on what HTML is, how it works, and the basics of Active Server Pages.

Summary

You covered a lot of ground in this chapter, and you're ready to get started building your site. You have

- Installed and configured software to change your pages, such as Visual InterDev or your text editor and FTP client.
- Learned enough HTML to build our basic home page. We've created the basic HTML structure, then added images and looked at their attributes. We also set the background color for the page.
- Created a very basic Active Server Page using an if-then-else statement and looked at how to debug a page, even if you don't have a debugging tool.

In Chapter 3 we'll look at adding content to the site. We'll also look at Server Side Includes and using components such as the Content Linking Component and the Ad Rotator Component.

In this chapter

- *The User Interface*
- *Typical Content*
- *Server Side Includes*
- *The Importance of Being Consistent*
- *Digging a Little Deeper*
- *The Content Linking Component*
- *Content Rotator*
- *Banner Ads and AdRotator*
- *The Page Counter Component*

Chapter 3

Creating Interactive Web Content

In Chapter 2 we discussed the basics of HTML and of using VBScript to create Active Server Pages. In this chapter, we're going to look at various ways to add content to your pages. These include server side includes and ASP components.

Now that you're comfortable with the basics, you can start putting together some of your content sections. You're going to start with the *News* and *Archives* sections and then take one more look at the home page.

The User Interface

The first thing you need to take care of is the user interface. If every page looked like the home page, there wouldn't be any room for content, so you're going to move the buttons up to the top of the page, next to the logo. You still want the buttons to be links. Ultimately, you want something like Figure 3.1.

User interface refers to the graphics and text that help the user navigate through an application or Web site.

A *Graphical User Interface* includes graphics, buttons, and other form elements that make it easier for a user to accomplish tasks with a system. Non-GUI interfaces are text-only, and rely heavily on keyboard commands.

GUI is short for Graphical User Interface.

Figure 3.1

Ultimately, your user interface will look something like this.

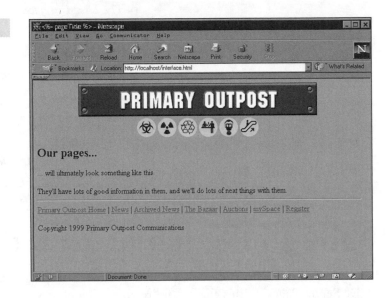

It's easiest to use index.asp as a starting point and customize from there. Make a copy of it and save it in the home directory as news.asp. (We'll eventually use this to replace the original news.asp file.) If you remove the text links and turn the buttons into two rows of three, your code looks like Listing 3.1.

Listing 3.1—news.asp: Adding the interface

```
1: <%@ LANGUAGE="VBSCRIPT" %>
2: <HTML>
3: <HEAD>
4: <TITLE>Primary Outpost</TITLE>
5: </HEAD>
6: <BODY bgcolor="32C800">
7:
8: <IMG SRC="images/logo.gif" ALT="Primary Outpost Logo" HEIGHT="67"
➥WIDTH="496">
9: <A href="news/news.asp">
10:<IMG SRC="images/news.gif" BORDER=0 ALIGN="middle" ALT="News" HEIGHT="39"
10a:WIDTH="39">
11:</A>
12:<A href="news/archives.asp">
13:<IMG SRC="images/archives.gif" BORDER=0 ALIGN="middle" ALT="Archived News"
13a:HEIGHT="39" WIDTH="39">
14:</A>
15:<A href="bazaar/bazaar.asp">
16:<IMG SRC="images/bazaar.gif" BORDER=0 ALIGN="middle" ALT="The Bazaar"
16a:HEIGHT="39" WIDTH="39">
17:</A>
18:
19:<BR>
```

```
20:
21:<A href="auction/auctions.asp">
22:<IMG SRC="images/auction.gif" BORDER=0 ALIGN="middle" ALT="Auctions"
22a:HEIGHT="39" WIDTH="39">
23:</A>
24:<A href="mySpace/mySpace.asp">
25:<IMG SRC="images/myspace.gif" BORDER=0 ALIGN="middle" ALT="mySpace"
25a:HEIGHT="39" WIDTH="39">
26:</A>
27:<A href="register.asp">
28:<IMG SRC="images/register.gif" BORDER=0 ALIGN="middle" ALT="Register"
28a:HEIGHT="39" WIDTH="39">
29:</A>
30:
31:</BODY>
32:</HTML>
```

 Note

When I have to break a line because it's too long for the page, I'll note it with a letter, like I'm doing here with lines 10 and 10a, 13 and 13a, etc. Unless otherwise indicated, it's up to you whether to break them up in your own pages.

If you look at this page in your browser, you'll see that the buttons don't quite line up the way you want them. This is because for now, the image can only have one line of information lined up next to it. You want to display multiple lines, with the image on the left. To do this, tell the browser that you want to align the logo image to the left, as shown on line 8 in Listing 3.2.

Listing 3.2—news.asp: Aligning the logo to the left

```
...
6: <BODY bgcolor="32C800">
7:
8: <IMG SRC="images/logo.gif" ALT="Primary Outpost Logo" HEIGHT="67"
8a:WIDTH="496" ALIGN="left">
9: <A href="news.asp">
...
```

Remember, the ellipses are not part of the code, they just show you that those lines haven't changed. Save the file and then reload it in your browser.

> If you notice tiny blue underlines, or artifacts, between your images, make sure that there are no spaces or returns between the end of your image tag, `<IMG>`, and the close link tag, `</A>`. If there are, your browser may treat it as a space and try to make a link out of it.
>
> We've done this with the listing we just created, in fact. By putting the link open and close tags on separate lines from the image to make the code more readable on lines 8 through 29, we included a return that the browser translates into a space and tries to turn into a link. (See Figure 3.2)

Figure 3.2

Including spaces or returns between an image and the close tag for a link can cause artifacts to appear on the page.

 An *artifact* is unintended visual dirt that appears on a page or image after processing.

This technique also works with multiple lines of text. You can align an image on the right side of the window by using `align="right"`. In this project, the next line of text is likely to wind up under the logo, but to make sure, use a special form of the break tag, as shown in Listing 3.3.

Listing 3.3—news.asp: Putting text under an image

```
...
28:<IMG SRC="images/register.gif" BORDER=0 ALIGN="middle" ALT="Register"
28a:HEIGHT="39" WIDTH="39"></A>
29:<BR clear="left">
30:Our news will go here.
...
```

This code tells the browser to skip down until the left side is clear of images or other items.

We're building the interface that you use throughout the rest of the site. It's fairly compact, and it allows users to get to almost anywhere from almost anywhere. One thing it doesn't allow, however, is for the user to get back to the home page. So to take care of that, turn the logo into a link to the home page, as shown in Listing 3.4.

Listing 3.4—news.asp: Adding a link back to the home page

```
7: <BODY bgcolor="32C800">
8: <A href="http://localhost/index.asp">
9: <IMG SRC="images/logo.gif" ALT="Primary Outpost Logo" HEIGHT="67" WIDTH="496"
➥ALIGN="left" 9a:border=0></A>
10:<A href="news.asp">
...
```

Adding a link back to the home page seems like a fairly trivial thing, but it's not. When designing your site, keep in mind that some customers will *not* enter your site by way of the home page. They might enter it from search engines and links from other sites, and there's no telling where these visitors will start out. Users need to be able to get back to the home page quickly and easily, or they will feel lost and leave.

Typical Content

Now that you've got the interface settled, it's time to add some content. On the CD, in the Chapter 3 folder, find a file called news.txt. This folder contains the news to add to this page, but it needs a bit of massaging before it's ready.

Open the file in your text editor. It looks fine there. Copy and paste it into your page, as shown in Listing 3.5.

Listing 3.5—news.asp: Adding news items

```
1: <%@ LANGUAGE="VBSCRIPT" %>
2: <HTML>
3: <HEAD>
4: <TITLE>Primary Outpost</TITLE>
5: </HEAD>
6: <BODY bgcolor="32C800">
7: <A href="http://localhost/index.asp">
8: <IMG SRC="images/logo.gif" ALT="Primary Outpost Logo" HEIGHT="67" WIDTH="496"
➥ALIGN="left" border=0></A>
9: <A href="news.asp">
10:<IMG SRC="images/news.gif" BORDER=0 ALIGN="middle" ALT="News" HEIGHT="39"
➥WIDTH="39"></A>
11:<A href="archives.asp">
12:<IMG SRC="images/archives.gif" BORDER=0 ALIGN="middle" ALT="Archived News"
➥HEIGHT="39" WIDTH="39"></A>
13:<A href="bazaar.asp">
14:<IMG SRC="images/bazaar.gif" BORDER-0 ALIGN="middle" ALT="The Bazaar"
➥HEIGHT="39" WIDTH="39"></A>
15:<BR>
16:<A href="auctions.asp">
```

continues

Listing 3.5—continued

```
17:<IMG SRC="images/auction.gif" BORDER=0 ALIGN="middle" ALT="Auctions"
➥HEIGHT="39" WIDTH="39"></A>
18:<A href="mySpace.asp">
19:<IMG SRC="images/myspace.gif" BORDER=0 ALIGN="middle" ALT="mySpace"
➥HEIGHT="39" WIDTH="39"></A>
20:<A href="auctions.asp">
21:<IMG SRC="images/register.gif" BORDER=0 ALIGN="middle" ALT="Register"
➥HEIGHT="39" WIDTH="39"></A>
22:<BR clear="left">
23: <h2>Breaking News</h2>
24:
25:The long awaited pilot "Mission to Destiny" will finally hit
26:the airwaves this coming Sunday night.
27:
28:The latest in Sorcha Wexford's Spell Makers saga is hitting the stores.
29:
30:The Unknown Gossip Columnist has another installment of news.
31:
32:Five hundred fans showed up last week with written petitions
33:to protest the cancelling of "Roller Rink Zombie Bimbos from
34:Jupiter" the sf comedy that has been aired on the APV network
35:for the last five years.  "It doesn't any  sense to kill the
36:show off now," said Megan Smith, president of the RRZBJ fan
37:club.  "Although the ratings did drop for a while, they're
38:back up now and better than ever."
39:
40:Alex Reed, star of "The T Men" will be in Tahiti next month
41:filming the opening episode of the new season.  "The 'T Men'
42:are having a very difficult time concentrating on thier lines
43:whenever the native dancers are on the set," said Alex.
44:
45:Jason Jennings will be making a guest appearance at the opening
46:of the new "Space Detectives' ride at the Sci-Fi Amusement Park
47:in Los Angeles, California next month. He will be signing autographs
48:and posing for pictures on October 15th.
49:
50:Fans have raised over $20,000(US) to donate to charity in honor
51:of  Chad Kelly, the late star of "Robert's Renagades".  Kelly
52:died last month from lung cancer.

53:
54:</BODY>
55:</HTML>
```

Save news.asp and open it in your browser. You'll notice that the text is all squished together (see Figure 3.3.) Remember, HTML ignores white space. You can fix this a couple of ways. The first way is to tell the browser to display the text exactly as you type it (see Listing 3.6). We do this with the preformatted text tags on lines 24 and 53.

Figure 3.3

Text might look fine in your text editor, but it requires formatting before it becomes HTML.

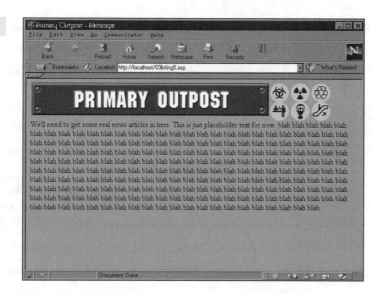

Listing 3.6—news.asp: Using preformatted text

```
...
21:<IMG SRC="images/register.gif" BORDER=0 ALIGN="middle" ALT="Register"
➥HEIGHT="39" WIDTH="39"></A>
22:<BR clear="left">
23: <h2>Breaking News</h2>
24:<pre>
25:The long awaited pilot "Mission to Destiny" will finally hit
26:the airwaves this coming Sunday night.
27:
28:The latest in Sorcha Wexford's Spell Makers saga is hitting the stores.
29:
30:The Unknown Gossip Columnist has another installment of news.
31:
32:Five hundred fans showed up last week with written petitions
33:to protest the canceling of "Roller Rink Zombie Bimbos from
34:Jupiter" the sf comedy that has been aired on the APV network
35:for the last five years.  "It doesn't any  sense to kill the
36:show off now," said Megan Smith, president of the RRZBJ fan
37:club.  "Although the ratings did drop for a while, they're
38:back up now and better than ever."
39:
40:Alex Reed, star of "The T Men" will be in Tahiti next month
41:filming the opening episode of the new season.  "The 'T Men'
42:are having a very difficult time concentrating on their lines
43:whenever the native dancers are on the set," said Alex.
44:
45:Jason Jennings will be making a guest appearance at the opening
```

continues

Listing 3.6—continued

```
46:of the new "Space Detectives' ride at the Sci-Fi Amusement Park
47:in Los Angeles, California next month. He will be signing autographs
48:and posing for pictures on October 15th.
49:
50:Fans have raised over $20,000(US) to donate to charity in honor
51:of  Chad Kelly, the late star of "Robert's Renegades".  Kelly
52:died last month from lung cancer.
53:</pre>
…
```

Let's take a look at the page. The line breaks and indents are there, all right, but the font isn't particularly attractive, and if you resize your browser window, the text doesn't adapt. Another way to lay out the text is to put horizontal lines between the news items, as shown in Listing 3.7.

Listing 3.7—news.asp: Adding horizontal lines between items

```
Done. --- Nick…
21:<IMG SRC="images/register.gif" BORDER=0 ALIGN="middle" ALT="Register"
➡HEIGHT="39" WIDTH="39"></A>
22:<BR clear="left">
23: <h2>Breaking News</h2>
24:
25:The long awaited pilot "Mission to Destiny" will finally hit
26:the airwaves this coming Sunday night.
27:<HR>
28:The latest in Sorcha Wexford's Spell Makers saga is hitting the stores.
29:<HR>
30:The Unknown Gossip Columnist has another installment of news.
31:<HR>
32:Five hundred fans showed up last week with written petitions
33:to protest the canceling of "Roller Rink Zombie Bimbos from
34:Jupiter" the sf comedy that has been aired on the APV network
35:for the last five years.  "It doesn't any  sense to kill the
36:show off now," said Megan Smith, president of the RRZBJ fan
37:club.  "Although the ratings did drop for a while, they're
38:back up now and better than ever."
39:<HR>
40:Alex Reed, star of "The T Men" will be in Tahiti next month
41:filming the opening episode of the new season.  "The 'T Men'
42:are having a very difficult time concentrating on their lines
43:whenever the native dancers are on the set," said Alex.
44:<HR>
45:Jason Jennings will be making a guest appearance at the opening
46:of the new "Space Detectives' ride at the Sci-Fi Amusement Park
47:in Los Angeles, California next month. He will be signing autographs
48:and posing for pictures on October 15th.
49:<HR>
```

```
50:Fans have raised over $20,000(US) to donate to charity in honor
51:of  Chad Kelly, the late star of "Robert's Renegades".  Kelly
52:died last month from lung cancer.
...
```

We've taken out the preformatted text tags and added horizontal rules on lines 27, 29, 31, 39, 44 and 49. These lines break up the items on the page while still allowing the layout to adjust if the user changes the size of the window. At this point, you could say that this page is done, but you shouldn't. It provides information, yes, but that's all it does. The nature of the Web is the interconnectedness of information. You've gotten users to come this far into the site and read the news, now lead them to other information.

You can create links to other news on your site. For example, maybe you have an article about "Mission to Destiny" on the site. You can create a link to that. Perhaps you have an episode guide to "Roller Rink Zombie Bimbos from Jupiter." You can create a link to that as well. Or maybe you just want to provide more information on a current story.

Before you add any of these links, you need the pages they're going to link to, which are included on the CD, but think a little bit about where to put them. On the one hand, it doesn't seem to matter where you put the files physically because you're going to be linking to them. But remember that other people are going to be linking to these files from their own sites. This means two things to you.

The first thing that it means is that after you put these pages out there, you want to leave them there indefinitely. Few things are more frustrating than finding a link to exactly what you want and then discovering that the information is no longer there.

The second thing that it means is that you want your URLs to make sense, so users looking at it can get a sense of where they are on the site. Because this is a fairly simple project, we've created a news directory for all your news items in your Web server's home directory. Drag the files destiny.asp, allissa.asp, and spoilers.asp into this directory.

Add some links to them from your news items, as shown in Listing 3.8.

Listing 3.8—news.asp: Adding links within the content

```
...
24:
25:The long awaited pilot <a href="news/destiny.asp">
25a:"Mission to Destiny"</a> will finally hit
26:the airwaves this coming Sunday night.
27:<HR>
```

continues

Listing 3.8—continued

```
28:The latest in Sorcha Wexford's Spell Makers
28a:<a href="news/allissa.asp">saga</a> is hitting the stores.
29:<HR>
30:The <a href="news/gossip.asp">Unknown Gossip Columnist</a>
30a:has another installment of news.
31:<HR>
32:Five hundred fans showed up last week with written petitions
33:to protest the canceling of "Roller Rink Zombie Bimbos from
34:Jupiter" the sf comedy that has been aired on the APV network
35:for the last five years.  "It doesn't any  sense to kill the
...
```

It's important to note that these links are relative links. The browser starts in the current directory, which in this case is the home directory, or "/", and looks for a directory called "news", and then looks for the file itself. Save news.asp, and then open in your browser. Click the link for Mission to Destiny, and it should bring you to

http://localhost/news/destiny.asp

Now call up the file by sending the browser to

http://localhost/news/news.asp

When you click the same link, you get an error message telling you the file can't be found. Why? You know the link works; you just used it! However, because it's a relative link, the browser looks for http://localhost/news/destiny.asp, which doesn't exist. How can you stop this? You could hard code the URLs, as shown in Listing 3.9.

Listing 3.9—news.asp: Hard-coding a link location.

```
...
24:
25:The long awaited pilot <a href="http://localhost/news/destiny.asp">
25a:"Mission to Destiny"</a> will finally hit
26:the airwaves this coming Sunday night.
27:<HR>
...
```

But then you'd have big problems if you moved the site to another machine, say, to an external host. Fortunately, you do have another solution. All you really need to do is tell the browser where to look in relation to the home directory by starting the URL with "/", as shown on line 25 of Listing 3.10.

Listing 3.10—news.asp: Relative versus Absolute Links

```
...
24:
25:The long awaited pilot <a href="/news/destiny.asp">
25a:"Mission to Destiny"</a> will finally hit
26:the airwaves this coming Sunday night.
27:<HR>
...
```

This solution works in any file in any directory because you provided a starting point that doesn't depend on where you already are.

3

> **Warning**
>
> Relative links will only work within a site. If you are pointing to a page on another server, you will have to use an absolute URL.

Server Side Includes

You probably noticed that the subpages you called up in the last section were... well, not particularly attractive. At the very least, they don't match the rest of the site. You need to get your interface onto each page. You could copy and paste the information. After all, you didn't do anything special with it, so it is appropriate for any of your subpages. But what if instead of 3 pages, you had 300 pages? Or 3000 pages? All of a sudden, copying and pasting doesn't make as much sense.

Instead, of copying and pasting, you can use a Server Side Include (SSI). An SSI is when the server takes information from one file and includes it as part of another file. For example, you can take all the HTML that makes up the top of your file and separate it into another text file. This file is called `pagetop.txt` on the CD, or you can create the file yourself. Drag it to your server's home directory. You can then tell the server that you want to include this file in `destiny.asp`, as shown in Listing 3.11.

Listing 3.11— destiny.asp: Adding the interface via SSI

```
1: <%@ LANGUAGE="VBSCRIPT" %>
2: <!--#include virtual="../pagetop.txt"-->
3: <h2>Mission to Destiny</h2>
4:
5: The best offering this fall seems to be the new sci-fi
6: pilot: "<b>Mission to Destiny</b>". The show is about a
7: seemingly innocent cargo ship that gets shot down and is
8: forced to makes an emergency landing on an uncharted
9: planet. Tension and emotions are running high among the
10:normally unshakeable crew. Will the 'Wind Star' be rescued
11:or will the crew be stranded? Can they survive by their
12:insticts, or will they turn on each other?
13:...
```

Save the file and open it in your browser by calling up `http://localhost/news/destiny.asp`. Bingo, everything is done for you—and more quickly than doing it by hand! Add it to `allissa.asp` and `gossip.asp`. While you're at it, replace the long version of it in `news.asp`, as shown in Listing 3.12.

Listing 3.12—news.asp: Changing the interface over to an SSI

```
0: <%@LANGUAGE=VBSCRIPT%>
1: <!--#include virtual="pagetop.txt"-->
2:
3: <h2>Breaking News</h2>
4:
5: The long awaited pilot <a href="news/destiny.asp">
6: "Mission to Destiny"</a> will finally hit
7: the airwaves this coming Sunday night.
8: <HR>
9: The latest in Sorcha Wexford's Spell Makers
10:<a href="news/allissa.asp">saga</a> is hitting the stores.
11:<HR>
12:The <a href="news/gossip.asp">Unknown Gossip Columnist</a>
13:has another installment of news.
14:<HR>
  <
...
```

This gives you a huge advantage. If you want to change the interface, for example, you move all the buttons to one line underneath the logo and center it all on the page, you make that change only once, in `pagetop.txt`, as shown in Listing 3.13.

Listing 3.13—pagetop.txt: Changing the interface

```
1: <HTML>
2: <HEAD>
3: <TITLE>Primary Outpost</TITLE>
4: </HEAD>
5: <BODY bgcolor="32C800">
6: <CENTER>
7: <A href="http://localhost/index.asp">
8: <IMG SRC="/images/logo.gif" ALT="Primary Outpost Logo" HEIGHT="67"
➥WIDTH="496" border=0></A>
9:<BR clear="left">
10:<A href="/news/news.asp">
11:<IMG SRC="/images/news.gif" BORDER=0 ALIGN="middle" ALT="News" HEIGHT="39"
➥WIDTH="39"></A>
12:<A href="/news/archives.asp">
13:<IMG SRC="/images/archives.gif" BORDER=0 ALIGN="middle" ALT="Archived News"
➥HEIGHT="39" WIDTH="39"></A>
14:<A href="/bazaar/bazaar.asp">
15:<IMG SRC="/images/bazaar.gif" BORDER=0 ALIGN="middle" ALT="The Bazaar"
➥HEIGHT="39" WIDTH="39"></A>
16:<A href="/auction/auctions.asp">
```

```
17:<IMG SRC="/images/auction.gif" BORDER=0 ALIGN="middle" ALT="Auctions"
➥HEIGHT="39" WIDTH="39"></A>
18:<A href="/mySpace/mySpace.asp">
19:<IMG SRC="/images/myspace.gif" BORDER=0 ALIGN="middle" ALT="mySpace"
➥HEIGHT="39" WIDTH="39"></A>
20:<A href="/register.asp">
21:<IMG SRC="/images/register.gif" BORDER=0 ALIGN="middle" ALT="Register"
➥HEIGHT="39" WIDTH="39"></A>
22:<BR clear="left">
23:<P>
24:</CENTER>
```

3

Here we've placed the buttons underneath the logo by adding a break tag on line 9. We've also removed the break tag that was between lines 15 and 16, then centered the whole thing using center tags on lines 6 and 24. Save the file and open `http://localhost/news/news.asp` in your browser. You see the change there. What about `http://localhost/news/destiny.asp`? It's there too. You'll find that the change is reflected in all four pages. This may not seem like a big deal, but it is.

The nature of the Web is change. What is new and hot today will be out of date in six months. What are you going to do then? Rekey every page? No way! You'd be tearing your hair out. This way, you can make the changes once (or maybe once per section) and be pretty much done with it.

The Importance of Being Consistent

One of the most important design considerations for your Web site is consistency. In general, two types of users visit the Web: novices and experts, but all users appreciate a coherent site. Web design should give users a sense of place. You hear it in the language people use. They leave one site and go to another. If your pages look consistent, the visitors are comfortable knowing that they are still where they started out, that they weren't suddenly thrown over to another site without expecting it.

This sense of place is something that new users have particular difficulty with. Many of them think that the entire Web comes from their browser as in, "You have to get on Netscape; it's great!" Other users think the Web comes from a particular search engine or directory, as in, "You wouldn't believe all the information that's on Yahoo!" Although, I'll grant you that most search engines and similar sites do have an increasing amount of content, that's not what these users mean. They do not realize that when they click a link in a search engine, they are going somewhere else.

EXCURSION

Look Before You Link

This brings up an important point. Many sites have dozens, even hundreds of links, but besides the danger of becoming overwhelming, from a business standpoint, you must consider that if you are going to have novice users, the content on the sites to which you are linking reflects on you. If you have a news item about the growing popularity of leather jackets, for instance, and you agree to link to leather retailers, you should see what other types of leather they sell. This is especially important in an age where online pornography is so pervasive. A novice user who links to that content from your site can easily believe it's yours.

It's always a good idea to check out a site before you link to it, but it's also a good idea to make sure that users understand what is and is not your content. Most large sites include a text statement disclaiming responsibility for content on linked sites, but that doesn't help users understand what is and is not external content. A better solution is to clearly mark an off-site link, usually with a small graphic.

One of the ways that you can build a consistent site is by using a template—a file that contains the basic elements that you want to include on every page. Listing 3.14 shows how to create one that you can use throughout this project.

Listing 3.14—template.asp: A starting point

```
<%@ LANGUAGE="VBSCRIPT" %>

<!--#include virtual="/pagetop.txt"-->

Add content here.

<!--#include virtual="/pagebottom.txt"-->
</BODY>
</HTML>
```

Save this file as `template.asp`, and make sure it's in your home directory. Right now, you don't have a `pagebottom.txt` file. Certain things should go on the bottom of every page, such as copyright information, or a text version of the menu. Listing 3.15 shows you how to create one. Open a new file, and add this text.

Listing 3.15—pagebottom.txt: A text version of the menu

```
<HR>
<A href="/index.asp">Primary Outpost Home</A> ¦
<A href="/news/news.asp">News</A> ¦
<A href="/news/archives.asp">Archived News</A> ¦
<A href="/bazaar/bazaar.asp">The Bazaar</A> ¦
<A href="/auction/auctions.asp">Auctions</A> ¦
<A href="/mySpace/mySpace.asp">mySpace</A> ¦
<A href="/register.asp">Register</A><BR>
<BR>
Copyright 1999 Primary Outpost Communications
```

Save this file as `pagebottom.txt` in your Web server's home directory. Then open the template file, at `http://localhost/template.asp` to see your entire interface.

EXCURSION

Ensuring Consistency With Cascading Style Sheets

Another way to make your life easier is to use Cascading Style Sheets (CSS) to help format your pages. For instance, if I wanted to make a headline red and very large, I could cheat and use the HTML:

```
<font size="+4" color="red">Breaking News</font>
```

This is the wrong way to go about it, however, for several reasons. First, that font tag doesn't identify your headline as something important, so it doesn't provide any information as to the structure of the page. A browser that doesn't understand the font tag won't do anything to set it off as a headline, and search engines and other tools that look for headlines won't count it as something important. Second, if you were to put this on every page and then decide that you wanted headlines to be blue, you'd be right back where you started before SSIs.

A better way to do it is with CCS, where you create a custom style, then apply it to the page. To create the style I used above, I could add Listing 3.15a to the page:

Listing 3.15a

```
<STYLE>
.headline {
        font-size:      24;
        font-weight:    bold;
        color:          red;
          }
.news {
        font-size:      12;
        color:          black;
          }

</STYLE>
```

This creates a class, or custom style, called `headline`. To use it, I could add it to my headline:

```
<H2 CLASS="headline">Breaking News</H2>
```

This way, the browser and other tools know it's important, but I still get my style information. What's more, if the browser doesn't understand style sheets—and only the newest browsers do—the text will still be legible. You can also apply a style to entire sections of a page, using `<div></div>`:

```
<DIV ID="news" CLASS="news">
Will Jane Dow be leaving her role as Major Pressman on "Dark Heroes"?  Rumor
has it
that she's been offered the starring role in a new pilot for another network.
</DIV>
```

The only remaining problem is the "cascading" part of Cascading Style Sheets. You could include the styles with an SSI, but CSS has its own way of linking pages, as in Listing 3.15b.

Listing 3.15b

```
1: <HTML>
2: <HEAD>
3: <TITLE>Breaking News</TITLE>
4:
5: <LINK REL="stylesheet" TYPE="text/css" HREF="outpost.css">
6:
7: </HEAD>
8: <BODY>
9: <H2 CLASS="headline">Breaking News</H2>
10:
11:<DIV ID="news" CLASS="news">
12:Will Jane Dow be leaving her role as Major Pressman on "Dark Heroes"?  Rumor
➥has it
13:that she's been offered the starring role in a new pilot for another network.
14:</DIV>
15:</BODY>
16:</HTML>
```

On line 5 we've linked to a style sheet that contains the headline and news styles. If we want to change what headlines or news text looks like, we can make the change once in outpost.css and it will cascade through the entire site.

CSS is part of HTML 4.0, so we won't be using it in this book, but you can get a good background at

```
http://www.w3.org/Style/
```

Once you've established the fundamentals, there are also many good books on the subject, such as *HTML 4 Unleashed, Second Edition*, by Rick Darnell.

Digging a Little Deeper

You can use Server Side Includes for much more than just including static HTML in a page. In fact, ASP is a kind of Server Side Include, in that the server takes an HTML file and looks for commands it needs to execute and insert before it sends the page back.

Using SSI you can display dates and other information, or embed the results of scripts into the page. The most common SSI command is as follows:

```
<!--#echo var="DATE_LOCAL"-->
```

This command enables you to display the current date on your page easily like you did in Chapter 1, "Planning and Designing A Professional Web Site." Examine how it works, so you can see what else it can do for you.

- The server reads the page.

- The server checks, or parses the page, looking for SSI commands.

- The server evaluates those commands and inserts the resulting text into the page.

- The server executes any ASP commands and returns the page to the browser.

It's important to note exactly what's going on here. The server takes the text returned by the SSI commands and inserts it into the page. After that happens, it doesn't matter where the text came from. So the text

```
<B>The current date is: <!—#echo var="DATE_LOCAL"—></B>
```

becomes

```
<B>The current date is:  July 22, 1999</B>
```

and this is how it's returned to the browser. It's pretty simple, but it's also pretty powerful, especially because there's nothing that says that when you include a text file, it can't have ASP commands in it.

For example, your `pagetop.txt` file is great, but there's one small problem with it. Every single page is going to have the exact same title. That's not too helpful to your users. To help solve this, you can change `pagetop.txt`, as shown in Listing 3.16.

Listing 3.16—pagetop.txt: Adding a dynamic page title

```
1: <HTML>
2: <HEAD>
3: <TITLE><%= pageTitle %></TITLE>
4: </HEAD>
5: <BODY bgcolor="32C800">
6: <CENTER>
7: <A href="http://localhost/index.asp">
8: <IMG SRC="/images/logo.gif" ALT="Primary Outpost Logo" HEIGHT="67"
➡WIDTH="496" border=0></A>
...
```

On line 3, `pageTitle` is a variable. That means you can assign a value to it, and whenever you call `pageTitle`, that value is substituted instead. Of course, because you haven't assigned any value to `pageTitle`, the server inserts nothing in its place. But if you set a value for `pageTitle` on every page, every page has its own title.

The most logical thing would be to assign `pageTitle` a value before you call `pagetop.txt`, as shown in Listing 3.17.

Listing 3.17—news.asp and pagetop.txt: Assigning a page title

```
0: <%@ LANGUAGE="VBSCRIPT" %>
1: <% pageTitle = "Outpost News" %>
2: <!--#include file="pagetop.txt"-->
3:
4: <h2>Breaking News</h2>
5:
6: The long awaited pilot <a href="news/destiny.asp">
…
```

Listing 3.18 shows how ASP sees the page when the page is called.

Listing 3.18—news.asp: Translating ASP commands in an SSI

```
0: <%@ LANGUAGE="VBSCRIPT" %>
1: <% pageTitle = "Outpost News" %>
2: <HTML>
3: <HEAD>
4: <TITLE><%= pageTitle %></TITLE>
5: </HEAD>
6: <BODY bgcolor="32C800">
7: <CENTER>
8: <A href="http://localhost/index.asp">
9: <IMG SRC="/images/logo.gif" ALT="Primary Outpost Logo" HEIGHT="67"
➥WIDTH="496" border=0></A>
10:<BR clear="left">
11:<A href="/news/news.asp">
12:<IMG SRC="/images/news.gif" BORDER=0 ALIGN="middle" ALT="News" HEIGHT="39"
➥WIDTH-"39"></A>
13:<A href="/news/archives.asp">
14:<IMG SRC="/images/archives.gif" BORDER=0 ALIGN="middle" ALT="Archived News"
➥HEIGHT="39" WIDTH="39"></A>
15:<A href="/bazaar/bazaar.asp">
16:<IMG SRC="/images/bazaar.gif" BORDER=0 ALIGN="middle" ALT="The Bazaar"
➥HEIGHT="39" WIDTH="39"></A>
17:<A href="/auction/auctions.asp">
18:<IMG SRC="/images/auction.gif" BORDER=0 ALIGN="middle" ALT="Auctions"
➥HEIGHT="39" WIDTH="39"></A>
19:<A href="/mySpace/mySpace.asp">
20:<IMG SRC="/images/myspace.gif" BORDER=0 ALIGN="middle" ALT="mySpace"
➥HEIGHT="39" WIDTH="39"></A>
20:<A href="/register.asp">
21:<IMG SRC="/images/register.gif" BORDER=0 ALIGN="middle" ALT="Register"
➥HEIGHT="39" WIDTH="39"></A>
22:<BR clear="left">
23:<P>
24:</CENTER>
3:
4: <h2>Breaking News</h2>
5:
6: The long awaited pilot <a href="news/destiny.asp">
…
```

You can include any ASP text in this same way. I often use it for VBScript that I need to place on multiple pages, for example for connecting to the database. This way I can make the change one time and it takes effect for the whole site.

The Content Linking Component

Even though an item may no longer be current, you still want to give users access to it. You do this with archives of this site. Users can view a list of all the files and click the item they want to read. While they're on that page, they can move forwards or backwards in the list. None of that is too complicated. In fact, you can do all that with the HTML you already know. But let's look at maintainability. Adding a new page means adding it to the contents page, which isn't difficult. You must also decide which pages go before and after it and add links to the new page, and then modify those pages to point to the new one. None of that is tough, but what if you reorganize the site and decide to reorder all those pages? You'd have to sort through each and every file.

Instead, you can use the Content Linking component, which is included with ASP, to simplify this process for you. The Content Linking component does two things for you. First, it allows you to generate a table of contents of sorts from a simple text file of the pages you want in the list. Second, it takes a page, figures out where it is on the list, and then automatically generates the correct Forward and Back links. This way, when you add a new page, you only have to add it to the list. This is certainly much better than sorting through tons of HTML!

Before you start, prepare your Archives page. You have a shell of an HTML page, but it doesn't use your interface elements, so make a copy of `template.asp` and save it in the news directory as `archives.asp`, overwriting the original file. Open the page in your text editor and add a heading describing the page, as well as a page title (see Listing 3.19).

Listing 3.19—archives.asp: Creating a new page from template.asp

```
<%@ LANGUAGE="VBSCRIPT" %>
<% pageTitle = "Outpost Archives" %>
<!--#include file="pagetop.txt"-->

<H1>Outpost Archives</H1>

<!--#include file="pagebottom.txt"-->
</BODY>
</HTML>
```

There, your page is complete with an interface, in much less time that we'd have spent building it from scratch.

Creating the List

The next thing that you have to create is the list of files in your archives. For each page, you need at least two things: the name of the file, and the description you want to use for the link. By using the single quote, you can also add comments so that later, when you try to figure out what's going on, you know what these files represented. Separate the three items by the Tab key. This is called a tab delimited file (see Listing 3.20).

Listing 3.20—archiveslist.txt: Specifying content

```
/news/destiny.asp  Mission to Destiny Finally Airs      'MtD Pilot
/news/gossip.asp   Dark Heroes, Millennium Mysteries, and a Baby    'Gossip
/news/allissa.asp  Review: Warrior Queen          'Review
```

Save this file in the news directory as `archiveslists.txt`. As far as ASP is concerned, your line ends just before the single quote. ASP ignores anything you put after it. (You use that later to comment your code.)

Code is the set of instructions the server executes. Taken together, these lines of code make up the program.

Commenting code means inserting text that does not execute, but lets you or other programmers know what you had in mind and what things represent. This is also known as documenting the code.

Creating an Object

I talked briefly about objects earlier, but now you're actually going to create one. When you deal with objects, you can create as many as you want of a single type. Each one is called an instance of the object, and you give each instance its own name. In the `archives.asp` file, add the code found in Listing 3.21.

Listing 3.21—archives.asp: Creating an instance of the Content Linking object

```
 0: <%@ LANGUAGE="VBSCRIPT" %>
 1: <% pageTitle = "Outpost Archives" %>
 2: <!--#include file="pagetop.txt"-->
 3:
 4: <H1>Outpost Archives</H1>
 5:
 6: <% set myTOC = Server.CreateObject("MSWC.NextLink") %>
 7:
 8: <!--#include virtual="pagebottom.txt"-->
 9: </BODY>
10:</HTML>
```

On line 6 we use the CreateObject method of the Server object to create an instance of the Content Linking object, called MSWC.Nextlink. In this case, MSWC is the package the object is part of, along with several other standard objects. This object has methods of its own, which you can use to accomplish various tasks. These methods enable you to do things, such as retrieve URLs and descriptions for files in the list. You're going to use them to create a table of contents for your archives section, but look at how the object works first. Add the code in Listing 3.22 to archives.asp.

Listing 3.22—archives.asp: Pulling URLs from archiveslist.txt

```
0: <%@ LANGUAGE="VBSCRIPT" %>
1: <% pageTitle = "Outpost Archives" %>
2: <!--#include file="pagetop.txt"-->
3:
4: <H1>Outpost Archives</H1>
5: <%  set myTOC = Server.CreateObject("MSWC.NextLink")  %>
6:
7: The first URL is:  <%= myTOC.GetNthURL("news/archiveslist.txt", 1) %>
8: <BR>
9: The first description is:  <%=
➥myTOC.GetNthDescription("news/archiveslist.txt", 1) %>
10:
11:<!--#include virtual="pagebottom.txt"-->
12:</BODY>
13:</HTML>
```

The method myTOC.GetNthURL does exactly that: It looks for the nth URL in the file and returns it. Likewise, GetNthDescription gives you the associated description, so you can use it in your links (see Figure 3.4).

Figure 3.4

The Content Linking component enables you to specify files and descriptions on a list and then pull them out as needed.

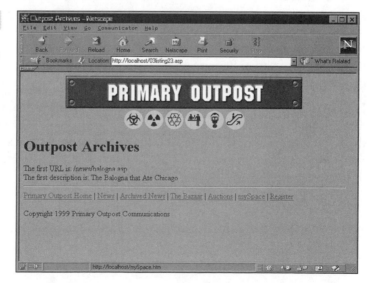

If that were all it did for you, it'd be useful, but not as useful as it could be. You can automate this process using a construct called a for-next loop. A for-next loop is basically a counter. It performs a set of instructions a set number of times. Let's look at a basic loop. Make these changes to your archives.asp file, save it and open it in your browser (see Listing 3.23).

Listing 3.23—archives.asp: Looping through the URLs in archiveslist.txt

```
0: <%@ LANGUAGE="VBSCRIPT" %>
1: <% pageTitle = "Outpost Archives" %>
2: <!--#include file="pagetop.txt"-->
3:
4: <H1>Outpost Archives</H1>

5: <%     set myTOC = Server.CreateObject("MSWC.NextLink")   %>
6:
7: <%     for N = 1 to 3   %>
8:         URL number <%= N %> is:   <%= myTOC.GetNthURL("news/archiveslist.txt",
➥N) %><BR>
9: <%     next       %>10:
11:<!--#include virtual="pagebottom.txt"-->
12:</BODY>
13:</HTML>
```

The for-next loop on lines 7 through 9 tells the server to do a specific set of tasks.

When the server gets to the code for N = on line 7 it assigns a value to the variable N, in this case the number 1.

The server continues on its merry way, executing instructions until the command next on line 9.

It returns to the beginning of the loop on line 7 and moves to the next number, 2.

Steps 1 through 3 are repeated until the server returns to the beginning and tries to set the value of N to 4. Because 4 isn't included in the numbers 1 to 3, the server skips the loop and moves to your final statements.

Let's look at turning this to your advantage. You can put as many files as you want into this table of contents, but you don't necessarily know how many files will be on the list at any given time. Fortunately, the object provides you with a way to get the number of pages in the list, so you can assign that number to a variable and use that in the for-next loop (see Listing 3.24).

Listing 3.24—archives.asp: Dynamically creating the table of contents

```
0: <%@ LANGUAGE="VBSCRIPT" %>
1: <% pageTitle = "Outpost Archives" %>
2: <!--#include file="pagetop.txt"-->
3:
4: <H1>Outpost Archives</H1>5: <% set myTOC =
Server.CreateObject("MSWC.NextLink")  %>
6: <% numPages = myTOC.GetListCount("/news/archiveslist.txt")
7:    for N = 1 to numPages  %>
8:        <A href="<%= myTOC.GetNthURL("/news/archiveslist.txt", N) %>">
9:        <%= myTOC.GetNthDescription("/news/archiveslist.txt", N) %></A>
10:       <BR>
11:<% next       %>
11:<!--#include virtual="pagebottom.txt"-->
12:</BODY>
13:</HTML>
```

On line 6 we set the value of numPages as the number of items in archiveslist.txt. We can then use that value as the maximum for the for-next loop on lines 7 through 9. On lines 8 and 9 we're using the URL and description to create a link on the page.

Now you can do anything you want to the list. You can add pages, remove pages, and move pages around, and the table of contents still works accurately.

Moving Among the Files

Now that you have the files in your table of contents, what happens when you choose one? You want to be able to send the user to the next page on the list, say the next day's news, or the previous page. The Content Linking component takes the URL of the current page—whatever it is—finds it in the list, and gives you the previous and next pages.

Open the destiny.asp file and add the links shown in Listing 3.25. Then save the file and open it in your browser.

Listing 3.25—destiny.asp: Adding Forward and Back links

```
...
40:<LI><B>David Sinclair</b>(Morgan) won't reveal his secret in the show, but
41:he told us in an interview: "It'll be really hard to figure out
42:the good guys from the bad ones." Whether he's a villain or not
43:remains to be seen.</LI>
44:<LI><B>Anitha Roshman</b>(Gemma) is a well known star in her own country.
45:Hot on the heels of her success as Laura in the made-for-TV movie,
46:<i>Day of the Eagle</i> this will be her second appearance in
47:the US. She is very happy and excited to be playing the
```

continues

Listing 3.25—continued

```
48:beautiful and exotic Gemma.</LI>
49:<P>
50:<% set myTOC = Server.CreateObject("MSWC.Nextlink") %>
51:    <A href="<%=myTOC.getPreviousURL("/news/archiveslist.txt")%>">
52:    Back to <%= myTOC.getPreviousDescription("/news/archiveslist.txt")%></A>
53:    <BR>
54:    <A href="<%=myTOC.getNextURL("/news/archiveslist.txt")%>">
55:    Forward to <%=myTOC.getNextDescription("/news/archiveslist.txt")%></A>
56:<P>
57:<!--#include virtual="/pagebottom.txt"-->
58:</BODY>
59:</HTML>
```

On lines 5 and 6 we're asking the server what the previous page is and creating a link to it, then on lines 8 and 9 we're doing the same for the next file on the list.

Because you're going to use this code over and over, you can put it into a file that you can include in other files. That way when you add a new page, you can include that file instead of coding it repeatedly. Put this new code into a file all by itself and save it as `archivelinks.asp` in the news directory. You can then include it in `allissa.asp` and `gossip.asp`, as shown in Listing 3.26.

Listing 3.26—gossip. asp: Adding Forward and Back links via an SSI

```
0: <%@ LANGUAGE="VBSCRIPT" %>
1: <% pageTitle = "Outpost Gossip" %>
2: <!--#include virtual="../pagetop.txt"-->
3:
4: <h2>The Unknown Gossip Columnist Rides Again</h2>
5: Will Jane Dow be leaving her role as Major Pressman on "Dark Heroes"?
6: Rumor has it she's been offered the starring role in a new pilot for another
7: network.
8: <HR>
9: "Millennium Mysteries" may be adding two new characters this season.  Word
10:is that Michael Arrans has been signed to play the new head of the Mystery
11:Team, and Andrew Peterson may be coming on board as an alien.
12:<HR>
13:A little bird told us that someone from the cast of  'Journey to Jeopardy'
14:is expecting a new baby next spring.  Wonder who she is?  Here's a clue:
15:she directed her first episode last month.
16:<HR>
17:Merridith Garett, star of the fur and feather epic "Misterra, Jungle
➥Princess",
18:is getting married next month to long time lover Keith Wild.  They plan to
19:settle down for a while and are looking for a show they can do together.
20:<P>
21:<!--#include virtual="/news/archivelinks.asp"-->
```

```
22:
23:<!--#include virtual="/pagebottom.txt" -->
24:</BODY>
25:</HTML>
```

Test it by moving back and forth in the list. You won't see the file `news.asp` show up because it's not in the list. Add it to `archiveslist.txt`, and try it again. You'll see that it comes up not only there, but also in the table of contents, and all you did was add it to a simple text file.

Content Rotator

Another way to display the news is to display a random news item on the home page, along with a link to the news page itself. The Content Rotator component enables us to set up a list of news items and let the server choose which to display when a user calls the home page. Before we add the code to display the news, however, we need to create the file that lists the news itself.

Listing 3.26b—content.txt: Listing the potential news items for the home page

```
1: %% #3 // Sky Surfers
2: The sequel to "Sky Surfers" will be coming out in theatres
3: next month.  A new team member will be added with special
4: powers, and a romance may be starting between Ilsa and Gripper.
5: %% #2 // Incredible Rocket
6: More movie news, Josh Collins best seller  "Adam Ansley's
7: Incredible Rocket" will be made into a movie.  The cast is
8: still being picked and filming starts sometime after the
9: New Year.
10:%% #3 // Salami
11:"The Salami That Ate Cleveland" is breaking box office records
12:everywhere.  Tickets have been sold out for days for the new
13:sf thriller comedy.  Be sure to see it if you love farce and
14:suspense.
15:%% #4 // Chase the Vision
16:Marrissa Denning's new book "Chase the Vision" will be released
17:this week.  It's the latest in her Dream Chaser series.
18:%% #3 // Eternity and Beyond
19:Look for a surprise season ender on "Eternity and Beyond".  Will
20:Russ finally tell Gena where he comes from?
```

Taking a look at line 1, the %% symbols signify a new entry. The number that follows is the weight for the item. A listing with a weight of 3 is going to appear more often than a listing with a weight of 2. You don't have to specify a weighting. If you leave it out, the server will assign it a weighting of 1. After the weighting you see two forward slashes (//). Anything on that line after the slashes is considered a comment and won't be displayed.

An item can be as many lines as you like, and can contain any HTML, including links and images.

To add the item to the page, we need to call the Content Rotator component by creating an instance of it. Open `index.asp` in your text editor and add the code in Listing 3.26c.

Listing 3.26c—index.asp: Adding a randomly generated news item

```
1: <HTML>
2: <HEAD>
3: <TITLE>Primary Outpost</TITLE>
4: </HEAD>
5: <BODY bgcolor="#32C800">
6:
7: <IMG SRC="images/logo.gif" ALT="Primary Outpost Logo" HEIGHT="67"
➥WIDTH="496">
8: <P>
9: <%
10:    set randomNews = Server.CreateObject("MSWC.ContentRotator")
11:    Response.Write randomNews.choosecontent("content.txt")
12:%>
13:<P>
14:<A href="news/news.asp">
15:<IMG SRC="images/news.gif" BORDER=0 ALIGN="middle" ALT="News" HEIGHT="39"
➥WIDTH="39">
16:News</A> -- find out the latest happenings
...
```

Line 10 creates the object, and line 11 pulls a random news item and prints it to the page. To change the news, we edit `content.txt` and the component takes care of the rest.

Banner Ads and AdRotator

In the beginning, there wasn't a lot of money floating around on the Web—certainly not as much as there is now! Most users got their access for free through universities and big business had yet to discover it. After the audience began to grow, of course big business began to look for ways to make money. (Many of the original users thought that this was appalling, actually, but it's this infusion of funds that helped drive prices down.) Early on, businesses settled on two main ways of making money: e-commerce and advertising. (The idea of subscription content was so heretical that it's still a tough sell in most industries.) At first the goal of advertising was to make money for those hosting the ads. Back then there weren't the millions of sites there are today. Just having a Web site was enough to distinguish you, in most cases. Today, with so many sites on the Web, it's almost crucial to have some sort of ad campaign going, even if you just join one of the free link exchanges.

We all know that a picture is worth a thousand words, so it should come as no surprise that advertising on the Web didn't take long to start incorporating images. The most common form of Web advertising these days is the banner ad. A banner ad is a more or less standard sized image (usually horizontal) that is also a clickable link to an advertiser's site (see Figure 3.5). At first, this was an effective tactic. Banner ads were new, so they attracted attention, and the click-through rate was good. These days, though with banners saturating the Web, users hardly notice them anymore, and the response rate is dropping. As such, big business has put a lot of time, effort, and money into determining ways to reverse this trend.

Figure 3.5

Banner ads, such as this one for InterGal Inc., are currently one of the most common methods of advertising on the Web.

One thing that came out of the ever-increasing pressure was the realization that the more times a user sees a particular banner, the less likely he or she is to click it. This led to the idea of a rotating banner. Every time users come to a page, they get a different ad. (Usually it's determined randomly from a pool.) Active Server Pages has a component, AdRotator, which enables you to insert banners easily. You can set up an ad and determine the banners that run, whether they are clickable, and how often they run relative to each other.

Using AdRotator

The AdRotator component actually consists of three main pieces in addition to the ads themselves:

- The actual AdRotator object itself
- The schedule file
- The redirection file

The first thing you need to do is gather the ads you're going to use. You'll find them on the CD, under ads in the Chapter 3 directory. Drag the whole folder into your Web server's home directory.

Next, you need to create a schedule file. This is the file that tells the AdRotator where to go and how often to go there. Create a new file called adRotatorSched.txt and save it in the ads directory. Put the text in Listing 3.27 in it. (Make sure you keep the asterisk on the first line.)

Listing 3.27—AdRotatorSched.txt: Determining which banners will run and how often

```
*
/ads/intergal.gif
http://localhost/ads/intergal.asp
Intergal, Inc.:  Get Safe, get insured.
3
/ads/korman.gif
http://localhost/Ads/korman.asp
Korman's Costume Shop:  Our costumes are out of this world
5
/ads/ad3.gif
http://localhost/Ads/intbooks.asp
Interplanetary Books:  Everything from Alpha to Zed
2
```

The four items in each listing are as follows:

- The image to be displayed.
- The URL of the sponsor's site.
- The ALT text to be included in the ad for people who can't/won't see the image.
- Relative weights for each ad. In this case, on the average for every 10 times the page is viewed, the first ad comes up 3 times, the second 5 times, and the last one 2 times.

Now you're ready to put the ad on your home page. Normally the banner ad goes at the top of the page, but it's also acceptable to put it on the bottom; so because you have a banner-type graphic at the top, that's what you should do. Open the index.asp file and add the entry in Listing 3.28 to create the AdRotator object and get the HTML for the ad.

Listing 3.28—index.asp: Adding a rotating banner

```
...
27:<A href="mySpace/mySpace.asp">
28:<IMG SRC="images/myspace.gif" BORDER=0 ALIGN="middle" ALT="mySpace"
➥HEIGHT="39" WIDTH="39">
29:mySpace</A> -- carve out your niche
```

```
30:<BR>
31:<A href="register.asp">
32:<IMG SRC="images/register.gif" BORDER=0 ALIGN="middle" ALT="Register"
➥HEIGHT="39" WIDTH="39">
33:Register</A> -- jump on board
34:<P>
35:<%
36:    set AdvObject = Server.CreateObject("MSWC.AdRotator")
37:    adHTML = AdvObject.GetAdvertisement("ads/AdRotatorSched.txt")
38:    Response.Write adHTML
39:%>
40:
41:</BODY>
42:</HTML>
```

On line 36 we create the AdRotator object, then on line 37 we get the HTML for an ad to display on line 38.

Save the file and open it in your browser. You can only guess which ad you'll see. If you reload the page, you'll probably see the ad change. Reload a few times and watch the frequency of each ad. You'll notice that the relative frequencies match the schedule file. Click the ad, and you'll be taken to the advertiser's site.

You could leave it like this, but from a business standpoint, you need to do one more thing. If you sell ad space, you need to provide the advertiser with a report of how many times their ad has been clicked. To do this, you need insert a step in this process. Instead of going directly to the advertiser's site, you go to a page of your own, where you can log the action, and then you send the browser on to the advertiser. To do this, you create a redirect file.

But first, tell the AdRotator thatyou're going to use a redirect file. You put three listings in the schedule file so far. Each one contains information that applies only to that ad. Now you add information that applies to all ads, unless you specifically change it when you call them (see Listing 3.29).

Listing 3.29—AdRotatorSched.txt: Setting up for redirection

```
1: REDIRECT http://localhost/ads/goToSponsor.asp
2: WIDTH 500
3: HEIGHT 72
4: BORDER 0
5: *
6: /ads/intergal.gif
7: http://localhost/ads/intergal.asp
8: Intergal, Inc.:  Get Safe, get insured.
9: 3
10:/ads/korman.gif
```

continues

Listing 3.29—continued

```
11:http://localhost/Ads/korman.asp
12:Korman's Costume Shop:  Our costumes are out of this world
13:5
14:/ads/ad3.gif
15:http://localhost/Ads/intbooks.asp
16:Interplanetary Books:  Everything from Alpha to Zed
17:2
```

Lines two and three are fairly obvious; they set the dimensions for the ad. Line 4 tells the AdRotator whether to set a border attribute. It's line 1, though, that's interesting. Save the schedule file and refresh the `index.asp` file. Click the ad and look at the location bar of your browser. The URL for the ad is now something like `http://localhost/goToSponsor.asp?url=http://localhost/ads/intergal.asp&image=/ads/intergal.gif`. It's important to take a look at what this means. The first part, `http://localhost/goToSponsor.asp` is pretty obvious. The rest of it,

`?url=http://localhost/ads/intergal.asp&image=/ads/intergal.gif`

is called the `querystring`. You learn more about `querystrings` in Chapter 4, "Database Access Using ASP," but for now, you need to understand only that this is one way to pass information to an Active Server Page. A series of name-value pairs is listed as part of the URL separated by asterisks.

Create a blank file—not a copy of `template.asp`—in the ads directory called `goToSponsor.asp` and add the text shown in Listing 3.30.

Listing 3.30—goToSponsor.asp: Redirecting the user to the sponsor's page

```
0: <%@ LANGUAGE="VBSCRIPT" %>
1: <%
2:     sponsorURL = Request.querystring("url")
3:     Response.Redirect sponsorURL
4: %>
```

First, understand that `Request` is an object, just like `Response`. On the line 2, you ask it to retrieve the value of `URL` from the `querystring` and assign that value to the variable `sponsorURL`. On line 3, you tell the server to send the browser to another page—literally to redirect it. So overall, this page finds out where to send the browser and sends it there.

In real life, you would want to record this information in a log or a database, but for now you just pass it on. The transaction is recorded in your access logs for you to retrieve later.

The Page Counter Component

Finally, you might want to get some idea of how frequently your page is being accessed without having to dig through the server logs. The Page Counter component enables you to do that with just a few lines of code. We can add this under the banner ad on index.asp with the code in Listing 3.31.

Listing 3.31—index.asp: Adding a hit counter

```
...
31:<A href="register.asp">
32:<IMG SRC="images/register.gif" BORDER=0 ALIGN="middle" ALT="Register"
HEIGHT="39" WIDTH="39">
33:Register</A> -- jump on board
34:<P>
35:<%
36:    set AdvObject = Server.CreateObject("MSWC.AdRotator")
37:    adHTML = AdvObject.GetAdvertisement("ads/AdRotatorSched.txt")
38:    Response.Write adHTML
39:%>
40:
41:<% set pageCount = Server.CreateObject("MSWC.PageCounter") %>
42:    This page has been accessed <%= pageCount.pageHit %> times.
43:
44:</BODY>
45:</HTML>
```

On line 41, we create the Page Counterobject, pageCount, then on line 42 we use the <%= %> syntax to print out the count. The PageHit method actually increments the counter, adding 1 every time the page is hit. To retrieve the count without incrementing, we could have used pageCount.hits instead of pageCount.pageHit. You can also reset the value number of hits for this page using the Reset method, so the command would be pageCount.Reset.

Next Steps

In this chapter, you learned

- How to include one file within another using Server Side Includes. These includes can also include ASP commands.
- How to create a template you can use multiple times
- How to use a for-next loop to automate page creation
- How to use the Content Linking component to bring together any number of individual pages with a table of contents and Forward and Back links
- How to use the Content Rotator component to display randomly chosen information on the page

- How to use the Ad Rotator component to rotate and record click-throughs for banner ads

- How to use the Page Counter component to get a quick idea of how often your page is being accessed

In Chapter 4, "Database Access Using ASP", you'll learn how to create an HTML form, retrieve the information a user enters, insert the data into a database, and pull the data back out again.

In this chapter

- *Creating the Database and ODBC DSN*
- *Inserting Records into the Database*
- *Creating a Connection to the Database*
- *SQL Basics: Insert*
- *Adding Interactivity with Forms*
- *Data Modeling*
- *Error Handling*
- *Completing the Form*
- *Tidying Up—HTML Tables*

Chapter 4

Database Access Using ASP

Now that you know that you can put together an Active Server Page and do a few semi-dynamic things with it, it's time to get down to business. True interactivity comes with information, and that information needs to be stored somewhere. More often than not in today's world, that somewhere is going to be a database.

Now, when this book was in the planning stages (and even afterwards, actually) almost every single person who reviewed it asked me the same question: "What database are you planning to use?"

My answer to all of them was the same: It really doesn't matter.

EXCURSION

ODBC and Database Choices

All databases have an Application Programming Interface (API) that allows programmers to talk to them, usually using C or C++. Each one is different, however, so an application that talks directly to a database can't talk to any other database. ODBC acts as a translator. A programmer can write to the ODBC API, and then ODBC translates those commands for the particular database using a driver that is specific to that database. That way an application works as long as the proper driver has been installed.

While this theory holds up in a learning situation, when you're deciding on the architecture for your production system, it does matter what you choose. Not all databases (or ODBC drivers, for that matter) support all features, and none completely conform to the ANSI SQL standard. For the sake of convenience, we will be using Microsoft Access in this book, but before choosing a system for your application, be sure to determine if it will have the features and capacity that you need.

Figure 4.1

Active Server Pages insulates you from the choice of a database by using a standard like ODBC to communicate.

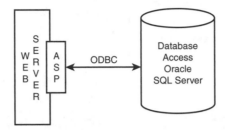

In this book, you use Microsoft Access for the underlying database because it's easy to use and because it's easy to obtain. In fact, if you don't mind creating tables and other objects using SQL, you don't even need Access to create and use a database with ASP! Many of you already have it installed as a part of Microsoft Office Professional. If you don't, and you want to use it to manipulate your database, install it now. I'll wait. While they're doing that, some of you might have a different database installed on your machine, such as Oracle or SQL Server. You will have no problem connecting to these databases as long as you have ODBC set up and working properly. Instructions for doing this are going to vary greatly according to your system, so you need to check the documentation. After you connect ASP to your database, there is little or no difference in the way you access it from within your pages.

> **Note**
>
> Not all databases support all features available in the ActiveX Data Object (ADO), which we'll be using, along with OLEDB and ODBC, to access them. Most of the issues are centered on techniques that are more advanced than those you use in this book, however.

In all likelihood, those of you who are hosting on an external machine were provided information on how to access the database. If not, you need to contact the administrator. Some of the things we are about to do aren't possible without access to the machine itself, but you can get around them with the proper information.

Creating The Database and ODBC DSN

At this point, I'll assume that you have Microsoft Access installed. Let's create the database for your project. Open Access and create a blank database called `outpost.mdb`. Take note of where you save it, because you'll need that in a couple of minutes. When you're done, exit Access. (You can also copy `outpost.mdb` from the CD-ROM to your machine instead of creating it from scratch.)

Now you need to create the Data Source Name (DSN) for the database you're using. You can think of a DSN as a set of ODBC configuration information our application will use to access the database. To do this, go to Start, Settings, Control Panel and double-click the Administrative Tools folder, then the Data Sources (ODBC) icon. Choose the System DSN tab along the top of the window (see Figure 4.2).

Figure 4.2

Choose the ODBC Administrator control panel, and click the System DSN tab.

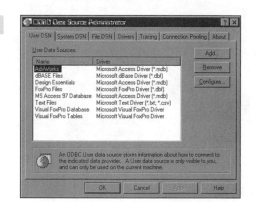

This shows you which DSNs exist on your machine. You're going to create a new one called outpost, so click Add (see Figure 4.3).

Figure 4.3

Insert the name and driver of the new DSN in the System DSN field and click Add.

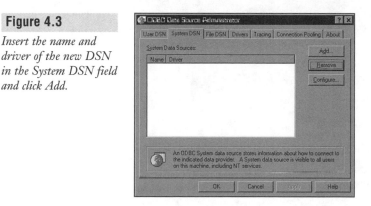

Choose the driver for the your database, in this case Access, and click Finish (see Figure 4.4).

At this point you're ready to pick your actual database, so fill in the name outpost as your Data Source Name. The description can be anything that you want (see Figure 4.5). Click Select and find the `outpost.mdb` file you created in Access, as shown in Figure 4.6. If you don't have a database installed, click Create to create an

Access database you can use for this project. If you get an error message telling you that the directory is invalid, make sure that you closed Access so it can release the database for other applications to use.

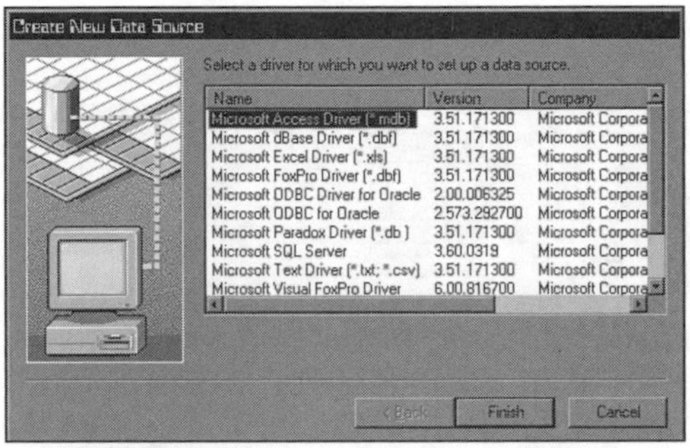

Figure 4.4

Choose the appropriate driver for your database and click Finish.

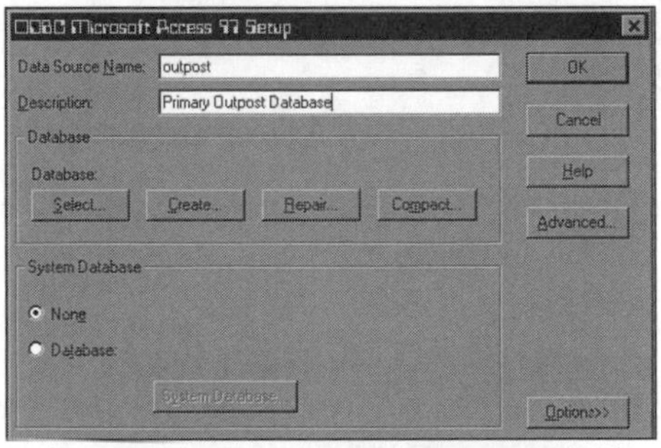

Figure 4.5

Name the new DSN and click Select to point it at your database.

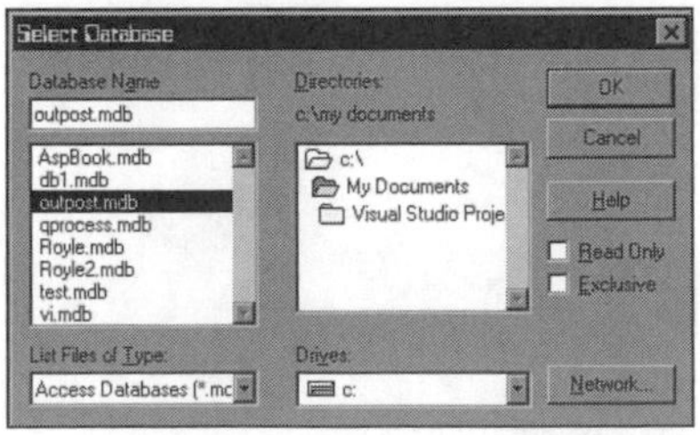

Figure 4.6

Navigate to the outpost.mdb file and select it.

That's all there is to it. Now you can use that DSN to access (no pun intended) your database from your pages.

Inserting Records into the Database

In Chapter 3, "Creating Interactive Web Content," you created a redirect file to track banner ads, but you didn't actually record the information. That's what you're going to do next. First open Access and choose the outpost database. If you get a warning that another application is using the database and you can't get exclusive access, that's fine; you don't want exclusive access anyway because you want ASP to be able to use it too.

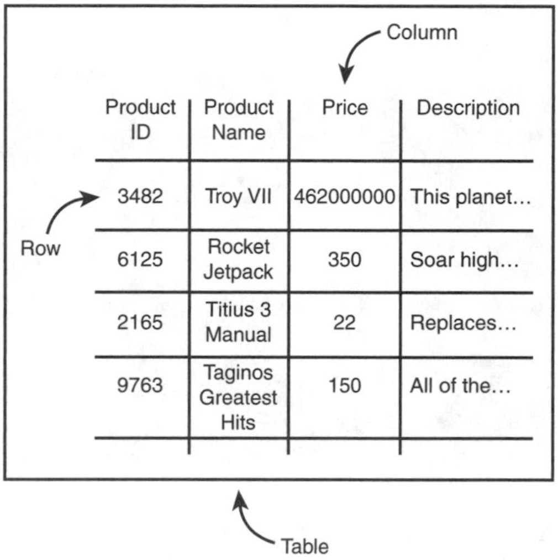

Figure 4.7

A database table consists of rows and columns of data.

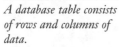

Right now you're just going to create a single table called ad_log. Let's consider that name for a minute. If you wanted to, you could put a space in the table name and still access it from ASP. But that's nonstandard, and later, when your site is a success (think positive!) you might want to upsize the database—duplicate the structure and the data into a more powerful database. In all likelihood, that database won't support the spaces in table names, so you would have to make numerous changes. Why set yourself up for that when you can see it coming?

Remember, if you stick to the standard as much as possible, you cause yourself fewer problems down the road.

If it's not already open, open Access and the outpost database. Click New to create a new table, and choose Design view.

In the Field Name column, type sponsor (see Figure 4.8). Press the Tab key to move to the Data Type column. Choose text, and set the field size to the maximum, which for Access is 255. This means that you created a column in your table that can hold up to 255 characters of text. Press Tab twice to go to the Field Name column on the next line. Type clickDate and set the date type to date/time.

Figure 4.8

Type the names of your columns and choose a data type.

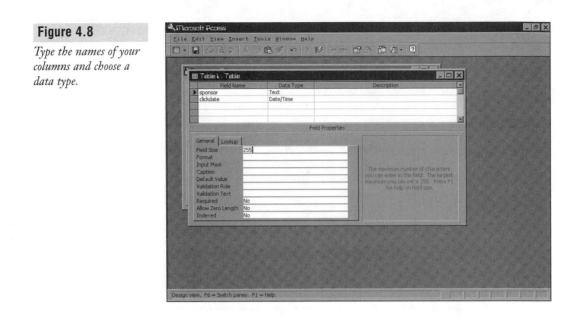

It's important to think about these data types. VBScript is not a strongly typed language, which means that you can assign any kind of data to a variable. But the database isn't like that. If you tell the database you want a column to hold numbers or a date, it doesn't accept a word. If you tell the database you want the field to be 50 characters long, it doesn't accept 51.

Close the window and save the table as `ad_log`. Access asks you whether you want a primary key for this table. I discuss primary keys and their uses later in this chapter, but for now click No.

Creating a Connection to the Database

Arguably the most important built-in components of Active Server Pages are the ActiveX Data Objects. These are COM objects that use ODBC and/or OLEDB to access databases and other stores of information, so they are language independent. They can be used not only from Active Server Pages but also from Visual Basic, Visual C++, and other programming environments. ADOs enable you to connect to a database to

- `Insert`: add new data to a table.
- `Update`: change data that's already in a table.
- `Delete`: remove data in a table.
- `Select`: look at data in a table.
- `Execute Stored Procedures`: many more advanced databases enable you to write code and store it directly in the database, where it's available to any connected program.

Before you can do any of that, however, you need to actually connect to the database. To do this, you create a Connection object.

Open the file goToSponsor.asp and add the following:

Listing 4.1—gotoSponsor.asp: Creating a connection

```
0: <%@ LANGUAGE="VBSCRIPT" %>
1: <%
2: sponsorURL = Request.querystring("url")
3:
4: 'Create the object
5: set outpostDB = Server.CreateObject("ADODB.Connection")
6: 'Open the connection
7: outpostDB.Open "outpost"
8:
9: 'Insert the record here
10:
11:'Close the connection
13:outpostDB.Close
14: 'Destroy the connection
15:set outpostDB = Nothing
16:
17:Response.Redirect sponsorURL
18:%>
```

You created the connection object on line 5, but you can't do anything with it until you open the connection. In this case, you open the DSN, outpost that you created earlier. If you need a username and password, put them after the DSN, separated by commas.

> **Tip**
>
> If your site is hosted externally, you may not be able to use a DSN without having an administrator set it up for you. In that case, you'll need to specify the information that would normally be found in the DSN, such as the type of database and location of the file. For instance, if I were to use a DSNless connection, Listing 4.1 becomes Listing 4.1a:
>
> ### Lising 4.1a—gotoSponsor.asp: Creating a DSNless Connection
>
> ```
> ...
> 4: 'Create the object
> 5: set outpostDB = Server.CreateObject("ADODB.Connection")
> 6: 'Open the connection
> 7: outpostDB.Open "DRIVER={Microsoft Access Driver
> ➥(*.mdb)};DBQ=C:\outpost.mdb"
> ...
> ```
>
> This method isn't as fast as using a System DSN, but it's a good alternative if you don't have that option. For more information on DSNless connections, see http://support.microsoft.com/support/kb/articles/q193/3/32.asp.

Opening a connection won't do any good unless we plan to use it. Later we'll be inserting the information as to what ad was clicked into the database, but for now add a comment to remind yourself that this is where it goes. It's important to comment your code, and as you go a little further along, you'll see a lot more of it.

When you finish making all changes, close the connection. This action tells the database you are finished so it can close the session. Otherwise, the database is swamped with connections that aren't doing anything but using up resources. This doesn't free up the resources on the Web server, though. To free up the memory used by the outpostDB object, you need to destroy any variables or other references to it. That's what you do on line 15 when you set outpostDB equal to Nothing. The Web server knows that once all variables associated with an object are set to Nothing it can use the object's resources for something else.

Now that we know how to connect to the database, we need to look at Structured Query Language (SQL), the command language that allows us to make changes, such as adding, changing, or removing data. SQL also allows us to retrieve information from the database, but let's start with inserting data.

SQL Basics: Insert

One nice thing about SQL is that it is a standard, so while each database has its own dialect that makes it unique, almost any database can understand the basic commands. Another nice thing about it is that if you look at it like a sentence, it almost makes sense. Over the course of this project you look at the four basic SQL statements: insert, update, delete, and select. But for now just look at insert. The most common form of insert statement is as follows:

```
insert into table_name (column_names) values (data_values)
```

Most databases enable you to leave out the column names under certain circumstances, but you're asking for trouble later if you do. So to insert the URL and the current date into the ad_loc table, use the following command:

```
insert into ad_loc (sponsor, clickDate) values (URL, Now)
```

This command tells the database to go to the table ad_loc and create a new record and put the value of URL in the sponsor column and the current date and time into the clickDate column.

To execute a simple command like this, use the execute method of the connection object, and feed it a string of text with the SQL command. Let's take a look at the string, as shown in Listing 4.2.

Listing 4.2—goToSponsor.asp: Creating an insert statement

```
0: <%@ LANGUAGE="VBSCRIPT" %>
1: <%
2: sponsorURL = Request.querystring("url")
3:
4: 'Create the object
5: set outpostDB = Server.CreateObject("ADODB.Connection")
6: 'Open the connection
7: outpostDB.open "outpost"
8:
9: 'Insert the record here
10:sqlText = "insert into ad_log (sponsor, clickDate) values ('"
11:sqlText = sqlText & sponsorURL
12:sqlText = sqlText & "', '"
13:sqlText = sqlText & Now
14:sqlText = sqlText & "')"
15:Response.Write sqlText
16:
17:'Close the connection
18:outpostDB.Close
19:'Destroy the connection
20:set outpostDB = Nothing
21:
22:'Response.Redirect sponsorURL
23:%>
```

Remember, the ellipses are not part of the code.

Before you look at the database, take a quick look at how you built that string of text: sqlText. I commented out the redirect by adding a single quote before it and added a line to print it to the page so you can see it. Without a debugger, the best way to look inside your program is to have it talk to you.

The string sqlText actually consists of five parts, some of which are plain text, and some of which you get from variables. In my case, when I ran it I got the following:

```
insert into ad_log (sponsor, clickDate) values
```

```
('http://localhost/ads/intergal.asp', '7/26/99 10:52:24 AM')
```

The text in bold came from the variables. Now that you know what you want to send to the database, send it, as shown in Listing 4.3.

Listing 4.3—goToSponsor.asp: Inserting data

```
...
9: 'Insert the record here
10:sqlText = "insert into ad_log (sponsor, clickDate) values ('"
11:sqlText = sqlText & sponsorURL
12:sqlText = sqlText & "', '"
```

continues

Listing 4.3—continued

```
13:sqlText = sqlText & Now
14:sqlText = sqlText & "')"
15:outpostDB.Execute(sqlText)
16:
17: 'Close the connection
18:outpostDB.Close
19: 'Destroy the connection
20:set outpostDB = Nothing
21:
22:Response.Redirect sponsorURL
23:%>
```

To test this, go to `http://localhost/index.asp` and click the banner ad; then open Access and look at the table. Your inserted record is there.

This is a very simple example of what you can do with the ADO. You'll get into more sophisticated examples as you go along.

Adding Interactivity with Forms

Considering that it was originally called interactive media, the Web really wasn't very interactive at first. About the most that could be said for it was that users got to choose where they were going, even if they didn't have much say about how they got there. As things have progressed, Web authors have searched for ways to include the user in the experience. Sites now routinely track users through the site, trying to surmise what interests them, so they can tailor the content appropriately. That's all terrific, and there's definitely a place for that. But you can do something a bit more straightforward to understand the user's preferences; you can ask.

One of the early innovations on the Web was the concept of an HTML form, which enables the user to submit information to a Web site, completing the circle of feedback.

A form is a page that includes elements allowing the user to input information, such as text boxes and radio buttons, and at least one element allowing the user to submit the form. These forms, which are specified with the <form></FORM> tags, can be used for almost anything, from user surveys to games to taking requests for search engines. Next, you'll build a form that takes a user's registration information and gathers information about their favorite kinds of science fiction.

EXCURSION

Gathering Information From Users

Users are becoming increasingly wary of sites that ask for personal information. If you want people to register, you have to earn their trust. One way to gain trust is with a privacy statement, which tells them what you will and will not do with their information, such as selling, renting, or lending it to other companies for their mailing lists. Also, research has shown that it's better to gather information from users a little at a time, instead of asking them to fill out long surveys at the beginning, when they're most likely to get frustrated and walk away.

In Chapter 3, "Creating Interactive Web Content", we created the file `archives.asp` by making a copy of `template.asp`. We're going to create `register.asp` the same way. Open `template.asp` in your text editor and save a copy called `register.asp` in the Web server's home directory. Next we add a simple form with a text box as in Listing 4.4.

Listing 4.4—register.asp: Creating a form

```
 0: <%@ LANGUAGE="VBSCRIPT" %>
 1: <% pageTitle = "Register" %>
 2: <!--#include virtual="/pagetop.txt"-->
 3:
 4: <H1>Register</H1>
 5: Fill in this form to become a member of Primary Outpost.
 6: <P>
 7: <FORM>
 8: Desired Username:   <INPUT TYPE="text">
 9: </FORM>
10:
11:<!--#include virtual="/pagebottom.txt"-->
12:</BODY>
13:</HTML>
```

Almost all elements you put into a form contain `<INPUT TYPE="type" …>`. Take a look at the page, as shown in Figure 4.9. Feel free to type in the Username text box. Because this is the only text box in the form, most browsers will submit it when you press Enter. Try it. You'll notice that far from performing some miraculous deed, it just takes you back to the original page. That's because you didn't give it anything else to do.

First we need to create a destination for the form. Open `template.asp` and save a copy as `take_registration.asp` in the Web server's home directory. Add some text to the body of it so that you recognize the page when it comes up.

Figure 4.9

Your basic form.

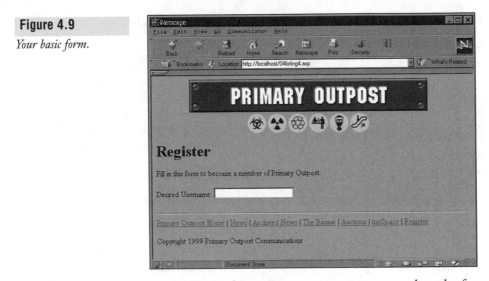

Return to register.asp. To send it to take_registration.asp when the form is submitted, we assign it an action as shown in Listing 4.5.

Listing 4.5—register.asp: Add an action

```
0: <%@ LANGUAGE="VBSCRIPT" %>
1: <% pageTitle = "Register" %>
2: <!--#include virtual="/pagetop.txt"-->
4:
5: <H1>Register</H1>
6: Fill in this form to become a member of Primary Outpost.
7: <P>
8: <FORM ACTIONFORM ACTION="/take_registration.asp">
9: Desired Username:  <INPUT TYPEINPUT TYPE="text">
10:</FORM>
11:
12:<!--#include virtual="/pagebottom.txt"-->
13:</BODY>
14:</HTML>
```

In this code, you tell the browser that when the form is submitted, you want it to go to that page. Save this page, reload it in your browser, and try again. This time you go to the page, as you had expected. However, notice the URL your browser is showing. Notice that question mark? It's the start of the querystring I mentioned in Chapter 3, "Creating Interactive Web Content" when I talked about the AdRotator redirect page. Unfortunately, there is no querystring. You neglected to assign a name to the text box, as shown on line 9 in Listing 4.6.

Listing 4.6—register.asp: Naming the username element

```
0: <%@ LANGUAGE="VBSCRIPT" %>
1: <% pageTitle = "Register" %>
2: <!--#include virtual="/pagetop.txt"-->
4:
5: <H1>Register</H1>
6: Fill in this form to become a member of Primary Outpost.
7: <P>
8: <FORM ACTIONFORM ACTION="/take_registration.asp">

9: Desired Username:  <INPUT TYPE="text" NAME="p_name">
10:</FORM>
11:
12:<!--#include virtual="/pagebottom.txt"-->
13:</BODY>
14:</HTML>
```

Save the file, reload it, and try again. Notice the URL you are presented with:

```
http://localhost/take_registration.asp?p_name=My+text
```

This is an important distinction; items that have names are submitted with the form, items that don't, aren't. Let's do two things now. Let's take a quick look at some of the attributes of the text box by setting the size, the maximum length of text, and an initial value when the page is first called up. While you're adding elements, also add two buttons (see Listing 4.7).

Listing 4.7—register.asp: Text field attributes and adding buttons

```
0: <%@ LANGUAGE="VBSCRIPT" %>
1: <!--#include virtual="/pagetop.txt"-->
2:
3: <H1>Register</H1>
4: Fill in this form to become a member of Primary Outpost.
5: <P>
6: <FORM ACTION="/take_registration.asp">
7: Desired Username:  <INPUT TYPE="text" NAME="p_name" SIZE=20 MAXLENGTH=15
➥VALUE="MyUserName">
8: <P>
9: <INPUT TYPE="submit" VALUE="Submit Registration"><INPUT TYPE="reset"
➥VALUE="Start Over">
10:</FORM>
11:
12:<!--#include virtual="/pagebottom.txt"-->
13:</BODY>
14:</HTML>
```

You haven't given either of these buttons names because you only have one submit button, so there's nothing to distinguish, but you did add values to them. As with the text box, adding a value to a button determines what the button says when you build the page. Unlike a text box, however, you can't change the value on a button.

Take a look at the text box (see Figure 4.10). Change the value to something more to your liking. Notice, that you can't put more than 15 characters in the box, however, because of the `maxlength` value that you set. This value is extremely handy, especially when you're ultimately putting the data into a database. Remember, if you say you want the column to be 50 characters long, that's all you get. It's much better to stop users from putting too many characters in the form than to let them get all the way through the form and send it back because their information doesn't fit.

Figure 4.10

You can specify starting values for your text boxes as well as set the text on the buttons.

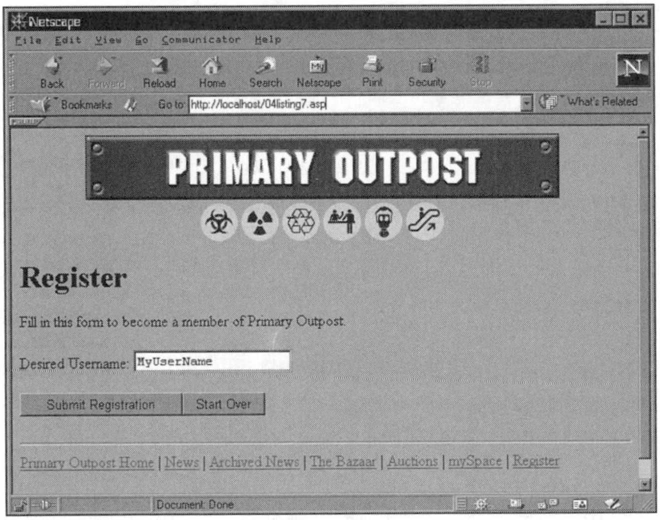

You've probably seen Reset buttons on the Web and noticed that they are used to clear a form. Most people don't realize, however, that clearing a form isn't exactly what the Reset button does. Click the Reset button, Start Over. Instead of clearing the form, it does something much more powerful; it returns the form to its original state.

Finally, there's the Submit button. It does exactly what you'd expect it to do, submit the form. You may not need it now because you only have one text field, but as soon as you add another one, the browser no longer submits when you press Enter.

Add the first part of your registration page (see Listing 4.8). You use all text boxes except for the two password entries. The password box is exactly like the text box, except that when you type in it you can't see the letters. This is to keep someone from looking over your shoulder and stealing your password when you're logging in.

Listing 4.8—register.asp: Add personal information

```
0: <%@ LANGUAGE="VBSCRIPT" %>
1: <!--#include virtual="/pagetop.txt"-->
2:
3: <H1>Register</H1>
4: Fill in this form to become a member of Primary Outpost.
5: <P>
6: <FORM ACTION="/take_registration.asp">
7: Desired Username:  <INPUT TYPE="text" NAME="p_name" SIZE=20 MAXLENGTH=15>
8: <BR>
9: Password:  <INPUT TYPE="password" NAME="p_pass1">
10:<BR>
11:Password (again):  <INPUT TYPE="password" NAME="p_pass2">
12:<BR>
13:First Name:  <INPUT TYPE="text" NAME="p_first">
14:<BR>
15:Last Name:  <INPUT TYPE="text" NAME="p_last">
16:<BR>
17:Email Address:  <INPUT TYPE="text" NAME="p_email">
18:<P>
19:<INPUT TYPE="submit" VALUE="Submit Registration"><INPUT TYPE="reset"
➥VALUE="Start Over">
20:</FORM>
21:
22:<!--#include virtual="/pagebottom.txt"-->
23:</BODY>
24:</HTML>
```

4

OK, now that you have a basic form, let's do something with it. Open your
take_registration.asp file. You're going to do two things here. First take your values and put them into variables, and print them to the screen to see them.

You might be wondering why you're doing that when you're ultimately going to put
the data into a database. Good question. Here's the answer: If you build a house,
would you build the whole thing, lay your carpet, bring in your furniture, and *then*
make sure the foundation was level? Of course not! (And if you would, please let me
know, so I don't hire you to build my house.) Instead, you'd check each step as you
went along so that you knew the work was solid before you built anything on it.
That's what you're doing here, and what you're going to do as you build your project. You'll check each step to make sure it works before you move on. That way, if
there's a problem, you'll only have to backtrack one or two steps to find out where it
is. Open the take_registration.asp file we created earlier with your text editor and
add the code in Listing 4.9.

Listing 4.9—take_register.asp: Getting information from the form

```
0: <%@ LANGUAGE="VBSCRIPT" %>
1: <!--#include virtual="/pagetop.txt"-->
2: <%
3:     p_userid = Request.querystring("p_name")
4:     p_pass1 = Request.querystring ("p_pass1")
5:     p_pass2 = Request.querystring ("p_pass2")
6:     p_first = Request.querystring ("p_first")
7:     p_last = Request.querystring ("p_last")
8:     p_email = Request.querystring ("p_email")
9: %>
10:
11:<H2>User Registration</H2>
12:
13:Userid:  <%= p_userid %> <BR>
14:Password:  <%= p_pass1 %> <BR>
15:Password (again):  <%= p_pass2 %><BR>
16:First Name:  <%= p_first %><BR>
17:Last Name:  <%= p_last %><BR>
18:Email:  <%= p_email %><BR>
19:
20:<!--#include virtual="/pagebottom.txt"-->
21:</BODY>
22:</HTML>
```

When you submit the form, you should see a listing of your form elements (see Figure 4.11).

Figure 4.11

After you extract the values from the request object, you can do whatever you want with them.

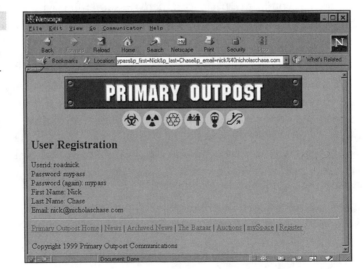

Now you add another type of form element (a radio button) to `register.asp`. Radio buttons are handy because they make sure that the user enters only one value, so the choices are mutually exclusive of each other. Let's add a yes or no question, as in Listing 4.10:

Listing 4.10—register.asp: Adding radio buttons

```
...
17:Email Address:  <INPUT TYPE="text" NAME="p_email">
18:<BR>
19:Do you believe in aliens?
20:<INPUT TYPE="radio" NAME="p_aliens" VALUE="yes" CHECKED>Absolutely
21:<INPUT TYPE="radio" NAME="p_aliens" VALUE="no">Don't be ridiculous
22:<P>
23:<INPUT TYPE="submit" VALUE="Submit Registration"><INPUT TYPE="reset"
VALUE="Start Over">
24:</FORM>
25:
26:<!--#include virtual="/pagebottom.txt"-->
27:</BODY>
28:</HTML>
```

Notice on lines 20 and 21 that you explicitly assigned a value to the radio button that doesn't match what you actually see on the page. It's this value that's going to be submitted with the form. The text on the page, or label, is there to help the user, and the form is oblivious to it. You could switch the answers, and the form would never know about it, submitting the value No when a user chooses Absolutely and vice versa.

The actual name for this is not radio button, but radio group, because the form groups them together based on their name to make sure that only one is active per group at any given time. Now add a second set of buttons asking about user preferences (see Listing 4.11).

Listing 4.11—register.asp: A second radio group

```
...
21:<INPUT TYPE="radio" NAME="p_aliens" VALUE="no">Don't be ridiculous
22:<P>
23:How do you enjoy your science fiction?<BR>
24:<INPUT TYPE="radio" NAME="p_medium" VALUE="television">Television<BR>
25:<INPUT TYPE="radio" NAME="p_medium" VALUE="movies">Movies<BR>
26:<INPUT TYPE="radio" NAME="p_medium" VALUE="books">Books<BR>
27:<INPUT TYPE="radio" NAME="p_medium" VALUE="comics">Comics<BR>
28:<INPUT TYPE="radio" NAME="p_medium" VALUE="online">Online<BR>
29:<INPUT TYPE="radio" NAME="p_medium" VALUE="fanzines">Fanzines<BR>
30:<P>
31:<INPUT TYPE="submit" VALUE="Submit Registration"><INPUT TYPE="reset"
➡VALUE="Start Over">
```

continues

Listing 4.11—continued

```
32:</FORM>
33:
24:<!--#include virtual="/pagebottom.txt"-->
35:</BODY>
36:</HTML>
```

Notice that because you didn't set any buttons as CHECKED to begin with, none of them were checked. However as soon as you click a button, you are committed to submitting at least one choice. There is no way to uncheck that element without selecting another in the group.

The trouble with a radio group, is that you can have only one element checked and you want to allow users to set multiple media, which you can do by changing the second set of radio buttons to check boxes (see Listing 4.12).

Listing 4.12—register.asp: Using check boxes instead of a radio group

```
...
22:<P>
23:How do you enjoy your science fiction?<BR>
24:<INPUT TYPE="checkbox" NAME="p_medium" VALUE="television">Television<BR>
25:<INPUT TYPE="checkbox" NAME="p_medium" VALUE="movies">Movies<BR>
26:<INPUT TYPE="checkbox" NAME="p_medium" VALUE="books">Books<BR>
27:<INPUT TYPE="checkbox" NAME="p_medium" VALUE="comics">Comics<BR>
28:<INPUT TYPE="checkbox" NAME="p_medium" VALUE="online">Online<BR>
29:<INPUT TYPE="checkbox" NAME="p_medium" VALUE="fanzines">Fanzines<BR>
30:<P>
31:<INPUT TYPE="submit" VALUE="Submit Registration"><INPUT TYPE="reset"
➥VALUE="Start Over">
32:</FORM>
33:
34:<!--#include virtual="/pagebottom.txt"-->
35:</BODY>
36:</HTML>
```

With the check boxes, users can choose as many options as they want, which brings up a whole new issue: How do you deal with this when you process the form?

Choose several of the medium items and submit the form. Take a look at the URL in your browser. You'll see p_medium several times, with different values. When your Active Server Page tries to evaluate the querystring and pull out a value for p_medium, it actually gets a series of values, a type of array (see Figure 4.12).

Figure 4.12

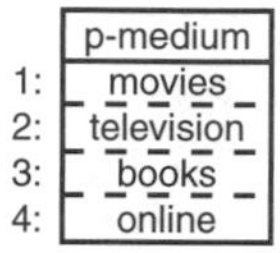

An array is a numbered series of related items.

Instead of figuring out how many items are in the array and looping through it, let ASP worry about it, as on lines 20 through 24 in Listing 4.13.

Listing 4.13—take_register.asp: Processing multiple check boxes with a `for each` loop

```
...
11:<H2>User Registration</H2>
12:
13:Userid:  <%= p_userid %> <BR>
14:Password:  <%= p_pass1 %> <BR>
15:Password (again):  <%= p_pass2 %><BR>
16:First Name:  <%= p_first %><BR>
17:Last Name:  <%= p_last %><BR>
18:Email:  <%= p_email %><BR>
19:<%
20:    for each p_medium in request.querystring("p_medium")
21:%>
22:        Preferred medium:  <%= p_medium %><BR>
23:<%
24:    next
25:%>
26:<!--#include virtual="/pagebottom.txt"-->
27:</BODY>
28:</HTML>
```

With a `for each` loop, VBScript loops through each item and assigns it to `p_medium`. This item might be text, as it is in this case, or a kind of object. When there are no more items to look at, the loop ends. This way, it doesn't matter how many elements a user chooses, the code will still work.

Now that you have all of your information, you need to start thinking about how you can store this information in the database. This process is called data modeling.

Data Modeling

One thing about building Web sites is that you hit upon a lot of different disciplines. Fortunately, you don't have to be an expert at all of them. I bring that up now because data modeling is another concept that could have a book of its own. In designing a database, there are a lot of factors to consider, from deciding what database to use in the first place, to how to lay out the files on the disks, to what tables to use. In this case, however, you have a very small database, so you can discount all but the tables themselves.

Two excellent books on data modeling are *Case Method: Entity Relationship Modeling (Computer Aided Systems Engineering)* by Richard Barker, and *Case Method: Function and Process Modeling* by Richard Barker and Cliff Longman.

Normally, you would design the entire database first, so that if one section affects the others, you don't have to make changes later. To keep things simple in this project, however, you design each section as it's needed.

Determining Entities

An entity is something of importance that needs to be tracked. In this case, you track users, but exactly what information about the users are you tracking? If you put everything in one table and laid it out spreadsheet style, it would look like Figure 4.13.

Figure 4.13

All user information in a single spreadsheet-like table.

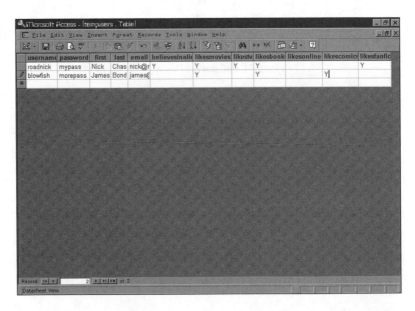

You certainly could track that way, but what if you add another preference? You'd have to add another column to the table. Plus, you'd have all that wasted space keeping track of preferences that don't apply to the user in question. Instead, consider the user and their preferences to be two different entities, related to each other (see Figure 4.14).

Figure 4.14

One member can have one or more preferences, and each preference can be owned by one or more members.

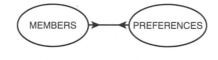

You could eliminate the wasted empty space and the problem of adding extra columns by listing it, as shown in Figure 4.15.

Figure 4.15

You need only one media column, really.

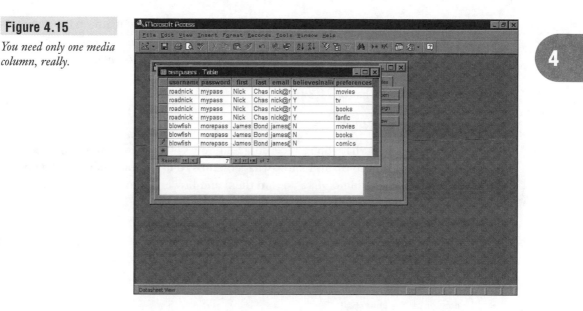

But then you waste even *more* space by listing the user's information over and over, when all you really need to know is which users owns each preference. We can do that with just two tables (see Figure 4.16).

Figure 4.16

By using two tables and linking them together with a key, such as the userid, *you give yourself a lot of flexibility.*

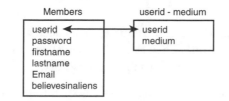

In this case, use the username as the key that links the information together.

EXCURSION

Primary Keys

In the members table, the username is the primary key. which means every member has to have a username, and each username must be unique. If you want a member's information, you can tell the database to look for the username, and it needs no other information.

As far as the `user_members` table is concerned, the username is a foreign key. That means that if you put a value in for the username, it has to match one that already exists in the members table.

Two words about naming things: be consistent. It doesn't really matter what your naming convention is, as long as you stick to it. It would be nice, though, if other people could understand what you were doing based on how you named things. That's why I named the second table `user_medium`. One glance and I know not only what it is, but also what else it's related to.

The Actual Tables

Now that you know what you're recording and how you're recording it, you need to finish designing the tables. You know what columns to use in each table; now you need to decide what kind of data goes in them and how much of it. The create scripts for these two tables would be as follows:

```
create table members (
    username    char(30),
    password    char(30),
    first_name    char(30),
    last_name    char(30),
    email    char(30),
    comments    char(500),
    believes_in_aliens    char(30)
    )

create table user_medium (
    username    char(30),
    medium    char(30)
    )
```

A create script allows you to create a database object such as a table without having to go through any special tools. They can be run anywhere that you can run SQL, and enable you to easily recreate your tables if necessary.

Assume that all your columns are going to hold text, and most of them are going to be 30 characters long; that's larger than you really need, but that's ok for now.

In your database, create two tables the same way you created the ad_log table. If you don't have a database installed in your system and you created an Access database when we set up the DSN, you can use the execute command to run the create scripts and create your tables.

Inserting the data

Now that you have the tables, you can insert your member data. You can do this exactly the same way that you did for the ad logs using the code in Listing 4.14.

Listing 4.14—take_registration.asp: Inserting data

```
0: <%@ LANGUAGE="VBSCRIPT" %>
1: <!--#include virtual="/pagetop.txt"-->
2: <%
3:     p_userid = Request.querystring("p_name")
4:     p_pass1 = Request.querystring ("p_pass1")
5:     p_pass2 = Request.querystring ("p_pass2")
6:     p_first = Request.querystring ("p_first")
7:     p_last = Request.querystring ("p_last")
8:     p_email = Request.querystring("p_email")
9:
10:    set outpostDB = Server.CreateOjbect("ADODB.Connection")
11:
12:    theSQL = "insert into members "
13:    theSQL = theSQL & "(username, password, first_name, last_name, "
14:    theSQL = theSQL & "email, believes_in_aliens)"
15:    theSQL = theSQL & " values ('"&p_userid&"', '"&p_pass1&"', '"
16:    theSQL = theSQL & p_first&"', '"&p_last &"','"&p_email&"', '"
17:    theSQL = theSQL & p_believes_in_aliens&"')"
18:
19:    outpostDB.Execute(theSQL)
20:
21:    for each p_medium in Request.querystring("p_medium")
22:         theSQL = "insert into userid_medium (userid, medium) values
➥('"&p_userid&"', '"&p_medium&"')"
23:         outpostDB.Execute(theSQL)
24:    next
25:
26:    outpostDB.close
27:    set outpostDB = Nothing
28:
29:%>
30:
31:<H2>User Registration</H2>
```

...

Now fill out a membership form and submit it, and check your tables. You're done with the registration form, right? Wrong. If you reload the page, you get another copy of your membership information in the tables, but you don't want more than one person to have the same username. You can handle this in two ways. One way is to simply check for duplicates before you do the insert, but that's an extra step to slow you down.

The other way to handle it is to designate the username column as a primary key in the database.

Set the username column in the members table as a primary key. If you're in Access, click the column and at the bottom of the column, where it says Indexed, choose Yes (No duplicates). Beside Required, choose Yes. (That's all a primary key really means: that it's unique and it's not empty.)

After you do that, the database won't let you insert duplicate records. All you have to do is try the insert and check for an error.

Error Handling

ASP provides you with several scripting objects that help with various tasks. One of them is the Err object, which helps you handle errors.

If you try to reload your page after you've already submitted it once, you get an error message. That message isn't very informative, however, and it's certainly not something we want our users to see. We can, however, handle this ourselves and avoid the error page.

You can handle the error with an On Error statement. What this means is that you tell ASP what to do if an error occurs. In VBScript, you don't have many error handling statements to choose from, but you can make do with On Error Resume Next. What this tells ASP is to keep going when it gets to an error. Add this to your page (see Listing 4.15).

Listing 4.15—take_registration.asp: Avoiding the error page

```
0: <%@ LANGUAGE="VBSCRIPT" %>
1: <!--#include virtual="/pagetop.txt"-->
2: <%
3:     On Error Resume Next
4:
5:     p_userid = Request.querystring("p_name")
6:     p_pass1 = Request.querystring ("p_pass1")
7:     p_pass2 = Request.querystring ("p_pass2")…
```

If you reload again, you won't get the error, but you won't get any indication that something bad happened, either. Now that you took that notification out of ASP's hands, you need to check for it yourself.

When an error occurs, three pieces of information are recorded in the Err object: the error number, a description of the error, and the source of the error. If there is no error, the error number is zero, so you can do the insert, and then check this value to see if it was successful, as in Listing 4.16.

Listing 4.16—take_registration.asp: Checking for errors

```
...
26:    for each p_medium in Request.querystring("p_medium")
27:         theSQL = "insert into userid_medium (userid, medium) values —
➥('"&p_userid&"', '"&p_medium&"')"
28:         outpostDB.Execute(theSQL)
29:    next
30:
31:    outpostDB.close
32:    set outpostDB = Nothing
33:%>
34:
35:<%  if Err.number = 0 then
36:
37:         'All is well with the world %>
38:
39:         <H2>User Registration</H2>
40:         Thank you for registering with Primary Outpost!
41:
42:<%  else %>
43:
44:         'There was a problem with their registration
45:
46:         <h2>Problem</h2>
47:         There was a problem with your registration.
48:         Please go back and choose a different username.
49:
50:<%  end if %>
51:
52:
53:<!--#include virtual="/pagebottom.txt"-->
54:</BODY>
55:</HTML>
```

On line 35 we check for any errors, then display the proper message. While you check for errors, make sure that the user didn't mistype his or her password before you allow them to register. We can do this with the second if-then-else statement on lines 12 and 53 through 58 of Listing 4.17.

4

Listing 4.17—take_registration.asp: Making sure the passwords match

```
0: <%@ LANGUAGE="VBSCRIPT" %>
1: <!--#include virtual="/pagetop.txt"-->
2: <%
3:      On Error Resume Next
4:
5:      p_userid = Request.querystring("p_name")
6:      p_pass1 = request. querystring ("p_pass1")
7:      p_pass2 = request. querystring ("p_pass2")
8:      p_first = request. querystring ("p_first")
9:      p_last = request. querystring ("p_last")
10:     p_email = request. querystring ("p_email")
11:
12:     if p_pass1 = p_pass2 then
13:
14:         set outpostDB = server.createObject("ADODB.Connection")
15:         outpostDB.open "outpost"
16:
17:         theSQL = "insert into members "
18:         theSQL = theSQL & "(username, password, first_name, last_name,
19:         theSQL = theSQL & "email, believes_in_aliens)"
20:         theSQL = theSQL & " values ('"&p_userid&"', '"&p_pass1&"', '"
21:         theSQL = theSQL & p_first&"', '"&p_last&"', '"&p_email&"', '"
22:         theSQL = theSQL & p_believes_in_aliens&"')"
23:
24:         outpostDB.Execute(theSQL)
25:
26:         for each p_medium in Request.form("p_medium")
27:             theSQL = "insert into userid_medium (userid, medium) values ('"
28:             theSQL = theSQL & p_userid&"', '"&p_medium&"')"
29:             outpostDB.Execute(theSQL)
30:         next
31:
32:         outpostDB.close
33:         set outpostDB = Nothing
34:%>
35:
36:<%       if Err.number = 0 then
37:
38:          'All is well with the world %>
39:
40:          <H2>User Registration</H2>
41:          Thank you for registering with Primary Outpost!
42:
43:<%       else %>
44:
45:          'There was a problem with their registration
46:
47:          <h2>Problem</h2>
48:          There was a problem with your registration.
49:          Please go back and choose a different username.
50:
```

```
51:<%        end if
52:
53:    else
54:         'p_pass1 doesn't match p_pass2
55:         <h2>Password Error</h2>
56:         Both entries for your password must match.
57:         Please try again.  Thank you!
58:    end if
59:%>
60:
61:
62:<!--#include virtual="/pagebottom.txt"-->
63:</BODY>
64:</HTML>
```

Notice that you nested the if-then statement. That means that you have statements one inside the other, like a Russian doll. This syntax is perfectly acceptable and is a good argument for commenting your code and keeping it neat. Few things are more frustrating than getting an error message and not knowing where it's coming from because your code is unintelligible.

Completing the Form

The form is almost complete; however, notice that all of the information you submitted, including your password, is in plain sight in the URL. That's fine for this example because you needed to see what the form was doing, but it's not a good idea in a real application. What you need to do is change the method that the form uses to send its information to the server.

Two methods are available: get and post. When a form is submitted using get, the information is put into the querystring. When a form is submitted using post the information is added to the request itself and processed in a different way.

If you don't specify one or the other, the browser uses get, and that's what you've been seeing. You want to use post. Add this to the <form> tag in register.asp, in this fragment of register.asp shown in Listing 4.18.

Listing 4.18—register.asp: Changing the form from get to post

```
0: <%@ LANGUAGE="VBSCRIPT" %>
1: <!--#include virtual="/pagetop.txt"-->
2:
3: <H1>Register</H1>
4: Fill in this form to become a member of Primary Outpost.
5: <P>
6: <FORM ACTION="/take_registration.asp" method="post">
7: Desired Username:  <INPUT TYPE="text" NAME="p_name" SIZE=20 MAXLENGTH=15>
...
```

That's all you have to do on the front end—the part the user sees—but you still need to modify the back end—the part that happens behind the scenes. When a form is submitted using post, it doesn't go into the URL, so there's no querystring. Instead, it goes into the form collection. So instead of using

```
Request.querystring("username")
```

you want to use

```
Request.form("username")
```

You can use your text editor to change every instance of querystring to form, so that take_registration.asp looks like Listing 4.19.

Listing 4.19—take_registration.asp: The final form

```
0: <%@ LANGUAGE="VBSCRIPT" %>
1: <!--#include virtual="/pagetop.txt"-->
2: <%
3:      On Error Resume Next
4:
5:      p_userid = Request.form("p_name")
6:      p_pass1 = Request.form("p_pass1")
7:      p_pass2 = Request.form("p_pass2")
8:      p_first = Request.form("p_first")
9:      p_last = Request.form("p_last")
10:     p_email = Request.form("p_email")
11:
12:     if p_pass1 = p_pass2 then
13:
14:         set outpostDB = server.createObject("ADODB.Connection")
15:         outpostDB.open "outpost"
16:
17:         theSQL = "insert into members "
18:         theSQL = theSQL & "(username, password, first_name, last_name,
19:         theSQL = theSQL & "email, believes_in_aliens)"
20:         theSQL = theSQL & " values ('"&p_userid&"', '"&p_pass1&"', '"
21:         theSQL = theSQL & p_first&"', '"&p_last&"', '"&p_email&"', '"
22:         theSQL = theSQL & p_believes_in_aliens&"')"
23:
24:         outpostDB.Execute(theSQL)
25:
26:         for each p_medium in Request.form("p_medium")
27:             theSQL = "insert into userid_medium (userid, medium) values ('"
28:             theSQL = theSQL & p_userid&"', '"&p_medium&"')"
29:             outpostDB.Execute(theSQL)
30:         next
31:
32:         outpostDB.close
33:         set outpostDB = Nothing
34:%>
35:
```

```
36:<%      if Err.number = 0 then
37:
38:            'All is well with the world %>
39:
40:            <H2>User Registration</H2>
41:            Thank you for registering with Primary Outpost!
42:
43:<%      else %>
44:
45:            'There was a problem with their registration
46:
47:            <H2>Problem</H2>
48:            There was a problem with your registration.
49            Please go back and choose a different username.
50:
51:<%      end if
52:
53:    else
54:        'p_pass1 doesn't match p_pass2
55:        <H2>Password Error</H2>
56:        Both entries for your password must match.
57:        Please try again.  Thank you!
58:    end if
59:%>
60:
61:
62:<!--#include virtual="/pagebottom.txt"-->
63:</BODY>
63:</HTML>
```

Save the file and test it. Notice that you no longer have all of that information in the URL. Instead it's passed as part of the request itself.

In real life, you want to use post as much as possible. It's not only more secure (because the information isn't in plain sight) but it's also more reliable. If you start passing large quantities of information as a get, you can cause server problems later.

Keep in mind, however, that because the information isn't in the URL, your user can't bookmark the page. This may be what you want, but if it's not, you'll need to use get.

Multi-purpose Forms

What if you need a form that works as both a get and a post? One advantage of get is that you can build a link that simulates a form. For instance, I could put together a link that goes to a search page and pre-selects a category:

```
<a href="search.asp?p_category=toys">Search for toys</a>
```

When the browser calls this page, it will be treated the same as a form submitted using get. If you used Request.querystring, however, you would not be able to build a search page that uses post to submit the form under normal circumstances. Fortunately, there is an alternative. If we were to change take_registration.asp in Listing 4.19a, it would work for both a get and a post:

Listing 4.19a—take_registration.asp: Using get or post

```
0: <%@ LANGUAGE="VBSCRIPT" %>
1: <!--#include virtual="/pagetop.txt"-->
2: <%
3:     On Error Resume Next
4:
5:     p_userid = Request("p_name")
6:     p_pass1 = Request("p_pass1")
7:     p_pass2 = Request("p_pass2")
8:     p_first = Request("p_first")
9:     p_last = Request("p_last")
10:    p_email = Request("p_email")
11:
12:    if p_pass1 = p_pass2 then
13:
14:        set outpostDB = server.createObject("ADODB.Connection")
15:        outpostDB.open "outpost"
16:
17:        theSQL = "insert into members "
18:        theSQL = theSQL & "(username, password, first_name, last_name,
19:        theSQL = theSQL & "email, believes_in_aliens)"
20:        theSQL = theSQL & " values ('"&p_userid&"', '"&p_pass1&"', '"
21:        theSQL = theSQL & p_first&"', '"&p_last&"', '"&p_email&"', '"
22:        theSQL = theSQL & p_believes_in_aliens&"')"
23:
24:        outpostDB.Execute(theSQL)
25:
26:        for each p_medium in Request("p_medium")
27:            theSQL = "insert into userid_medium (userid, medium) values ('"
28:            theSQL = theSQL & p_userid&"', '"&p_medium&"')"
29:            outpostDB.Execute(theSQL)
30:        next
31:
32:        outpostDB.close
33:        set outpostDB = Nothing
```

On lines 5 though 10 and 26, we're using a syntax that will allow VBScript to use whichever data is available. If there is not querystring, it will check the form collection. This way we can use the form action in either situation.

Tidying Up—HTML Tables

Finally, let's look at the registration form itself. It's pretty ugly right now, with nothing lining up. You can try to line up the form fields with spaces, but that's ineffective. Instead, use HTML tables.

HTML tables, like database tables, are made up of rows and columns, but they don't have anything to do with data or databases, except that they are the perfect way to format data on the page. You need to know three basic sets of tags:

> <TABLE></TABLE> starts and ends the table itself.
>
> <TR></TR> defines the table rows and contains cells of data.
>
> <TD></TD> defines the table data cells and contains the actual information you're displaying.

You use these tags to make your text boxes line up on the form, as shown in Listing 4.20.

Listing 4.20—register.asp: Cleaning up the page layout with HTML tables

```
0: <%@ LANGUAGE="VBSCRIPT" %>
1: <!--#include virtual="/pagetop.txt"-->
2:
3: <H1>Register</H1>
4: Fill in this form to become a member of Primary Outpost.
5: <P>
6: <FORM ACTION="/take_registration.asp" method="post">
7: <TABLE BORDER=1>
8: <TR>
9:    <TD>Desired Username:  </TD>
10:    <TD><INPUT TYPE="text" NAME="p_name" SIZE=20 MAXLENGTH=15></TD>
11:</TR>
12:<TR>
13:    <TD>Password:  </TD>
14:    <TD><INPUT TYPE="password" NAME="p_pass1"></TD>
15:</TR>
16:<TR>
17:    <TD>Password (again):  </TD>
18:    <TD><INPUT TYPE="password" NAME="p_pass2"></TD>
19:</TR>
20:<TR>
21:    <TD>First Name:  </TD>
22:    <TD><INPUT TYPE="text" NAME="p_first"></TD>
23:</TR>
24:<TR>
25:    <TD>Last Name:  </TD>
26:    <TD><INPUT TYPE="text" NAME="p_last"></TD>
```

continues

Listing 4.20—continued

```
27:</TR>
28:<TR>
29:    <TD>Email Address:  </TD>
30:    <TD><INPUT TYPE="text" NAME="p_email"></TD>
31:</TR>
32:</TABLE>
33:Do you believe in aliens?
...
```

On line 7, at the start of the table, I included a border, so you can see what's happening. You take it out in a minute, but first look at what's going on here. Each item has its own row and its own cell (see Figure 4.17). All the text boxes are in the second column, so they line up with each other. While you're adjusting the layout, you can also neaten up the preferences (see Listing 4.21).

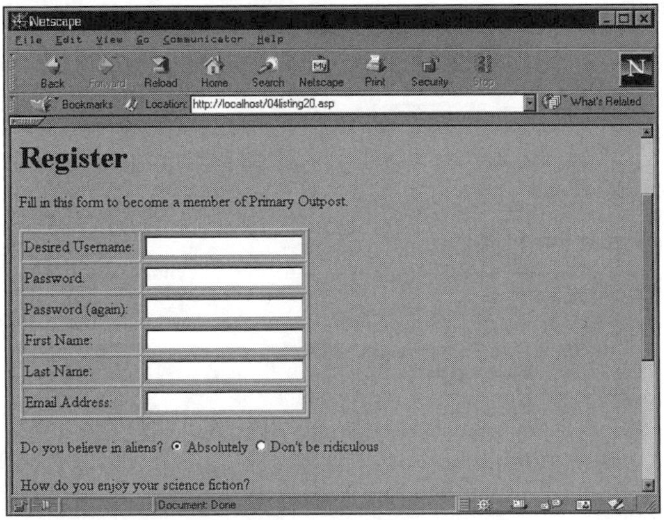

Figure 4.17

HTML tables help neaten up a page by lining up elements.

Listing 4.21—register.asp: Cleaning up the preferences

```
...
7: <TABLE BORDER=0>
8: <TR>
9:     <TD>Desired Username:  </TD>
10:    <TD><INPUT TYPE="text" NAME="p_name" SIZE=20 MAXLENGTH=15></TD>
11:</TR>
12:<TR>
13:    <TD>Password:  </TD>
14:    <TD><INPUT TYPE="password" NAME="p_pass1"></TD>
...
```

```
35:How do you enjoy your science fiction?<BR>
37:<TABLE BORDER = 1>
38:    <TR>
39:        <TD><INPUT TYPE="checkbox" NAME="p_medium" VALUE= "television"></TD>
40:        <TD>Television</TD>
41:        <TD><INPUT TYPE="checkbox" NAME="p_medium" VALUE= "movies"></TD>
42:        <TD>Movies</TD>
43:    </TR>
44:    <TR>
45:        <TD><INPUT TYPE="checkbox" NAME="p_medium" VALUE= "books"></TD>
46:      <TD>Books</TD>
47:        <TD><INPUT TYPE="checkbox" NAME="p_medium" VALUE= "comics"></TD>
48:        <TD>Comics</TD>
49:    </TR>
50:    <TR>
51:        <TD><INPUT TYPE="checkbox" NAME="p_medium" VALUE= "online"></TD>
52:        <TD>Online</TD>
53:        <TD><INPUT TYPE="checkbox" NAME="p_medium" VALUE= "fanzines"></TD>
54:        <TD>Fanzines</TD>
55:    </TR>
56:    <TR>
57:        <TD><INPUT TYPE="submit" VALUE="Submit Registration"></TD>
58:        <TD><INPUT TYPE="reset" VALUE="Start Over"></TD>
59:    </TR>
60:</TABLE>
61:<P>
62:</FORM>
63:
64:<!--#include virtual="/pagebottom.txt"-->
65:</BODY>
66:</HTML>
```

Again I turned on the border for the bottom table on line 37, so you can see what's going on (see Figure 4.18).

Figure 4.18

HTML tables adjust to the data you provide them.

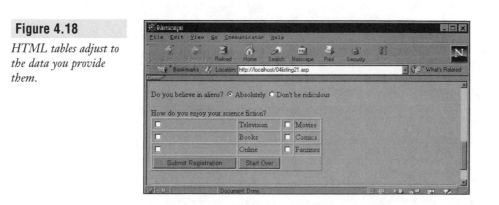

Notice the following about HTML tables:

- The table automatically adjusts to the fact that you had more than two columns and treats them accordingly.
- The table adjusts the first column to make room for the Submit button, moving everything to the right.
- The table doesn't mind that the last row only had two columns, and the rest of them had four. It adjusts to fit the longest row.

If you want to neaten things more, you could have the Submit Registration and Start Over buttons span two columns each. Fortunately, you can place the following attribute on the table data tag on lines 57 and 58 of Listing 4.22:

Listing 4.22—register.asp: Spanning two columns

```
...
56:    <TR>
57:       <td colspan=2><INPUT TYPE="submit" VALUE="Submit Registration"></TD>
58:       <td colspan=2><INPUT TYPE="reset" VALUE="Start Over"></TD>
59:    </TR>
60:</TABLE>
61:<P>
62:</FORM>
...
```

A similar attribute called rowspan lets us make a cell more than one row high.

Keep one very important thing in mind about tables. Because the browser doesn't display any part of the table until it knows where to put everything, it doesn't display anything until it receives the </TABLE> tag. That means that if you have a table that takes a while to download, the user is looking at empty space, and this is a *bad thing*. You can avoid this by breaking your content into smaller tables and always making sure to specify the height and width of images.

Save register.asp and open it in the browser to check the layout.

Summary

In this chapter, I covered

- Creating a Data Source Name (DSN) using the Control Panels to allow ASP to connect to a database.
- Connecting to the database using the ADODB.Connection object.
- Using SQL insert statements to add data to a database table.

- Using HTML forms to get information from the user and tables to lay out the information on the page.
- Data modeling—creating tables.

In the next chapter, you will look at customizing your site using cookies. We'll also be selecting information from the database and introducing RecordSets.

4

Chapter 5

In this chapter

- *Why Personalize?*
- *Introduction to Cookies*
- *Querying the Database*
- *Cookie Expiration Dates*
- *Customizing* mySpace
- *Putting it All Together*

Personalizing the Site Using Cookies and Database Information

Why Personalize?

At this point we've created content for our users, but we'd like to make sure that they keep coming back. One way sites accomplish this is with personalized content so that our users feel at home. This can take a variety of forms, such as keeping track of content a user has already seen and giving him or her additional content based on those actions or by just asking users their preferences and using those preferences to decide what to offer.

We're going to customize the site by building mySpace, an area that contains customized content based on the user's preferences. This area is going to have three sections:

- **myNews**: Users will specify the categories of news they're interested in, and that will be given the highest priority.
- **myLinks**: Our intent is for our users to set this page as their starting point on the Web, or portal. We'll provide a list of links that they can choose to include on their page and give them an opportunity to add their own links.
- **myAuctions**: Users can track the items that they are selling or buying from this page.

myAuctions, will be added later, after we've built that section, but we have plenty to work with here.

Introduction to Cookies

When it comes to Web development, I can't think of a single item that has caused more confusion and controversy than cookies. There are a number of reasons for this, some justified and some not. Let's start by dispelling some myths about what cookies are and are not.

Cookies are small amounts of text a site leaves on your computer so that it recognizes you when you come back. A cookie is not a virus, and because it's just text (not executable) it's not capable of spreading viruses. Because a site can *only* read the cookies it's left you (and not anybody else's), one site can't steal another's information. Limitations on how big a cookie can be (4K) and how many a particular site can send you (a maximum of 20) mean that a malicious site would have a hard time filling up your hard drive.

Information is stored within cookies as name-value pairs. There's a variable name and a value for it, as well as information on when the cookie was sent, and by whom. Here's an excerpt from my one cookie file, cookies.txt. (If you're using Internet Explorer, they're each in a separate file in the cookies directory, and if you're on the Macintosh, look for a file named MagicCookie.)

Figure 5.1

A sample cookie.txt file.

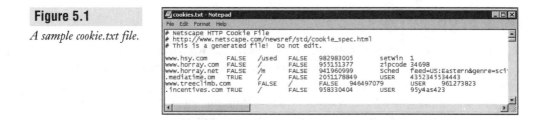

Let's take a look at these entries in Figure 5.1. In addition to the name of the site that sent them, such as www.hsy.com there is a unique identifier and information as to whether or not the cookie must be sent securely (we'll cover security later). The important part, however, is the last two items, the name and value.

Notice that in most of these cases, all that is stored is something to identify me. After the site knows what user I am, any additional information is stored on the site itself. This is how it should be. In some cases, like horray.com, the information itself is stored in the cookie. This isn't too bad, as long as you don't go overboard. It's one thing to store a lot of information in a single cookie; I've seen them several hundred characters long on occasion, but try to limit the number of cookies that you send.

Notice that I have three different ids from `mediatime.com`, `treeclimb.com`, and `incentives.com`. This may not seem strange until you realize that they're all the same site, Media Enterprises. But remember what I said earlier: A site can only read its own cookies, and that's determined by the domain name. Because these three sections have different domain names, they can't share the cookies.

Note also that I have two here from `hooray.com`. If I set up my browser to warn me before accepting a cookie, I'm going to get two warnings on every page. More than that, and it gets annoying quickly.

Cookies and Privacy Concerns

If cookies are so benign (and they are), why wouldn't I want to just accept them as a matter of course, as most of us do? There are several reasons that some people get a little nervous about cookies. After you get over the myths that we discussed earlier, there's one issue left: privacy.

When you go to some major sites and get a banner ad, that ad isn't necessarily coming from the site itself. It may be coming from a service that is cashing in on the idea of one-to-one marketing—finding your customer's preferences and playing to them. When I go to one of these sites, they take note of where I went, or perhaps what I asked a search engine to find for me. They probably know a good bit about user number 9a1f38a3. There is one thing they don't know, though: Who is user number 9a1f38a3? Unless I provide it in some way, they have no name to put with the number. (Of course, there are numerous ways that I can unknowingly provide it, most of which start with "Fill out this form to get your FREE…") The grocery store where I have one of those discount cards probably knows more about me than they do.

But this is an issue and an issue that some people feel very strongly about. Personally, if I have to look at ads, I'd rather they were ads I might be interested in, but the privacy implications are significant.

To ease their concerns, your users can set up their browsers to warn them before accepting a cookie, and then they can decide whether or not to accept it. If they decide not to and your site depends on cookies to function properly, they will experience problems. Personally, I always wanted to use a cookie something like the one you see in Figure 5.2 explaining why they're necessary so that users wouldn't dismiss them out of hand.

Figure 5.2

Users can set their browsers to warn them before accepting a cookie, or even disable cookies completely.

Cookies and Collections

We're not going to do anything extremely complicated with cookies. We're just going to store two pieces of information: one that tells us who the user is so we can welcome them back, and one that tells us that the user has logged in so we don't have to continuously ask for a username and password.

Cookies are a two-way street: they have to be sent to the browser as part of a page, and they have to be sent to the server as part of a request. As such, we actually see cookies in both the Request object and the Response object. They take the form of a collection.

A collection, or dictionary, is similar to an array, except that instead of being indexed by a number, the information is indexed by a word. Dictionary is probably a very good term for it, because it's rather like a word and it's definition. This can make things a lot easier on us when we're programming as well, as we can refer to things directly. Let's take a look at setting up a collection and pulling information out of it. Make a copy of template.asp and call it counter.asp, and then add the text in Listing 5.1:

Listing 5.1—counter.asp: Creating a collection

```
0: <%@ LANGUAGE="VBSCRIPT" %>
1: <% pageTitle = "Counter" %>
2: <!--#include virtual="/pagetop.txt"-->
3: <%
4:     set myCol = Server.CreateObject("Scripting.Dictionary")
5:
6:     myCol("first") = "This is the first value"
7:     myCol("second") = "This is the second value"
8:     myCol("third") = "This is the third value"
9:
10:     Response.Write myCol("second")
11:%>
12:
13:<!--#include virtual="/pagebottom.txt"-->
14:</BODY>
15:</HTML>
```

On line 3 we're creating the collection as a dictionary object. (The dictionary is one of the Scripting tools that ASP provides.) After we've done that, we can set any value that we want, and then call it back again using the correct key.

Cookies are set up the same way, as collections in the Request and Response objects. Let's take a look at setting up a very simple cookie, the classic page counter. We want to check to see if the user has ever been to this page, and if so, how many times. Replace lines 3 through 11 with lines 4 through 11 of Listing 5.2.

Listing 5.2—Counter.asp: Checking for the presence of a cookie

```
0: <%@ LANGUAGE="VBSCRIPT" %>
1: <% pageTitle = "Counter" %>
2: <!--#include virtual="/pagetop.txt"-->
3:
4: <%  if Request.cookies.count = 0 then       %>
5:          Welcome!  I see this is your first time here!
6: <%          Response.cookies("howmany") = 1
7:      else     %>
8:          Welcome!  I see you've been here
9:          <%= Request.cookies("howmany") %> times before.
10: <%         Response.cookies("howmany") = Request.cookies("howmany") + 1
11:      end if %>
12:
13:<!--#include virtual="/pagebottom.txt"-->
14:</BODY>
15:</HTML>
```

The first thing we're doing, on line 4, is looking to see if there are any cookies as part of the request. Remember, the Request object is coming from the browser to the server, so it would contain any cookies that are already there. If there aren't any, it displays a first time welcome, and then sets the howmany cookie to a value of 1. If there are cookies, it displays the current value, and then it updates the value. It does this by setting the value in the Response object, which goes from the server to the browser.

There's just one problem with all this: it won't work this way. This is because of the way that Web pages in general and cookies in particular are sent back and forth.

When your browser asks for a Web page, there is a lot more information sent than just the content that you actually see. This information is in the headers—information that is just for the browser's use. These headers contain information, such as the type of data (so the browser knows what to do with it) and the amount of data (so the browser knows what percentage it's already downloaded). Because of this, they must always be the first thing sent to the browser. Fortunately, the Response object handles all this for us. It knows what it needs to send, and when it's done sending headers, it starts sending our content.

Cookies are part of this header information that's managed by the Response object. As such, if you're going to send any, you've got to send them before you start sending content. After the Response object starts sending content, it's too late. That's why you'll get an error if you try to run Listing 5.2 as is (see Figure 5.3). The browser was perfectly happy reading the cookie, but as soon as we tried to send one back, we had a problem. Instead, we need to move the cookies so they're sent before any page text as in Listing 5.3.

Figure 5.3

Cookies must always be sent before any content.

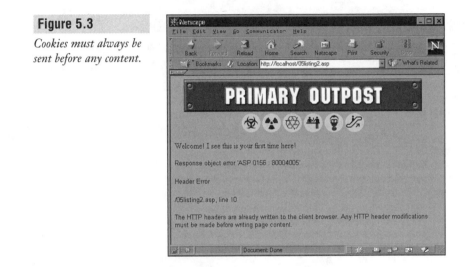

Listing 5.3—counter.asp: Sending the cookies first

```
0: <%@ LANGUAGE="VBSCRIPT" %>1: <%  if Request.cookies.count = 0 then
2:          howmany = 0
3:          Response.cookies("howmany") = 1
4:      else
5:          howmany = Request.cookies("howmany")
6:          Response.cookies("howmany") = Request.cookies("howmany") + 1
7:      end if  %>
8: <% pageTitle = "Counter" %>
9: <!--#include virtual="/pagetop.txt"-->
10:
11:<%    if howmany = 0 then     %>
12:        Welcome!  I see this is your first time here!
13:<%    else      %>
14:        Welcome!  I see you've been here <%= howmany %> times before.
15:<%    end if %>
16:
17:<!--#include virtual="/pagebottom.txt"-->
18:</BODY>
19:</HTML>
```

Note that even though `pagetop.txt` is a Server Side Include, it needs to come *after* the cookies are sent. Even a blank line is considered content in this case.

Save this page and call it up with your browser. Reload a few times and watch the values change. You've just set a cookie. In a little while, we'll set some cookies for the site. In the meantime, let's take a look at how we find out who our users are so that we have some information to save.

Querying the Database

In the last chapter, we inserted information into the database. In this chapter, we're going to pull it out again. To do this, the ActiveX Data Objects (ADO) includes a special kind of object for us to use. It's called a recordset, and it's just that: a set of records from the database. We're going to use a recordset to check the username and password a user submits when logging into the site.

First let's create the form they're going to use. Make a copy of `template.asp` called `login.asp` and save it in the Web server home directory. All we really need from the user at this point is their username and password. If they're really who they say they are and they've registered, we'll have all their other information already. We also want to give them a chance to register if they haven't already (see Figure 5.4). Add the code for the login form in Listing 5.4 to `login.asp`.

Listing 5.4—login.asp: Getting the username and password from the user

```
 0: <%@ LANGUAGE="VBSCRIPT" %>
 1: <% pageTitle = "Outpost Login Page" %>
 2: <!--#include virtual="/pagetop.txt"-->
 3:
 4: <H2>Member Login</H2>
 5:
 6: <FORM ACTION="login_action.asp" METHOD="post">
 7:     Username:  <INPUT TYPE="text" NAME="p_username"><BR>
 8:     Password:  <INPUT TYPE="text" NAME="p_password"><BR>
 9:     <BR>
10:     <INPUT TYPE="submit" VALUE="Log In">1
11:     <P>
12:</FORM>
13:
14:Don't have a username and password?  You can
15:<A HREF="register.asp">register</a> for free
16:and get your own space!
17:<P>
18:
19:<!--#include virtual="/pagebottom.txt"-->
20:</BODY>
21:</HTML>
```

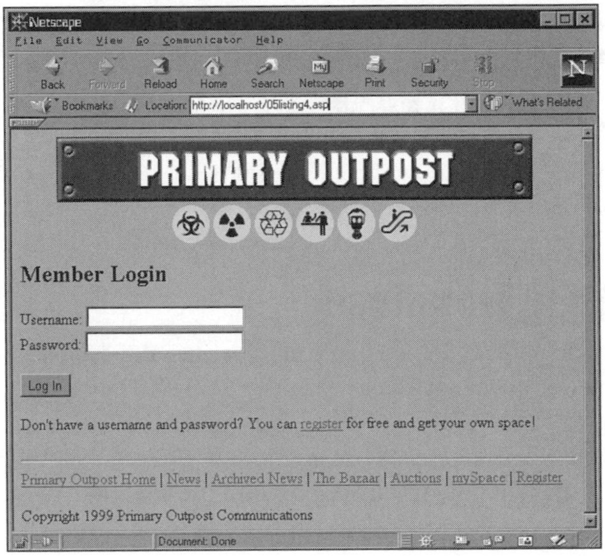

Figure 5.4

To identify our users, we need to give them a place to log in.

Now is a good time to discuss naming conventions. It doesn't matter what you call things, as long as you're consistent. There are lots of recommended methods out there, but the overriding goal is to produce code that's readable not only by you, but by the programmers that come after you.

My own personal naming convention goes like this: the name of a form action should always contain the name of the form, and _action. In this case, the form `login.asp` has as its action `login_action.asp`. This way just looking at the pages, I can tell what's what. What's more, when I name my variables, especially the ones that hold information that came in via a form, I try to start them with p_, as in `p_username`. I do this so that I always know what variables belong to the page, and what variables are, say, column names or other types of objects.

Now that we've created the login page, we're ready to create the action page. We want to do the following on this page:

- Check to make sure users used a valid username.
- Check to make sure their password matches.
- If everything checks out, bring them to the customization page. If not, send them back to the login page, preferably with some sort of message telling them that something is wrong.

Create a copy of `template.asp` called `login_action.asp`. On lines 5 and 6 of Listing 5.5 we extract the information that the user has put into the form (see Figure 5.5).

Listing 5.5—login_action.asp: Retrieving login information

```
0: <%@ LANGUAGE="VBSCRIPT" %>
1: <% pageTitle = "Outpost Login" %>
2: <!--#include virtual="/pagetop.txt"-->
3:
4: <%    p_username = Request.form("p_username")
5:       p_password = Request.form("p_password")
6:
7:       Response.Write "Username = " & p_username & "<BR>"
8:       Response.Write "Password = " & p_password & "<BR>"
9: %>
10:
11:<!--#include virtual="/pagebottom.txt"-->
12:</BODY>
13:</HTML>
```

Figure 5.5

It's important to test as you go to prevent burying yourself later.

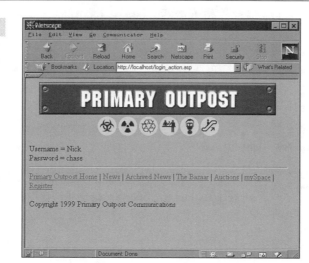

After we've made sure that the values are coming through, we can start to look at using them. If they're not, check to make sure that you haven't mistyped a name, either in the form or in the action. This is part of the debugging process. Debugging means exactly what it sounds like; the process of removing bugs from a program.

A *bug* is a problem in a program that causes something unexpected or undesirable to happen. The name actually dates back to the earliest room-sized computers when problems were caused by actual insects that got into the machinery. (These days they're also referred to as glitches, gremlins, or undocumented features.)

The best way to debug is to catch things as they happen. This extra step may seem time consuming, but it's certainly less time consuming than combing through hundreds of lines of code to find out you spelled username as unserame. I have a reputation as a very fast coder, largely because my testing time isn't taken up looking for little glitches I was unable to catch in the beginning.

At any rate, we're ready to move on. We are going to select data from the table, but we'll have to put it somewhere. The ADO provides us with a special kind of object called a *recordset* to store our set of records. After we've populated our recordset, we can find out how many records are in it, move around in it, and even update the information. There are several types of recordsets, but we're only dealing with the simplest right now. For now we're going to satisfy ourselves with checking the members table for this username and password.

We're going to use a bit of a shortcut here. Instead of creating the recordset directly, as we did with the dictionary and other objects we've created, we're going to let ASP do it for us. When we select the information from the database, ASP has to have somewhere to put it, so it will create the recordset and populate it for us on line 12 of Listing 5.6.

Listing 5.6—login_action.asp: Selecting login information from the database

```
0: <%@ LANGUAGE="VBSCRIPT" %>
1: <% pageTitle = "Outpost Login" %>
2: <!--#include virtual="/pagetop.txt"-->
3:
4: <%  p_username = Request.form("p_username")
5:      p_password = Request.form("p_password")
6:
7:      set outpostDB = Server.CCreateObject("ADODB.Connection")
8:      outpostDB.Open"outpost"
9:
10:     sqlText = "select * from members where username = '" & p_username & "'"
11:     Response.Write sqlText
12:     set userSet = outpostDB.Execute(sqlText)
13:%>
14:
15:<!--#include virtual="/pagebottom.txt"-->
16:</BODY>
17:</HTML>
```

EXCURSION

When I first did this code, I actually typed in line 10 as it appears in Listing 5.7:

Listing 5.7—login_action.asp: A common mistake

```
0: <%@ LANGUAGE="VBSCRIPT" %>
1: <% pageTitle = "Outpost Login" %>
2: <!--#include virtual="/pagetop.txt"-->
3:
4: <%  p_username = Request.form("p_username")
5:      p_password = Request.form("p_password")
6:
7:      set outpostDB = Server.CreateObjectCreateObject("ADODB.Connection")
8:      outpostDB.OpenOpen "outpost"
```

```
 9:
10:    sqlText = "select * from members where username = " & p_username
11:      Response.Write sqlText
12:      set userSet = outpostDB.Execute(sqlText)
13: %>
14:
15: <!--#include virtual="/pagebottom.txt"-->
16: </BODY>
17: </HTML>
```

This code causes an error. Perhaps you will know right off the bat what the problem is, but right now here is the information given to me in the error message:

```
Error Type:
    Microsoft OLE DB Provider for ODBC Drivers (0x80040E10)
    [Microsoft][ODBC Microsoft Access Driver] Too few parameters.
    Expected 1.
    /login_action.asp, line 12
```

Now, I could have just fixed this and moved on, but instead I want to talk a little more about debugging, and this seems like the perfect opportunity.

One nice thing about ASP is that while the error messages can be vague, they at least pin-point the line at which the error occurs. This makes it a lot easier to track down problems. In this case, the offending piece of code is

```
set userSet = outpostDB.Execute(sqlText)
```

Now, just looking at this isn't going to give us the answer. For one thing, there's nothing wrong with that statement. Let's look at the error code again. It specifically mentions Access, so it's probably got something to do with the database. Maybe our SQL statement has a problem. In previous versions of IIS we would be able to see any text that has been output before the error, but with IIS 5.0 this is no longer the default behavior. To see the text, we comment out line 12 by placing a single quote (') at the start of the line. This way the error won't occur and we'll see the output. The statement:

```
select * from members where username = Nick
```

isn't quite a correct statement. We don't want to compare `username` to a variable called `Nick`. We want to compare it to the actual string of letters, `'Nick'`. What we really want the string to say is

```
select * from members where username = 'Nick'
```

To do that, we have to change line 10. We want to add the single quote just before `p_user-name`, and that's easy. But what about the one that comes afterwards? That's easy too. We just have to add another string of characters after it. It just so happens that that string has only one character, and it's a single quote. So let's change it as shown in Listing 5.8.

Listing 5.8—login_action.asp: Passing a value to a SQL statement

```
0: <%@ LANGUAGE="VBSCRIPT" %>
1: <% pageTitle = "Outpost Login" %>
2: <!--#include virtual="/pagetop.txt"-->
```

continues

Listing 5.8—continued

```
 3:
 4: <%   p_username = Request.form("p_username")
 5:      p_password = Request.form("p_password")
 6:
 7:      set outpostDB = Server.CreateObject("ADODB.Connection")
 8:      outpostDB.Open "outpost"
 9:
10:      sqlText = "select * from members where username = '" & p_username & "'"
11:    Response.Write sqlText
12:      set userSet = outpostDB.Execute(sqlText)
13:
14:%>
15:
16:<!--#include virtual="/pagebottom.txt"-->
17:</BODY>
18:</HTML>
```

That solves the problem. The question is why did we get the error on line 12 instead of line 10? After all, that's where we made the changes. The reason is because up until line 12, `sqlText` was just a string of text. There was nothing special about it or what it was sup- posed to do. On line 12, we were actually asking ASP to do this:

```
set userSet = outpostDB.Execute("select * from members where username = Nick")
```

ASP doesn't care that the select statement came from a variable we set two lines earlier. It just cares that it doesn't work, and that's when we get the error.

So now that we've created a recordset, what do we do with it? First let's take a look at what we actually have. Let's say, for the sake of argument, that we had selected three records from the members table. Conceptually, the data in the recordset would look something like Table 5.1:

Table 5.1

BOF		
1st Record:	userSet.Fields.	item(0) = "roadNick"
	userSet.Fields.	item(1) = "mypassword"
	userSet.Fields.	item(2) = "Nick"
	userSet.Fields.	item(3) = "Chase"
	userSet.Fields.	item(4) = "aspfs@nicholaschase.com"
	userSet.Fields.	item(5) = "No comments right now"
	userSet.Fields.	item(6) = "Yes"
2nd Record:	userSet.Fields.	item(0) = "sarah"
	userSet.Fields.	item(1) = "herpassword"
	userSet.Fields.	item(2) = "Sarah"

	userSet.Fields.	item(3) = "Chase"
	userSet.Fields.	item(4) = "sarahsaddress@nicholaschase.com"
	userSet.Fields.	item(5) = "I've got lots of comments"
	userSet.Fields.	item(6) = "Yes"
3rd Record:	userSet.Fields.	item(0) = "seanman"
	userSet.Fields.	item(1) = "hispassword"
	userSet.Fields.	item(2) = "Sean"
	userSet.Fields.	item(3) = "Chase"
	userSet.Fields.	item(4) = "seanboy@nicholaschase.com"
	userSet.Fields.	item(5) = "What's a comment?"
	userSet.Fields.	item(6) = "No"

EOF

Each of these items corresponds to a column. Item(0) is username; item(1) is password, and so on. BOF represents beginning of file, and EOF represents end of file. True, this isn't really a file, but it's leftover terminology. When you're at BOF or EOF, there is no current record.

Getting back to our login page, there are two things we need to do: we need to check and see whether the username is valid, and we need to make sure that the given password is the password for that username. We do this in Listing 5.9.

Listing 5.9—Login_action.asp: Checking login information against the database

```
0: <%@ LANGUAGE="VBSCRIPT" %>
1: <% pageTitle = "Outpost Login" %>
2: <!--#include virtual="/pagetop.txt"-->
3:
4: <%  p_username = Request.form("p_username")
5:     p_password = Request.form("p_password")
6:
7:     set outpostDB = Server.CreateObject("ADODB.Connection")
8:     outpostDB.Open "outpost"
9:
10:    sqlText="select * from members where username='"&p_username&"'"
11:    Response.Write sqlText
12:    set userSet = outpostDB.Execute(sqlText)
13:    if userSet.EOF then
14:        'No such username, so the recordSet is empty
15:        Response.Write "No such username. Please <A HREF="/login.asp">try
            ➥again</a>."
```

continues

Listing 5.9—continued

```
16:     else
17:         'The username is good, now let's check the password
18:         real_password = trim(userSet.fields.item(1))
19:
20:         if p_password = real_password then
21:             'Password is good
22:             Response.Write "Great!  Welcome back!"
23:         else
24:             'Username is good, but password is wrong
25:             Response.Write "Bad password.  Please <A HREF="/login.asp">try
➥again</a>."
26:         end if
27:     end if
28:%>
29:
30:<!--#include virtual="/pagebottom.txt"-->
31:</BODY>
32:</HTML>
```

Let's assume for a moment that there is no such username. Since there would be no records matching our request, the recordset would be empty, so it would be pointing at both BOF and EOF. Fortunately, we can check for that on line 13. EOF and BOF are properties of the recordset, and have a value of either True or False, so we can use it in an if-then statement as the condition.

If the username is found, userSet.EOF will return False because the recordset will be pointing at the first (and in this case only) record. That will take us to the else section starting on line 16. From there, on line 20, we check the password that they entered (p_password) against the real password. There is one more thing we need to do, however. Depending on the database and how you define and populate the table, there may be extra spaces on the end of your data to fill out the fields. (In other words, if you defined it as char(50) and you have a five-letter word in the column, it will come back to you as 5 letters and 45 spaces.) To get rid of these extra spaces, we use the trim() function on line 18.

Of course, userSet.fields.item(1) isn't exactly what we would call intuitive. Fortunately, there's some shorthand we can use. Instead of specifying the order of the field, we can use the name, making it

```
userSet.fields.item("password")
```

That makes it a little easier, but we can shorten it even more. The default property for fields is item, so if we don't specify anything, that's what it will use. The default for a recordset is fields, so we could actually cut this down to

```
UserSet.fields("password")
```

or even

```
userSet("password")
```

which is much easier to read.

Now that we know how to find out if the login is okay, we need to decide what to do with it. Ultimately, we want to be able to know that this user has logged in and also to know who they are. We can do that by setting a cookie with their username. If the cookie is there, we know this user has logged in. If the cookie is not there, we know that he or she is not logged in.

Because we can't send the cookie after we've sent page text, however, we're going to have to rearrange things a little bit, as in Listing 5.10.

Listing 5.10—login_action.asp: Sending the user back to the login page

```
 0: <%@ LANGUAGE="VBSCRIPT" %>
 1: <%  p_username = Request.form("p_username")
 2:     p_password = Request.form("p_password")
 3:
 4:     set outpostDB = Server.CreateObject("ADODB.Connection")
 5:     outpostDB.Open "outpost"
 6:
 7:     sqlText="select * from members where username='"&p_username&"'"
 8:     set userSet = outpostDB.Execute(sqlText)
 9:   if userSet.EOF then
10:        'No such username, so the recordSet is empty
11:        Response.Redirect " /login.asp?retry=username"
12:    else
13:        'The username is good, now let's check the password
14:        real_password = trim(userSet("password"))
15:        if p_password = real_password then
16:           'Password is good, too
17:           Response.cookies("isLoggedInAs") = p_username
18:        else
19:           'Username is good, but password is wrong
20:           Response.Redirect " /login.asp?retry=password"
21:        end if
22:    end if
23:%>
24 <% pageTitle = "Counter" %>
25:<!--#include virtual="/pagetop.txt"-->
26:
27:Welcome back, <%= userSet("first_name")%>!
28:
29:<!--#include virtual="/pagebottom.txt"-->
30:</BODY>
31:</HTML>
```

5

What we've done here is move all of the logic for the page so that it happens before any text is output on line 25, so that we can set our cookie for a successful login on line 17. As long as we've done that, we might as well send users back to the login page if their usernames and passwords don't match. (I've added a code that we could have the login page check, but it's not absolutely necessary.)

Because we're redirecting the user for unsuccessful logins on lines 11 and 20, only the successful logins will make it to line 27, so we can just welcome the user. While we're at it, we've added a little personalization. When we selected all columns to find the username, we got all of the user information, not just the password, so the first name was available to us.

At this point, we have to look at a very common error that could cause us problems later. Because we're the only ones working here, it's unlikely to have reared its ugly head yet, but we've been creating objects left and right and not getting rid of them. The problem with this is the potential for the draining of resources. If you open a connection to the database and don't close it, it will sit there until it times out, which can be a drain on your system. What's more, even after we've closed an object, it's still sitting there in memory, taking up space. To really clean things up, we need to destroy the object when we're done with it, as on lines 29 through 33 of Listing 5.11.

Listing 5.11—login_action.asp: Closing objects

```
0: <%@ LANGUAGE="VBSCRIPT" %>
1: <%     p_username = Request.form("p_username")
2:        p_password = Request.form("p_password")
3:
4:        set outpostDB = Server.CreateObject("ADODB.Connection")
5:        outpostDB.Open "outpost"
6:
7:        sqlText="select * from members where username='"&p_username &"'"
8:        set userSet = outpostDB.Execute(sqlText)
9:        if userSet.EOF then
10:               'No such username, so the recordSet is empty
11:               Response.Redirect " /login.asp?retry=username"
12:        else
13:               'The username is good, now let's check the password
14:               real_password = trim(userSet("password"))
15:               if p_password = real_password then
16:                      'Password is good, too
17:                      Response.cookies("isLoggedInAs") = p_username
18:               else
19:                      'Username is good, but password is wrong
20:                      Response.Redirect " /login.asp?retry=password"
21:               end if
22:        end if
23: %>
24: <% pageTitle = "Counter" %>
```

```
25: <!--#include virtual="/pagetop.txt"-->
26:
27: Welcome back, <%= userSet("first_name")%>!
28:
29: <%  userSet.Close
30:     set userSet = Nothing
31:
32:     outpostDB.Close
33:     set outpostDB = Nothing
34: %>
35:
36: <!--#include virtual="/pagebottom.txt"-->
37: </BODY>
38: </HTML>
```

This way we've closed and destroyed our objects on lines 29 through 33, so all of their resources are freed.

Cookie Expiration Dates

Now that we've set our cookie, let's do something with it. After users have logged in, we don't need for them to log in again, so we'll tell the login page to check for our cookie in Listing 5.12, and display a different message if it finds it.

Listing 5.12—login.asp: Checking to see if the user is already logged in

```
0: <%@ LANGUAGE="VBSCRIPT" %>
1: <% pageTitle = "Outpost Login" %>
2: <!--#include virtual="/pagetop.txt"-->
3:
4: <%
5: 'First check to see if user is already logged in
6: if Request.cookies("isLoggedInAs") = "" then  %>
7:
8:      <H2>Member Login</H2>
9:
10:     <% if Request.querystring("retry") = "password" then %>
11:         <h3>Invalid Password</h3>
12:     <% elseif Request.querystring("") = "username" then %>
13:         <h3>Invalid username</h3>
14:     <% end if %>
15:
16:     <FORM ACTION="login_action.asp" METHOD="post">
17:     Username:  <INPUT TYPE="text" NAME="p_username"><BR>
18:     Password:  <INPUT TYPE="password" NAME="p_password"><BR>
19:     <BR>
20:     <INPUT TYPE="submit" VALUE="Log In">
21:     </FORM>
22:     <P>
```

continues

Listing 5.12—continued

```
23:     Don't have a username and password?  You can
24:     <A HREF="register.asp">register</a> for free
25:     and get your own space!
26:
27:<% else  %>
28:
29:     <H2><%= RRequest.cookies("isLoggedInAs") %>'s Personal Space</H2>
30:
31:     If you are not <%= RRequest.cookies("isLoggedInAs") %>,
32:     <A HREF="/logoff.asp">click here</a>.
33:
34:<% end if %>
35:
36:<P>
37:<!--#include virtual="/pagebottom.txt"-->
38:</BODY>
39:</HTML>
```

On line 6 we check for the value of our cookie. If it's not there, it will come up as nothing, so we know that the users has not logged in yet and we need to display the login page on lines 7 through 26. On lines 10 through 14, we check to see if the user has been sent back to this page because his or her login information was wrong and we display the appropriate message.

If the cookie isn't empty on line 6, we know the user is logged in. We can display the username and give the user the option of logging off if this isn't his or her account on lines 31 and 32.

Now, this cookie is going to remain in the browser for as long as the browser remains open. After users quit their browsers, they're logged out. But how can we log them out earlier?

Ironically, we can make the cookie go away before the browser is closed using the same method we'd use to make it stay after the browser is closed: explicitly setting an expiration date and time. Cookies are not forever. If we don't set this date, they won't be saved when the browser is closed. If we do set this date, they will expire when that time has come and gone. So to remove a cookie, we simply set the expiration time to be some time in the past, and then it goes away on its own.

Make a copy of template.asp and call it logoff.asp, and then add the changes in Listing 5.13.

Listing 5.13—logoff.asp: Expiring a cookie

```
0: <%@ LANGUAGE="VBSCRIPT" %>
1: <%
2: Response.cookies("isLoggedInAs").expires=#January 1, 1980 00:00:00#
3: %>
4: <% pageTitle = "Outpost Log Off" %>
5: <!--#include virtual="/pagetop.txt"-->
6:
7: Thank you for visiting with us!  If you wish, you may
8: <A HREF="login.asp">log in again</a>.
9:
10:<!--#include virtual="/pagebottom.txt"-->
11:</BODY>
12:</HTML>
```

We're using a new notation here on line 2. Using the number symbol (#) tells VBScript to take the information inside and translate it into a date. This way we don't have to worry about what the proper date format is. The actual date we've used isn't important, as long as it's far enough in the past that you're sure nobody's got his or her system clock set before it.

Call up your `login.asp` page and log in if you haven't already done so. Then reload to see that the cookie was set. Click the link to log off, and try the login page again; you'll see that the cookie is now gone.

We can also offer the user a chance to keep the cookie on their machine, so they don't have to log in every time by setting the expiration date. Add the changes from Listing 5.14 to `login.asp`.

Listing 5.14—login.asp: Asking the user if they want their login information saved

```
...
16:     <FORM ACTION="login_action.asp" METHOD="post">
17:     Username:  <INPUT TYPE="text" NAME="p_username"><BR>
18:     Password:  <INPUT TYPE="password" NAME="p_password"><BR>
19:     <BR>
20:     <INPUT TYPE="checkbox" NAME="p_save" VALUE="yes">
21:     Save my username and password
22:     <P>
23:     <INPUT TYPE="submit" VALUE="Log In">
24:     </FORM>
...
```

On line 20, we add an element the user can check to signal that he or she wants the login information saved. Of course, it's not going to do us any good unless we add this functionality to `login_action.asp`, as shown in Listing 5.15.

5

Listing 5.15—login_action.asp: Saving login information

```
0: <%@ LANGUAGE="VBSCRIPT" %>
1: <% pageTitle = "Counter" %>
2: <%    p_username = Request.form("p_username")
3:       p_password = Request.form("p_password")
4:       p_save = Request.form("p_save")
...
15:      if p_password = real_password then
16:           'Password is good, too
17:           Response.cookies("isLoggedInAs") = p_username
18:           if p_save = "yes" then
19:               Response.cookies("isLoggedInAs").expires = _
20:                   #December 31, 2001 00:00:00#
21:           end if
22:      else
23:           'Username is good, but password is wrong
24:           Response.Redirect "http://localhost/login.asp?retry=password"
25:      end if
...
```

 Note   An underscore(_) at the end of a line means that the line is continued below.

This time we've done the exact opposite; we set the expiration date far in the future, but only if the user asks us to.

Other Cookie Properties

The expiration date isn't the only one of those properties we saw in `cookies.txt` that we can set. The others are as follows:

- `Response.cookies(`*cookiename*`).domain`: If we don't set this, it's taken to mean our current machine, and only that machine can access it, as we mentioned earlier. We can, however, set a cookie so that it's accessible by any machine in our domain. For instance, I can set a cookie from `www.nicholaschase.com` that's readable from `orders.nicholaschase.com` by setting the domain as `".nicholaschase.com"`. Note that the first `period (.)` is required.

- `Response.cookies(`*cookiename*`).path`: We can set a cookie for a particular path, such as `/mySpace` or `/auctions`.

- `Response.cookies(`*cookiename*`).secure`: If we set this to `True`, the cookie will only be sent over a secure connection, so we don't have to worry about storing passwords or other sensitive information. (We'll talk more about secure connections in Chapter 8.)

There is one more thing that we can do with cookies: We can set multiple values in a single cookie. For instance, although it's nice that we recognize our users when they've already logged in, it would be nice if we could greet them by their first names instead of their usernames. Fortunately, we can store both values in a single cookie, as shown in Listing 5.16. Make the following addition to `login_action.asp`:

Listing 5.16—login_action.asp: Saving the login information

```
0: <%@ LANGUAGE="VBSCRIPT" %>
1: <% pageTitle = "Counter" %>
2: <%   p_username = Request.form("p_username")
3:       p_password = Request.form("p_password")
4:       p_save = Request.form("p_save")
5:
6:       set outpostDB = Server.CreateObject("ADODB.Connection")
7:       outpostDB.Open "outpost"
8:
9:       sqlText="select * from members where username='"&p_username &"'"
10:      set userSet = outpostDB.Execute(sqlText)
11:      if userSet.EOF then
12:          'No such username, so the recordSet is empty
13:          Response.Redirect " /login.asp?retry=username"
14:      else
15:          'The username is good, now let's check the password
16:          real_password = trim(userSet("password"))
17:      if p_password = real_password then
18:          'Password is good, too
19:          Response.cookies("isLoggedInAs")("username") = p_username
20:          Response.cookies("isLoggedInAs")("first_name") _
20a:             = userSet("first_name")
21:          if p_save = "yes" then
22:              Response.cookies("isLoggedInAs").expires =_
22a:                  #December 31, 2001 00:00:00#
23:          end if
24:      else
25:          'Username is good, but password is wrong
26:          Response.Redirect "http://localhost/login.asp?retry=password"
27:      end if
...
```

On line 22, we set the date for the cookie to be in the future, so the cookie will persist after the browser is closed. We're also adding a second value for the `isLoggedInAs` cookie on lines 19 and 20. We can use this syntax to store multiple values in a single cookie, making it less annoying for users who are confirming each one as its sent. These users still won't be able to use the personalized features of the site if they don't accept the cookies, but they'll be less likely to get frustrated and leave.

To accommodate this change, we need to add the code in Listing 5.17 to `login.asp`:

Listing 5.17

```
...
24:    <A HREF="register.asp">register</a> for free
25:    and get your own space!
26:
27:<% else  %>
28:
29:    <H2><%= Request.cookies("isLoggedInAs")("first_name") %>'s Personal
➥Space</H2>
30:
31:    If you are not <%= Request.cookies("isLoggedInAs")("first_name") %>,
32:    <A HREF="/logoff.asp">click here</a>.
33:
34:<% end if %>
35:
36:<P>
37:<!--#include virtual="/pagebottom.txt"-->
38:</BODY>
39:</HTML>
```

You can store as many values as you want in a single cookie, as long as it is not more than 4Kb in size. As a practical matter, however, your cookies should be much, much smaller than that because they are passed back and forth between the server and the browser with every request.

Customizing mySpace

Now that the users are logged in, we are ready for them to start customizing their space. In this chapter, we are going to allow them to customize two items: myLinks and myNews. In both cases, they are going to choose a number of items from a list that we give them. In the case of myLinks, they also have the opportunity to add their own links.

The first thing that we need to do is create the database tables for this section. Let's look at myLinks first. We need two tables: one for the standard links that everyone gets, and one for custom links. Listing 5.18 shows the create scripts for these tables. For a review of creating tables in Access, see Chapter 4, "Database Access Using ASP."

Listing 5.18—mylinks: Create scripts

```
create table links (
    link_id     numeric(18,0) PRIMARY KEY,
    link_name   char(255),
    link_desc   char(255),
    link_url    char(255)
```

```
    )

create table user_links (
    username    char(30),
    link_id     numeric(18,0)
    )
```

Note that in many cases we may want to accept more than 255 characters for link names and descriptions. However Access can't handle more than that, so unless we upsize our database, we're stuck. For now it's not an issue. We'll just leave it at 255. Go ahead and create these tables in your database.

Note the naming convention here. The user_links table ties the users and links together, and I can tell that just by the name.

After the tables are created, go ahead and create a few items in the links table, so we have something to offer.

 Note

If you don't have Access, you can create these records with the same types of insert statements we used to add users to the database.

Now we're ready to let our user choose some items. Make a copy of `template.asp` called `mySpace_custom.asp` and save it in the mySpace directory. Add the code in Listing 5.19.

Listing 5.19—mySpace_custom.asp: Enabling the user to choose links

```
0: <%@ LANGUAGE="VBSCRIPT" %>
1: <% pageTitle = "Customize mySpace" %>
2: <!--#include virtual="/pagetop.txt"-->
3:
4: <h1>Customize your space</h1>
5:
6: <% if Request.cookies("isLoggedInAs")("username") = "" then
7:     'user is not logged in, so they don't get to do anything %>
8:
9:     This area is only for registered members of Primary Outpost.
10:    Please <A HREF="/login.asp">log in</a>.  Thank you!
11:
12:<% else
13:
14:    'Open the connection to the database
15:    set outpostDB=Server.CreateObject("ADODB.Connection")
16:    outpostDB.Open "outpost"
17:
18:    'Create and populate our recordset
```

continues

Listing 5.19—continued

```
19:     set linkSet = outpostDB.Execute("select * from links")
20:
21:     'Our link list will go here in a minute
22:
23:     'Clean everything up
24:     linkSet.Close
25:     set linkSet = Nothing
26:
27:     outpostDB.Close
28:     set outpostDB = Nothing
29:
30:end if %>
31:
32:<!--#include virtual="/pagebottom.txt"-->
33:</BODY>
34:</HTML>
```

There is nothing new here, so let's just review quickly what we've done.

It's possible for a user to get to this page without having logged in, so on line 6 we're checking to see whether users have logged in by checking for the presence of our cookie. If they haven't, we're sending them back to the login page on lines 9 and 10. (We could have simply redirected them to the login page, as well.)

If users are logged in, we're preparing to give them a list to choose from by opening a connection to the database on line 15 and creating a recordset that has all of our links in it on line 19. Then we're closing our objects and destroying them on lines 24 through 29, so we're not holding up resources that we're not using.

Now that that's taken care of, we want to create a form that is going to list all of the items in the links table along with check boxes so users can decide which ones they want. We do this on lines 21 through 26 of Listing 5.20.

Listing 5.20—mySpace_custom.asp: Creating the list of links

```
...
14:     'Open the connection to the database
15:     set outpostDB=Server.CreateObject("ADODB.Connection")
16:     outpostDB.Open "outpost"
17:
18:     'Create and populate our recordset
19:     set linkSet = outpostDB.Execute("select * from links")
20:
21:     while not linkSet.EOF
22:
23:         Response.Write linkSet("link_name") & "<BR>"
24:
25:         linkSet.MoveNext
```

```
26:    wend
27:
28:    'Clean everything up
29:    linkSet.Close
30:    set linkSet = Nothing
31:
32:    outpostDB.Close
33:    set outpostDB = Nothing
34:
35:end if %>
36:
37:<!--#include virtual="/pagebottom.txt"-->
38:</BODY>
39:</HTML>
…
```

Before we set up the form, let's look at stepping through the records. As we know, if there are no records in the recordset when we create it, linkSet.EOF will be True. Because we populated the table, however, there will be records in it, and the recordset will be pointing to the first one. Therefore linkSet.EOF will be False on line 21. This means that not linkSet.EOF will be True because not automatically switches a value from False to True, and vice versa.

So ASP comes to line 21 and sees that as long as we're not at the end of the recordset, it needs to perform a particular set of actions. It does the first, printing the name of our first link and a link break and then on line 25 we see something new.

BOF and EOF are properties of a recordset; MoveNext is an example of a method of a recordset. Recall that we defined methods as units of work that an object can perform. In this case, we're telling it to move to the next record.

Then we come to the wend statement, which is one of the few statements in VBScript that really doesn't make a lot of sense to the English speaker because it's not a word, as almost everything else we've seen has been. Fortunately, though, it's not too convoluted. wend is just short for while end, or the end of the while loop. So when ASP comes to the wend statement, it goes back to the beginning of the loop on line 21.

When I populated my table, I put in three links, so let's assume for a moment that that's how many we all have. When ASP goes back to line 21, it's pointing to the second record, so not linkSet.EOF is still True. It prints out the second name (because that's where the recordset is pointing) and moves on to the third. It then hits the wend statement on line 26 and goes back to the beginning.

Once more it prints out the name, and moves down one record. The difference is that this time, there *is* no next record, so linkSet is at the end of file, and linkSet.EOF is now True. So when ASP hits the wend statement and goes back to the beginning, not linkSet.EOF is False, so it skips the loop altogether and moves on with the rest of the page, starting on line 27.

Now we're ready to print the rest of the form. Add the code in Listing 5.21 to
mySpace_custom.asp.

Listing 5.21—mySpace_custom.asp: Completing the form

```
0: <%@ LANGUAGE="VBSCRIPT" %>
1: <% pageTitle = "Customize mySpace" %>
2: <!--#include virtual="/pagetop.txt"-->
3:
4: <FORM ACTION="mySpace_custom_action.asp" METHOD="post">
5: <h1>Customize your space</h1>
6:
7: <% if Request.cookies("isLoggedInAs")("username") = "" then
8:     'user is not logged in, so they don't get to do anything %>
9:
10:    This area is only for registered members of Primary Outpost.
11:    Please <A HREF="/login.asp">log in</a>.  Thank you!
12: <% else
13:
14:    'Open the connection to the database
15:    set outpostDB=Server.CreateObject("ADODB.Connection")
16:    outpostDB.Open "outpost"
17:
18:    'Create and populate our recordset
19:    set linkSet = outpostDB.Execute("select * from links")
20:
21:    while not linkSet.EOF %>
22:        <INPUT TYPE="checkbox" NAME="p_link_id"
23:            VALUE="<%=linkSet("link_id")%>" CHECKED>
24:        <A HREF="<%=linkSet("link_url")%>"><%= linkSet("link_name") %>
➥</a><BR>
25:        <%= linkSet("link_desc") %><BR>
26:<%        linkSet.moveNext
27:    wend
28:
29:    'Clean everything up
30:    linkSet.Close
31:    set linkSet = Nothing
32:
33:    outpostDB.Close
34:    set outpostDB = Nothing
35:
36:end if %>
37:<P>
38:<INPUT TYPE="submit">
39:</FORM>
40:<!--#include virtual="/pagebottom.txt"-->
41:</BODY>
42:</HTML>
```

On line 22, we use the recordset to dynamically generate not only the names of the links but the values of the checkboxes. Similarly, on line 24, we pull the destination for the link directly from the database.

So now we have a form that users can use to select their own links from our list (see Figure 5.6).

Figure 5.6

We can give the user a chance to decide which links to include in mySpace.

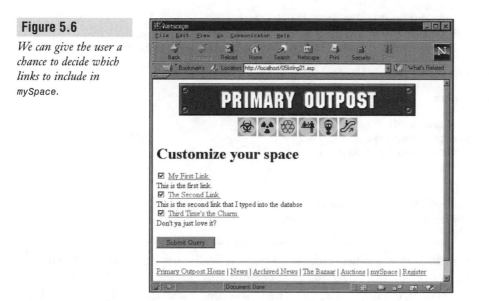

Now let's make the action page to accept this form. Copy `template.asp` to `mySpace_custom_action.asp` and save it in the mySpace directory. Add the code from Listing 5.22.

Listing 5.22—mySpace_custom_action.asp: Saving myLinks preferences

```
0: <%@ LANGUAGE="VBSCRIPT" %>
1: <% pageTitle = "Customize mySpace" %>
2: <!--#include virtual="/pagetop.txt"-->
3:
4: <%
5: 'First figure out what user we're looking at
6: p_username = Request.cookies("isLoggedInAs")("username")
7:
8: if p_username = "" then
9:     'user is not logged in, so they don't get to do anything
10:%>
11:     This area is only for registered members of Primary Outpost.
12:     Please <A HREF="login.asp">log in</a>.  Thank you!
```

continues

Listing 5.22—continued

```
13:<%
14:else
15:    'Connect to the database
16:    set outpostDB = Server.CreateObject("ADODB.Connection")
17:    outpostDB.Open "outpost"
18:
19:    'Now put each value into the database
20:    for each p_link_id in Request.form("p_link_id")
21:        sqlText = "insert into user_links(username, link_id) values ('" _
22:            & p_username & "', " & p_link_id & ")"
23:        Response.Write sqlText & "<BR>"
24:        outpostDB.Execute(sqlText)
25:    next
26:
27:    'Clean up
28:    outpostDB.Close
29:    set outpostDB = Nothing
30:end if
31:%>
32:
33:<!--#include virtual="/pagebottom.txt"-->
34:</BODY>
35:</HTML>
```

As far as this listing is concerned, there's nothing really new here. We're checking to see whether the user is logged in, we're opening and closing the database, we're looping through the check boxes, and we're inserting the data. All of this we've done before. The only thing new is on line 21. The underscore character (_) is used to tell ASP that our command continues on the next line.

Of course, we did all this assuming that our user didn't have any choices already in the database. Ideally, when we bring up the page with choices, links a user has already chosen will be checked. But this can be a problem. The way we have the tables set up, we'd have to loop through the list of links, and for each one search the user_links table to see whether the user has chosen it. This is terribly inefficient. There's a better way.

Essentially, we have two sets of records: the full set of links, and those that the user has already chosen. If we sort both of them by link_id as shown in Table 5.2, we can compare them easily. Let's say that there are six links, and our user has chosen 2 and 5.

Table 5.2   Comparing two recordsets

linkSet	hasLinkSet
1	
2	2
3	
4	
5	5
6	

We display link number 1, and because it doesn't match the current value of hasLinkSet (which is 2) we don't set it to be checked. Then we display the second link. This one does match, so we mark the check box as checked and move hasLinkSet to the next record, which is 5. There it sits until linkSet catches up. In mySpace_custom.asp, it looks like Listing 5.23.

Listing 5.23—mySpace_custom.asp: Showing the user's current choices

```
0: <%@ LANGUAGE="VBSCRIPT" %>
1: <% pageTitle = "Customize mySpace" %>
2: <!--#include virtual="/pagetop.txt"-->
3:
4: <FORM ACTION="mySpace_custom_action.asp" METHOD="post">
5: <h1>Customize your space</h1>
6:
7: <% if Request.cookies("isLoggedInAs")("username") = "" then
8:      'user is not logged in, so they don't get to do anything %>
9:
10:     This area is only for registered members of Primary Outpost.
11:     Please <A HREF="login.asp">log in</a>.  Thank you!
12:
13:<% else
14:
15:     'Get username for use later.
16:     p_username = Request.cookies("isLoggedInAs")("username")
17:
18:     'Open the connection to the database
19:     set outpostDB = Server.CreateObject("ADODB.Connection")
20:     outpostDB.Open "outpost"
21:
22:'Create and populate our recordSet
23:     set linkSet = outpostDB.Execute("select * from links order by link_id")
24:     set hasLinkSet = outpostDB.Execute("select * from user_links " _
25:         & "where username = '" _& p_username & "' order by link_id")
26:
```

continues

Listing 5.23—continued

```
27:     while not linkSet.EOF %>
28:         <INPUT TYPE="checkbox" NAME="p_link_id"
➥VALUE="<%=linkSet("link_id")%>"
29:         <% if not hasLinkSet.EOF then
30:                 if linkSet("link_id") = hasLinkSet("link_id") then %>
31:                     CHECKED
32:         <%          hasLinkSet.moveNext
33:                 end if
34:             end if %>
35:         >
36:         <A HREF="<%=linkSet("link_url")%>"><%= linkSet("link_name") %>
➥</a><BR>
37:         <%= linkSet("link_desc") %><BR>
38:<%         linkSet.moveNext
39:     wend
40:
41:     'Clean everything up
42:     linkSet.Close
43:     set linkSet = Nothing
44:
45:     hasLinkSet.Close
46:     set hasLinkSet = Nothing
47:
48:     outpostDB.Close
49:     set outpostDB = Nothing
50:
51:end if %>
52:<P>
53:<INPUT TYPE="hidden" NAME="p_username" VALUE="<%=p_username%>">
54:<INPUT TYPE="submit">
55:</FORM>
56:<!--#include virtual="/pagebottom.txt"-->
57:</BODY>
58:</HTML>
```

On line 24 we create hasLinkSet from the user_links table. The while loop on lines 27 through 39 behaves the same way it did before, except that before marking the check box as checked on line 31 we're comparing linkSet against hasLinkSet. Note that if we try to look at the value of a recordset that is not pointing to a current record, we'll get an error, so on lines 29 and 34 we look at hasLinkSet.EOF. If it's true, we don't even try the comparison.

We are going to need one more type of SQL statement: Delete. We've added records to the user_links table, but we haven't taken into account that this may not be the first time the user has been here. As it stands right now, when a user returns to this page, he or she will wind up adding the same link multiple times, and that's not what we want. We have two choices here. We can either do something similar to what we did for the form (check two sets of records against each other) or, because we're just adding all the records anyway, we can simply delete the user's current set before we add anything new. To do this, we just add one statement to `mySpace_custom_action.asp`, as shown on lines 23 and 24 of the code fragment in Listing 5.24.

Listing 5.24—mySpace_custom_action.asp: Deleting the user's previous choices

```
...
20:    outpostDB.Open "outpost"
21:
22:    'First delete existing values
23:    outpostDB.Execute("delete from user_links " & _
24:        " where username = '" & p_username & "'")
24:
25:    'Now put each value into the database
...
```

`Delete` is one of those commands that is a standard SQL command, but is implemented differently in different databases. In Microsoft products, you can say `delete from myTable where …` but in Oracle, you would instead say `delete myTable where…`.

The work we've done so far should take care of customizing the `myLinks` section, but what about actually displaying it? We need to create a new `mySpace.asp` page. To simplify matters, save a copy of `mySpace_custom.asp` as `mySpace.asp` in the mySpace directory. From there it's just a matter of removing the form and reformatting the display ever so slightly. The finished page should look like Listing 5.25.

Listing 5.25—mySpace.asp: Displaying the user's choices

```
0: <%@ LANGUAGE="VBSCRIPT" %>
1: <% pageTitle = "mySpace" %>
2: <!--#include virtual="/pagetop.txt"-->
3:
4:<h1>mySpace</h1>
5:
6: <H2>myLinks</H2>
7: <% if Request.cookies("isLoggedInAs")("username") = "" then
8:     'user is not logged in, so they don't get to do anything %>
9:
10:    This area is only for registered members of Primary Outpost.
11:    Please <A HREF="login.asp">log in</a>.  Thank you!
12:
13:<% else
14:
15:    'Get username for use later.
16:    p_username = Request.cookies("isLoggedInAs")("username")
17:
```

continues

Listing 5.25—continued

```
18:     'Open the connection to the database
19:     set outpostDB = Server.CreateObject("ADODB.Connection")
20:     outpostDB.Open "outpost"
21:
22:     'Create and populate our recordset
23:     set linkSet = outpostDB.Execute("select * from links order by link_id")
24:     set hasLinkSet = outpostDB.Execute("select * from user_links " _
25:         & " where username = '" & p_username & "' order by link_id")
26:
27:     while not linkSet.EOF %>
28:         <% if not hasLinkSet.EOF then
29:                 if linkSet("link_id") = hasLinkSet("link_id") then %>
30:                     <A HREF="<%=linkSet("link_url")%>"><%=
➡linkSet("link_name") %> </a><BR>
31:                     <%= linkSet("link_desc") %><BR>
32:
33:         <%          hasLinkSet.moveNext
34:                 end if
35:             end if %>
36:<%         linkSet.moveNext
37:     wend
38:
39:     'Clean everything up
40:     linkSet.Close
41:     set linkSet = Nothing
42:
43:     hasLinkSet.Close
44:     set hasLinkSet = Nothing
45:
46:     outpostDB.Close
47:     set outpostDB = Nothing
48:
49:end if %>
50:<P>
51:<!--#include virtual="/pagebottom.txt"-->
52:</BODY>
53:</HTML>
```

The only significant difference is in lines 28 through 35. Instead of using hasLinkSet to decide if an item should be checked, we're using it to decide if the item should be displayed in the first place. We've also removed the formfrom the page. (see Figure 5.7).

Figure 5.7

After a user decides what links to display, only their choices will show up in myspace.

That takes care of the myLinks section of mySpace.

Now let's take a look at myNews. There's nothing really new here, except that we need to create the data model for this section.

The idea here is to allow users to specify categories for which they want to receive news. This means that we have three pieces of information we need to keep track of: the categories of news, which categories a user has chosen, and which news items belong to which category. As for the news itself, we will note each item in the database, along with a headline, a blurb, the appropriate category, and a URL for the full article.

We'll use the following tables, as shown in Listing 5.26:

Listing 5.26—MyNews: Create scripts

```
create table news (
    news_id      numeric(18,2) PRIMARY KEY,
    news_cat_id     numeric(18,2),
    news_headline    char(255),
    news_blurb    char(255),
    news_url    char(255)
)

create table news_categories (
    cat_id    numeric(18,2) PRIMARY KEY,
    cat_name    char(255),
    cat_desc    char(255)
```

continues

5

Listing 5.26—continued

```
)

create table user_news_cat (
    username      char(30),
    news_cat_id      numeric(18,2)
)
```

Because we're just building right now, we're going to use extremely general categories, but when building your site, you could actually get quite specific. Use Access or the appropriate database tool to add categories to news_categories. We've added

- Books
- Movies
- Television
- Other

Feel free to be as specific as you like in adding your categories. Now add some placeholder news items. Again, we're just building right now, so they don't have to be real news items. We just want something in our categories, so we have something to test with. They can be complete gibberish.

Now we want to give our users a chance to pick the categories they'd like to see. Because what we're doing is virtually identical what we did in myLinks, we can use virtually the same code. Open mySpace_custom.asp and add the code shown in Listing 5.27.

Listing 5.27—mySpace_custom.asp: Adding customization for myNews

```
0: <%@ LANGUAGE="VBSCRIPT" %>
1: <% pageTitle = "mySpace" %>
2: <!--#include virtual="/pagetop.txt"-->
3:
4: <h1>Customize your space</h1>
5:
...
38:
39:     'Clean everything up
40:     linkSet.Close
41:     set linkSet = Nothing
42:
43:     hasLinkSet.Close
44:     set hasLinkSet = Nothing
45:%>
46:<%'----- End of myLinks, beginning of myNews ----- %>
47:
48:<H2>myNews</H2>
```

```
49:
50:<%
51:    'Create and populate our recordset
52:    set newsCatSet = outpostDB.Execute("select * from news_categories " _
53:        & " order by cat_id")
54:    set hasNewsSet = outpostDB.Execute("select * from user_news_cat " _
55:        & " where username = 0: '" & p_username & "' order by news_cat_id")
56:
57:    while not newsCatSet.EOF %>
58:        <INPUT TYPE="checkbox" NAME="p_cat_id"
59:            VALUE="<%=newsCatSet("cat_id")%>"
60:        <% if not hasNewsSet.EOF then
61:            if newsCatSet("cat_id") = hasNewsSet("news_cat_id") then %>
62:                CHECKED
63:        <%            hasNewsSet.moveNext
64:            end if
65:          end if %>
66:        >
67:        <%= newsCatSet("cat_name") %><BR>
68:        <%= newsCatSet("cat_desc") %><BR>
69:<%      newsCatSet.moveNext
70:    wend
71:
72:    'Clean everything up
73:    newsCatSet.Close
74:    set newsCatSet = Nothing
75:
76:    hasNewsSet.Close
77:    set hasNewsSet = Nothing
78:
79:
80:    outpostDB.Close
81:    set outpostDB = Nothing
82:
83:end if %>
84:<P>
85:<INPUT TYPE="hidden" NAME="p_username" VALUE="<%=p_username%>">
86:<INPUT TYPE="submit">
87:</FORM>
88:<!--#include virtual="/pagebottom.txt"-->
89:</BODY>
90:</HTML>
```

All I've done here is copy the myLinks section exactly, changing the names and removing the anchor tag. If you pull up the page, you'll find a listing just like the one for myLinks, except that the names of the categories are not links (because there's nothing to link to). We can do virtually the same thing with mySpace_custom_action.asp as shown in Listing 5.28:

Listing 5.28—mySpace_custom_action.asp: Saving myNews category choices

```
0: <%@ LANGUAGE="VBSCRIPT" %>
1: <% pageTitle = "Customize mySpace" %>
2: <!--#include virtual="/pagetop.txt"-->
3:
4: <%
5: 'First figure out what user we're looking at
6: p_username = Request.cookies("isLoggedInAs")("username")
7:
8: if p_username = "" then
9:     'user is not logged in, so they don't get to do anything
10:%>
11:    This area is only for registered members of Primary Outpost.
12:    Please <A HREF="login.asp">log in</a>.  Thank you!
13:<%
14:else
15:    'Connect to the database
16:set outpostDB = Server.CreateObject("ADODB.Connection")
17:    outpostDB.Open "outpost"
18:
19:    'First delete existing values
20:    outpostDB.Execute("delete from user_links where username = '" &
p_username & "'")
21:
22:    'Now put each value into the database
23:    for each p_link_id in Request.form("p_link_id")
24:        sqlText = "insert into user_links(username, link_id) values ('" _
25:            & p_username & "', " & p_link_id & ")"
26:        Response.Write sqlText & "<BR>"
27:        outpostDB.Execute(sqlText)
28:    next
29:'------------------End of myLinks, beginning of myNews ------------------
30:    outpostDB.Execute("delete from user_news_cat " _
31:        & " where username = '" & p_username & "'")
32:
33:    'Now put each value into the database
34:    for each p_cat_id in Request.form("p_cat_id")
35:        sqlText = "insert into user_news_cat(username, news_cat_id)" _
36:            & " values ('" & p_username & "', " & p_cat_id & ")"
37:        Response.Write sqlText & "<BR>"
38:        outpostDB.Execute(sqlText)
39:    next
40:
41:    'Clean up
42:    outpostDB.Close
43:    set outpostDB = Nothing
44:end if
45:%>
46:
47:<!--#include virtual="/pagebottom.txt"-->
48:</BODY>
49:</HTML>
```

Again, all we did was copy, paste, and change the names, and it worked right out of the box, so to speak. However, mySpace.asp is going to need slightly more extensive changes to accommodate myNews. First let's list the categories, which is just copying and pasting, as before. Add the new code in Listing 5.29 to mySpace.asp.

Listing 5.29—mySpace.asp: Adding myNews

```
0: <%@ LANGUAGE="VBSCRIPT" %>
1: <% pageTitle = "mySpace" %>
2: <!--#include virtual="/pagetop.txt"-->
3:
4: <h1>mySpace</h1>
5:
...
42:
43:    hasLinkSet.Close
44:    set hasLinkSet = Nothing
45:%>
46:<%'--------End of myLinks, beginning of myNews--------%>
47:
48:<H2>myNews</H2>
49:
50:<%    'Create and populate our recordset
51:    set newsCatSet = outpostDB.Execute("select * from news_categories"_
52:        & " order by cat_id")
53:    set hasNewsSet = outpostDB.Execute("select * from user_news_cat"_
54:        & "  where username = '" & p_username & "' order by news_cat_id")
55:
56:    while not newsCatSet.EOF %>
57:        <% if not hasNewsSet.EOF then
58:            if newsCatSet("cat_id") = hasNewsSet("news_cat_id") then %>
59:                <%= newsCatSet("cat_name") %><BR>
60:
61:        <%        hasNewsSet.moveNext
62:            end if
63:        end if %>
64:<%        newsCatSet.moveNext
65:    wend
66:
67:    'Clean everything up
68:    newsCatSet.Close
69:    set newsCatSet = Nothing
70:
71:    hasNewsSet.Close
72:    set hasNewsSet = Nothing
73:
74:    outpostDB.Close
75:    set outpostDB = Nothing
76:
```

continues

Listing 5.29—continued

```
77:end if %>
78:<P>
79:<!--#include virtual="/pagebottom.txt"-->
80:</BODY>
81:</HTML>
```

Now that we've got our categories, we also want to show the news items within each of those categories. To do this, we create a *nested loop*. A nested loop is a loop within another loop. In this case, for each category that the user has chosen, we are going to loop through and get all of the appropriate news items as shown in Listing 5.30.

Listing 5.30—mySpace.asp: Getting individual news stories

```
...
53:     set hasNewsSet = outpostDB.Execute("select * from user_news_cat"_
54:         & "  where username = '" & p_username & "' order by news_cat_id")
55:
56:     while not newsCatSet.EOF %>
57:         <% if not hasNewsSet.EOF then
58:             if newsCatSet("cat_id") = hasNewsSet("news_cat_id") then
59:                 'Output category header
60:                 Response.Write "<H3>" & newsCatSet("cat_name") & "</H3>"
61:                 'Now get each news item
62:                 set newsSet = outpostDB.Execute("select * from news"_
63:                     &"  where news_cat_id = " & newsCatSet("cat_id"))
64:                 while not newsSet.EOF
65:                     'For each news item %>
66:                     <B><%= newsSet("news_headline")%></B><BR>
67:                     <%= newsSet("news_blurb") %><BR>
68:                     <A HREF="<%= newsSet("news_url") %>">Full Story</a><P>
69:<%                  newsSet.moveNext
70:                 wend
71:                 newsSet.Close
72:                 set newsSet = Nothing
73:                 hasNewsSet.moveNext
74:         end if
...
```

So for each category that the user has chosen (as determined on line 58), we create a new recordset to pull out the news on lines 62 and 63. On lines 64 through 70, we display the news, and on lines 71 and 72 we close and destroy the recordset. (This isn't the most efficient way to do it, but it'll do for now.)

Putting It All Together

Let's take a look at what we've done in this chapter. We've allowed users to log in, and we've looked at setting a cookie on their machine when they do. We've set cookie expiration dates and used that cookie to recognize whether a user has access to members-only material, such as the ability to view and customize their own space.

Now that we have all the pieces, it's time to clean everything up and link every-thing together. Essentially, we have three files to worry about: mySpace.asp, mySpace_custom.asp, and mySpace_custom_action.asp.

In Listing 5.32, we've taken mySpace.asp and cleaned up the layout a bit using tables and then added a link that will take users to mySpace_custom.asp, which we've also cleaned up somewhat. Finally, we've linked mySpace_custom_action.asp back to the other two files to complete the chain.

Let's look at Listing 5.31, the complete mySpace.asp, first:

Listing 5.31—mySpace.asp: The final page

```
0:  <%@ LANGUAGE="VBSCRIPT" %>
1:  <% pageTitle = "mySpace" %>
2:  <!--#include virtual="/pagetop.txt"-->
3:
4:  <h1 align="center">mySpace</h1>
5:
6:  <table width=100%>
7:  <tr><td valign="top">
8:
9:  <H2>myLinks</H2>
10: <% if Request.cookies("isLoggedInAs")("username") = "" then
11:     'user is not logged in, so they don't get to do anything %>
12:
13:     This area is only for registered members of Primary Outpost.
14:     Please <A HREF="login.asp">log in</a>.  Thank you!
15:
16: <% else
17:
18:     'Get username for use later.
19:     p_username = Request.cookies("isLoggedInAs")("username")
20:
21:     'Open the connection to the database
22:     set outpostDB = Server.CreateObject("ADODB.Connection")
23:     outpostDB.Open "outpost"
24:
25:     'Create and populate our recordset
26:     set linkSet = outpostDB.Execute("select * from links"_
27:         & "  order by link_id")
28:     set hasLinkSet = outpostDB.Execute("select * from user_links"_
29:         & " where username = '" & p_username & "' order by link_id")30:
31:     while not linkSet.EOF %>
32:         <% if not hasLinkSet.EOF then
33:             if linkSet("link_id") = hasLinkSet("link_id") then %>
```

continues

Listing 5.31—continued

```
34:                              <A HREF="<%=linkSet("link_url")%>">
35:                              <%= linkSet("link_name") %> </a><BR>
36:                              <%= linkSet("link_desc") %><BR>
37:
38:              <%        hasLinkSet.moveNext
39:                  end if
40:               end if %>
41: <%        linkSet.moveNext
42:      wend
43:
44:      'Clean everything up
45:      linkSet.Close
46:      set linkSet = Nothing
47:
48:      hasLinkSet.Close
49:      set hasLinkSet = Nothing
50: %>
51: <P>
52: <A HREF="mySpace_custom.asp">Customize myLinks</a><P>
53:
54: </td>
55:
56: <%'-----End of myLinks, beginning of myNews-----%>
57:
58: <td valign="top">
59: <H2>myNews</H2>
60:
61: <%     'Create and populate our recordset
62:      set newsCatSet = outpostDB.Execute("select * from news_categories"_
63:          & " order by cat_id")
64:      set hasNewsSet = outpostDB.Execute("select * from user_news_cat"_
65:          & " where username = '" & p_username & "' order by news_cat_id")
66:
67:      while not newsCatSet.EOF %>
68:          <% if not hasNewsSet.EOF then
69:              if newsCatSet("cat_id") = hasNewsSet("news_cat_id") then
70:                  'Output category header
71:                  Response.Write "<H3>" & newsCatSet("cat_name") & "</H3>"
72:                  'Now get each news item
73:                  set newsSet = outpostDB.Execute("select * from news"_
74:                      & " where news_cat_id = " & newsCatSet("cat_id"))
75:                  while not newsSet.EOF
76:                      'For each news item %>
77:                      <B><%= newsSet("news_headline")%></B><BR>
78:                      <%= newsSet("news_blurb") %><BR>
79:                      <A HREF="<%= newsSet("news_url") %>">Full Story</a><P>
80: <%                   newsSet.moveNext
81:                  wend
82:                  newsSet.Close
83:                  set newsSet = Nothing
```

```
84:                   hasNewsSet.moveNext
85:              end if
86:            end if %>
87: <%       newsCatSet.moveNext
88:    wend
89:
90:    'Clean everything up
91:    newsCatSet.Close
92:    set newsCatSet = Nothing
93:
94:    hasNewsSet.Close
95:    set hasNewsSet = Nothing
96:
97:    outpostDB.Close
98:    set outpostDB = Nothing
99:
100:end if %>
101:<P>
102:<A HREF="mySpace_custom.asp">Customize myNews</a>
103:<P>
104:</td></tr>
105:</table>
106:<!--#include virtual="/pagebottom.txt"-->
107:</BODY>
108:</HTML>
```

What we've done is add the two links and put the page content into a table, so the two sections are side by side (see Figure 5.8).

Figure 5.8

The final mySpace.

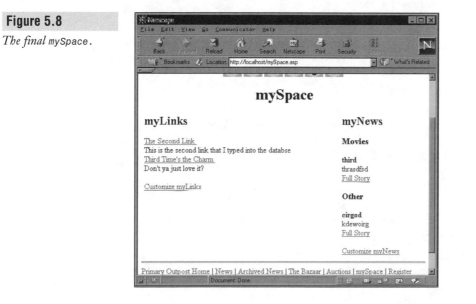

Now let's look at the final mySpace_custom.asp, in Listing 5.32:

Listing 5.32—mySpace_custom.asp: The final page

```
0: <%@ LANGUAGE="VBSCRIPT" %>
1: <% pageTitle = "Customize mySpace" %>
2: <!--#include virtual="/pagetop.txt"-->
3:
4: <FORM ACTION="mySpace_custom_action.asp" METHOD="post">
5: <h1 align="center">Customize your space</h1>
6:
7: <% if Request.cookies("isLoggedInAs")("username") = "" then
8:     'user is not logged in, so they don't get to do anything %>
9:
10:     This area is only for registered members of Primary Outpost.
11:     Please <A HREF="login.asp">log in</a>.  Thank you!
12:
13: <% else %>
14: <table cellspacing="10" cellpadding="10">
15: <tr><td valign="top" width="50%">
16:
17: <H2>myLinks</H2>
18: Check the links you wish to include in mySpace.<P>
19:
20: <%     'Get username for use later.
21:     p_username = Request.cookies("isLoggedInAs")("username")
22:
23:     'Open the connection to the database
24:     set outpostDB = Server.CreateObject("ADODB.Connection")
25:     outpostDB.Open "outpost"
26:
27:     'Create and populate our recordset
28:     set linkSet = outpostDB.Execute("select * from links"_
29:         & " order by link_id")
30:     set hasLinkSet = outpostDB.Execute("select * from user_links"_
31:         & " where username = '" & p_username & "' order by link_id")
32:
33:     while not linkSet.EOF %>
34:         <INPUT TYPE="checkbox" NAME="p_link_id"
35:             VALUE="<%=linkSet("link_id")%>"
36:         <% if not hasLinkSet.EOF then
37:             if linkSet("link_id") = hasLinkSet("link_id") then %>
38:                 CHECKED
39:         <%        hasLinkSet.moveNext
40:             end if
41:         end if %>
42:         >
43:         <A HREF="<%=linkSet("link_url")%>"><%= linkSet("link_name") %>
➥</a><BR>
44:         <%= linkSet("link_desc") %><BR>
45: <%        linkSet.moveNext
```

```
46:      wend
47:
48:      'Clean everything up
49:      linkSet.Close
50:      set linkSet = Nothing
51:
52:      hasLinkSet.Close
53:      set hasLinkSet = Nothing
54: %>
55: </td>
56: <%'--- End of myLinks, beginning of myNews ----- %>
57: <td valign="top" width="50%">
58: <H2>myNews</H2>
59: Check the categories of news you'd like to receive.<P>
60: <%
61:      'Create and populate our recordset
62:      set newsCatSet = outpostDB.Execute("select * from news_categories"_
63:          & " order by cat_id")
64:      set hasNewsSet = outpostDB.Execute("select * from user_news_cat"_
65:          & " where username = '" & p_username & "' order by news_cat_id")
66:
67:      while not newsCatSet.EOF %>
68:          <INPUT TYPE="checkbox" NAME="p_cat_id"
69:              VALUE="<%=newsCatSet("cat_id")%>"
70:          <% if not hasNewsSet.EOF then
71:              if newsCatSet("cat_id") = hasNewsSet("news_cat_id") then %>
72:                      CHECKED
73:          <%          hasNewsSet.moveNext
74:              end if
75:          end if %>
76:          >
77:          <%= newsCatSet("cat_name") %><BR>
78:          <%= newsCatSet("cat_desc") %><BR>
79: <%          newsCatSet.moveNext
80:      wend
81:
82:      'Clean everything up
83:      newsCatSet.Close
84:      set newsCatSet = Nothing
85:
86:      hasNewsSet.Close
87:      set hasNewsSet = Nothing
88:
89:
90:      outpostDB.Close
91:      set outpostDB = Nothing
92:
93: end if %>
94: </td></tr>
95: </table>
96: <P>
```

continues

Listing 5.32—continued

```
97: <center><INPUT TYPE="submit"></center>
98: </FORM>
99: <!--#include virtual="/pagebottom.txt"-->
100:</BODY>
101:</HTML>
```

Again, we've put the two sections side by side in a table and cleaned up the layout a little, as well as added directions for the user (see Figure 5.9).

Figure 5.9

The final
mySpace_custom.asp.

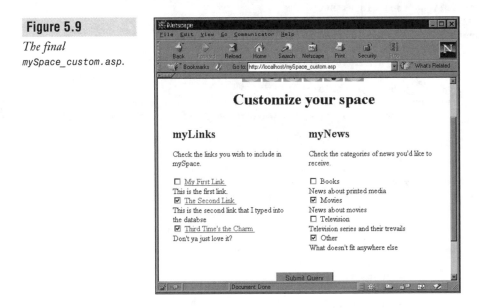

Finally, there's mySpace_custom_action.asp in Listing 5.33.

Listing 5.33—mySpace_custom_action.asp: The final page

```
0: <%@ LANGUAGE="VBSCRIPT" %>
1: <% pageTitle = "Customize mySpace" %>
2: <!--#include virtual="/pagetop.txt"-->
3:
4: <%
5: 'First figure out what user we're looking at
6: p_username = Request.cookies("isLoggedInAs")("username")
7:
8: if p_username = "" then
9:     'user is not logged in, so they don't get to do anything
10:%>
11:    This area is only for registered members of Primary Outpost.
12:    Please <A HREF="login.asp">log in</a>.  Thank you!
```

```
13:<%
14:else
15:    'Connect to the database
16:    set outpostDB = Server.CreateObject("ADODB.Connection")
17:    outpostDB.Open "outpost"
18:
19:    'First delete existing values
20:    outpostDB.Execute("delete from user_links"_
21:        & " where username = '" & p_username & "'")
22:
23:    'Now put each value into the database
24:    for each p_link_id in Request.form("p_link_id")
25:        sqlText = "insert into user_links(username, link_id) values ('" _
26:            & p_username & "', " & p_link_id & ")"
27:        outpostDB.Execute(sqlText)
28:    next
29:'-----------------End of myLinks, beginning of myNews -----------------
30:    outpostDB.Execute("delete from user_news_cat"_
31:        & " where username = '" & p_username & "'")
32:
33:    'Now put each value into the database
34:    for each p_cat_id in Request.form("p_cat_id")
35:        sqlText = "insert into user_news_cat(username, news_cat_id) "_
36:        & " values ('" & p_username & "', " & p_cat_id & ")"
37:        outpostDB.Execute(sqlText)
38:    next
39:    'Clean up
40:
41:    outpostDB.Close
42:    set outpostDB = Nothing
43:end if
44:%>
45:
46:<H1>Changes Accepted</h1>
47:
48:Your changes have been saved.  You may
49:<A HREF="mySpace_custom.asp">customize mySpace some more</a> or
50:<A HREF="mySpace.asp">go to mySpace</a>.
51:<P>
52:
53:<!--#include virtual="/pagebottom.txt"-->
54:</BODY>
55:</HTML>
```

Here we removed the Response.Write statements that were printing our sqlText, and we've added directions for users after they've saved their changes (see Figure 5.10).

Figure 5.10

The final
*mySpace_custom_*
action.asp.

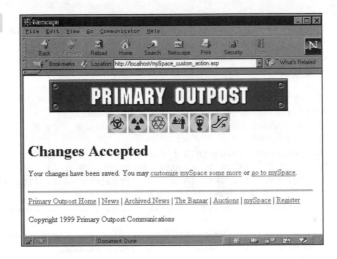

Summary

In this chapter, we created and set expiration dates for cookies. We also created and looped through recordsets, and deleted records.

Now that we've created a personalized area for our users and allowed them to log into and out of the site, we're going to look at adding the next of our special areas, person-to-person auctions. We'll be looking at the Application object, as well as some third-party components and how we can integrate them into our projects.

Chapter 6

In this chapter

- *Auction Data Model*
- *More on RecordSets*
- *Moving On*
- *Seeing Our Auctions*
- *Personalizing Our Site Through* myAuctions
- *One More Step: Third Party Components and Emailing Users*

Adding Person-To-Person Auction Capabilities

In this chapter, we are going to build a person-to-person auction house. Users will be able to put items up for sale, bid on items others are selling, and get a report on all auctions in which they're involved. We're also going to look at sending email from our application using third party components, or programs that we can plug into our application.

Auction Data Model

The first thing that we need to do is decide how we're going to store all of this information in the database. Let's look at the entities involved:

Figure 6.1

Entities for the auction section. Sellers may place for sale one or more items. Items must be placed by exactly one seller. Each item may have one or more bids, each of which must apply to one and only one item, and bidders may place one or more bids.

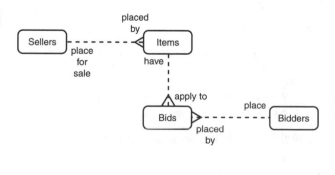

This entity relationship diagram (ERD) can be read like a sentence: Each seller may be selling one or more items, each of which may have one or more bids. Each bidder may place one or more bids, but each of them must apply to one and only one item.

Our first decision will be whether buyers and sellers are also members. We could allow people to place bids and sell items without becoming members, but then we'd have to store them separately. Therefore, for simplicity's sake, we're going to assume that buyers and sellers are the same as members.

That leaves us two entities to worry about: items and bids. We're going to store them in two tables: auction_items and auction_bids (see Listing 6.1).

Listing 6.1—myAuction create scripts

```
create table auction_items (
  auction_id  numeric(18,0),
  seller      char(30),
  item_name   char(255),
  item_desc   char(255),
  image_URL   char(255),
  opening     numeric(18,2),
  current     numeric(18,2),
  startdate   datetime,
  enddate     datetime
  )

create table auction_bids (
  auction_id  numeric(18,0),
  buyer       char(30),
  maxprice    numeric(18,2),
  bidtime     datetime
  )
```

EXCURSION

Foreign Keys and Data Integrity

If we were going to be strictly proper and adhere to the rules of data integrity, the buyer and seller columns would be a foreign key referencing the primary key of username in the members table. This means that if the columns have a value, such as roadnick or night-flyer, that value must also exist in the members table.

In this case, the create scripts would contain the additions in Listing 6.1a.

Listing 6.1a—myAuction create scripts with foreign keys

```
create table auction_items (
    auction_id  numeric(18,0),
    seller      char(30) references members(username),
    item_name   char(255),
```

```
    item_desc   char(255),
    image_URL   char(255),
    opening     numeric(18,2),
    current     numeric(18,2),
    startdate    datetime,
    enddate      datetime
    )

create table auction_bids (
    auction_id  numeric(18,0),
    buyer       char(30) references members(username),
    maxprice    numeric(18,2),
    bidtime     datetime
    )
```

Before we go any further, go ahead and create these two tables in your database, so we're ready to allow users to list items for sale.

As before, let's start with a form that users can fill out. Copy `template.asp` to `auction_sellitem.asp` in the auction directory and add the form shown in Listing 6.2.

Listing 6.2—auction_sellitem.asp: Enabling the user to enter item information

```
 1: <%@ LANGUAGE="VBSCRIPT" %>
 2: <!--#include virtual="/pagetop.txt"-->
 3: <% if Request.cookies("isLoggedInAs")("username") = "" then
 4:     'user is not logged in, so they don't get to do anything %>
 5:
 6:     To list items for sale on the Primary Outpost Auction Block,
 7:     you must be a member. Membership is free, and only takes a
 8:     moment! Please <A HREF="login.asp">log in</A>. Thank you!
 9:
10:<% else %>
11:
12:     <H2>List an Item for Sale</H2>
13:
14:     <FORM ACTION="auction_sellitem_action.asp" METHOD="post">
15:     <TABLE>
16:     <TR>
17:        <TD>Item Name: </TD>
18:        <TD> <INPUT TYPE="text" NAME="p_name"><BR> </TD>
19:     </TR>
20:     <TR>
21:        <TD VALIGN="top">Item Description: </TD>
22:        <TD>
23:           <TEXTAREA NAME="p_desc" COLS=30 ROWS=5></TEXTAREA><BR>
24:        </TD>
25:     </TR>
26:     <TR>
27:        <TD>Image Location: </TD>
```

continues

Listing 6.2—continued

```
28:        <TD>
29:            <INPUT TYPE="text" NAME="p_image" VALUE="http://"><BR>
30:        </TD>
31:    </TR>
32:    <TR>
33:        <TD>Opening Bid: </TD>
34:        <TD> <INPUT TYPE="text" NAME="p_min"><BR></TD>
35:    </TR>
36:    <TR>
37:        <TD>Auction Length:</TD><TD> <SELECT NAME="p_length">
38:                        <OPTION VALUE="3">3 days
39:                        <OPTION VALUE="5">5 days
40:                        <OPTION VALUE="7">7 days
41:                        <OPTION VALUE="10">10 days
42:                        </SELECT> </TD>
43:    </TR>
44:    </TABLE>
45:    <INPUT TYPE="submit" VALUE="Add To Auction">
46:    <INPUT TYPE="reset" VALUE="Clear Changes">
47:    </FORM>
48:
49:<% end if %>
50:
51:<!--#include virtual="/pagebottom.txt"-->
52:</BODY>
53:</HTML>
```

Nothing here is new, in principle. Lines 3 through 10 were copied and pasted from
mySpace_custom.asp. I customized the wording somewhat so as not to scare off any
users who just came for the auctions, as opposed to any other content, however.

Lines 12 through 43 are a simple form, much like all of the other forms that we've
done except that I've gone ahead and formatted it nicely from the beginning instead
of waitinguntil we were all done (see Figure 6.2).

On line 14, we're setting up the form; then on 15 we're opening the table into which
we're putting all of this information. We ask for the name of the item and then for
the description on line 22. This is something new for us, a textarea as opposed to
text input box. Notice that we can control how high and how wide this box is.
Unfortunately, unlike a text box, we can't limit how much text our users put into the
textarea, so we're going to have to make sure and trim it down ourselves after it's
submitted and before we try and put it into the database.

We don't want people actually uploading their images to our server, so instead we're
going to let them give us the URL of an image they want to use and we're starting
them out with http:// in the field so they get the idea.

Figure 6.2

Users can enter all pertinent information about their items on the completed page.

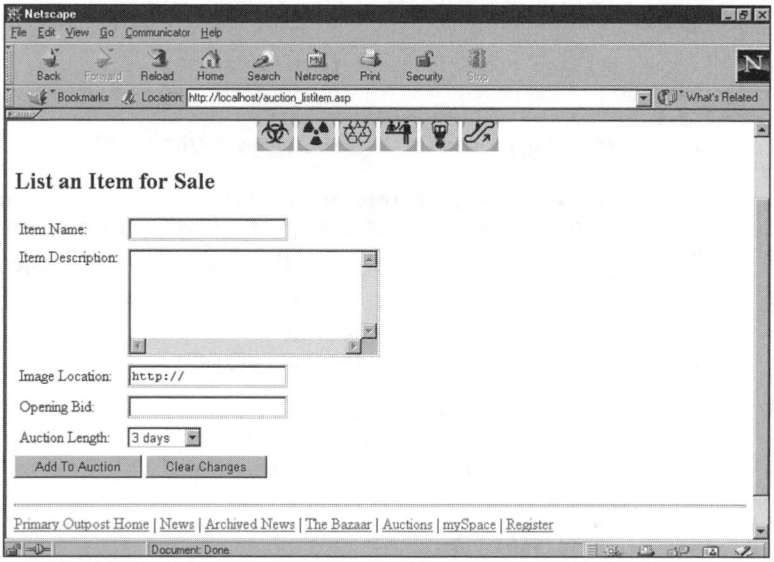

Finally, we need for them to specify the opening bid and the amount of time they want this auction to run.

Now that we have the form, we need the action. We're actually going to do this in two steps. First we're going to let the user preview the page as it would appear, and then, if they like it, they can save it. If they don't like it, we'll take them back to the original form. Copy `template.asp` to `auction_sellitem_action.asp` in the auction directory and enter the code shown in Listing 6.3.

Listing 6.3—auction_sellitem_action.asp: Previewing the auction

```
0: <%@ LANGUAGE="VBSCRIPT" %>
1: <% pageTitle = "Outpost Auction Preview" %>
2: <!--#include virtual="/pagetop.txt"-->
3: <% if Request.cookies("isLoggedInAs")("username") = "" then
4:      'user is not logged in, so they don't get to do anything %>
5:
6:      To list items for sale on the Primary Outpost Auction Block, you
7:      must be a member. Membership is free, and only takes a moment!
8:      Please <A HREF="login.asp">log in</A>. Thank you!
9:
10:<% else
11:
12:      'First we extract our form variables
13:      p_name = cstr(Request.form("p_name"))
14:      p_min = cstr(Request.form("p_min"))
15:      p_length = cstr(Request.form("p_length"))
16:      p_desc = cstr(Request.form("p_desc"))
```

continues

Listing 6.3—continued

```
17:      p_image = cstr(Request.form("p_image"))
18:
19:%>
20:      <h1 align="center">Auction Preview</h1>
21:
22:      Please check your information for accuracy, then click "Save
23:      Item" to add your auction or "Edit Item" to make changes.
24:
25:      <HR>
26:      <H2><%=p_name%></H2>
27:      Starting bid: <%=p_min%><BR>
28:      Auction length: <%=p_length%> days<P>
29:      <HR>
30:      <% if len(p_desc) > 255 then
31:            p_desc = left(p_desc, 255) %>
32:            (Descriptions are limited to 255 characters.)<P>
33:      <% end if %>
34:      <%= p_desc %>
35:      <BR clear="left">
36:      <IMG SRC="<%=p_image%>">
37:      <HR>
38:
39:      <FORM ACTION="auction_save.asp" METHOD="post">
40:      <INPUT TYPE="hidden" NAME="p_name" VALUE="<%=p_name%>">
41:      <INPUT TYPE="hidden" NAME="p_min" VALUE="<%=p_min%>">
42:      <INPUT TYPE="hidden" NAME="p_length" VALUE="<%=p_length%>">
43:      <INPUT TYPE="hidden" NAME="p_desc" VALUE="<%=p_desc%>">
44:      <INPUT TYPE="hidden" NAME="p_image" VALUE="<%=p_image%>">
45:
46:      <INPUT TYPE="submit" NAME="p_button" VALUE="Save Item">
47:      <INPUT TYPE="submit" NAME="p_button" VALUE="Edit Item">
48:      </FORM>
49:
50:<% end if %>
51:
52:<!--#include virtual="/pagebottom.txt"-->
53:</BODY>
54:</HTML>
```

On lines 13 through 17, we're extracting the information that was submitted on the form, even though we're not going to add it to the database just yet. Because we're going to be dealing with information as strings of text, or simply strings, we need to convert it using cstr (short for convert to string). Remember, request.form(p_name) is actually request.form.fields.item(p_name), or an item object. Most of the time conversions will be done for us, but it never hurts to cover the bases.

Next, we're displaying the information in a format similar to the way it will ultimately appear. Because we can't (easily) limit the number of characters a user can enter into the text box, on line 30 we need to check and make sure the text string is not too long after it's been submitted. If it is, we're taking only the first 255 characters using the `left()` function on line 31. The `left()` function takes the specified number of characters from the left side of a string that we give it. There's also the `right()` function, which does the same thing, except that it takes the characters off the end. Of course, if we ARE going to truncate someone's text, we need to tell them why so that a) they don't think it's a problem with the site, and b) they know how to correct it.

After we've displayed their information, we've got to find some way to get it back into the database. We do this by creating another form. There are a few things to notice about this form.

First is the name of the action on line 39. I know I'm violating my own rule about naming files, but `auction_sellitem_action_action.asp` looks like a mistake, and we don't want someone to delete it in a cleaning frenzy. The same is true for `auction_sellitem_action_save.asp`. So instead I've chosen something that will be at least indicative of what we're trying to achieve. The important thing is that rules are guidelines. Following them too closely can lead you to filenames such as `member_submit_keyword_action_keyword_action_desc.asp`—boy, was I sorry about that one!

Notice also that this form doesn't actually have any boxes or buttons that the user can see; all the information is in hidden fields on lines 40 through 44. The only way the user even knows that there's a form is the buttons that we've added to the bottom of the page.

In this case, we've added two buttons on lines 46 and 47, and we've done something special. Not only have we specified what the buttons should say, we've given them names so that their values will be submitted. We've done this so that we know which button they've clicked and we know what to do with the data.

Next we need to create the page that takes this data and either sends it back to `auction_sellitem.asp` or saves it to the database. Let's save ourselves some time by copying not `template.asp`, but `auction_sellitem_action.asp` to `auction save.asp`, also in the auction directory, and modifying it to match Listing 6.4.

Listing 6.4—auction_save.asp: Retrieving the hidden information

```
0: <%@ LANGUAGE="VBSCRIPT" %>
1: <% if Request.cookies("isLoggedInAs")("username") = "" then
2:     'user is not logged in, so they don't get to do anything %>
3:
4:     To list items for sale on the Primary Outpost Auction Block,
```

continues

Listing 6.4—continued

```
5:      you must be a member. Membership is free, and only takes a
6:      moment! Please <A HREF="login.asp">log in</A>. Thank you!
7:
8: <% else
9:      'First we extract our form information
10:     p_name = cstr(Request.form("p_name"))
11:     p_min = cstr(Request.form("p_min"))
12:     p_length = cstr(Request.form("p_length"))
13:     p_desc = cstr(Request.form("p_desc"))
14:     p_image = cstr(Request.form("p_image"))
15:     p_button = cstr(Request.form("p_button"))
16:     p_user = Request.cookies("isLoggedInAs")("username")
17:
18:     Response.write "p_NAME=" & p_name & "<BR>"
19:     Response.write "p_min=" & p_min & "<BR>"
20:     Response.write "p_length=" & p_length & "<BR>"
21:     Response.write "p_desc=" & p_desc & "<BR>"
22:     Response.write "p_image=" & p_image & "<BR>"
23:     Response.write "p_button=" & p_button & "<BR>"
24:     Response.write "p_user=" & p_user & "<P>"
25:
26:     if p_button = "Edit Item" then
27:         Response.write "Redirect to edit page"
28:     else
29:         Response.write "Save to the database"
30:%>
31:         <% pageTitle = "Outpost Auction Added" %>
32:         <!--#include virtual="/pagetop.txt"-->
33:         Item Added.
34:         <!--#include virtual="/pagebottom.txt"-->
35:         </BODY>
36:         </HTML>
37:
38:<%
39:     end if 'Button Choice
40:
41:  end if 'Logged in or not
42:%>
```

Here we've done another intermediate step to make sure things are going all right before we move on (see Figure 6.3). Because we may be redirecting the user back to the edit page on line 27, I've moved the top of the interface down to the bottom. This will let us do any processing we need to do before sending text to the browser. Remember, after we've sent text to the browser, we can't do anything that changes the headers, such as sending cookies or redirecting to another page.

Figure 6.3

Before we add our functionality, we need to make sure our logic is working.

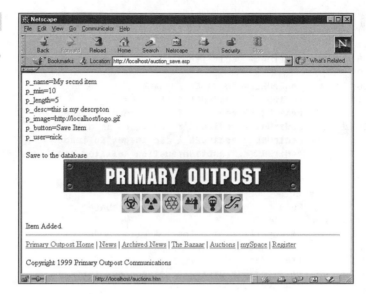

After we check to make sure the user is logged in, we're printing out our values on lines 18 through 24 to make sure they're all making it to the form. Then on lines 27 and 29 we're displaying which of the two outcomes we're going to be processing: either adding the item to the database or redirecting to the edit form. Try the page a couple of times, pressing each button to make sure you are getting the proper response. After we know the logic is working, it's time to add the functionality. Let's take the redirect first (see Listing 6.5).

Listing 6.5—auction_save.asp: Sending the user back to the edit page

```
0: <%@ LANGUAGE="VBSCRIPT" %>
1: <% if Request.cookies("isLoggedInAs")("username") = "" then
2:     'user is not logged in, so they don't get to do anything %>
3:
4:     To list items for sale on the Primary Outpost Auction Block,
5:     you must be a member. Membership is free, and only takes a
6:     moment! Please <A HREF="login.asp">log in</A>. Thank you!
7:
8: <% else
9:     'First we extract our form information
10:     p_name = cstr(Request.form("p_name"))
11:     p_min = cstr(Request.form("p_min"))
12:     p_length = cstr(Request.form("p_length"))
13:     p_desc = cstr(Request.form("p_desc"))
14:     p_image = cstr(Request.form("p_image"))
15:     p_button = cstr(Request.form("p_button"))
16:     p_user = Request.cookies("isLoggedInAs")("username")
```

continues

Listing 6.5—continued

```
17:
18:    if p_button = "Edit Item" then
19:
20:        redirURL = "p_NAME="&p_name
21:        redirURL = redirURL & "&p_min="&p_min
22:        redirURL = redirURL & "&p_length="&p_length
23:        redirURL = redirURL & "&p_desc="&p_desc
24:        redirURL = redirURL & "&p_image="&p_image
25:        redirURL = "/auction/auction_sellitem.asp?"&redirURL
26:        Response.Redirect redirURL
27:
28:    else
29:        Response.write "Save to the database"
30:%>
31:        <% pageTitle = "Outpost Auction Added" %>
32:        <!--#include virtual="/pagetop.txt"-->
33:        Item Added.
34:        <!--#include virtual="/pagebottom.txt"-->
35:        </BODY>
36:        </HTML>
37:
38:<%
39:    end if 'Button Choice
40:
41: end if 'Logged in or not
42:%>
```

Since we know the logic is working, we removed the output statements. Next we're assembling the URL we want to redirect to; then we're sending the browser there. However, if you try this, the chances are good that you're going to get an error. To find out why, change line 26 to

```
Response.write redirURL
```

so we can see what's going on. In all likelihood, you've got spaces in your URL because they were part of what you had submitted to the original form as an item description. Because you can't submit a URL with a space in it (see Figure 6.4), we're going to need to do something about that. "But wait a minute," you may be asking, "Why did the original form work, then?" Excellent question! The original form worked because when it submits a form, the browser automatically encodes the information. That means that it translates spaces and other objectionable characters into something that's permissible in a URL. For instance, a space becomes a + sign. When the server gets the request, it's automatically decoded back to its original form, so we didn't have to worry about it.

Figure 6.4

We have to encode our requests properly, or the browser won't be able to understand them.

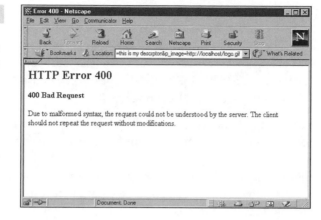

Now we have to worry about it. Fortunately, instead of writing a routine that goes through the string and translates characters into their encoded equivalents, we can use a function that's provided to us by ASP as part of the server object, as shown in Listing 6.6.

Listing 6.6—auction_save.asp: Encoding the URL

```
...
15:    p_button = cstr(Request.form("p_button"))
16:    p_user = Request.cookies("isLoggedInAs")("username")
17:
18:    if p_button = "Edit Item" then
19:
20:     redirURL = "p_NAME="&Server.URLencode(p_name)
21:     redirURL = redirURL & "&p_min="&Server.URLencode(p_min)
22:     redirURL = redirURL & "&p_length="&Server.URLencode(p_length)
23:     redirURL = redirURL & "&p_desc="&Server.URLencode(p_desc)
24:     redirURL = redirURL & "&p_image="&Server.URLencode(p_image)
25:     redirURL = "/auction/auction_sellitem.asp?"&redirURL
26:     Response.Redirect redirURL
27:
28:   else
29:     Response.write "Save to the database"
:%>
...
```

Warning

It is possible to go overboard with this. The whole idea of encoding is to make sure our data is not confused with part of the URL. If we also encode, say, the equal (=) sign, the URL won't be interpreted properly.

Because it's the production of the actual URL that we're testing, just reloading isn't going to do the trick. You're going to have to click the Back button on your browser to go back to the preview page and click Edit Item again. This time it should work. (Make sure to change `Response.Write` back to `Response.Redirect`!) If not, or if you're just curious to see what URLEncode does, you can use `Response.write` to print the URL to the page and take a look at it.

So now we're getting them back to the edit page, but the information isn't showing up on the form. There's a very good reason for this: we haven't told it to! Open up `auction_sellitem.asp` and take a look at it. We've got the form, now we want to insert prefilled information in it the same way we prefilled the image box with "http:// originally. To do this, we're going to copy the text to extract the form values from `auction_sellitem_action.asp`—why type more than we have to?—and modify it for our new purposes; then we're going to use it to place values in the fields (see Listing 6.7).

Listing 6.7—auction_sellitem.asp: Displaying previous information

```
0: <%@ LANGUAGE="VBSCRIPT" %>
1: <% pageTitle = "Outpost Auctions" %>
2: <!--#include virtual="/pagetop.txt"-->
3: <% if Request.cookies("isLoggedInAs")("username") = "" then
4:     'user is not logged in, so they don't get to do anything %>
5:
6:     To list items for sale on the Primary Outpost Auction Block,
7:     you must be a member. Membership is free, and only takes a
8:     moment! Please <A HREF="login.asp">log in</A>. Thank you!
9:
10:<% else
11:     p_name = cstr(Request.querystring("p_name"))
12:     p_min = cstr(Request.querystring("p_min"))
13:     p_length = cstr(Request.querystring("p_length"))
14:     p_desc = cstr(Request.querystring("p_desc"))
15:     p_image = cstr(Request.querystring("p_image"))
16:     if p_image = "" then
17:         p_image = "http://"
18:     end if
19:%>
20:
21:     <H2>List an Item for Sale</H2>
22:
23:     <FORM ACTION="auction_sellitem_action.asp" METHOD="post">
24:     <TABLE>
25:     <TR>
26:         <TD>Item Name: </TD>
27:         <TD>
28:             <INPUT TYPE="text" NAME="p_name" VALUE="<%=p_name%>">
29:             <BR>
```

```
30:            </TD>
31:        </TR>
32:        <TR>
33:            <TD VALIGN="top">Item Description: </TD>
34:            <TD> <TEXTAREA NAME="p_desc" COLS=30 ROWS=5>
35:<%=p_desc%>
36:                </TEXTAREA><BR>
37:                </TD>
38:        </TR>
39:        <TR>
40:            <TD>Image Location: </TD>
41:            <TD>
42:                <INPUT TYPE="text" NAME="p_image" VALUE="<%=p_image%>">
43:                <BR>
44:            </TD>
45:        </TR>
46:        <TR>
47:            <TD>Opening Bid: </TD>
48:        <TD>
49:            <INPUT TYPE="text" NAME="p_min" VALUE="<%=p_min%>">
50:            <BR>
51:        </TD>
52:    </TR>
53:    <TR>
54:        <TD>Auction Length:</TD><TD> <SELECT NAME="p_length">
55:                            <OPTION VALUE="3"
56:                                <% if p_length = "3" then %>
57:                                    SELECTED
58:                                <% end if %>
59:                                >3 days
60:                                <OPTION VALUE="5"
61:                                <% if p_length = "5" then %>
62:                                    SELECTED
63:                                <% end if %>
64:                                >5 days
65:                                <OPTION VALUE="7"
66:                                <% if p_length = "7" then %>
67:                                    SELECTED
68:                                <% end if %>
69:                                >7 days
70:                                <OPTION VALUE="10"
71:                                <% if p_length = "10" then %>
72:                                    SELECTED
73:                                <% end if %>
74:                                >10 days
75:                                </SELECT> </TD>
76:    </TR>
77:    </TABLE>
78:    <INPUT TYPE="submit" VALUE="Add To Auction">
79:    <INPUT TYPE="reset" VALUE="Clear Changes">
80:    </FORM>
```

continues

Listing 6.7—continued

```
81:
82:<% end if %>
83:
84:<!--#include virtual="/pagebottom.txt"-->
85:</BODY>
86:</HTML>
```

The first thing that we had to dowas change `request.form` to `request.querystring`. Because we're redirecting and not coming in from a form, we need to put all of the information the form needs into the URL. This is the same situation as a form that uses the `get` method. Next, we take a look at `p_image` on lines 15 through 18. Remember, if this is the first time the user is pulling up the form, we still want the Image URL box to say http://. Instead of putting the `if-then` statement in the middle of the text box, we create a variable and then just put the appropriate value, whatever it is, in the text box on line 42.

Adding these values to our form is pretty straightforward. We've seen it before for text boxes, but what's going on with that textarea on lines 34 through 36? Well, it turns out that this is another one of the ways that a textarea is different from a simple text box. Instead of setting an actual value as we did with a text box, we insert information into a textarea by placing the text between the open and close tags. There's one catch, though. This text is displayed like preformatted text, so any tabs, carriage returns, or even spaces are going to be displayed. That's why I've broken my rules about formatting the code and placed it all the way to the left. If I didn't (and originally I didn't) the text would have a series of spaces before it in the box. (Go ahead and try it!)

Finally we have the select box on lines 54 through 75. Unfortunately, this is one place where we couldn't (easily) avoid having the `if-then` statements in the text. For a choice to be selected, it has to have the `SELECTED` keyword as part of the `OPTION` tag.

When all is said and done, we have a form that serves two purposes: it will enable us to create an item if we don't give it any information, and it will enable us to edit an item if we do.

So that takes care of the `auction_sellitem_action.asp`'s Edit Item button. What about the Save Item button? Let's go back to `auction_save.asp` (see Listing 6.8).

Listing 6.8—auction_save.asp: Saving the auction data

```
0: <%@ LANGUAGE="VBSCRIPT" %>
1:<% if Request.cookies("isLoggedInAs")("username") = "" then
2:    'user is not logged in, so they don't get to do anything %>
3:
4:    To list items for sale on the Primary Outpost Auction Block,
```

```
5:    you must be a member. Membership is free, and only takes a
6:    moment! Please <A HREF="login.asp">log in</A>. Thank you!
7:
8:<% else
9:    'First we extract our form information
10:   p_name = cstr(Request.form("p_name"))
11:   p_min = cstr(Request.form("p_min"))
12:   p_length = cstr(Request.form("p_length"))
13:   p_desc = cstr(Request.form("p_desc"))
14:   p_image = cstr(Request.form("p_image"))
15:   p_button = cstr(Request.form("p_button"))
16:   p_user = Request.cookies("isLoggedInAs")("username")
17:
18:   if p_button = "Edit Item" then
19:
20:       redirURL = "p_NAME="&p_name
21:       redirURL = redirURL & "&p_min="&p_min
22:       redirURL = redirURL & "&p_length="&p_length
23:       redirURL = redirURL & "&p_desc="&p_desc
24:       redirURL = redirURL & "&p_image="&p_image
25:       redirURL = "/auction/auction_sellitem.asp?"&redirURL
26:       Response.Redirect redirURL
27:
27:   else
29:
30:       p_auction_id = 1
31:       p_start = Now
32:       p_end = DateAdd("d", p_length, Now)
33:
34:       set outpostDB = Server.CreateObject("ADODB.Connection")
35:       outpostDB.Open "outpost"
36:
37:       sqlText = "insert into auction_items "
38:       sqlText = sqlText & "(auction_id, seller, item_name,"
39:       sqlText = sqlText & "item_desc, image_URL, opening, "
40:       sqlText = sqlText & "current, startdate, enddate)"
41:       sqlText = sqlText & " values ("
42:       sqlText = sqlText & p_auction_id & ", " 'auction_id
43:       sqlText = sqlText & "'" & p_user & "', " 'seller
44:       sqlText = sqlText & "'" & p_name & "', " 'item_name
45:       sqlText = sqlText & "'" & p_desc & "', " 'item_desc
46:       sqlText = sqlText & "'" & p_image & "', " 'image_URL
47:       sqlText = sqlText & p_min & ", " 'opening
48:       sqlText = sqlText & p_min & ", " 'current
49:       sqlText = sqlText & "'" & p_start & "', " 'start
50:       sqlText = sqlText & "'" & p_end & "')" 'end
51:
52:       Response.write sqlText
53:       Response.write "<P>"
54:
55:       outpostDB.Close
```

continues

Listing 6.8—continued

```
56:        set outpostDB = Nothing
57:
58:%>
59:        <% pageTitle = "Auction Saved" %>
60:        <!--#include virtual="/pagetop.txt"-->
61:        Item Added.
62:        <!--#include virtual="/pagebottom.txt"-->
63:        </BODY>
64:        </HTML>
65:
66:<%
67:        end if 'Button Choice
68:
69:    end if 'Logged in or not
70:%>
```

The first thing that we need to do is get our data together. Most of it is coming in from the form on lines 10 through 16, but there are a few items we still need to deal with. The first, p_auction_id, we're going to handle separately in a little while. The start time and date for the auction (p_start), is set to the current date and time using the keyword Now on line 31. Because p_end is supposed to be a certain number of days after the start time we can use the function DateAdd().

DateAdd() is an extremely useful function because it takes care of figuring out whether you've gone into another month or year, whether you need to consider leap year, and so on. On line 32, we're telling DateAdd() that we want to add days (d) to our date. The number of days that we want to add is p_length, and our starting date is Now. (Other inputs we can use for DateAdd() are w for weeks, y for years, h for hours and so on.)

Now let's deal with the auction_id. This is a perfect opportunity to talk about user-defined Functions and Subroutines.

We've been dealing with built-in functions, such as DateAdd(). We supply them with input, and they return us a value that we can use, either directly or by assigning them to a variable to use later. Functions are handy because we don't have to interrupt the flow of what we're doing with a lot of logic. This makes our code a lot easier to read and debug. Another handy thing about functions is that we have to write them only once and we can use them over and over again. (This would have been handy when we were deciding whether to mark the pull-down menu options as selected.)

Perhaps the biggest advantage of using functions and subroutines is for modularity. Modularity is the process of chunking your code into pieces that are essentially independent of each other. For instance, we're going to create a function to give us the next auction_id, and we're going to insert that value into the database. Later on, we can change the way that we get that value, and the rest of our program won't care. All it will know is that it gets a value. It doesn't matter how or from where.

For now we're going to create the function nextAuctionID and assign it to p_auction_id (see Listing 6.9).

Listing 6.9—auction_save.asp: Using a function

```
0: <%@ LANGUAGE="VBSCRIPT" %>
1: <%
2: Function nextAuctionID
3:
4:     Randomize
5:     nextAuctionID = int(Rnd * 1000000)
6:
7: end Function
8: %>
9: <% if Request.cookies("isLoggedInAs")("username") = "" then
10:    'user is not logged in, so they don't get to do anything %> …
27:    else
28:        p_auction_id = nextAuctionID
29:        p_start = Now
20:        p_end = DateAdd("d", p_length, Now)
21:
…
```

It is customary in most languages to put functions and subroutines either at the top of the file or the bottom of the file, so we've gone ahead and put it at the top as is customary in ASP. Let's look at what's going on. When ASP comes down to line 28, it knows it needs to evaluate the function nextAuctionID to get a value. It goes to line 2 and starts processing. Line 4, Randomize, tells the system that we're about to request a random number. This allows it to seed the random function. The random function, Rnd, will generate a long decimal number between 0 and 1; so because we want a number between 0 and 1000000, that's what we multiply it by.

Finally, on line 5 we tell ASP what to return to our program by assigning the value to nextAuctionID because that's the name of the function.

Now that we've set our values, we're going to have to put them into the table, of course. As in the past, we need to insert the data into the table, so we've created an insert statement with all of our data, including the values that we just created. Note that some of them are surrounded by single quotes, and some of them aren't. The ones that aren't are the numeric values. If we try to surround them with single quotes, the database won't like it.

Go ahead and create an auction, and take a look at the SQL statement we get back.

Now we're going to have the page insert into the database. Change the redirect.write to a database command (see Listing 6.10).

Listing 6.10—auction_save.asp: Saving the item

```
...
48:     sqlText = sqlText & p_min & ", " 'current
49:     sqlText = sqlText & "'" & p_start & "', " 'start
50:     sqlText = sqlText & "'" & p_end & "')" 'end
51:
52:     Response.write sqlText
53:     Response.write "<P>"
54:     outpostDB.Execute(sqlText)
55:
56:     outpostDB.Close
57:     set outpostDB = Nothing
...
```

Now try and submit it to the database by reloading the page (if you were looking at auction_save.asp) or entering in a new auction (if you weren't). One of two things is going to happen.

The first possibility is that it's going to work flawlessly, and you'll get a page telling you that your item has been added. The second possibility, particularly if you had any single or double quotes in your item name or description, is that your are going to get an error complaining about the form of the SQL statement. If it worked, change p_auction_id to 2; then go back and try to add another auction, putting an apostrophe in the name,(for example, "Nick's stuff"). You'll get the error too.

Let's see why. Comment out line 54 and reload the page. If you take a look at the SQL statement printed across the top of the page, it will look something like this:

```
insert into auction_items (auction_id, seller, item_name,
item_desc, image_URL, opening, current, startdate, enddate) values
(1, 'Nick', 'Nick's test item', 'This is my test item',
'http://localhost/images/myimage.gif', 10, 10,
'8/15/99 2:14:46 PM', '8/20/99 2:14:46 PM')
```

Notice where it says 'Nick's test item'. That single quote throws off the whole line, because the database thinks it's the end of the item. It's expecting a comma, not more data.

This is probably *the* most common issue among new ASP programmers. How do you handle quotes in an insert statement? If you look at the newsgroups, you'll find this question asked over and over again. Sooner or later someone hits on the idea of using the "replace()" function to turn that single quote into two single quotes. Since SQL interprets that as a single quote within a string, that will solve the problem, but there are other issues. For instance, how do you handle a double quote? There is no corresponding easy answer.

Fortunately, there is a way to get around all of that, but it requires us to know a bit more about the recordsets.

More on RecordSets

There are actually several kinds of recordsets. Some are read-only, meaning we can't change the data within them. Some allow us to scroll up and down among the data; some don't. We can control all of those attributes of a recordset when we create it directly using a `CreateObject` statement instead of letting ASP do it for us, as we have been doing.

Let's look at the issues we need to take into consideration, and then we'll look at syntax. When we create a recordset using

```
set mySet = Server.CreateObject("ADODB.RecordSet")
```

we need to set several attributes about it. These attributes will be discussed in the following sections.

Source

The first attribute is the source of the data—where is it coming from? So far we've been using SQL statements, a one kind of source that we can feed a recordset. There are actually three other types, however.

The first, and simplest, is to simply feed the recordset a table. In this case, we give the recordset a table name and it takes in all rows and columns—similar to sending it `select * from mytable`. We can then filter out the records we don't want after we have them.

Another source for a recordset would be a stored procedure. In Access, this would be the same as a saved query. This is code that is part of the database, as opposed to being part of your actual pages. It can be called from any environment that is able to access (no pun intended) the database. A stored procedure can also take parameters, or run-time values. For instance, say we wanted to provide upgraded access to members who contributed to the site, either monetarily or by volunteering. There may be several things we need to do in the database to make this happen. We can make an Active Server Page to handle the changes, but what if we also had people accessing the database directly? In this case, we'd want to put the code into the database itself so it could be called, but we'd want to specify what user to upgrade when the time came. We would do this by specifying the username as a parameter.

If we are going to specify parameters, we'll probably want to use our last source for recordsets, the `Command` object. The `Command` object functions similarly to the `Connection` object, in that we can specify a SQL statement and execute it, but it's much more powerful than just that. With a `Command` object, not only can we specify the `CommandText` (what it's actually going to do) and `ActiveConnection` (the Connection it's going to use to do it), but we can also set other properties, such as the number of seconds to wait for a response. And, of course, we can add parameters to use with a stored procedure.

6

We're going to use a `Command` object a little bit later when we set the current bid for an item.

ActiveConnection

ActiveConnection is pretty straightforward. It is possible to have more than one database connection open at any given time, so the `ActiveConnection` is simply the connection to use to execute whatever statement it is we are using. Typically, if we use a `Command` object, we'll set it there, but if not, we need to set it explicitly for the recordset itself.

CursorType

The most common use of the word cursor is to describe a set of records that we've selected and are going to look at, but it actually describes any set of rows that the database has singled out, such as for updating. It's called a cursor because, like the cursor on your screen, it points to a specific place where the next action will take place. (Some people will also tell you that it stands for CURrent Set Of Rows, but that's probably apocryphal.) The recordsets that we have been using have two qualities about them that didn't bother us before, but have suddenly become an issue: We can only move forward, and we can't change anything. This is the default type of cursor, a Forward-only, or firehose cursor.

With ADO, however, we also have the option to create cursors that enable us to add or update records, or see changes that have been made to the database by other users since we first made our selections. The four `CursorTypes` are as follows:

- Forward-only: This is the default type, meaning that if you don't specify something else, this is what you're going to get. We've been scrolling down our recordsets using `MoveNext`, but we can't scroll up a Forward-Only cursor. We also can't add records or see changes that other people have made since we opened it. (We always get a current set when we open the cursor, however, so we would see other people's changes the next time we opened it.) The `CursorType` for this is `0`.

- Static: A static cursor is similar to the Forward-Only, with the exceptions that we can also scroll up and we can add records. We still can't see other people's changes. The `CursorType` is `3`.

- Keyset: With this cursor, we can finally see changes that other people have made, but only to records that existed when we opened the recordset. Records that were added afterwards won't be visible. We can also add records and scroll in any direction. The `CursorType` is `1`.

- Dynamic: This is a full-featured cursor. It enables us to make changes and add records, as well as move in any direction and see changes made by other people. It also sees records that have been added by other people since we opened the recordset. The `CursorType` is 2.

You may be wondering why you would need anything besides a Dynamic cursor. After all, you can do anything with it! There are two reasons. The first and simplest reason is that different databases support different kinds of cursors. For instance, the Visual Basic database, Jet, doesn't support Dynamic cursors. The second and more relevant reason is performance. It takes a lot of resources to maintain a Dynamic cursor. If all we're going to do is run through the set of data once, why should we take all of those resources? A good rule of thumb is to use a Forward-only cursor unless you really need functionality that it doesn't provide.

LockType

Before we talk about the different types of locks, let's talk for a moment about locking in general, and why it's used in databases.

In most relational databases, when you make a change, that change doesn't take effect right away. For instance, if I were to go and change all of our members' names to Joe and then look at the table, I'd see that they were all named Joe—but nobody else would. These changes would be pending until I commit them, or make them permanent. Why is this? This is because there are circumstances where I don't *want* to commit my changes.

> **Note**
>
> In Active Server Pages, we need to take specific steps to keep changes from being committed immediately if that's not what we want. We'll discuss those steps in Chapter 9.

The classic example is bank transfers. Let's say I deduct money from one account in order to add it to another account. If for any reason I can't add it to that second account, I want to cancel the original deduction (especially if it's my money!). This is called a rollback. In a rollback, all pending changes are discarded, and the database remains in its original state, which enables us to handle changes as a single transaction. Either all the changes are made, or none of them are.

We can commit or rollback transactions using the `Connection` object, but in general we're not going to worry about that. When we close the `Connection` object, our changes are automatically committed.

Commit means to make changes to a database permanent.

Rollback means to discard changes made to a database, leaving it in its original state

A *transaction* is a complete set of changes—either it all works, or none of it does. A transaction stretches from the first change to a commit or rollback.

So what does this mean for us? It means that if we've made a change to a record, we don't want anybody else to make changes to it until we've either committed the change or rolled it back. In a database, we do this using locking. When we lock a record, nobody can make changes to it, or delete it.

ASP provides us with several types of locks:

- Read-only: In this case, the records are not actually locked to other people, but you can't make changes; you can just read the data. (The rule of thumb is that writers don't block readers, and readers don't block writers.) This LockType is 1.

- Pessimistic locking: ASP assumes that the moment you make a change, you're eventually going to commit it, so it locks the record to other people. This LockType is 2.

- Optimistic locking: ASP doesn't lock the record until you Update the recordset to send your changes to the database. This LockType is 3.

- Optimistic batch updates: ASP makes all of the changes at once, as opposed to updating each time. This LockType is 4.

When a program tries to update a record that has been locked, it normally sits and waits for the lock to be released, so it's a good idea not to keep records locked any longer than necessary.

Options

We can specify a lot of different things with options, such as advanced actions we do and do not want to support. In our case, however, the Options property of a record-set really is more like the CommandType parameter we'll see with a Command object. It specifies what kind of action we're trying to perform. Are we just sending an SQL statement or specifying a table? There are four values for Option:

- Unknown—If we don't specify a type, this is what is used. In this case, the database needs to look at what we've sent and figure out what it is, which slows things down considerably. This value is 0.

- Command Text—This is a SQL statement and is submitted to the database exactly as-is. This value is 1.

- Table name—Tells the database we just want the rows from a table. This value is 2.

- Stored Procedure—Tells the database we are looking for a stored procedure or a query. This value is 4.

Constants

You've probably noticed that there are an awful lot of numbers to remember for all of this. It's actually not as bad as it seems because there are generally only three or four per item. To make it even easier, however, you can include a file of constants and just use their names. The file is called adovbs.inc, and should be in the directory c:\Program Files\Common Files\SYSTEM\ADO. You can use it as a server-side include and reference the values by their names.

For instance, if I copy this file to my Web server's home directory, I can use:

```
<!--#include file="adovbs.inc"-->
```

After I do that, instead of using 2 to tell the database I'm using the name of a table, I can use adCmdTable. It's a little more typing, of course, but it's a whole lot easier to remember. I've included the file on the CD, but Listing 6.11 provides a sample.

Listing 6.11—adovbs.inc: Constants

```
'---- CursorTypeEnum Values ----
Const adOpenForwardOnly = 0
Const adOpenKeyset = 1
Const adOpenDynamic = 2
Const adOpenStatic = 3

'---- LockTypeEnum Values ----
Const adLockReadOnly = 1
Const adLockPessimistic = 2
Const adLockOptimistic = 3
Const adLockBatchOptimistic = 4
```

Moving On

What all of this has been leading up to is a way to insert data into the database without worrying about whether or not it has punctuation that will interfere with an SQL statement. What we're going to do is create an updateable recordset, add a record to it, and set the values of that record.

Open auction_save.asp and make the changes shown in Listing 6.12.

Listing 6.12—auction_save.asp: Using a the constants include file

```
0: <%@ LANGUAGE="VBSCRIPT" %>
1: <!--#include file="adovbs.inc"-->
2: <%
3: Function nextAuctionID
4:
5:      Randomize
6:      nextAuctionID = int(Rnd * 1000000)
7:
8: end Function
9: %>
10:<% if Request.cookies("isLoggedInAs")("username") = "" then
11:     'user is not logged in, so they don't get to do anything %>
12:
13:     To list items for sale on the Primary Outpost Auction Block,
14:     you must be a member. Membership is free, and only takes a
15:     moment! Please <A HREF="login.asp">log in</A>. Thank you!
16:
17:<% else
18:     'First we extract our form information
19:     p_name = cstr(Request.form("p_name"))
20:     p_min = cstr(Request.form("p_min"))
21:     p_length = cstr(Request.form("p_length"))
22:     p_desc = cstr(Request.form("p_desc"))
23:     p_image = cstr(Request.form("p_image"))
24:     p_button = cstr(Request.form("p_button"))
25:     p_user = Request.cookies("isLoggedInAs")("username")
26:
27:     if p_button = "Edit Item" then
28:
29:         redirURL="p_NAME="&Server.URLencode(p_name)
30:         redirURL=redirURL&"&p_min="&Server.URLencode(p_min)
31:         redirURL=redirURL&"&p_length="&Server.URLencode(p_length)
32:         redirURL=redirURL&"&p_desc="&Server.URLencode(p_desc)
33:         redirURL=redirURL&"&p_image="&Server.URLencode(p_image)
34:         redirURL="http://localhost/auction_sellitem.asp?"&redirURL
35:         Response.Redirect redirURL
36:
37:     else
38:         p_auction_id = nextAuctionID
39:         p_start = Now
40:         p_end = DateAdd("d", p_length, Now)
41:
42:         set outpostDB = Server.CreateObject("ADODB.Connection")
43:         outpostDB.Open "outpost"
44:
45:         set insertSet = Server.CreateObject("ADODB.RecordSet")
46:         insertSet.Open "auction_items", outpostDB, _
47:                 adOpenStatic, adCmdTable
48:
49:         insertSet.AddNew
```

```
50:        insertSet("auction_id") = p_auction_id
51:        insertSet("seller") = p_user
52:        insertSet("item_name") = p_name
53:        insertSet("item_desc") = p_desc
54:        insertSet("image_URL") = p_image
55:        insertSet("opening") = p_min
56:        insertSet("current") = p_min
57:        insertSet("startdate") = p_start
58:        insertSet("enddate") = p_end
59:        insertSet.Update
60:
61:        insertSet.Close
62:        set insertSet = Nothing
63:
64:        outpostDB.Close
65:        set outpostDB = Nothing
66:
67:%>
68:        <% pageTitle = "Save Auction" %>
69:        <!--#include virtual="/pagetop.txt"-->
70:        Item Added.
71:        <!--#include virtual="/pagebottom.txt"-->
72:        </BODY>
73:        </HTML>74:<%
75:    end if 'Button Choice

76: end if 'Logged in or not
77:%>
```

6

On line 1, right after declaring the language, we import our variable definition file. This is not strictly necessary. We could have just as easily used the numbers directly, but let's make this thing as easy to read as possible.

Moving down to lines 45 through 59, notice that the incredibly ugly SQL statement is gone. If that were the only benefit we got out of this, it'd probably be worth it!

On line 45, we create the recordset just as we would create any other object. Previously, this was done for us when we assigned the recordset the results of a select statement.

Next we need to actually open the recordset. There are several different ways for us to do this. On lines 46 and 47 we've assigned the recordset the contents of the auction_items table, but we could just as easily have assigned it the results of select * from auction_items. The important thing is that we have a set of records that belong to the auction_items table, so we can add to it.

That's what we've done on line 49. When we execute the AddNew method, we are adding another record to the recordset. On line 59, when we update, the database is going to take into account all changes to the recordset, including that additional record, and it will add it to the database.

When we add the new record, it then becomes the current record. It is, however, just an empty record waiting for us to give it some information. That's what we're doing on lines 50 through 58. Earlier we accessed the information that was in those fields, now we can assign information to them. The nice thing is that now we're dealing with our inputted information as objects; it no longer matters whether they have objectionable characters, such as single or double quotes.

Finally, on line 59, we update the recordset, which sends the changes to the database. Then all that's left to do is close the recordset and destroy it so we free up our resources.

This method for adding records to the database is always preferable to just sending an SQL string, unless you're absolutely certain that nothing is going to interfere with it. It would be a good idea for us to go back to our registration page and change the insertion of member information to work this way, so we don't have problems with O'Briens or O'Malleys.

If we move to an existing record instead of adding a new one, we can also use this method for updating records.

And compared to those hideous SQL statements, it's so much easier to read and maintain!

Seeing Our Auctions

Now that we have finally succeeded in saving an item for auction, go ahead and add a few more.

Next we're going to get a list of all of the items that are available for sale. At first, we'll make this a general list. A little later, we'll make it more generic it so we can use it for multiple purposes.

Copy `template.asp` to `auction_listitems.asp` in the auction directory and add the code shown in Listing 6.13.

Listing 6.13—auction_listitems.asp: Getting a list of all auction items

```
0: <%@ LANGUAGE="VBSCRIPT" %>
1:<!--#include file="adovbs.inc"-->
2: <% pageTitle = "Outpost Auction Block" %>
3:<!--#include virtual="/pagetop.txt"-->
4:<%
5:    set outpostDB = Server.CreateObject("ADODB.Connection")
6:    outpostDB.Open "outpost"
7:
8:    set itemSet = Server.CreateObject("ADODB.RecordSet")
9:    itemSet.Open "select * from auction_items", outpostDB,
```

```
10:        adOpenForwardOnly, adCmdText
11:
12:    while not itemSet.EOF
13:       Response.write itemSet("item_name") & "<BR>"
14:       itemSet.MoveNext
15:    wend
16:
17:    itemSet.Close
18:    set itemSet = Nothing
19:
20:    outpostDB.Close
21:    set outpostDB = Nothing
22:%>
23:<!--#include virtual="/pagebottom.txt"-->
24:</BODY>
25:</HTML>
```

Here we're creating a recordset using an SQL statement. We could have just specified the table name, or even created the recordset indirectly using outpostDB.Execute(), as we have been doing, but let's get the practice. In this case, we're printing out the name of each item just to make sure that everything is working.

If you are getting an error, make sure that you've included adovbs.inc. If you don't have it or don't want to include it, you can go ahead and just use the numbers (in this case, 0 and 1). You may also need to check and make sure you don't have a problem with your SQL statement.

Now that we know we can cycle through our items, let's think about what we want to display for each of them. Obviously, we want to display the name of the item. We'll probably also want to display how much time is left on the auction, and what the current bid is. We'll also want things to line up nicely, so we're going to use HTML tables. Finally, we'll want to order the auctions, so that those that are about to end are at the top of the list. These changes are shown in Listing 6.14.

Listing 6.14—auction_listitems.asp: Completing the auction listings

```
0: <%@ LANGUAGE="VBSCRIPT" %>
1:<!--#include file="adovbs.inc"-->
2: <% pageTitle = "Outpost Auction Block" %>
3:<!--#include virtual="/pagetop.txt"-->
4:<%
5:    set outpostDB = Server.CreateObject("ADODB.Connection")
6:    outpostDB.Open "outpost"
7:
8:    set itemSet = Server.CreateObject("ADODB.RecordSet")
9:    itemSet.Open "select * from auction_items order by enddate", _
```

continues

Listing 6.14—continued

```
10:      outpostDB, adOpenForwardOnly, adCmdText
11:%>
12:
13:<TABLE border=0>
14:    <TR>
15:        <th>Item</th><th>Current Bid</th><th>Auction Ends at</th>
16:    <TR>
17:
18:<%    while not itemSet.EOF  %>
19:          <TR>
20:              <TD><%=itemSet("item_name")%></TD>
21:              <TD ALIGN="center">$<%=itemSet("current")%></TD>
22:              <TD><%=itemSet("enddate")%></TD>
23:          </TR>
24:<%       itemSet.moveNext
25:   wend     %>
26:</TABLE>
27:
28:<% itemSet.Close
29:    set itemSet = Nothing
30:
31:    outpostDB.Close
32:    set outpostDB = Nothing
33:%>
34:<!--#include virtual="/pagebottom.txt"-->
35:</BODY>
36:</HTML>
```

On line 9 we added an order by clause to the SQL statement. This tells the database that we want to order our output by the value in this column, in this case end. Because this made the line very long, we also added the underscore (_), which tells ASP that the line is continued below.

On lines 13 through 16 we set up the table and the header row. We set the border equal to zero so it doesn't show up, but you could just as easily have made it visible by setting it to 1 or some other integer value.

Because every item in the database (and hence every row in the recordset) is going to be a new row in the table, we're opening and closing the table rows *inside* the while loop on lines 19 and 23, as well as pulling our data out and displaying it on lines 20 through 22. Finally, on line 26, when we've finished with every row in the table, we close the table.

Of course, this list has limited usefulness. It would be better if we could get to the auction page from this list. We're going to create a page for each item called auction_item.asp, so we can create a link in this page (see Listing 6.15).

Listing 6.15—auction_listitems.asp: Adding a link to the item page

```
...
18:<%  while not itemSet.EOF  %>
19:        <TR>
20:           <TD>
21:              <A HREF="auction_item.asp?p_auction_id=<%
22:                          Response.Write itemSet("auction_id")
23:                       %>">
24:                 <%=itemSet("item_name")%>
25:              </A>
26:           </TD>
27:           <TD ALIGN="center">$<%=itemSet("current")%></TD>
28:           <TD><%=itemSet("enddate")%></TD>
29:        </TR>
30:<%    itemSet.MoveNext
31: wend   %>
...
```

On lines 21 through 25, we've made the item name a link to the page
auction_item.asp. We've also fed auction_item.asp the auction_id, so we know
what item to display when we get there.

This page is complete for now, so let's move on to auction_item.asp. Copy
template.asp, as usual, and add the code shown in Listing 6.16.

Listing 6.16—auction_item.asp: Displaying the item for sale

```
0: <%@ LANGUAGE="VBSCRIPT" %>
1: <% pageTitle = "Outpost Auctions" %>
2: <!--#include virtual="/pagetop.txt"-->
3: <%
4:     'First we extract our form information
5:     p_auction_id = cstr(Request.querystring("p_auction_id"))
6:
7:     'Now that we know what we're looking for, let's go get it
8:     set outpostDB = Server.CreateObject("ADODB.Connection")
9:     outpostDB.Open "outpost"
0:
11:    sqlText = "select * from auction_items where auction_id="_
12:        & p_auction_id
13:    set itemSet = outpostDB.Execute(sqlText)
14:
15:    if itemSet.EOF then
16:        Response.Write "Auction "&p_auction_id&" does not exist."
17:    else
18:        p_name = itemSet("item_name")
19:        p_desc = itemSet("item_desc")
20:        p_image = itemSet("image_URL")
21:        p_min = itemSet("opening")
```

continues

Listing 6.16—continued

```
22:        p_current = itemSet("current")
23:        p_start = itemSet("startdate")
24:        p_end = itemSet("enddate")
25:        p_seller = itemSet("seller")
26:
27:        p_next = p_current + 1.00
28:
29:%>
30:        <h1 align="center"><%=p_name%></h1>
31:
32:        <HR>
33:
34:        <TABLE width=100%>
35:        <TR><td width=60%>
36:
37:        <%= p_desc %>
38:        <P>
39:        <IMG SRC="<%=p_image%>">
40:
41:        </TD><TD>
42:
43:        <h3>Bid on This Item</h3>
44:
45:        Seller: <%=p_seller%><BR>
46:        Starting bid: <%=p_min%><BR>
47:        Current bid: <%=p_current%><BR>
48:        Bidding ends at: <%=p_end%><P>
49:
50:        <FORM ACTION="auction_biditem.asp" METHOD="post">
51:
52:        <INPUT TYPE="hidden" NAME="p_auction_id"
53:        VALUE="<%=p_auction_id%>">
54:        <INPUT TYPE="hidden" NAME="p_current"
55:            VALUE="<%=p_current%>">
56:
57:        Your bid: <INPUT TYPE="text" NAME="p_bid" size=10
58:            VALUE="$<%=p_next%>"><P>
59:        <INPUT TYPE="submit" VALUE="Enter Bid">
60:
61:        </FORM>
62:
63:        </TD></TR>
64:        </TABLE>65:
66:<%    end if %>
67:
68:<!--#include virtual="/pagebottom.txt"-->
69:</BODY>
70:</HTML>
```

First let's take a look at what we're *not* doing. We're not requiring the user to be logged in to see this page. We want to bring in the largest possible audience for our auctions. We can check to see if they're logged in before we accept their bid.

On lines 11 through 15, we're selecting our information from the database, and checking to make sure it's really there. It's possible that users could be using a bookmark to look at an auction that we have removed because it's long over, or that they could have mistyped. Instead of giving them an error, we are letting them know that the auction doesn't exist on line 16.

On lines 18 through 27, we're taking the data that we pulled out of the database and making it a bit easier to work with. We've got enough symbols flying around without making more! We are also setting a minimum next bid by adding $1.00 to the current bid.

When we display the information, which we're doing on lines 34 through 64, we're going to put it side-by-side in a table (see Figure 6.5). The table has only one row, but it has two columns. This allows us to separate the information easily. By setting widths as percentages, we can also control how much of the page is taken up by each cell without worrying about different browser window sizes.

Figure 6.5

The information page for an item should allow a user to bid.

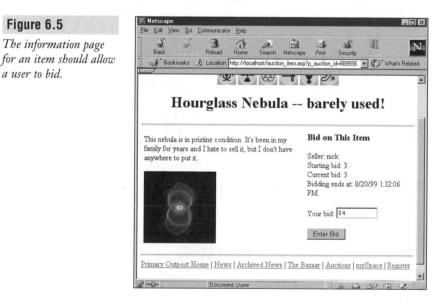

Our first cell is pretty straightforward, being just the description and the image. The second cell is where the action is. We're listing the current information, including the ending time for the auction, as well as including a form for the user to enter his or her bid.

We should probably do a little bit of clean up, though, at least as far as the bid amounts go, to make sure that they're always displayed ad currency, with two decimal places, as in Listing 6.17.

Listing 6.17—auction_item.asp: Formatting currency

```
...
43:     <h3>Bid on This Item</h3>
43:
43:     Seller: <%=p_seller%><BR>
43:     Starting bid: $<%=formatNumber(p_min, 2)%><BR>
43:     Current bid: $<%=formatNumber(p_current, 2)%><BR>
43:     Bidding ends at: <%=p_end%> <P>
43:
50:     <FORM ACTION="auction_biditem.asp" METHOD="post">
51:
52:     <INPUT TYPE="hidden" NAME="p_auction_id"
53:         VALUE="<%=p_auction_id%>">
54:     <INPUT TYPE="hidden" NAME="p_current"
55:         VALUE="<%=p_current%>">
56:
57:     Your bid: <INPUT TYPE="text" NAME="p_bid" size=10
58:         VALUE="$<%=formatNumber(p_next, 2)%>"><P>
59:     <INPUT TYPE="submit" VALUE="Enter Bid">
60:
61:     </FORM>
62:
63:     </TD></TR>
64:     </TABLE>
...
```

Here we've taken the currencies and told formatNumber that we want two digits. This way if the bid is three dollars, it won't show up as $3, but $3.00. We don't bother with the hidden value on line 54 because all we're worried about there is the value, not how it looks.

But enough with the item page, let's take some bids! After all, that's why we were doing all this, right? Before we copy template.asp anywhere, let's make a slight change to it. Open it up and add the code highlighted in Listing 6.18.

Listing 6.18—template.asp: Adding commonly used elements

```
0: <%@ LANGUAGE="VBSCRIPT" %>
1: <!--#include file="adovbs.inc"-->
2: <% pageTitle = "" %>
3: <!--#include virtual="/pagetop.txt"-->
4: <%
5:     set outpostDB = Server.CreateObject("ADODB.Connection")
6:     outpostDB.Open
7: %>
```

```
8:
9: Add content here.
10:
11:<%
12:   outpostDB.Close
13:   set outpostDB = Nothing
14:%>
15:<!--#include virtual="/pagebottom.txt"-->
16:</BODY>
17:</HTML>
```

Because we're using the database on most pages, it makes sense to add the database commands to the template. The variables file included on line 2 is a little less certain, but we can always remove it if we're not going to use it. The point is that as you go along you may find that your template files need to be changed to fit the way life really works, as opposed to the way you thought it worked.

Now copy `template.asp` to `auction_biditem.asp` in the auction directory. We're going to check to make sure that the submitted bid is higher than the current bid, and if it is, we're going to record it and make that the current bid (see Listing 6.19).

Listing 6.19—auction_biditem.asp: Accepting a bid

```
0: <%@ LANGUAGE="VBSCRIPT" %>
1: <!--#include file="adovbs.inc"-->
2: 1: <% pageTitle = "Counter" %>
3: <!--#include virtual="/pagetop.txt"-->
4: <%
5: p_username = Request.cookies("isLoggedInAs")("username")
6: if p_username = "" then
7: %>
8:
9: You must be logged in to bid on a Primary Outpost
10:auction. Please <A HREF="login.asp">login</A>.
11:Don't have a username and password? It only takes
12:a minute to <A HREF="register.asp">register</A>,
13:and it's free!
14:
15:<%
16:else 'Login Check
17:     p_auction_id = request.form("p_auction_id")
18:     p_bid = cDbl(Request.form("p_bid"))
19:     p_current = cDbl(Request.form("p_current"))
20:
21:     if not (p_bid > p_current) then
22:%>
23:        Your bid must be greater than $<%=p_current%>.
24:
25:<%   else 'Bid Check
```

continues

Listing 6.19—continued

```
26:
27:        set outpostDB = Server.CreateObject("ADODB.Connection")
28:        outpostDB.Open "outpost"
29:%>
30:
31:        Save bid here.
32:
33:<%
34:        outpostDB.Close
35:        set outpostDB = Nothing
36:
37:    end if 'Bid Check
38:
39:end if 'Login Check
40:%>
41:<!--#include virtual="/pagebottom.txt"-->
42:</BODY>
43:</HTML>
```

As usual, we're checking along the way to make sure that everything is working. On lines 5 and 6 we're making sure that the user is logged in. If he or she isn't, we don't want to do any of the rest of the page, so all of that is part of the else clause. Because we're going to have nested if-then statements, we've labeled the elses and end ifs so we know what goes with what.

On lines 18 and 19, we're retrieving the current and proposed bids from the form, and converting them to numbers. Double is a kind of number, but unlike an integer (Remember cInt?) it has decimal places. We'll use cDbl to convert the form inputs for us so we can compare them as numbers.

We're doing that comparison a little differently than usual on line 21. We don't really care whether the new bid is equal to the old one or less than the old one. All we care about is whether it's greater than the old one. So the same way that we used not in our while statements, we can use it here in our if-then statement. If it's not greater, we tell our users so they can go back and correct it. If it is, we prepare the way to record the new bid, which we take care of in Listing 6.20.

Listing 6.20—auction_biditem.asp: Checking the bid price

```
...
25:<% else 'Bid Check
26:
27:    set outpostDB = Server.CreateObject("ADODB.Connection")
28:    outpostDB.Open "outpost"
29:
30:    outpostDB.Execute("update auction_items set current = "&p_bid& _
31:        " where auction_id = "&p_auction_id)
```

```
32:
33:   set bidSet = Server.CreateObject("ADODB.RecordSet")
34:   bidSet.Open "auction_bids", outpostDB, adOpenStatic,
35:       adLockPessimistic, adCmdTable
36:   bidSet.AddNew
37:   bidSet("auction_id") = p_auction_id
38:   bidSet("buyer") = p_username
39:   bidSet("maxprice") = p_bid
40:   bidSet("bidtime") = Now
41:   bidSet.Update
42:   bidSet.Close
43:   set bidSet = Nothing
44:%>
45:
46:Your bid has been recorded. Thank you!
47:
48:<%
49:   outpostDB.Close
50:   set outpostDB = Nothing
51:
52:   end if 'Bid Check
53:
54:end if 'Login Check
...
```

So now we've done two things. On lines 30 and 31 we've updated the auction_items table to reflect the new bid, and table on lines 33 through 43 we've recorded the new bid in the auction_bids. None of this in itself is new, but there's one thing we're not taking into consideration: how can we guarantee that we're always taking the highest bid?

Consider this: two people, Luke and Jake, both want the same used starship currently going for $50. Luke enters a bid of $55, and Jake enters a bid of $52. They both hit the submit button at the same time. The system now has two copies of auction_biditem.asp running. They both check to see if the bid is high enough, and they both see that it is, so they know they can make the change. But what happens if Luke's change goes through first? He's now placed a bid of $55 and a moment later it's being replaced by a bid of $52.

This is a bad thing. This is known as the concurrency issue. What we need to do is make sure that after one person checks to make sure their bid is good, nobody else can check until the auction is updated with the new information. Fortunately, there is an easy way for us to do this.

So far we've dealt with several of the objects built into ASP, such as Response, Redirect, Server, and Session. There is another that we're going to use here: Application.

The Application object does two things for us. First, it enables us to store global Application-level data. For instance, we could store a counter that got updated every time there was a new member, and that information would be available from any session. The second thing that it does for us is to provide a lock similar to the locking we discussed earlier with regards to databases.

After we lock the Application object, nobody else can lock it. If someone tries, they will sit and wait until our lock is released. Let's take the previous example. Both Luke and Jake got item description pages telling them that the current bid was $50. They both submit their pages. Luke's page locks the Application object. Jake's page tries to lock the Application object, but can't because Luke's got the lock, so it waits. Luke's page checks and sees that his bid of $55 is higher than the current bid of $50, so it makes the change and then unlocks the Application object.

The moment the Application object is unlocked, Jake's page grabs the lock and checks his bid. Now it sees that his bid of $52 is not higher than the current bid of $55, and it tells Jake he's got to increase his bid.

To implement this, we're going to have to move a couple of things around (see Listing 6.21).

Listing 6.21—auction_biditem.asp: Concurrency

```
0: <%@ LANGUAGE="VBSCRIPT" %>
1: <!--#include file="adovbs.inc"-->
2: <% pageTitle = "Outpost Auction " %>
3: <!--#include virtual="/pagetop.txt"-->
4: <%
5: p_username = Request.cookies("isLoggedInAs")("username")
6: if p_username = "" then
7: %>
8:
9: You must be logged in to bid on a Primary Outpost
10:auction. Please <A HREF="login.asp">login</A>.
11:Don't have a username and password? It only takes
12:a minute to <A HREF="register.asp">register</A>,
13:and it's free!
14:
15:<%
16:else 'Login Check
17:
18:    p_auction_id = request.form("p_auction_id")
19:    p_bid = cDbl(Request.form("p_bid"))
20:
21:    set outpostDB = Server.CreateObject("ADODB.Connection")
22:    outpostDB.Open "outpost"
23:
24:    Application.Lock
25:
26:    set currentSet = outpostDB.Execute("select * from "_
```

```
27:        & " auction_items where auction_id = "_
28:        & p_auction_id)
29:   if currentSet.EOF then
30:     p_current = 0
31:   else
32:      p_current = cDbl(currentSet("current"))
33:   end if
34:
35:
36:   if not (p_bid > p_current) then
37:%>
38:    Your bid must be greater than $<%=p_current%>.
39:
40:<% else 'Bid Check
41:
42:     outpostDB.Execute("update auction_items set current = "_
43:         &p_bid&" where auction_id = "&p_auction_id)
44:
45:     set bidSet = Server.CreateObject("ADODB.RecordSet")
46:     bidSet.Open "auction_bids", outpostDB, adOpenStatic, _
47:         adLockPessimistic, adCmdTable
48:     bidSet.AddNew
49:        bidSet("auction_id") = p_auction_id
50:        bidSet("buyer") = p_username
51:        bidSet("maxprice") = p_bid
52:        bidSet("bidtime") = Now
53:     bidSet.Update
54:     bidSet.Close
55:     set bidSet = Nothing
56:%>
57:
58:Your bid has been recorded. Thank you!
59:
60:<%
61:     end if 'Bid Check
62:
63:     Application.Unlock
64:
65:     outpostDB.Close
66:     set outpostDB = Nothing
67:
68:end if 'Login Check
69:%>
70:<!--#include virtual="/pagebottom.txt"-->
71:</BODY>
72:</HTML>
```

The first thing we did was to move the connection to the database. Because we need a live view of the current bid, we needed to move it out of the bid check if-then statement. Of course, after we did that, we needed to make sure that the statements where we closed and got rid of the connection would get closed, even if the bid was too low, so we've moved them to lines 65 and 66.

On line 24, just before we check the current value, we lock the Application object. From now until we unlock the Application object on line 63, anybody who places a bid will have to wait for us.

We check the current value; then update the auction_items table (if the bid was good) and add the new bid to the auction_bids table. Finally, we unlock the application and get rid of the database connection.

Personalizing Our Site Through myAuctions

At this point we have a functioning auction house, but we still need to tie things together somewhat. For instance, we need a list of all the auctions involving our user for their mySpace page. This includes the items that they're selling as well as the items they're trying to buy.

Copy auction_listitems.asp (it has a lot of what we want to do already in it) to myAuctions.asp. Unaltered, this will list all of the auctions, but we're going to set the recordset to filter out everything that's not being sold by our user (see Listing 6.22).

Listing 6.22—myAuctions.asp: The user as seller

```
 0: <%@ LANGUAGE="VBSCRIPT" %>
 1: <!--#include file="adovbs.inc"-->
 2: <% pageTitle = "myAuctions" %>
 3: <!--#include virtual="/pagetop.txt"-->
 4: <%
 5:    p_username = Request.cookies("isLoggedInAs")("username")
 6:
 7:    set outpostDB = Server.CreateObject("ADODB.Connection")
 8:    outpostDB.Open "outpost"
 9:
10:    set itemSet = Server.CreateObject("ADODB.RecordSet")
11:    itemSet.Open "select * from auction_items order by enddate", _
12:       outpostDB, adForwardOnly, adCmdText
13:
14:    itemSet.filter = "seller = '" & p_username & "'"
15:%>
16:
17:<TABLE border=0>
18:    <TR>
19:     <th>Item</th><th>Current Bid</th><th>Auction Ends at</th>
20:    <TR>
21:
22:<%    while not itemSet.EOF %>
23:       <TR>
24:       <TD>
25:        <A HREF="auction_item.asp?p_auction_id=<%=itemSet("auction_id")%>">
26:           <%=itemSet("item_name")%>
```

```
27:        </A>
28:        </TD>
29:        <td align="center">$<%=itemSet("current")%></TD>
30:        <TD><%=itemSet("enddate")%></TD>
31:        </TR>
32:<%     itemSet.MoveNext
33:    wend
34:%>
35:</TABLE>
36:
37:<% itemSet.Close
38:    set itemSet = Nothing
39:
40:    outpostDB.Close
41:    set outpostDB = Nothing
42:%>
43:<!--#include virtual="/pagebottom.txt"-->
44:</BODY>
45:</HTML>
```

We've really made only very minor changes here. We're not actually checking to see if the user is logged in, because ultimately this page is going to become part of mySpace.asp, so we'll have checked it already.

On line 14, we're setting the filter property of the recordset. After we do that, only the auctions that match our criteria will be available.

If we only wanted the user's auctions, why didn't we select only those from the database in the first place?

Well, we certainly could have, but it would have made our second job a lot harder. We've easily accomplished our first task; we've displayed the items being sold by our user. But what about those our user is trying to buy? That information isn't stored in auction_items, so we're going to have to pull it from two separate tables. First, in Listing 6.23, we get the information on auctions in which the user is participating.

Listing 6.23—myauctions.asp: The user as buyer

```
...
32:<%     itemSet.moveNext
33:    wend
34:%>
35:</TABLE>
36:
37:<h3>Items I'm Trying to Buy</h3>
38:
39:<%  set buyerSet = outpostDB.Execute("select "_
40:          & " distinct(auction_id) from " _
41:          & "auction_bids where buyer = '"&p_username&"'")
```

continues

Listing 6.23—continued

```
42:    while not buyerSet.EOF
43:
44:        Response.Write buyerSet.fields.item(0)
45:        Response.Write "<BR>"
46:
47:        buyerSet.MoveNext
48:    wend
49:    buyerSet.Close
50:    set buyerSet = Nothing
51:%>
52:
53:<% itemSet.Close
54:   set itemSet = Nothing
55:
...
```

The information on which auctions our user is bidding on is in the `auction_bids` table, but we need to take into account the fact that our user may have more than one bid on a particular item. On line 39 we're creating a recordset to list the items that they're buying, but by using the SQL keyword `distinct` we're telling the database that we want each `auction_id` listed only once. Then, when we have the information, we're outputting the `auction_ids`, which is the only information we have at this point.

So how can we get the rest of the information, such as the item name, current bid, and so on? We could take each `auction_id` and do a search on the database, but that's probably not going to be our most efficient use of resources. Besides, we already have all of that information in `itemSet`, if only we could get to it.

Fortunately (as I'm sure you've guessed by now) we can. We do this with the `Find` method, which is used in Listing 6.24.

Listing 6.24—myAuctions.asp: Retrieving information on a buyer's items

```
0: <%@ LANGUAGE="VBSCRIPT" %>
1: <!--#include file="adovbs.inc"-->
2: <% pageTitle = "myAuctions" %>
3: <!--#include virtual="/pagetop.txt"-->
4: <%
5:    p_username = Request.cookies("isLoggedInAs")("username")
6:
7:    set outpostDB = Server.CreateObject("ADODB.Connection")
8:    outpostDB.Open "outpost"
9:
10:    set itemSet = Server.CreateObject("ADODB.RecordSet")
11:    itemSet.Open "select * from auction_items order by enddate", _
12:     outpostDB, adOpenStatic, adCmdText
```

```
13:
14:
15:    itemSet.filter = "seller = '" & p_username & "'"
16:%>
17:<h3>Items I'm Selling</h3>
18:<TABLE border=0>
19:    <TR>
20:    <th>Item</th><th>Current Bid</th><th>Auction Ends at</th>
21:    <TR>
22:
23:<%    while not itemSet.EOF %>
24:        <TR>
25:        <TD>
26:         <A HREF="auction_item.asp?p_auction_id=<%=itemSet("auction_id")%>">
27:            <%=itemSet("item_name")%>
28:         </A>
29:        </TD>
30:        <td align="center">$<%=itemSet("current")%></TD>
31:        <TD><%=itemSet("enddate")%></TD>
32:        </TR>
33:<%        itemSet.moveNext
34:    wend
35:%>
36:</TABLE>
37:
38:<h3>Items I'm Trying to Buy</h3>
39:
40:<%    'First we'll remove the original filter so we have
41:        'access to all auctions
42:    itemSet.filter = adFilterNone
43:%>
44:    <TABLE border=0>
45:        <TR>
46:            <th>Item</th>
47:            <th>Current Bid</th>
48:            <th>Auction Ends at</th>
49:        <TR>
50:
51:<%  set buyerSet = outpostDB.Execute("select distinct(auction_id)"_
52:        & " from auction_bids where buyer = '"&p_username&"'")
53:    while not buyerSet.EOF
54:        p_auction_id = buyerSet.fields.item(0)
55:
56:        'For each item, find the right record in itemSet
57:        'and display it
58:        itemSet.MoveFirst
59:        itemSet.Find "auction_id = " & p_auction_id
60:%>        <TR>
61:                <TD>
62:            <A HREF="auction_item.asp?p_auction_id=<%
63:                    Response.Write itemSet("auction_id")%>">
```

continues

Listing 6.24—continued

```
64:                     <%=itemSet("item_name")%>
65:                 </A>
66:                 </TD>
67:                 <td align="center">$<%=itemSet("current")%></TD>
68:                 <TD><%=itemSet("enddate")%></TD>
69:                 </TR>
70:<%          buyerSet.MoveNext
71:     wend
72:     buyerSet.Close
73:     set buyerSet = Nothing
74:%>
75:     </TABLE>
76:
77:<% itemSet.Close
78:     set itemSet = Nothing
79:
80:     outpostDB.Close
81:     set outpostDB = Nothing
82:%>
83:<!--#include virtual="/pagebottom.txt"-->
84:</BODY>
85:</HTML>
```

We've really done very little extra typing here.

The first thing that we needed to do was change itemSet to a Static cursor instead of Forward-Only, because we're going to be moving up and down the list looking for particular auctions. We did that on line 12. Next, we needed to remove the filter we'd originally put on so we can see all of the auctions, not just those our user is selling, which we did on line 42. AdFilterNone is actually just a constant equal to zero.

On lines 44 through 75, we set up our table, just as we did for the first set of auctions. In fact, both tables are exactly the same except for the records we chose to display in them.

On line 54, we just pull out each auction_id and put it into a convenient variable. Because we are using an SQL function (distinct) we don't have a handy name that we can use as shorthand as we've been doing.

Unless we tell it otherwise, the Find method of a recordset on line 59 is going to start looking at the current record in a recordset, so for each pass we tell it to move to the first record in the set, *then* Find the record. The criteria we're using here, just like the criteria we used for filtering, is just like the where clause in an SQL statement (only without the word where). After it finds the right record in the set, it displays the information normally on lines 60 through 69, just as it did when we scrolled through it in order.

Finally, we close the table, and we're done with this page!

OK, we're almost done. We still need to put this into the mySpace.asp page. Right now mySpace.asp has a table with one row and two cells. The first cell is myLinks, and the second cell is myNews. We are going to add a row to this table, but because we have only one cell to add, we're going to have that one cell span the whole row, and we'll center our information in it (see Listing 6.25).

Listing 6.25—myspace.asp: Adding myAuctions

```
0: <%@ LANGUAGE="VBSCRIPT" %>
1: <% pageTitle = "mySpace" %>
2: <!--#include virtual="/pagetop.txt"-->
3:
4: <h1 align="center">mySpace</h1>
5:
6: <TABLE width=100%>
7: <TR><TD VALIGN="top">
8:
9: <H2>myLinks</H2>
10: <% if Request.cookies("isLoggedInAs")("username") = "" then
11:     'user is not logged in, so they don't get to do anything %>
12:
13:     This area is only for registered members of Primary Outpost.
14:     Please <A HREF="login.asp">log in</A>. Thank you!
15:
16: <% else
17:
18:     'Get username for use later.
19:     p_username = Request.cookies("isLoggedInAs")("username")
20:
21:     'Open the connection to the database
22:     set outpostDB = Server.CreateObject("ADODB.Connection")
23:     outpostDB.Open "outpost"
24:
25:     'Create and populate our RecordSet
26:     set linkSet = outpostDB.Execute("select * from links "_
27:         & " order by link_id")
28:     set hasLinkSet = outpostDB.Execute("select * from user_links" _
29:         & " where username = '"&p_username&"' order by link_id")
30:
31:     while not linkSet.EOF %>
32:         <% if not hasLinkSet.EOF then
33:             if linkSet("link_id") = hasLinkSet("link_id") then %>
34:                 <A HREF="<%=linkSet("link_url")%>">
35:                     <%= linkSet("link_name") %> </A><BR>
36:                 <%= linkSet("link_desc") %><BR>
37:
38:         <%         hasLinkSet.moveNext
39:             end if
```

continues

Listing 6.25—continued

```
40:            end if %>
41: <%      linkSet.moveNext
42:      wend
43:
44:      'Clean everything up
45:      linkSet.Close
46:      set linkSet = Nothing
47:
48:      hasLinkSet.Close
49:      set hasLinkSet = Nothing
50: %>
51: <P>
52: <A HREF="mySpace_custom.asp#myLinks">Customize myLinks</A><P>
53:
54: </TD>
55:
56: <%'--------End of myLinks, beginning of myNews--------%>
57:
58: <TD VALIGN="top">
59: <H2>myNews</H2>
60:
61: <%     'Create and populate our RecordSet
62:      set newsCatSet = outpostDB.Execute("select * from"_
63:          & " news_categories order by cat_id")
64:      set hasNewsSet = outpostDB.Execute("select * from"_
65:          & " user_news_cat where username = '" & p_username & _
66:          & "' order by news_cat_id")
67:
68:      while not newsCatSet.EOF %>
69:          <% if not hasNewsSet.EOF then
70:              if newsCatSet("cat_id")=hasNewsSet("news_cat_id") then
71:                  'Output category header
72:                  Response.write "<H3>"&newsCatSet("cat_name")&"</H3>"
73:                  'Now get each news item
74:                  set newsSet = outpostDB.Execute("select * from"_
75:                      & " news where news_cat_id = " _
76:                      & newsCatSet("cat_id"))
77:                  while not newsSet.EOF
78:                      'For each news item %>
79:                      <B><%= newsSet("news_headline")%></B><BR>
80:                      <%= newsSet("news_blurb") %><BR>
81:                      <A HREF="<%= newsSet("news_url") %>">
82:                          Full Story</A><P>
83: <%                     newsSet.moveNext
84:                  wend
85:                  newsSet.Close
86:                  set newsSet = Nothing
87:                   hasNewsSet.moveNext
88:              end if
89:          end if %>
```

```
90: <%          newsCatSet.moveNext
91:     wend
92:
93:     'Clean everything up
94:     newsCatSet.Close
95:     set newsCatSet = Nothing
96:
97:     hasNewsSet.Close
98:     set hasNewsSet = Nothing
99:
100:
101:
102: end if %>
103: <P>
104: <A HREF="mySpace_custom.asp#myNews">Customize myNews</A>
105: <P>
106: </TD></TR>
107: <%'-----------End of myNews, beginning of myAuctions----------%>
108: <TR><td colspan="2" align="center">
109:
110: <!--#include file="adovbs.inc"-->
111: <H2>myAuctions</H2>
112: <%
113:     p_username = Request.cookies("isLoggedInAs")("username")
114:
115:     set itemSet = Server.CreateObject("ADODB.RecordSet")
116:     itemSet.Open "select * from auction_items order by enddate", _
117:         outpostDB, adOpenStatic, adCmdText
118:
119:     itemSet.filter = "seller = '" & p_username & "'"
120: %>
121: <h3>Items I'm Selling</h3>
122: <TABLE border=0>
123:     <TR>
124:      <th>Item</th><th>Current Bid</th><th>Auction Ends at</th>
125:     <TR>
126:
127: <%     while not itemSet.EOF %>
128:         <TR>
129:         <TD>
130:          <A HREF="auction_item.asp?p_auction_id=<%=itemSet("auction_id")%>">
131:            <%=itemSet("item_name")%>
132:          </A>
133:         </TD>
134:         <td align="center">$<%=itemSet("current")%></TD>
135:         <TD><%=itemSet("enddate")%></TD>
136:         </TR>
137: <%     itemSet.moveNext
138:     wend
139: %>
140: </TABLE>
```

continues

Listing 6.25—continued

```
141:
142: <h3>Items I'm Trying to Buy</h3>
143:
144: <%   'First we'll remove the original filter so we have
145:       'access to all auctions
146:    itemSet.filter = adFilterNone
147: %>
148:    <TABLE border=0>
149:       <TR>
150:        <th>Item</th><th>Current Bid</th><th>Auction Ends at</th>
151:       <TR>
152:
153: <%  set buyerSet = outpostDB.Execute("select"_
154:       & " distinct(auction_id) from auction_bids"_
155:       & " where buyer = '"&p_username&"'")
156:    while not buyerSet.EOF
157:       p_auction_id = buyerSet.fields.item(0)
158:
159:       'For each item, find the right record in itemSet
160:       'and display it
161:       itemSet.moveFirst
162:       itemSet.find "auction_id = " & p_auction_id
163: %>         <TR>
164:       <TD>
165:           <A HREF="auction_item.asp?p_auction_id=<%=itemSet("auction_id")%>">
166:             <%=itemSet("item_name")%>
167:           </A>
168:          </TD>
169:          <td align="center">$<%=itemSet("current")%></TD>
170:          <TD><%=itemSet("enddate")%></TD>
171:          </TR>
172: <%       buyerSet.moveNext
173:    wend
174:    buyerSet.Close
175:    set buyerSet = Nothing
176: %>
177:    </TABLE>
178:
179: <% itemSet.Close
180:    set itemSet = Nothing
181: %>
182:
183: </TD></TR>
184: </TABLE>
185:
186: <%
187:    outpostDB.Close
188:    set outpostDB = Nothing
189:
190: %>
191: <!--#include virtual="/pagebottom.txt"-->
192: </BODY>
193: </HTML>
```

Because we're part of a bigger page, we don't need our own copy of `pagebottom.txt` and `pagetop.txt`, so we've pulled those out of the section that we've copied. Likewise for the language definition and the creation of the database connection, but we've left the include of the constants file on line 110 because this is the first time on this page that it's being used. We've also moved the closing of the database connection to after our inserted text so that it's still available for us to use.

One More Step: Third Party Components and Emailing Users

Now that we've got our auctions set up, there's one more nice thing that we can do for our users: we can email them if they've been outbid, so they are prompted to come back to our site and take another look. (After all, getting them to come back is why we did all this!) Of course, we can't send email directly with what ASP provides for us. Instead we have to use a third-party component.

Components are one of the really great things about Active Server Pages. You can build a component in just about any language and then plug it in to your application and call it from your pages to do things that you normally couldn't do.

In this case we want to send email. There are lots of components out there. We're going to use one called `AspEmail` from Persits software.

Before we can use it, we need to install it and register it. We've included a copy on the CD, but you can also download it directly from `http://www.aspemail.com/download.html`. Installing the component involves the following steps:

1. Download the software or locate it on the CD.

2. Unzip the files to a directory on your hard drive.

3. Register the component. This involves making a change to the Registry on your machine so that PWS (or IIS, for that matter) knows what we're talking about when we call on it. (Not all components require this step.) To register the component, either open a DOS window or go to Start, Run and type

   `regsvr32 c:\aspemail\AspEmail.dll`

   (Persits also includes a trial copy of their `AspUpload` component, which you can register with the command `regsvr32 c:\aspemail\AspEmail.dll`.)

4. Prepare the environment: AspEmail needs certain session-level items available to it. Fortunately, we can tell the Web server to create them when a new session starts. We do this through the `global.asa` file. This file is normally

created when you install PWS, but if not, or if it's been deleted, you can go ahead and create it for yourself. The global.asa file is where we can create scripts that are to run when a session starts or ends, or when the application itself starts or ends. One of the files included with AspEmail is global.asa. You'll need to copy the information from there and put it into your own global.asa file. An example of a fairly minimal global.asa file that has the information for AspEmail is shown in Listing 6.26.

This is actually my very own global.asa file, with the information that was in it after I installed Windows 2000 (lines 1 and 2) and the information taken from the AspEmail file (lines 4 through 17).

5. Test the component. AspEmail comes with a file called SendMail.asp. Copy it to your Web server's home directory. On line 11 of this file, you will need to change the value of Mail.Host to your own mail server. The easiest way to find out what this should be would be to check the options you have listed in your email client. The SMTP host, our Outgoing Mail host is what we're looking for. After you have that set, send your browser to

```
http://localhost/SendMail.asp
```

and test it by sending yourself an email.

Listing 6.26—global.asa: Preparing for ASPEmail

```
 1: <OBJECT RUNAT=Server SCOPE=Session ID=MyInfo PROGID="MSWC.MyInfo">
 2: </OBJECT>
 3:
 4: <SCRIPT LANGUAGE=VBScript RUNAT=Server>
 5:
 6: Sub Session_OnStart
 7:     Set Session("arrTo")=SServer.CreateObject("Scripting.Dictionary")
 8:     Set Session("arrCC")=Server.CreateObject("Scripting.Dictionary")
 9:     Set Session("arrBCC")=Server.CreateObject("Scripting.Dictionary")
10:     Set Session("arrFiles")=Server.CreateObject("Scripting.Dictionary")
11:     Session("Count")=0' to generate unique keys for the dictionaries
12: end sub
13:
14: Sub Session_OnEnd
15:
16: end sub
17:
18: </SCRIPT>
```

When you've got the component itself working, it's time for us to add it to our auction.

You've Been Outbid

What we need to do now is go back to auction_biditem.asp. When we add a new bid, we will check for an old one, and if there is one, we send an email. This operation takes place in Listing 6.27.

Listing 6.27—auction_biditem.asp: Sending the "You've been outbid" message

```
...
29:    set currentSet = outpostDB.Execute("select * from"_
30:        & " auction_items where auction_id = "&p_auction_id)
31:    if currentSet.EOF then
32:        p_current = 0
33:    else
34:        p_current = cDbl(currentSet("current"))
35:        p_item_name = currentSet("item_name")
36:    end if
37:
38:    if not (p_bid > p_current) then
39:%>
40:    Your bid must be greater than $<%=p_current%>.
41:
42:<% else 'Bid Check
43:
44:    set outbidSet = outpostDB.Execute("select buyer"_
45:        & " from auction_bids" _
46:        & " where auction_id="&p_auction_id _
47:        &" order by bidtime desc")
48:
49:    if outbidSet.EOF then
50:        'This is our first bidder, so there's nobody to notify
51:    else 'Outbid check
52:        p_lastbidder = outbidSet("buyer")
53:        set lastbidderSet = outpostDB.Execute("select * from"_
54:            & " members where 5username = '"&p_lastbidder&"'")
56:        p_email = lastbidderSet("email")
57:
58:%>
59:    <OBJECT RUNAT=SERVER PROGID="Persits.MailSender" ID="Mail">
60:    </OBJECT>
61:
62:<%      Set arrTo = Session("arrTo")
63:        Mail.Host = "mail.myprovider.net"
64:        Mail.AddAddress p_email
65:
66:        Mail.From = "auctions@primaryoutpost.com"
67:        Mail.FromName = "Outpost Auctions"
68:        Mail.Subject = "You've Been Outbid!"
69:
70:        p_body = "A moment ago, you were the high bidder "
71:        p_body = p_body & "for the "& p_item_name
```

continues

Listing 6.27—continued

```
72:        p_body = p_body & " up for auction at Primary"
73:        p_body = p_body & " Outpost. Now someone has placed "
74:
75:        p_body = p_body & " a bid of $" & p_bid
76:        p_body = p_body & " and unless you want to match it, "
77:        p_body = p_body & "they're going to be the lucky "
78:        p_body = p_body & " winner. You can increase your bid "
79:        p_body = p_body & " by going to "
80:        p_body = p_body & "http://localhost/auction_item.asp"
81:        p_body = p_body & "?p_auction_id=" & p_auction_id &"."
82:
83:        Mail.Body = p_body
84:        On Error Resume Next
85:        if not Mail.Send Then
86:        Response.write Err.Description
87:        Else
88:            arrTo.RemoveAll
89:        End If
90:        On Error Goto 0
91:    end if 'Outbid Check
92:
93:    outpostDB.Execute("update auction_items set current = " _
94:        &p_bid&" where auction_id = "&p_auction_id)
95:
96:    set bidSet = Server.CreateObject("ADODB.RecordSet")
97:    bidSet.Open "auction_bids", outpostDB, adOpenStatic, _
98:        adLockPessimistic, adCmdTable
99:    bidSet.addNew
100:        bidSet("auction_id") = p_auction_id
101:        bidSet("buyer") = p_username
...
```

Starting on line 44, we're checking to see if there are any previous bidders. Because what we're really interested in is the very last bidder prior to this one, we're going to tell the database to sort them by bid time, starting with the last one (in other words, in descending order). If there are no previous bidders, outbidSet.EOF will be true, and we don't have to worry about sending an email.

If there is a user being outbid, we pull their email address from the members table on lines 53 through 56 and get ready to send him or her a message. The first thing we need to do is create the Mail object. On lines 59 and 60 you see an alternate syntax for creating an object. This is exactly the same as

```
set Mail = Server.CreateObject("Persits.MailSender")
```

I've included it in this alternative form because that's how Persits does it in their example, and I want you to understand that they are exactly the same. This alternative form is also useful for creating objects in the browser, or client.

After we've created the object, we're going to provide it with the information it needs to send out the mail on lines 62 through 68. The `arrTo` object will be used to hold our addresses, so we need to create it, even though we don't call it directly. Instead, `Mail.Addaddress` is going to add the address to it on line 64.

On line 63, you will need to set your `mailhost`, just as you did with `SendMail.asp`. Lines 32 through 83 are just building the information and populating the `Mail` object with it.

On line 84, we're going to do something a little different. Normally, when ASP encounters an error in processing, everything stops. If you've been following along with the examples, chances are you've seen that by now! In this case, however, there are lots of things that can cause an error, and many of them are not in our control. A user may have entered an incorrect email address, a server may be down; any number of things can prevent an email from going through. If the page stopped here, not only would we get an ugly error page, but the new bid wouldn't even be recorded!

To prevent that, we've added the command

```
On Error Resume Next
```

This command tells ASP that no matter what happens, it should keep going. This way if the mail can't be sent, the script will keep going and everything else will process properly.

Finally, on line 85, we send the mail. Here's how it works: ASP tries to evaluate the `if-then` statement. When it gets to `Mail.Send`, it tries to execute it, and gets a result of either `true` (meaning it was sent successfully) or `false` (meaning there was an error). Because it's been executed there, we don't need to do it again; we just need to evaluate the results.

Here we're printing out the error, but in the real world you probably wouldn't want to. You will need to clear things out if it was sent properly, however, and that's what we're doing on line 88.

Finally, on line 90, we turn off the `On Error Resume Next` statement, so if there are any *further* errors, we'll know.

That's just a very simple example of what you can do with components in general and the AspEmail component in particular. Take a look at the sample script,

6

`SendMail.asp`, for more in-depth information on how to use this component.

Next Steps

We have covered a lot of ground in this chapter. In the process of putting together a simple auction house, we have learned

- How to explicitly create recordsets and filter and move around within them
- How to create a record without using an `insert` statement, avoiding problems with punctuation.
- How to encode information so we can pass it along on a URL.
- How to generate random numbers.
- What a database transaction is, and how it effects us.
- How to lock the `Application` object to ensure consistency in our data.
- How to register a third-party component.
- How to use a third-party component, specifically to send email from within the

Chapter 7

In this chapter

- *Category Listings*
- *Searching For Products*
- *Taking Orders*

Creating Electronic Storefronts and Implementing Shopping Carts

When big business started to think about making money on the Web, the first thing they thought of (naturally) was selling things. Companies like Amazon.com reinforced this impression, and the first indicators people looked at for success were based on sales revenue.

These days, companies are beginning to realize that selling products is only one way to make money on the Internet, but it's still a very important way. Basically, there are two ways to make money by selling products. The first, and most obvious, is to sell a lot of products and make a profit on them. The second, and less obvious, is to use the products as a draw—even, in some cases, pricing items *below* cost—to get customers to your site to make money via advertising and other avenues.

In either case, your goals are the same: the customer should be able to find what they need (or want) quickly and easily and should be able to part with their money as painlessly as possible. Presenting your products is fairly straightforward. The tricky part is keeping track of the items customers want. Ideally, they would be able to select an item as they are looking at it, then choose something else, and so on until they were ready to check out. This type of system is known as a shopping cart, and there is no shortage of programs out there that will do it for you. In order to understand the issues involved in implementing one of these systems, we're going to build one of our own.

Our store is going to have the following capabilities:

- Products will be categorized and may fit into more than one category.
- Searches will be possible by category, product name, product description, or price level.
- Orders will be taken online, although we will be using manual credit card processing instead of automatic.

In order to do all this, see the basic model in Figure 7.1.

Figure 7.1

Our storefront entities.

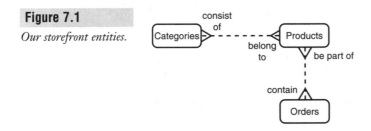

Each category may consist of one or more products, each of which must belong to one or more categories. Each product may be a part of one or more orders, each of which may contain one or more products. These are all many-to-many relationships, and we'll need to create some tables specifically to manage them. Create the tables shown in Listing 7.1.

Listing 7.1—Bazaar table create scripts

```
create table baz_categories (
    cat_id      integer,
    cat_name    char(100)
)

create table baz_products(
    prod_id     integer,
    prod_name   char(100),
    prod_desc   char(255),
    prod_image  char(100),
    prod_price  numeric(18,2)
)

create table baz_product_categories (
    prod_id     integer,
    cat_id      integer
)

create table baz_orders (
    order_id    integer,
    first_name  char(100),
    last_name   char(100),
    address1    char(255),
```

```
    address2    char(255),
    city    char(255),
    state       char(100),
    postalcode  char(50),
    country    char(100),
    phone       char(20),
    shipping    numeric(18,2),
    total       numeric(18,2)
    cc_type    char(50),
    cc_number    char(20),
    cc_exp      char(5),
    cc_nameoncard char(100),
    status     char(25)
)

create table baz_order_items (
    order_id    integer,
    prod_id     integer,
    quantity    integer
)
```

First of all, we're starting all of our table names with `baz_` to indicate that they're part of the Bazaar, the same way we started our tables with `auction_` in the previous chapter. This way we don't have any conflicts between our product categories and any other categories, such as our news.

Please note that even though we only have three entities (categories, products, and orders) we actually need five tables to tie them all together. This gives us the flexibility to create multiple associations between items; a product can belong to more than one category, and an order can have any number of items. This is one of the advantages of relational databases. If we tried to do this all in one table, we'd have to anticipate a maximum number of items per order, and so on.

After you've gotten the tables created, go into your database and create some categories and products. Try to create some that will fit into more than one category. Some suggestions are in Table 7.1:

Table 7.1

	Machinery	*Planets*	*Clothing*	*Vehicles*
Planet Rover				X
Fransisco V		X		
Laser Shielding Vest	X		X	
Titius VI Rocket	X		X	X
Jet Pack				
Power Torch	X			
Troy VII		X		
Vanguard Fighter				X

You might also consider giving them different price ranges so we can search on them later.

Not only do we have to create the categories and the products, we have to create the records that tie them all together (see Figure 7.2). For instance, the Titius IV Rocket Jet Pack will actually have three records in the `baz_product_categories` table—one for each category it belongs to.

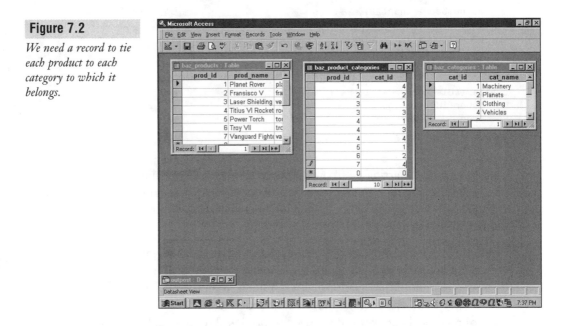

Figure 7.2

We need a record to tie each product to each category to which it belongs.

Ultimately, we can do all of this maintenance over the Web, and we'll take a look at that in our next chapter. For now, though, we'll concentrate on the task at hand: building an online storefront.

Category Listings

When we first come to the store, we of course will want to know what's for sale. Because we're concentrating on the technology, we won't worry too much about the presentation, but we will need a single start page for the store, in this case `bazaar.asp`. This page can have any specials that we're running, but should also list (at a minimum) the categories of products that we have for sale. We already have a file called `bazaar.asp` in the bazaar directory, but let's overwrite it with a copy of `template.asp` anyway because it already has the database information that we need. We customize bazaar.asp for the Bazaar and add the category listings in Listing 7.2.

Listing 7.2—bazaar.asp: Adding Category Listings

```
 0: <%@ LANGUAGE="VBSCRIPT" %>
 1: <!--#include file="adovbs.inc"-->
 2: <!--#include virtual="/pagetop.txt"-->
 3: <%
 4:     set outpostDB = Server.CreateObject("ADODB.Connection")
 5:     outpostDB.Open "outpost"
 6: %>
 7: <H1>The Bazaar</H1>
 8: If you can't find it here, you can't find it anywhere in the
 9: universe!
10:<P>
11:<CENTER>
12:<%
13:     set catSet = outpostDB.Execute("select * from baz_categories")
14:     while not catSet.EOF
15:%>
16:         <%= catSet("cat_name") %><BR>
17:<%
18:         catSet.MoveNext
19:     wend
20:     catSet.Close
21:     set catSet = Nothing
22:
23:     outpostDB.Close
24:     set outpostDB = Nothing
25:%>
26:<P>
27:</CENTER>
28:<!--#include virtual="/pagebottom.txt"-->
29:</BODY>
30:</HTML>
```

We haven't done anything new or special here, just looped through the list of categories and printed them to the page. The next thing that we're going to want to do is make those listings links. When we click the link, we want to get a page that lists all of the products in that category.

Now let's think about this. The best name for that page will probably be something like baz_category_products.asp or some such thing, and we'll probably want to pass it a parameter, such as what category we're looking at, as indicated by the cat_id. We could go ahead and add the links right now, but let's think for another moment. (Just because we're not doing detailed plans doesn't mean we should turn our brain off entirely!) When we get to this page, what are we going to want to see? We would like to see the products, of course, but what about the name of the category? Sure, we could use the cat_id to look it up when we get there, but why should we incur all that extra overhead when we already have the name and we can just pass it as part of the URL along with the category ID?

The point I'm trying to make is that we should always be looking for ways to improve performance and avoid duplicating effort. Naturally, we wouldn't want to pass tons of information as part of the URL, but this is one time where you'd have a hard time convincing me that we shouldn't do it. So let's go ahead and add those links, as shown in Listing 7.3.

Listing 7.3—bazaar.asp: Adding category links

```
…
11: <%
12:     set catSet = outpostDB.Execute("select * from baz_categories")
13:     while not catSet.EOF
14: %>
15:         <A HREF="baz_category_products.asp?p_cat_id=<%
16:             Response.Write catSet("cat_id") %>&p_cat_NAME=<%
17:             Response.Write Server.URLencode(catSet("cat_name"))%>">
18:         <%= catSet("cat_name") %>
19:         </A>
20:         <BR>
21: <%
22:         catSet.MoveNext
23:     wend
24:     catSet.Close
25:     set catSet = Nothing
26: …
```

We've created the link, and we've fed it, as parameters, p_cat_id and p_cat_name. Remember, though, because the category name is to become part of the URL, we need to make sure we don't run into problems if we have a category with, say, a space in it. Therefore, on line 17 we use Server.URLEncode to prevent problems with the link.

So now we have our main page, and we're ready to go ahead and create our category pages. Go ahead and copy template.asp to baz_category_products.asp in the bazaar directory. In this case, we're going to list the products, but we already know where we're going to be linking to the product page. So let's go ahead and add the information while we're there, as in Listing 7.4.

Listing 7.4—baz_category_products.asp: Listing the category's products

```
0: <%@ LANGUAGE="VBSCRIPT" %>
1: <!--#include file="adovbs.inc"-->
2: <!--#include virtual="/pagetop.txt"-->
3: <%
4:     p_cat_id = Request.querystring("p_cat_id")
5:     p_cat_name = Request.querystring("p_cat_name")
6: %>
7: <H2 ALIGN="center"><%=p_cat_name%></H2>
8:
```

```
9: <%
10:    set outpostDB = Server.CreateObject("ADODB.Connection")
11:    outpostDB.Open "outpost"
12:
13:    set prodInfoSet = Server.CreateObject("ADODB.RecordSet")
14:    prodInfoSet.Open "baz_products", outpostDB, adOpenStatic, _
15:       adCmdTable
16:
17:    set prodIDSet = outpostDB.Execute("select prod_id from " _
18:       & "baz_product_categories where cat_id = "&p_cat_id)
19:    while not prodIDSet.EOF
20:       p_prod_id = prodIDSet("prod_id")
21:       prodInfoSet.Find "prod_id = " & p_prod_id
22:%>
23:       <A HREF="baz_product.asp?p_prod_id=<%= p_prod_id%>">
24:          <%= prodInfoSet("prod_name") %>
25:       </A>
26:       <BR>
27:
28:<%       prodIDSet.MoveNext
29:    wend
30:
31:    prodInfoSet.Close
32:    set prodInfoSet = Nothing
33:
34:    outpostDB.Close
35:    set outpostDB = Nothing
36:%>
37:<P>
38:<!--#include virtual="/pagebottom.txt"-->
39:</BODY>
40:</HTML>
```

The first thing that we're doing here is extracting the information from the previous page on lines 4 and 5 and displaying our header telling the user what category they're looking at on line 7.

Next we're going to make a choice. To find out what products to display, we're going to go to the baz_category_products table, which will give us the appropriate prod_id numbers on lines 17 and 18. After we have them, though, we will need to get the rest of the information, such as the name of the product. We could do a search of the baz_product table for each and every item, but that would be a terrible waste of resources.

Instead, on lines 14 and 15 we're creating a static recordset with all of our products. This way ASP has to go to the database for this information only once.

Then, on lines 19 through 29, we loop through all of the records in baz_product_categories that have the right cat_id. For each one, we let ASP find the right record on line 21, and we display the appropriate information, including a link to a product information page.

7

Now we're ready to tackle `baz_product.asp`. Since we are already retrieving all of the product information from the database, we could pass it all through this URL and save ourselves a trip to the database after we get to `baz_product.asp`. That, however, would be too much of a good thing, in my opinion, for two reasons. First, that's a bit too much information to be passing on a regular basis. Second, the product information page is one place where you want to make sure that all the information is as up to date as possible. If you included all of the product information in the URL, a user could bookmark the page and any changes, such as a change in price, wouldn't be reflected. Once again copy `template.asp`, this time to `baz_product.asp` in the auction directory. Add the highlighted code in Listing 7.5.

Listing 7.5—The product information page

```
0: <%@ LANGUAGE="VBSCRIPT" %>
1: <!--#include file="adovbs.inc"-->
2: <!--#include virtual="/pagetop.txt"-->
3: <%
4:     p_prod_id = Request.querystring("p_prod_id")
5:
6:     set outpostDB = Server.CreateObject("ADODB.Connection")
7:     outpostDB.Open "outpost"
8:
9:     set prodInfoSet = outpostDB.Execute("select * from " & _
10:         baz_products where prod_id="&p_prod_id)
11:     if prodInfoSet.EOF then
12:         Response.Write "Product Number " & p_prod_id & _
13:             " does not exist."
14:     else
15:         p_name = prodInfoSet("prod_name")
16:         p_desc = prodInfoSet("prod_desc")
17:         p_image = prodInfoSet("prod_image")
18:         p_price = prodInfoSet("prod_price")
19:
20: %>
21:         <CENTER>
22:         <H2><%= p_name %></H2>
23:         <%= p_desc %>
24:         <P>
25:         <IMG SRC="/images/products/<%= p_image %>">
26:         <P>
27:         Price: $<%= formatNumber(p_price, 2) %>
28:         <P>
29:         </CENTER>
30: <%
31:     end if
32:     prodInfoSet.Close
33:     set prodInfoSet = Nothing
34:
35:     outpostDB.Close
```

```
36:  set outpostDB = Nothing
37:%>
38:<!--#include virtual="/pagebottom.txt"-->
39:</BODY>
40:</HTML>
```

On line 4 we retrieve the product ID, then on lines 9 and 10 we look for the product in our database. If it's not there, we return a message one lines 12 and 13. If it is there, we're going to print out the information about it on lines 15 through 29. We didn't have to extract the information into variables, but it sure makes our code a whole lot easier to read.

Congratulations! You've created an online catalog! You should feel a tremendous sense of accomplishment. In the early years of the Web, people got paid tens, or even hundreds of thousands of dollars to do what you just did with three pages and a few database tables. Ok, so it's not a very good catalog and those people put considerably more time, effort, and design skills into it, but you should feel good anyway.

Let's look at how we can make this a much better catalog. The most obvious problem is that there's currently no way to actually order anything, but before we get to that point, let's tweak this product page just a tiny bit to make the catalog a little more enticing.

One thing to keep in mind is that there is an entire industry devoted to the idea that if you can deduce what the customer is likely to want next, you can more easily sell it to them. This is called, depending on the context, database marketing, one-to-one marketing, customer relationship management, or whatever the catch phrase happens to be this week.

You can see it at work on some of the larger sites. Probably the most obvious is at Amazon.com. Let's say that you did a search and were looking at the description page for `Special Edition: Using Oracle 8/8I`. It's simple enough to offer links to various subcategories of `Computers and Internet`, which they do. But they also make note of what else people have bought when they've bought this book. So if you like this author, you'll probably like that author. If you're interested in this book, you'll probably also be interested in that one.

This is a science in and of itself and we're not going to get that in-depth, but it's something to remember when you're putting together your strategy. It would be a simple matter for us to point people back to relevant items by category, as we did in Listing 7.6.

Listing 7.6—Adding related categories

```
...
28:
29:        </CENTER>
30:<%
31:    end if
32:    prodInfoSet.Close
33:    set prodInfoSet = Nothing
34:%>
35:    <H3>You can find products similar to this one in:</H3>
36:<%
37:    set catSet = Server.CreateObject("ADODB.RecordSet")
38:    catSet.Open "baz_categories", outpostDB, adOpenStatic,
39:        adLockOptimistic, adCmdTable
40:
41:    set prodCatSet = outpostDB.Execute("select * from " _
42:        & "baz_product_categories where prod_id=" & p_prod_id)
43:    while not prodCatSet.EOF
44:    catSet.MoveFirst
45:    catSet.Find "cat_id = " & prodCatSet("cat_id")
46:%>
47:    <A HREF="baz_category_products.asp?p_cat_id=<%
48:        Request.Write catSet("cat_id") 8%>&p_cat_NAME=<%
49:        Request.Write Server.URLencode(catSet("cat_name"))%>">
50:    <%= catSet("cat_name") %>
51:    </A>
52:    <BR>
53:<%
54:        prodCatSet.MoveNext
55:  wend
56:  prodCatSet.Close
57:  set ProdCatSet = Nothing
58:
59:  catSet.Close
60:  set catSet = Nothing
61:
62:  outpostDB.Close
63:  set outpostDB = Nothing
64:%>
65:<P>
66:<!--#include virtual="/pagebottom.txt"-->
67:</BODY>
68:</HTML>
```

After we display the product information, on line 37 we're creating a recordset with all the category information, so we can display it when the time comes—kind of like the category products page, only in reverse.

Then, rather than selecting all of the products in the category, we're selecting all of the categories for the product. We have one table, baz_product_categories, and two great things we can do with it. After we have the categories, we're displaying them along with a link to a listing of all the products in that category. These lines, 47 through 51, were actually taken from bazaar.asp, without the slightest modification. (Of course, that's because we used the same names for our recordsets.)

The nice thing about dynamically generated pages like these is that after we make the change to the product page, it takes effect for all products. Go ahead and surf through your products. You'll be able to go from category to category, right from the product pages.

Searching For Products

In addition to allowing our users to find products by category, we want to give them the option of searching for a product by its name, description, or price range. Instead of making a separate page, let's go ahead and put it right on bazaar.asp for now, as in Listing 7.7.

Listing 7.7—Preparing to add the search form

```
0: <%@ LANGUAGE="VBSCRIPT" %>
1: <!--#include file="adovbs.inc"-->
2: <!--#include virtual="/pagetop.txt"-->
3: <%
4:     set outpostDB = Server.CreateObject("ADODB.Connection")
5:     outpostDB.Open "outpost"
6: %>
7: <H1>The Bazaar</H1>
8: If you can't find it here, you can't find it anywhere in the
9: universe!
10:<P>
11:<CENTER>
12:<%
13:     set catSet = outpostDB.Execute("select * from baz_categories")
14:%>
15:<TABLE<TABLE WIDTH=""75%"">
16:<TR><TD<TD WIDTH="30%">
17:<%
18:     while not catSet.EOF
19:%>
20:         <A HREF="baz_category_products.asp?p_cat_id=<%
21:             Request.Write catSet("cat_id") %>&p_cat_NAME=<%
22:             Request.Write Server.URLencode(catSet("cat_name")) %>">
23:         <%= catSet("cat_name") %>
24:         </A>
25:         <BR>
26:<%
```

continues

Listing 7.7—continued

```
27:        catSet.MoveNext
28: wend
29:%>
30:</TD><TD>
31:
32:Our Form Will Go Here.
33:
34:</TD></TR>
35:</TABLE>
36:<%
37:   catSet.Close
38:   set catSet = Nothing
39:
40:   outpostDB.Close
41:   set outpostDB = Nothing
42:%>
43:<P>
44:</CENTER>
45:<!--#include virtual="/pagebottom.txt"-->
46:</BODY>
47:</HTML>
```

The first thing that we've done is set up the form to make sure the format is correct. To set the categories and the form side-by-side, we've put them into a one-row table (see Figure 7.3). If we'd just left it at that, what'd have a very narrow table with everything squished together. So instead, we've set the width on the table to 75 percent of the page, and the width of the category cell to 30 percent of the table. That should space things out nicely.

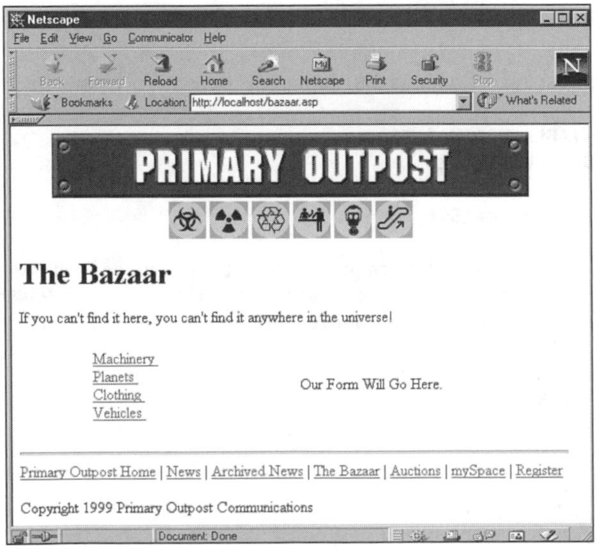

Figure 7.3

Using an HTML table, we can place our elements side-by-side, but external formatting doesn't take effect within the table itself.

Remember how we centered the categories when we first created this page? We haven't gotten rid of the <CENTER></CENTER> tags, but you'll notice that the categories are no longer centered. Instead, the entire table is centered, and the categories are aligned to the left. This is because each cell is independent as far as formatting goes. We'd need to re-apply the center tags within the cell for us to see the change.

Aside from the formatting, there is one important programming issue to take notice of. We're opening catSet on line 15, before the table, but we're not closing it until line 38, after the table. We could have opened it, displayed the information, and closed it all inside the cell, but we're going to use that recordset again for the search formed, so why destroy it?

Now let's create the form we're going to use (see Listing 7.8).

Listing 7.8—Creating the search form

```
0: <%\\@ LANGUAGE="VBSCRIPT" %>
1: <!--#include file="adovbs.inc"-->
2: <!--#include virtual="/pagetop.txt"-->
3: <%
4:   set outpostDB = Server.CreateObject("ADODB.Connection")
5:   outpostDB.Open "outpost"
6: %>
7: <H1>The Bazaar</H1>
8: If you can't find it here, you can't find it anywhere in the
9: universe!
10:<P>
11:<CENTER>
12:<%
13:   set catSet = outpostDB.Execute("select * from baz_categories")
14:%>
15:<TABLE<TABLE WIDTH=""75%"">
16:<TR><TD<TD WIDTH="30%">
17:<%
18:   while not catSet.EOF
19:%>
20:     <A HREF="baz_category_products.asp?p_cat_id=<%
21:       Response.Wrie catSet("cat_id") %>&p_cat_NAME=<%
22:       Resoinse.Write Server.URLencode(catSet("cat_name"))%>">
23:     <%= catSet("cat_name") %>
24:     </A>
25:     <BR>
26:<%
27:     catSet.MoveNext
28:   wend
29:%>
30:</TD><TD>
31:
```

continues

Listing 7.8—continued

```
32:    <H3>Search our catalog</H3>
33:    <FORM ACTION="baz_search_action.asp" METHOD="post">
34:
35:        <INPUT TYPE="checkbox" NAME="p_usetext" VALUE="yes"> Look for:
36:        <INPUT TYPE="text" NAME="p_text">
37:        <BR>
38:    <INPUT TYPE="checkbox" NAME="p_useprice" VALUE="yes"> Price Range:
39:    <SELECT NAME="p_price">
40:        <OPTION VALUE="all">All Price Levels
41:        <OPTION VALUE="100">Under $100
42:        <OPTION VALUE="1000"> Under $1000
43:        <OPTION VALUE="10000"> Under $10,000
44:        <OPTION VALUE="100000"> Under $100,000
45:    </SELECT>
46:    <BR>
47:    <INPUT TYPE="checkbox" NAME="p_usecat" VALUE="yes"> In Category:
48:    <SELECT NAME="p_cat">
49:    <%
50:        catSet.MoveFirst
51:        while not catSet.EOF
52:    %>
53:            <OPTION VALUE="<%= catSet("cat_id") %>"><%
54:                Response.Write catSet("cat_name")%>
55:    <%
56:            catSet.MoveNext
57:        wend
58:    %>
59:    </SELECT>
60:    <P>
61:    <INPUT TYPE="submit">
62: </FORM>
63:
64:</TD></TR>
65:</TABLE>
66:<%
67:    catSet.Close
68:    set catSet = Nothing
69:
70:    outpostDB.Close
71:    set outpostDB = Nothing
72:%>
73:<P>
74:</CENTER>
75:<!--#include virtual="/pagebottom.txt"-->
76:</BODY>
77:</HTML>
```

First we're going ahead and opening the form on line 33. Because
bazaar_action.asp doesn't really describe what the action does, we're going to call
the it baz_search_action.asp. We want to give the customer a chance to not only

search by several different qualities, but also to pick and choose which should apply. We're going to do that with check boxes on lines 35, 38, and 47 (see Figure 7.4). If the check box is selected, we search on that criteria. If not, we don't.

Figure 7.4

The Search form.

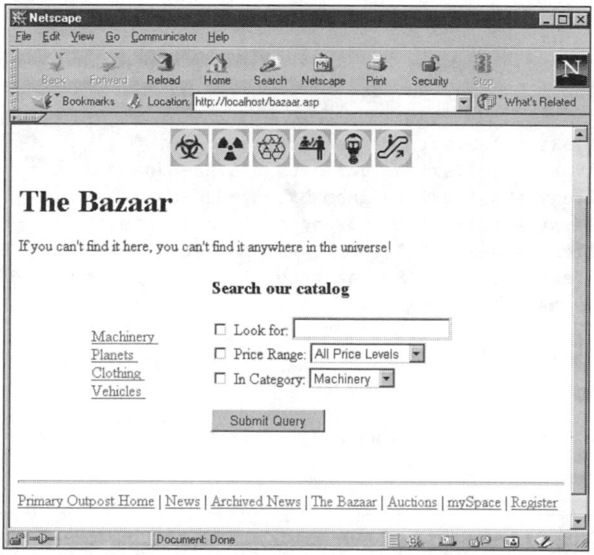

So we create a check box and a text box for the text, and a check box and a pull-down menu for the price levels. Finally, we want a check box and a pull-down menu for the categories. This is why we didn't close the recordset after we used it the first time. Before we get to line 50, `catSet` is at the end of file, so we bring it back to the beginning using `MoveFirst`. We can then loop through it as usual, without the overhead of re-creating it. What we're doing when we loop through the categories on lines 51 through 57 is creating the options for our pull-down menu, specifying the `cat_id` as our value.

So now that we have our form, we can create the action to service it. Copy `template.asp` to `baz_search_action.asp` in the bazaar directory and add the new code in Listing 7.9.

Listing 7.9—Preparing to process the search form

```
0: <%@ LANGUAGE="VBSCRIPT" %>
1: <!--#include file="adovbs.inc"-->
2: <!--#include virtual="/pagetop.txt"-->
3: <%
4:     p_usetext = Request.form("p_usetext")
5:     p_text = Request.form("p_text")
```

continues

Listing 7.9—continued

```
 6:        p_useprice = Request.form("p_useprice")
 7:        p_price = Request.form("p_price")
 8:        p_usecat = Request.form("p_usecat")
 9:        p_cat = Request.form("p_cat")
10:
11:        set outpostDB = Server.CreateObject("ADODB.Connection")
12:        outpostDB.Open "outpost"
13:
14:        sqlText = "select baz_products.prod_id, "
15:        sqlText = sqlText & "baz_products.prod_name "
16:        sqlText = sqlText & "from baz_products, "
17:        sqlText = sqlText & "baz_product_categories "
18:        sqlText = sqlText & "where baz_products.prod_id = "
19:        sqlText = sqlText & "baz_product_categories.prod_id"
20:        Response.Write sqlText
21:
22:        outpostDB.Close
23:        set outpostDB = Nothing
24:%>
25:<!--#include virtual="/pagebottom.txt"-->
26:</BODY>
27:</HTML>
```

On lines 4 throught 9 we're retrieving our form values, as usual, but before we even think about hitting the database, let's talk strategy. So far every time we've queried the database with a select statement, we've asked for information from just one table. In some cases, this has meant that we then had to go to a second table or a second recordset for more information, and we could do that this time as well.

What we're doing here, however, is called dynamic SQL. That means that until we get to the page, we don't know what we're looking for. So in this case, we're going to join the product and the product_categories tables together into a single batch of information that we can query all at once.

Let's dissect the SQL statement on lines 14 through 19. The first thing that we need to do is specify what information it is that we want. All we're going to do with the information is generate a list of links to product pages, so we need the prod_id (for the URL) and the prod_name (for the link). You may notice the products. in front of the names. That's to tell the database which table we're referring to, because there's a prod_id column in both of the tables we're selecting from. Because there's only one product_name column, we could have gotten away without specifying the table name there, but it's good practice to always include it.

Next, on lines 16 and 17, we're telling the database what tables we want to select from, in this case baz_products and baz_product_categories. Now, if we wanted to, we could leave it here, but that would be a bad thing. The reason is that this SQL statement, as it stands, would join every line in the baz_products table with every line in the baz_product_categories table. Our tables only have 7 and 4 lines, respectively, which would mean only 28 lines in the resulting set, but imagine if you have thousands of products and hundreds of categories. This condition is called a *Cartesian Join*, and you can bring an entire machine down with it, if you're not careful.

The way that we get around this is to add a join condition linking the appropriate rows together, on lines 18 and 19. This way, the only lines we get back for each product are those that list the categories to which it actually belongs.

We've still got some work to do on this SQL statement. After all, if we run it right now, it will return us all of our products, no matter what our search asked for! Let's do it, though, just to test things out and make sure they're working, as in Listing 7.10.

Listing 7.10—Joining two tables

```
...
11:  set outpostDB = Server.CreateObject("ADODB.Connection")
12:  outpostDB.Open "outpost"
13:
14:  sqlText = "select distinct(baz_products.prod_id), "
15:  sqlText = sqlText & "baz_products.prod_name "
16:  sqlText = sqlText & "from baz_products, "
17:  sqlText = sqlText & "baz_product_categories "
18:  sqlText = sqlText & "where baz_products.prod_id = "
19:  sqlText = sqlText & "baz_product_categories.prod_id"
20:
21:  set prodSet = outpostDB.Execute(sqlText)
22:  while not prodSet.EOF
23:%>    <A HREF="baz_product.asp?p_prod_id=<%
24:          Response.Write prodSet("prod_id") %>">
25:      <%= prodSet("prod_name") %>
26:      </A><BR>
27:<%    prodSet.MoveNext
28:  wend
29:  prodSet.Close
30:  set prodSet = Nothing
31:
32:  outpostDB.Close
33:  set outpostDB = Nothing
34:...
```

Note

If this were virtually any other database, we could clean this up with table aliases, making the SQL statement:

```
select distinct(p.prod_id), p.prod_name from baz_products p,
    baz_product_categories c where p.prod_id = c.prod_id
```

Unfortunately, Access doesn't support table (or for that matter column) aliases, so we're stuck with the long ones. Feel free to use what works in your database, however.

Before we go about displaying any products, we need to make sure that we're going to get at most one listing for each product. Remember, with a join, if there are three categories that a product belongs to, it's going to show up in three rows. We eliminate that problem by telling the database that we want distinct product IDs, as noted on line 14. Then we create a simple recordset and display our product links.

Now we're ready to start narrowing things down based on our search criteria. Listing 7.11 shows how we create the dynamic where clause for the search.

Listing 7.11—Creating a dynamic SQL statement

```
0:  <%@ LANGUAGE="VBSCRIPT" %>
1:  <!--#include file="adovbs.inc"-->
2:  <!--#include virtual="/pagetop.txt"-->
3:  <%
4:      p_usetext = Request.form("p_usetext")
5:      p_text = Request.form("p_text")
6:      p_useprice = Request.form("p_useprice")
7:      p_price = Request.form("p_price")
8:      p_usecat = Request.form("p_usecat")
9:      p_cat = Request.form("p_cat")
10:
11:     p_textWhere = ""
12:     p_priceWhere = ""
13:     p_catWhere = ""
14:
15:     if p_usetext = "yes" then
16:         p_textWhere = " and (prod_name = '"&p_text&"'"
17:         p_textWhere = p_textWhere&" or prod_desc = '"&p_text &"')"
18:         Response.Write "p_textWhere = "&p_textWhere&"<BR>"
19:     end if
20:
21:     if p_useprice = "yes" and p_price <> "all" then
22:         p_priceWhere = " and prod_price < "&p_price
23:         Response.Write "p_priceWhere = "&p_priceWhere&"<BR>"
24:     end if
25:
26:     if p_usecat = "yes" then
```

```
27:          p_catWhere = " and cat_id = "&p_cat
28:          Response.Write "p_catWhere = "&p_catWhere&"<BR>"
29:      end if
30:
31:      set outpostDB = Server.CreateObject("ADODB.Connection")
32:      outpostDB.Open "outpost"
33:
34:      sqlText = "select distinct(baz_products.prod_id), "
35:      sqlText = sqlText & "baz_products.prod_name "
36:      sqlText = sqlText & "from baz_products, "
37:      sqlText = sqlText & "baz_product_categories "
38:      sqlText = sqlText & "where baz_products.prod_id = "
39:      sqlText = sqlText & "baz_product_categories.prod_id"
40:      sqlText = sqlText & p_textWhere & p_priceWhere & p_catWhere
41:
42:      Response.Write "<P>sqlText = " & sqlText & "<P>"
43:
44:      set prodSet = outpostDB.Execute(sqlText)
45:      while not prodSet.EOF
...
```

What we're doing here is conditionally building an SQL statement. On lines 34 through 39, we've built the complete set of records. Now we want to narrow it down using the criteria from the form, which we are adding on line 40.

Let's look at how we're building those Where clauses. On lines 11 through 13, we're initializing the statements. If we don't have anything to add to them, they'll remain blank and won't affect the results.

On line 15, we decide whether to worry about the text search. If the user didn't click the check box, it doesn't matter what they entered in the text box; we're not going to search on it anyway. If they did, however, we need to compare it against two things: the product name and the product description. Let's take a look at what we actually receive. If I were to do a search and ask it to look for Rocket, line 18 would print out

```
p_textWhere = and (prod_name = 'Rocket' or prod_desc = 'Rocket')
```

This means that this part of the Where clause would be true if the product name or the product description was Rocket. If this were the only item I'd checked off, the complete Where clause would be

```
... where baz_products.prod_id = baz_product_categories.prod_id
and (prod_name = 'Rocket' or prod_desc = 'Rocket')
```

Let's look at what this means. For every record that is returned by our two tables, the database is going to ignore every record that doesn't fit the following:

```
Condition 1 AND Condition 2
Condition 1 is just
baz_products.prod_id = baz_product_categories.prod_id
Condition 2 is
(prod_name = 'Rocket' or prod_desc = 'Rocket')
```

So a record has to satisfy our Join clause, and it has to have Rocket in the name or the description. But what if we left out the parenthesis? In that case, we'd have

Condition 1	And	Condition 2	Or	Condition 3
baz_products. prod_id = baz_ product_ categories. prod_id		prod_name = ' Rocket'		prod_desc = 'Rocket'

In this case, a record would be included if the description was Rocket, even if it didn't satisfy any of the other conditions—like the join condition.

Fortunately for us, our other situations are a bit more straightforward. On line 21, we're going to decide whether or not to search on the price. Not only do we need for users to have clicked the check box, we need for them to have chosen a price level. After all, if they don't care what the price is, there's no point searching on it, now is there! We also saved ourselves a bit of time when we chose the values for our pull-down menu. We could have set the values as Level 1, Level 2, and so on, but then we'd have to translate that into actual prices here. Instead we set it as the actual price we need to come in under, so we can put it right into the SQL statement.

Finally, we set the category, if the user picked it. Just to make sure everything's working the way that we expect, we are also printing out our Where clauses and the final SQL statement. This way we can see what's actually making it to the form, and if we get strange results, we can see exactly where they're coming from (see Figure 7.5).

Figure 7.5

By printing our Where clauses and the final SQL statement to the page, we can see why products are being selected or excluded.

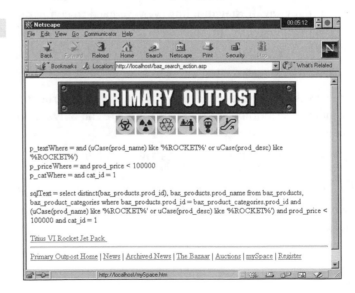

We still have one problem. The chances are that the user is not going to enter the exact name of a product, let alone the description. We need to take that into account, and put in wildcards, as in Listing 7.12.

Listing 7.12—Adding wildcards to the search

```
0:  <%@ LANGUAGE="VBSCRIPT" %>
1:  <!--#include file="adovbs.inc"-->
2:  <!--#include virtual="/pagetop.txt"-->
3:  <%
4:    p_usetext = Request.form("p_usetext")
5:    p_text = cstr(Request.form("p_text"))
6:    p_text = uCase(p_text)
7:    p_useprice = Request.form("p_useprice")
8:    p_price = Request.form("p_price")
9:    p_usecat = Request.form("p_usecat")
10:   p_cat = Request.form("p_cat")
11:
12:   p_textWhere = ""
13:   p_priceWhere = ""
14:   p_catWhere = ""
15:
16:   if p_usetext = "yes" then
17:     p_textWhere = " and (uCase(prod_name) like '%"&p_text&"%'"
18:     p_textWhere = p_textWhere & " or uCase(prod_desc) like '%"_
19:       & p_text & "%')"
20:     Response.Write "p_textWhere = " & p_textWhere & "<BR>"
21:   end if
22:
23:
```

With these changes, we're accounting for both wild cards and case-sensitivity. On line 6 we're converting the string that our customer is searching on to all uppercase letters. Then we also convert the text in the database to all uppercase letters, so no matter what the user enters the case will match. To take care of the wildcards, we're using the `like` operator on line 18 instead of the equal sign, and adding percent signs, which act as wildcards.

Note

> The best way to accomplish case insensitivity for your search is going to depend on what database you're using. For instance, if we were using Oracle or another more advanced database, we could have just said
>
> ```
> p_textWhere = " and (upper(prod_name) like upper('%" &p_text& "%)"
> _& " or upper(prod_desc) like upper('%" & p_text & "%'))"
> ```
>
> but Access won't allow you to use conversion functions with the `like` operator.

If we remove our debugging statements, as we do in Listing 7.13, we have a fully functional (although fairly basic) search engine for our catalog.

Listing 7.13—Completing the search engine

```
0:  <%@ LANGUAGE="VBSCRIPT" %>
1:  <!--#include file="adovbs.inc"-->
2:  <!--#include virtual="/pagetop.txt"-->
3:  <%
4:    p_usetext = Request.form("p_usetext")
5:    p_text = cstr(Request.form("p_text"))
6:    p_text = uCase(p_text)
7:    p_useprice = Request.form("p_useprice")
8:    p_price = Request.form("p_price")
9:    p_usecat = Request.form("p_usecat")
10:   p_cat = Request.form("p_cat")
11:
12:   p_textWhere = ""
13:   p_priceWhere = ""
14:   p_catWhere = ""
15:
16:   if p_usetext = "yes" then
17:     p_textWhere = " and (uCase(prod_name) like '%"&p_text&"%'"
18:     p_textWhere = p_textWhere & " or uCase(prod_desc) like '%"_
19:       & p_text & "%')"
20:   end if
21:
22:   if p_useprice = "yes" and p_price <> "all" then
23:     p_priceWhere = " and prod_price < " & p_price
24:   end if
25:
26:   if p_usecat = "yes" then
27:     p_catWhere = " and cat_id = " & p_cat
28:   end if
29:
30:   set outpostDB = Server.CreateObject("ADODB.Connection")
31:   outpostDB.Open "outpost"
32:
33:   sqlText = "select distinct(baz_products.prod_id), "
34:   sqlText = sqlText & "baz_products.prod_name "
35:   sqlText = sqlText & "from baz_products, "
36:   sqlText = sqlText & "baz_product_categories "
37:   sqlText = sqlText & "where baz_products.prod_id = "
38:   sqlText = sqlText & "baz_product_categories.prod_id"
39:   sqlText = sqlText & p_textWhere & p_priceWhere & p_catWhere
40:
41:   set prodSet = outpostDB.Execute(sqlText)
42:   while not prodSet.EOF
43:%>    <A HREF="baz_product.asp?p_prod_id=<%
44:        Response.Write prodSet("prod_id") %>">
45:    <%= prodSet("prod_name") %>
46:    </A><BR>
```

```
47:<%    prodSet.MoveNext
48:  wend
49:  prodSet.Close
50:  set prodSet = Nothing
51:
52:  outpostDB.Close
53:  set outpostDB = Nothing
54:%>
55:<!--#include virtual="/pagebottom.txt"-->
56:</BODY>
57:</HTML>
```

Now that we have this thing, it's a shame that we can only get to it from `bazaar.asp`. It would be very handy for our customers if they could do a search from anywhere in the catalog. Fortunately for us, anywhere in the catalog consists of basically three ASP pages: `bazaar.asp`, `baz_category_products.asp`, and `baz_product.asp`. From a maintainability standpoint, it'd be a nightmare to have the form on all three pages, though. Every time we made a change, we'd have to make sure it was made on all pages. Or would we? We could have it on all three pages, but in only one file, if we used Server Side Includes. The include file needs just the actual form itself (see Listing 7.14).

Listing 7.14—Creating a file that can be included on other pages

```
1:    <H3>Search our catalog</H3>
2:    <FORM ACTION="baz_search_action.asp" METHOD="post">
3:
4:        <INPUT TYPE="checkbox" NAME="p_usetext" VALUE="yes">
5:        Look for:
6:        <INPUT TYPE="text" NAME="p_text">
7:        <BR>
8:        <INPUT TYPE="checkbox" NAME="p_useprice" VALUE="yes">
9:        Price Range:
10:       <SELECT NAME="p_price">
11:           <OPTION VALUE="all">All Price Levels
12:           <OPTION VALUE="100">Under $100
13:           <OPTION VALUE="1000"> Under $1000
14:           <OPTION VALUE="10000"> Under $10,000
15:           <OPTION VALUE="100000"> Under $100,000
16:       </SELECT>
17:       <BR>
18:       <INPUT TYPE="checkbox" NAME="p_usecat" VALUE="yes">
19:       In Category:
20:       <SELECT NAME="p_cat">
21:       <%
22:           set catSet = outpostDB.Execute("select * from " & _
23:               baz_categories")
24:           while not catSet.EOF
```

continues

7

Listing 7.14—continued

```
25:     %>
26:                 <OPTION VALUE="<%= catSet("cat_id") %>"><%
27:                     Response.Write catSet("cat_name")%>
28:     <%
29:             catSet.MoveNext
30:         wend
31:         catSet.Close
32:         set catSet = Nothing
33:     %>
34:     </SELECT>
35:     <P>
36:     <INPUT TYPE="submit">
37: </FORM>
```

We don't need any of the declarations or page headers and footers because we're going to be including this file in pages that already have them, but because we can't count on having the category recordset, we need to create and destroy it within this section, on lines 22, 23, 31 and 32. Copy this from bazaar.asp into the file baz_search.inc and add the recordset information. We've removed catSet.MoveFirst because it is no longer necessary, but it wouldn't have hurt anything to leave it there.

Now we can include this form anywhere we want. Add the include file to bazaar.asp as shown in Listing 7.15.

Listing 7.15—Adding the include file

```
0: <%@ LANGUAGE="VBSCRIPT" %>
1: <!--#include file="adovbs.inc"-->
2: <!--#include virtual="/pagetop.txt"-->
3: <%
4:     set outpostDB = Server.CreateObject("ADODB.Connection")
5:     outpostDB.Open "outpost"
6: %>
7: <H1>The Bazaar</H1>
8: If you can't find it here, you can't find it anywhere in the
9: universe!
10:<P>
11:<CENTER>
12:<%
13:     set catSet = outpostDB.Execute("select * from baz_categories")
14:%>
15:<TABLE<TABLE WIDTH=""75%"">
16:<TR><TD<TD WIDTH="30%">
17:<%
18:     while not catSet.EOF
19:%>
20:             <A HREF="baz_category_products.asp?p_cat_id=<%
```

```
21:                    Response.Write catSet("cat_id") %>&p_cat_NAME=<%
22:                    Response.Write Server.URLencode(catSet("cat_name"))%>">
23:           <%= catSet("cat_name") %>
24:           </A>
25:           <BR>
26:<%
27:           catSet.MoveNext
28:      wend
29:      catSet.Close
30:      set catSet = Nothing
31:%>
32:</TD><TD>
33:
34:<!--#include file="baz_search.inc"-->
35:
36:</TD></TR>
37:</TABLE>
38:<%
39:      outpostDB.Close
40:      set outpostDB = Nothing
41:%>
42:<P>
43:</CENTER>
44:<!--#include virtual="/pagebottom.txt"-->
45:</BODY>
46:</HTML>
```

Because we are going to have to create and destroy the category recordset within the include, we'll go ahead and destroy the first instance of it when we're done with it on lines 29 and 30. Yes, we'll be hitting the database one more time than we have to, but we're trading off for flexibility. We'll add the search include file to our other pages as we go along.

Taking Orders

At this point our customers can do everything but actually order products. Because that's the whole idea, let's go ahead and give them that opportunity.

Ordering products basically consists of three steps:

- Adding a product to your cart
- Reviewing the order
- Submitting the order

Adding a Product to Your Cart

The best time for us to get a customer to add a product to their cart is when they're actually looking at it. With that in mind, we want to add a button to the product page that will allow them to do this as painlessly as possible. Let's open baz_product.asp and prepare the layout, taking into account the addition of the search form (see Listing 7.16).

Listing 7.16—Preparing to add the shopping cart

```
0: <%@ LANGUAGE="VBSCRIPT" %>
1: <!--#include file="adovbs.inc"-->
2: <!--#include virtual="/pagetop.txt"-->
3: <%
4:      p_prod_id = Request.querystring("p_prod_id")
5:
6:      set outpostDB = Server.CreateObject("ADODB.Connection")
7:      outpostDB.Open "outpost"
8:
9:      set prodInfoSet = outpostDB.Execute("select * from " & _
10:         "baz_products where prod_id = " & p_prod_id)
11:      if prodInfoSet.EOF then
12:         Response.Write "Product Number "&p_prod_id&" does not exist."
13:      else
14:         p_name = prodInfoSet("prod_name")
15:         p_desc = prodInfoSet("prod_desc")
16:         p_image = prodInfoSet("prod_image")
17:         p_price = prodInfoSet("prod_price")
18:
19:%>
20:         <TABLE WIDTH="100%">
21:         <TR><TD WIDTH="75%">
22:
23:            <CENTER>
24:            <H2><%= p_name %></H2>
25:            <%= p_desc %>
26:            <P>
27:            <IMG SRC="/images/products/<%= p_image %>">
28:            <P>
29:            Price: $<%= formatNumber(p_price, 2) %>
30:            <P>
31:
32:            OUR ADD TO ORDER BUTTON WILL GO HERE
33:
34:            </CENTER>
35:
36:         </TD><TD>
37:
38:              <!--#include file="baz_search.inc"-->
39:
40:         </TD></TR>
41:         </TABLE>
42:<%
43:         end if
44:         prodInfoSet.Close
45:         set prodInfoSet = Nothing
46:%>
```

```
47:          <H3>You can find products similar to this one in:</H3>
48:<%
49:          set catSet = Server.CreateObject("ADODB.RecordSet")
50:          catSet.Open "baz_categories", outpostDB, adOpenStatic, _
51:              adLockOptimistic, adCmdTable
52:
53:          set prodCatSet = outpostDB.Execute("select * from " _
54:              baz_product_categories where & "prod_id=" & p_prod_id)
55:          while not prodCatSet.EOF
56:              catSet.MoveFirst
57:              catSet.Find "cat_id = " & prodCatSet("cat_id")
58:%>
59:              <A HREF="baz_category_products.asp?p_cat_id=<%
60:                  Response.Write catSet("cat_id") %>&p_cat_NAME=<%
61:                  Response.Write Server.URLencode(catSet("cat_name"))%>">
62:              <%= catSet("cat_name") %>
63:              </A>
64:              <BR>
65:<%
66:              prodCatSet.MoveNext
67:          wend
68:          prodCatSet.Close
69:          set ProdCatSet = Nothing
70:
71:          catSet.Close
72:          set catSet = Nothing
73:
74:          outpostDB.Close
75:          set outpostDB = Nothing
76:%>
77:<P>
78:<!--#include virtual="/pagebottom.txt"-->
79:</BODY>
80:</HTML>
```

Again we've laid things out in a table, but because the product information is the most important, we've made sure that it gets the lion's share of the real estate.

Real estate refers to screen area. Like land in the physical world, there is only so much available.

Now that we know where things are going, let's add the form. We want the customer to be able to not only add a product, but specify a quantity. (Some sites make you wait until you get to the order page to do this, but in my experience this gives users a bit of uneasiness. Use your judgment.) We also want to make sure that they can check out without having to order anything else. We're adding this functionality in Listing 7.17.

Listing 7.17—Adding the shopping cart

```
...
20:    <TABLE WIDTH="100%">
21:    <TR><TD WIDTH="75%">
22:
23:        <CENTER>
24:        <H2><%= p_name %></H2>
25:        <%= p_desc %>
26:        <P>
27:        <IMG SRC="/images/products/<%= p_image %>">
28:        <P>
29:        Price: $<%= formatNumber(p_price, 2) %>
30:        <P>
31:
32:        <FORM ACTION="baz_add_action.asp" METHOD="post">
33:        <TABLE border=1>
34:        <TR><TD ALIGN="center">
35:            <FONT SIZE=-1>
36:            <INPUT TYPE="hidden" NAME="p_prod_id"
37:                VALUE="<%=p_prod_id%>">
38:            Add
39:            <INPUT TYPE="text" SIZE="3" NAME="p_quant"
40:                VALUE="1">
41:            to my order
42:        <BR>
43:        <INPUT TYPE="submit" VALUE="Add to Cart">
44:        <P>
45:        <A HREF="baz_order_review.asp">
46:        Review My Order and/or Check Out</A>
47:        </FONT>
48:    </TD></TR>
49:    </TABLE>
50:    </FORM>
51:
52:        </CENTER>
53:
54:    </TD><TD>
55:
56:        <!--#include file="baz_search.inc"-->
57:
58:    </TD></TR>
59:    </TABLE>
60:
```

We want to call attention to the ability to add the product to the cart, but we don't want to be obnoxious about it, so we've put the form into a single-celled table and given it a border of 1 on line 33. We also shrank the size of the text (see Figure 7.6) on line 35. Ultimately, these are all decisions for our designer, of course.

Figure 7.6

Our completed product page.

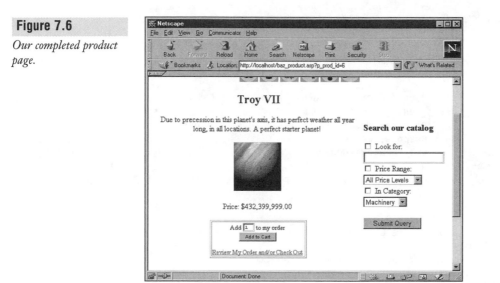

The form itself is pretty straightforward. All we need to pass are the product ID and the quantity. We'll take care of the order number in the form's action.

Copy `template.asp` to `baz_add_action.asp` in the auction directory. We'll start by checking to see if there's an existing order (see Listing 7.18).

Listing 7.18—Recording the addition of a product to an order

```
0: <%@ LANGUAGE="VBSCRIPT" %>
1: <!--#include file="adovbs.inc"-->
2: <!--#include virtual="/pagetop.txt"-->
3: <%
4:      '-------------------------------------------------
5:      Sub sub_CreateNewOrder
6:
7:          Response.Write "We will create a new order here."
8:          Response.Write "<P>"
9:          Response.Write "Product ID = " & p_prod_id
10:         Response.Write "<BR>"
11:         Response.Write "Quantity = " & p_quant
12:
13:     End Sub
14:     '-------------------------------------------------
15:%>
16:<%
17:     'Main Program actually starts here
18:     p_prod_id = Request.form("p_prod_id")
19:     p_quant = Request.form("p_quant")
```

continues

Listing 7.18—continued

```
20:
21:    set outpostDB = Server.CreateObject("ADODB.Connection")
22:    outpostDB.Open "outpost"
23:
24:    p_order_id = Session("order_id")
25:    if p_order_id = "" then
26:        Response.Write "There is no current order."
27:        Response.Write "<P>"
28:        sub_CreateNewOrder
29:    else
30:        Response.Write "The Current Order Number Is: "& p_order_id
31:    end if
32:
33:    outpostDB.Close
34:    set outpostDB = Nothing
35:%>
36:<!--#include virtual="/pagebottom.txt"-->
37:</BODY>
38:</HTML>
```

Even though we have new information on line 5, ASP doesn't actually begin processing (aside from our Server Side Includes) until line 16. This is because lines 5 through 13 are a subroutine, designated by the keyword Sub. Even though they're at the top of the page, they won't be executed until the main program explicitly calls them.

After our main program starts out as usual by retrieving our form values, it checks for a session value. Session values are exactly what the name implies. They are values that are available to this customer for the duration of his or her session, even though that session may consist of lots of individual pages.

EXCURSION

Sessions versus Cookies

Because they persist between a user's page requests, session values are similar to cookies. In fact, the Web server uses cookies to help keep track of them. Unlike cookies, however, we can set our sessions to time out after a specific period of inactivity, as opposed to waiting for users to close their browser. (This value is set in the Web server itself, or using the Session.Timeout property.)

We actually dealt with session values earlier when we were setting up the email component. In that case, arrays were created when the new session began and were available whenever we were ready for them. In this case, on lines 25 and 25, we are checking to see whether there's an existing value for order_id, and if there isn't, we are going to want to create one.

We're going to create our `order_id` on line 28 using the subroutine `sub_CreateNewOrder`. It's not necessary to start the name with `sub_`, but I use it as a naming convention for clarity. When we call `sub_CreateNewOrder`, ASP goes back up to the start of the subroutine on line 5 and executes everything until it gets to `end Sub`. We can have as many subroutines as we want, and they're a good idea for a more complicated application than this one, where modularity becomes extremely important.

Modular code is designed so that one piece does not depend on how another is implemented, just on what it returns. That way if the implementation changes, the dependent code doesn't suffer. Modular code is also much easier to maintain.

In this case, we've just had the subroutine print out the form values on lines 7 through 11, so we're killing two birds with one stone. We're testing the subroutine, and we're testing to make sure that the values are coming through.

A subroutine can be a world unto itself. Consider Listing 7.19.

Listing 7.19—Global Scope

```
0: <%@ LANGUAGE="VBSCRIPT" %>
1: <!--#include file="adovbs.inc"-->
2: <!--#include virtual="/pagetop.txt"-->
3: <%
4:     '------------------------------------------------------
5:     Sub sub_CreateNewOrder
6:
7:         myValue = 1
8:         Response.Write "myValue = " & myvalue
9:         Response.Write "<P>"
10:
11:     End Sub
12:     '------------------------------------------------------
13:%>
14:<%
15:     'Main Program actually starts here
16:     p_prod_id = Request.form("p_prod_id")
17:     p_quant = Request.form("p_quant")
18:
19:     set outpostDB = Server.CreateObject("ADODB.Connection")
20:     outpostDB.Open "outpost"
21:
22:     p_order_id = Session("order_id")
23:     if p_order_id = "" then
24:
25:         Response.Write "There is no current order."
26:         Response.Write "<P>"
```

continues

Listing 7.19—continued

```
27:
28:        myvalue = 2
29:        sub_CreateNewOrder
30:        Response.Write "myValue = " & myvalue
31:    else
32:        Response.Write "The Current Order Number Is: " _
33:            & p_order_id
34:    end if
35:
36:    outpostDB.Close
37:    set outpostDB = Nothing
38:%>
39:<!--#include virtual="/pagebottom.txt"-->
40:</BODY>
41:</HTML>
```

What value would you expect to see when it's printed to the screen? Initially, on line 28, we're setting the value of myValue to 2. Then we call the subroutine, which sets the value to 1, and prints it out. Then, when we return from the subroutine, we print it out again. In this case, it's 1, because we've changed the value within the subroutine (see Figure 7.7). This is an example of a global variable. Changes made to the variable anywhere in the program will affect the data. With a slight change, however, we can make two copies of myValue, one global variable outside the subroutine, and one inside it (see Figure 7.8). This is called a local variable, because it's local to the subroutine.

In Listing 7.20 we are going to Dim, or dimension, the variable. What this means is that instead of letting VBScript create the variable as it's needed, we are specifically telling it to create a place in memory for this data.

> **Tip**
>
> In some programming languages, you must always declare a variable before you can use it. One advantage to this is that typos in variable names are caught more quickly, as the misspelled variable has not been declared. You can mimic this behavior in VBScript by starting your programs with the command
>
> ```
> Option Explicit
> ```
> In this case, you must Dim every variable before you can use it.

Figure 7.7

myValue as a global variable.

Figure 7.8

myValue as a local variable.

Listing 7.20—Local Scope

```
0: <%@ LANGUAGE="VBSCRIPT" %>
1: <!--#include file="adovbs.inc"-->
2: <!--#include virtual="/pagetop.txt"-->
3: <%
4:      '-------------------------------------------------
5:      Sub sub_CreateNewOrder
6:          Dim myValue
7:          myValue = 1
8:          Response.Write "myValue = " & myvalue
9:          Response.Write "<P>"
10:
11:     End Sub
12:     '-------------------------------------------------
13:%>
14:<%
```

continues

Listing 7.20—continued

```
15:    'Main Program actually starts here
16:    p_prod_id = Request.form("p_prod_id")
17:    p_quant = Request.form("p_quant")
18:
19:    set outpostDB = Server.CreateObject("ADODB.Connection")
20:    outpostDB.Open "outpost"
21:
22:    p_order_id = Session("order_id")
23:    if p_order_id = "" then
24:
25:        Response.Write "There is no current order."
26:        Response.Write "<P>"
27:
28:        myvalue = 2
29:        sub_CreateNewOrder
30:        Response.Write "myValue = " & myvalue
31:    else
32:        Response.Write "The Current Order Number Is: " _
33:            & p_order_id
34:    end if
35:
36:    outpostDB.Close
37:    set outpostDB = Nothing
38:%>
39:<!--#include virtual="/pagebottom.txt"-->
40:</BODY>
41:</HTML>
```

We added only a single line, and yet if you reload the page, you'll get a different answer. When we declared the variable within the subroutine, we created a local variable. It exists only in that subroutine and is totally unaffected by anything that happens on the outside. The scope of the variable is the subroutine. Anything outside it is outside the variable's scope. But what about the original myValue? It's a global variable, available from anywhere—unless there's a local variable with the same name.

Scope is a very important concept. It defines when and where objects, values, and variables are defined. Our session variables have a scope of session. After they are defined, they exist throughout the whole of the session, and nowhere outside of it.

That's great, but what if we want a variable that's accessible from any session? You may see this on a site that tells you how many people are logged on. That information is available throughout all sessions in the application. In other words, the application is its scope.

We can declare variables with a scope of application by using application variables. (Hence the name.) Application variables are just like session variables. After we declare them, we can use them from anywhere, but because of their scope, we can use them from any session.

That's how we can handle the order ID issue. We're going to store the next available `order_id` in an application variable. Then when we need it we can grab it and increment it. That way the next customer will get the next number.

In the `baz_add_action.asp` file, add the code shown in Listing 7.21 to the subroutine.

Listing 7.21—Using Application Variables

```
0: <%@ LANGUAGE="VBSCRIPT" %>
1: <!--#include file="adovbs.inc"-->
2: <!--#include virtual="/pagetop.txt"-->
3: <%
4:     '------------------------------------------------
5:     Sub sub_CreateNewOrder
6:         Application.lock
7:         if Application("order_id") = "" then
8:             Application("order_id") = 1
9:         end if
10:
11:         p_order_id = Application("order_id")
12:         Session("order_id") = p_order_id
13:         outpostDB.Execute("insert into baz_orders "_
14:           & " (order_id, status) values " _
15:           & " ("&p_order_id&", 'OPEN')")
16:
17:         Application("order_id") = Application("order_id") + 1
18:         Application.Unlock
19:     End Sub
20:     '------------------------------------------------
21:%>
22:<%
23:     'Main Program actually starts here
24:     p_prod_id = Request.form("p_prod_id")
25:     p_quant = Request.form("p_quant")
26:
27:     set outpostDB = Server.CreateObject("ADODB.Connection")
28:     outpostDB.Open "outpost"
29:
30:     p_order_id = Session("order_id")
31:     if p_order_id = "" then
32:
33:         Response.Write "There is no current order."
34:         Response.Write "<P>"
35:
36:         sub_CreateNewOrder
37:     else
```

continues

Listing 7.21—continued

```
38:        Response.Write "The Current Order Number Is: " _
39:            & p_order_id
40:    end if
41:
42:    outpostDB.Close
43:    set outpostDB = Nothing
44:%>
45:<!--#include virtual="/pagebottom.txt"-->
46:</BODY>
47:</HTML>
```

We can access application variables the same way we accessed session variables, so the first thing that we're doing—after locking the application object on line 6—is checking to make sure that Application("order_id") exists, and if it doesn't, we're creating it on line 8.

Next we're setting both of our variables—the local and the session copies—and creating a new record in the baz_orders table on lines 13 through 15. Finally, we're incrementing the application variable on line 17 and unlocking the application object so the next person can use it on line 18. We don't have to lock the application object to use application variables, but the situation is similar to the one we encountered when we were recording bids. We don't want two people contributing to the same order!

This works, but it has one (huge) flaw. If application("order_id") doesn't exist, we're setting it to 1. That's fine this time, but what about next time we run this after, say, rebooting the server? Ideally, the application object would reinitialize this value when it starts up.

Fortunately, there is a special subroutine, Application_OnStart, which runs every time the application starts up. We define it in the global.asa file. What we want to do is find out what the next available order ID is. Open global.asa and add the subroutine shown in Listing 7.22.

In a real-life environment, it's crucial to test your application level subroutine code *before* you put it into the global.asa file, so you don't find yourself with an application that won't run at all.

Listing 7.22— Initializing Application("order_id")

```
0:  <OBJECT RUNAT=Server SCOPE=Session ID=MyInfo PROGID="MSWC.MyInfo">
1:  </OBJECT>
2:
3:  <SCRIPT LANGUAGE=VBScript RUNAT=Server>
4:
5:  Sub Application_OnStart
6:
7:      set outpostDB = Server.CreateObject("ADODB.Connection")
8:      outpostDB.Open "outpost"
9:
10:     set maxOrderSet = outpostDB.Execute("select order_id from"_
11:         " baz_orders " & "order by order_id desc")
12:     if maxOrderSet.EOF then
13:         Application("order_id") = 1
14:     else
15:         Application("order_id") = maxOrderSet("order_id") + 1
16:     end if
17:     maxOrderSet.Close
18:     set maxOrderSet = Nothing
19:
20:     outpostDB.Close
21:     set outpostDB = Nothing
22:
23:End Sub
24:
25:Sub Session_OnStart
26:    Set Session("arrTo")=Server.CreateObject("Scripting.Dictionary")
27:    Set Session("arrCC")=Server.CreateObject("Scripting.Dictionary")
28:    Set Session("arrBCC")=Server.CreateObject("Scripting.Dictionary")
29:    Set Session("arrFiles")=Server.CreateObject("Scripting.Dictionary")
30:    Session("Count")=0 'to generate unique keys for the dictionaries
31:end sub
32:
33:Sub Session_OnEnd
34:
35:end sub
36:
37:</SCRIPT>
```

Since nothing else is run until Application_OnStart is finished, we don't need to lock the application before getting the highest order ID in the baz_orders table on lines 10 and 11. We set the application variable on line 13 of 15, then close and destroy the objects we've created on lines 17 through 21. Now, when we start the application, we'll have the proper number.

> As you might imagine, there's also an `Application_OnEnd` routine that you can use to clean things up before you close the application. Keep in mind, however, that while this subroutine runs automatically when you shut down the Web server, it does not run at all if the Web server or the machine crashes.

Counters

Some versions of ASP, including the version of ASP 3.0 that comes with Windows 2000 Professional, include a Counters component that can make this job a lot easier. (The documentation for all versions says it's included, but for some servers, such as Personal Web Server 4.0 for Windows 95, it's not.) To find out if you have it, do a search for `counters.dll`.

The counters component allows you to specify any number of individual counters to keep track of, and the component will handle initializing, incrementing, and saving the values. To start using it, add the following lines to your `global.asa` file:

```
<OBJECT RUNAT=Server SCOPE=Application ID=Counter PROGID="MSWC.Counters">
</OBJECT>
```

This creates an object called Counter that you can use throughout the application. For instance, `baz_add_action.asp` can be changed to use the counters using the code in Listing 7.22b:

Listing 7.22b—Using Counters

```
0: <%@ LANGUAGE="VBSCRIPT" %>
1: <!--#include file="adovbs.inc"-->
2: <!--#include virtual="/pagetop.txt"-->
3: <%
4:      '-------------------------------------------------
5:      Sub sub_CreateNewOrder
6:          Application.lock
7:          Session("order_id") = Counter.get("order_id")
8:          Counter.increment("order_id")
9:          Application.Unlock
10:     End Sub
11:     '-------------------------------------------------
12:%>
13:<%
14:     'Main Program actually starts here
…
```

On line 7, we get the current value of the `order_id` counter, and on line 8 we increment that counter so it's ready for the next order. We still lock and unlock the `application` object to prevent conflicts between orders, but if all orders were created in this way, we don't have to check the `baz_orders` table to make sure there aren't any duplicates.

Notice also that because this was built modularly, the rest of the application is totally unaffected by this change. It also eliminates the need to initialize the application variable in `Application_OnStart`.

You can also set the `order_id` counter to a specific value using

```
Counter.set("order_id", 10)
```

Now that we've taken care of that, let's go back to `baz_add_action.asp`. If there is no existing order for the session we're creating one, but we still haven't added our item to it! Continuing our modularity theme, we'll do it in another subroutine (see Listing 7.23).

Listing 7.23—Adding products to the order

```
 0: <%@ LANGUAGE="VBSCRIPT" %>
 1: <!--#include file="adovbs.inc"-->
 2: <!--#include virtual="/pagetop.txt"-->
 3: <%
 4:     '--------------------------------------------------
 5:     Sub sub_CreateNewOrder
 6:         Application.lock
 7:         Session("order_id") = Counter.get("order_id")
 8:         Counter.increment("order_id")
 9:         Application.Unlock
10:     End Sub
11:
12:     Sub sub_AddToOrder(the_order_id, the_prod_id, the_quant)
13:
14:         sqlText = "insert into baz_order_items " _
15:             & "(order_id, prod_id, quantity) " _
16:             & "values (" _
17:             & the_order_id&", "&the_prod_id&", "&the_quant&")"
18:         outpostDB.Execute(sqlText)
19:
20:     End Sub
21:
22:     '_ _ _ _ _ _ _ _ _ _ _ _ _ _ _ _ _ _ _ _ _ _ _ _ _
23:%>
24:<%
25:     'Main Program actually starts here
26:     p_prod_id = Request.form("p_prod_id")
27:     p_quant = Request.form("p_quant")
28:
29:     set outpostDB = Server.CreateObject("ADODB.Connection")
30:     outpostDB.Open "outpost"
31:
32:     p_order_id = Session("order_id")
33:     if p_order_id = "" then
```

continues

Listing 7.23—continued

```
34:            sub_CreateNewOrder
35:        end if
36:
37:        sub_AddToOrder p_order_id, p_prod_id, p_quant
38:%>
39:
40:<TABLE<TABLE WIDTH="100%">
41:<TR><TD ALIGN="center">
42:        The item has been added to your order.
43:        <P>
44:        <A HREF="baz_product.asp?p_prod_id=<%=p_prod_id%>">Back</A>
45:        <P>
46:        <A HREF="baz_order_review.asp">Review your order and/or check out</A>
47:        <P>
48:    </TD><TD>
49:        <!--#include file="baz_search.inc"-->
50:        <P>
51:</TD></TR>
52:</TABLE>
53:
54:<%
55:    outpostDB.Close
56:    set outpostDB = Nothing
57:%>
58:<!--#include virtual="/pagebottom.txt"-->
59:</BODY>
60:</HTML>
```

The first thing that we did was clean up the code that we're not using anymore. Because we're handling the actual ordering separately, on lines 33 through 35 all we need to do is see whether we need a new order created and instruct the subroutine to create one if necessary. From there, it doesn't matter where the order ID came from, we're just going to use it.

On line 37, we're calling the subroutine sub_AddToOrder, and we're giving it three parameters: the order ID, the product ID, and the quantity. Truth be told, because those are all global variables, we didn't have to send them in as parameters, but I wanted to show you how it works.

When ASP gets to line 37, it jumps up to line 12, and the values in p_order_id, p_prod_id, and p_quant are copied to the_order_id, the_prod_id, and the_quant, respectively. These are local variables. Their scope is the subroutine.

From here we actually have a choice. We could insert the item into the baz_orders_table using an SQL statement, or we could create a recordset and add it that way. I chose to use an SQL statement on lines 14 though 18 because there was no benefit to creating a potentially large recordset when we didn't need any of the information in it. So from a resources standpoint, this was the better choice.

When the subroutine is finished, we come back down to line 39, where we display the page the user will see when all of our processing is finished. We are providing our customers with three options. They can go back to the product page they were just on; they can go on to review their order, or they can search for another product. Notice that all we had to do to include the search form was include the `baz_search.inc` file on line 49 (see Figure 7.9).

Figure 7.9

After we've added the product to the order, we need to give the customer somewhere to go.

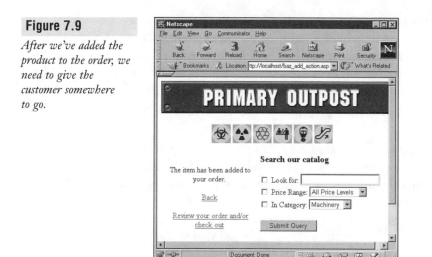

Security in an Insecure World (Wide Web)

Now that we can add items to our order, it's time to look at how to retrieve the order to be confirmed and (of course) paid for. This requires a special touch.

It is the nature of the Internet that messages pass through many different servers before they get to their destination. Unfortunately, any one of those places, or even in between, is a chance for thieves to steal data. That may not sound like a big deal until you realize that data could easily be your credit card number.

To combat this, we can use Secure Sockets Layer, or SSL, technology. This technology encrypts the information that passes between you and the server, so that only the two of you can read it. What's more, SSL guarantees that the site that's receiving your information really is who it says it is and some unscrupulous individuals are not claiming to be your favorite book store.

Entire books have been devoted to security, but we will cover the basics here in this section.

7

Remember when you were a kid and you made up secret codes? You were, in a very simple way, doing what your Web browser is doing when it goes to an e-commerce site. You were making up a message that could be read only by someone who had the key. You were encrypting it.

This was a symmetric key system. If you wanted to trade messages with your friend, both of you had the same key, which could both encrypt and decrypt the messages.

SSL is based on an asymmetric key system. There are two keys, and a message encrypted by one can only be decrypted by the other, and vice versa. The system is called public key-private key encryption because one key is private, kept only by the owner and the other is published, like a phone number. If I look up my friend Bill's number in the phone book and call it, I expect to get Bill on the phone. Likewise, if he calls me and I see his number on my Caller ID, I expect it to be him on the other end.

Let's say Bill and I want to discuss something private in email. I can get his public key, because it's published. If I encrypt my message with that public key, it can only be decrypted with the private key. That means that only Bill can read it. Similarly, if I get encrypted mail and I can decrypt it with the public key, I know it was encrypted with the private key, so I know it came from Bill. I could also send Bill a new shared key that only he could decrypt. We could then use that shared key for any further messages.

It works the same for an e-commerce site. My browser gets the public key for the site (through a series of events that are not important right now) and sends a shared key to the server to use on subsequent requests. It then encrypts my credit card information with that shared, or session key. Now, no matter where that message goes on its way to the site, only the Web server can read it.

To create SSL connections with our Web server, we need to have a public and private key and we need to get a digital ID from a certifying authority (CA), such as Verisign (`http://www.verisign.com`). The certifying authority takes your information and issues a digital ID. This ID, which is electronically signed by the CA, vouches for your authenticity as well as providing your public key so the browser can make a secure connection. There are products, such as Microsoft Certificate Services 2.0, which will enable you to create your own certificates, but those certificates won't be trusted by the user. For an external commercial site, you will need to obtain a digital ID from a third-party CA. This process can take days or weeks, depending on the current workload, and can cost several hundred dollars or more depending on the type of ID.

The process of requesting and installing a digital ID, or SSL certificate, varies from product to product. To request an install certificate for IIS 5.0, first go to the Internet Services Manager. Right click on the site you wish to secure and choose

Properties. Choose the Directory Security tab and click Server Certificate. This brings up a wizard that will step you through the process of creating a certificate request which you will then send to the CA according to their instructions. When the certificate arrives, the same wizard will walk you through the process of installing it.

It's easy to tell whether a connection is secure; you can see it in the URL. For instance, if we had installed a digital ID, we could tell the browser to establish a secure connection using

```
https://localhost/baz_order_review.asp
```

That's not a typo. The URL really does start with https, short for Secure HyperText Transmission Protocol.

Reviewing the Order

In reviewing the order, users should be able to change quantities or even delete products altogether before they give us their credit card information. This is pretty straightforward. Copy template.asp to baz_order_review.asp in the bazaar directory (see Listing 7.24).

Listing 7.24—Reviewing the customer's order

```
0: <%@ LANGUAGE="VBSCRIPT" %>
1: <!--#include file="adovbs.inc"-->
2: <!--#include virtual="/pagetop.txt"-->
3: <%
4:     set outpostDB = Server.CreateObject("ADODB.Connection")
5:     outpostDB.Open "outpost"
6:
7:     if Session("order_id") = "" then
8:         Response.Write "There is no current order. If you had "
9:         Response.Write "previously added items to your order, "
10:        Response.Write "your session may have timed out."
11:        Response.Write "<P>"
12:%>
13:        <!--#include file="baz_search.inc"-->
14:<%    else
15:        p_order_id = Session("order_id")
16:
17:        sqlText = "select baz_products.prod_id, prod_name, " _
18:            & "prod_price, quantity from baz_products, " _
19:            & "baz_order_items where " _
20:            & "baz_products.prod_id = baz_order_items.prod_id "_
21:            & "and baz_order_items.Order_id = " & p_order_id
22:
23:        set reviewSet = outpostDB.Execute(sqlText)
```

continues

Listing 7.24—continued

```
24:        while not reviewSet.EOF
25:            Response.Write reviewSet("prod_name")
26:            Response.Write "<BR>"
27:            reviewSet.MoveNext
28:        wend
29:        reviewSet.Close
30:        set reviewSet = Nothing
31:
32:    end if
33:    outpostDB.Close
34:    set outpostDB = Nothing
35:
36:%>
37:<!--#include virtual="/pagebottom.txt"-->
38:</BODY>
39:</HTML>
```

On line 7 we're checking to see whether the customer even *has* an order! After all, there's a link to this form on the product page. If there is no order, we're simply telling the customer why and giving them a way to find something to buy.

If there is an order, we're extracting the order ID and creating a recordset with a join on the baz_products and baz_order_items. It's true that we could have used the two-recordset method we used earlier, but there's no reason to select every product in the database when only a few of them will matter. We have two parts to the Where clause, the join condition and a condition that limits the returned rows to just our order number.

> **Note**
>
> In actuality, we could also have copied the relevant information to the baz_order_items table when we added it to the order and not be worried about it now at all.

On lines 24 through 28 we're displaying the name of each product in the order, and then we're closing things up.

This is great, but we need to find a way for the customer to confirm his or her order, and we need it to look neat. We need to display quantities and final prices taking into account those quantities. We will do this in Listing 7.25.

Listing 7.25—Order confirmation information

```
0: <%@ LANGUAGE="VBSCRIPT" %>
1: <!--#include file="adovbs.inc"-->
2: <!--#include virtual="/pagetop.txt"-->
```

```
 3: <%
 4:    set outpostDB = Server.CreateObject("ADODB.Connection")
 5:    outpostDB.Open "outpost"
 6:
 7:    if Session("order_id") = "" then
 8:        Response.Write "There is no current order. If you had "
 9:        Response.Write "previously added items to your order, "
10:        Response.Write "your session may have timed out."
11:        Response.Write "<P>"
12:%>
13:        <!--#include file="baz_search.inc"-->
14:<% else
15:        p_order_id = Session("order_id")
16:
17:        sqlText = "select baz_products.prod_id, prod_name, " _
18:            & "prod_price, quantity from baz_products, " _
19:            & "baz_order_items where " _
20:            & "baz_products.prod_id = baz_order_items.prod_id "_
21:            & "and baz_order_items.Order_id = " & p_order_id
22:%>
23:        <H2>Review Your Order</H2>
24:        Please review your order to be certain it is correct.
25:        To remove an item, set the quantity to zero.
26:        <FORM ACTION="baz_order_review_action.asp" METHOD="post">
27:        <TABLE<TABLE WIDTH="100%">
28:        <TR>
29:            <TH ALIGN="left">Quantity</TH>
30:            <TH ALIGN="left">Product Name</TH>
31:            <TH ALIGN="left">Unit Price</TH>
32:            <TH ALIGN="left">Extended Price</TH>
33:    </TR>
34:<%  set reviewSet = outpostDB.Execute(sqlText)
35:    while not reviewSet.EOF
36:        p_prod_id = reviewSet("prod_id")
37:        p_prod_name = reviewSet("prod_name")
38:        p_prod_price = reviewSet("prod_price")
39:        p_quant = reviewSet("quantity")
40:%>
41:        <TR>
42:            <TD>
43:                <INPUT NAME="quant<%=p_prod_id%>" TYPE="text"
44:                    SIZE=3 VALUE="<%=p_quant%>">
45:            </TD><TD>
46:                <%=p_prod_name%>
47:            </TD><TD ALIGN="right">
48:                $<%= formatNumber(p_prod_price, 2) %>
49:            </TD><TD ALIGN="right">
50:                $<%= formatNumber((p_quant * p_prod_price), 2) %>
```

continues

Listing 7.25—continued

```
51:                </TD>
52:             </TR>
53: <%        reviewSet.MoveNext
54:      wend
55:      reviewSet.Close
56:      set reviewSet = Nothing
57: %>    </TABLE>
58:
59:         <INPUT TYPE="submit" NAME="p_button" VALUE="Update Totals">
60:         <INPUT TYPE="submit" NAME="p_button" VALUE="Complete Order">
61:         </FORM>
62:<% end if
63:
64:      outpostDB.Close
65:      set outpostDB = Nothing
66:%>
67:<!--#include virtual="/pagebottom.txt"-->
68:</BODY>
69:</HTML>
```

Most of what we did here was formatting. On lines 27 through 57 we're creating a table, giving it headers, and then displaying the product information in the table cells. On some sites, when you change quantities, the totals will automatically update, but that's client-side scripting, and that's not what we're here for, so instead we'll settle for asking the user to submit the form to recalculate.

There is one very important nonformatting issue we tackled here, though: how to create a form, on-the-fly to give us the fields we want and can identify. We're accomplishing this by looping through the product IDs for the order and then appending them to the name of each quantity text field on line 43. That way, when we get the form back, we can just pull in the fields explicitly by name because we know what they should be called.

Another thing that we're missing here is a grand total. Let's go ahead and add it in (see Listing 7.26).

Listing 7.26—Adding the totals

```
...
38:      p_prod_price = reviewSet("prod_price")
39:      p_quant = reviewSet("quantity")
40:      p_total = p_total + (p_quant * p_prod_price)
41: %>
42:      <TR>
43:         <TD>
44:         <INPUT NAME="quant<%=p_prod_id%>" TYPE="text"
45:             SIZE=3 VALUE="<%=p_quant%>">
```

```
46:            </TD><TD>
47:…
48:    reviewSet.Close
49:    set reviewSet = Nothing
50:%>
51:    <TR>
52:        <TD>Total:</TD>
53:        <TD COLSPAN="3" ALIGN="right">
54:            $<%= formatNumber(p_total,2) %>
55:        </TD>
56:    </TR>
57:
58:    </TABLE>
59:    <INPUT TYPE="submit" NAME="p_button" VALUE="Update Totals">
60:    <INPUT TYPE="submit" NAME="p_button" VALUE="Complete Order">
61:    </FORM>
…
```

This is a useful tactic. We could have had the database give us a total, but because we're doing the calculations on-the-fly, we can keep a running total on line 40 as we go along.

So that's our completed order review page. Now we have to decide what happens when a customer submits the form. Copy template.asp to baz_order_review_action.asp (see Listing 7.27).

Listing 7.27—Making changes to the order

```
0: <%@ LANGUAGE="VBSCRIPT" %>
1: <!--#include file="adovbs.inc"-->
2: <!--#include virtual="/pagetop.txt"-->
3: <%
4:
5: set outpostDB = Server.CreateObject("ADODB.Connection")
6:     outpostDB.Open "outpost"
7:
8:
9:     if Session("order_id") = "" then
10:         Response.Write "There is no current order. If you had "
11:         Response.Write "previously added items to your order, "
12:         Response.Write "your session may have timed out."
13:         Response.Write "<P>"
14:%>
15:         <!--#include file="baz_search.inc"-->
16:<% else
17:
18:         p_order_id = Session("order_id")
19:
20:         set prodSet = Server.CreateObject("ADODB.RecordSet")
21:         prodSet.Open "select * from baz_order_items " _
```

continues

Listing 7.27—continued

```
22:                  & "where order_id="& p_order_id, _
23:                  outpostDB, adOpenDynamic, adLockPessimistic, adCmdText
24:          while not prodSet.EOF
25:
26:              p_element = "quant" & prodSet("prod_id")
27:              p_quant = Request.form(p_element)
28:
29:              if p_quant <> "" and isNumeric(p_quant) then
30:                  if p_quant = 0 then
31:                      prodSet.Delete
32:                  else
33:                      prodSet("quantity") = p_quant
34:                  end if
35:              end if
36:              prodSet.Update
37:              prodSet.MoveNext
38:          wend
39:          prodSet.Close
40:          set prodSet = Nothing
41: end if
42:
43: outpostDB.Close
44: set outpostDB = Nothing
45:%>
46:<!--#include virtual="/pagebottom.txt"-->
47:</BODY>
48:</HTML>
```

On lines 9 through 15 we're checking for an existing order, and actually this was just copied from baz_order_review.asp. The meat really starts on line 20, as we create a recordset of the order items. Because we will be deleting records from this recordset if the customer has set the quantity to zero, we need a dynamic cursor. We'll also set the recordset to use pessimistic locking because we're making such radical changes.

When we set up the quantity text boxes, we set them up with names that consisted of quant and the product ID. Now on lines 24 through 38 we will loop through the product ID's in the baz_order_items table and re-create those names, checking each item as we go.

There's always the possibility that the user has added more items to their order in another window, in which case Request.form(p_element) is going to come back empty, so we need to check for that on line 29. There's also the possibility that what the customer entered wasn't a number, so we need to check for that too using the built-in function isNumeric().

If the entry passes both of those tests, there's still one more hurdle. If the customer set the quantity to zero, we want to delete the record on line 31, otherwise we want to update the quantity of the items ordered on line 33. Finally, we update the database on line 36 and move on to the next record.

Now that we've updated the information, so we need to give some feedback to the customer besides a blank page. If the customer just wanted to update the totals, we need to send them back to the review page. If they wanted to check out, we need to provide them a final listing and gather their credit card information. We'll make that distinction in Listing 7.28.

Listing 7.28—baz_order_review_action.asp: Using Server.Transfer

```
0:  <%@ LANGUAGE="VBSCRIPT" %>
1:  <!--#include file="adovbs.inc"-->
2:  <%
3:      set outpostDB = Server.CreateObject("ADODB.Connection")
4:      outpostDB.Open "outpost"
5:
6:      if Session("order_id") = "" then
7:  %>
8:          <!--#include virtual="/pagetop.txt"-->
9:  <%
10:         Response.Write "There is no current order. If you had "
11:         Response.Write "previously added items to your order, "
12:         Response.Write "your session may have timed out."
13:         Response.Write "<P>"
14:%>
15:         <!--#include file="baz_search.inc"-->
16:         <!--#include virtual="/pagebottom.txt"-->
17:         </BODY>
18:         </HTML>
19:<%     else
20:
21:         p_order_id = Session("order_id")
22:
23:         set prodSet = Server.CreateObject("ADODB.RecordSet")
24:         prodSet.Open "select * from baz_order_items " _
25:             & "where order_id="& p_order_id, _
26:             outpostDB, adOpenDynamic, adLockPessimistic, adCmdText
27:         while not prodSet.EOF
28:
29:             p_element = "quant" & prodSet("prod_id")
30:             p_quant = Request.form(p_element)
31:
32:             if p_quant <> "" and isNumeric(p_quant) then
33:                 if p_quant = 0 then
34:                     prodSet.Delete
```

continues

Listing 7.28—continued

```
35:                      else
36:                          prodSet("quantity") = p_quant
37:                      end if
38:              end if
39:              prodSet.Update
40:              prodSet.MoveNext
41:          wend
42:
43:          if Request.form("p_button") = "Update Totals" then
44:
45:              prodSet.Close
46:              set prodSet = Nothing
47:
48:              outpostDB.Close
49:              set outpostDB = Nothing
50:
51:              Server.Transfer " /bazaar/baz_order_review.asp"
52:          else
53:%>
54:              <!--#include virtual="/pagetop.txt"-->
55:              Credit Card Form goes here
56:              <!--#include virtual="/pagebottom.txt"-->
57:              </BODY>
58:              </HTML>
59:<%
60:              prodSet.Close
61:              set prodSet = Nothing
62:
63:          end if
64:
65:   end if
66:
67:   outpostDB.Close
68:   set outpostDB = Nothing
69:%>
```

Because we're going to redirect to the review page, we've had to move some things around. Remember, we can't send any text to the browser before the redirect, so we've now made each section it's own page, with it's own copies of the includes for the top and bottom of the page. (There's an easier way to do this, which we'll talk about in the next chapter.)

On line 43 we're checking to see which button the users clicked to get to this point. If it was the Update totals button, we know we want to send them back to the review page, but we need to clean things up before we go on line 51.

After we've closed and destroyed the recordset and the database connection, we're ready to redirect to the new page. Instead of using `Response.Redirect`, which we've used before, we're using `Server.Transfer`.

The difference between them is in how the request is processed. With `Response.Redirect`, the browser receives a command to go to a new URL. It then calls up the URL and proceeds normally. The location line displays the new address, and all is well. The only drawbacks of this method are that the browser must be able to redirect (which is sometimes a problem for users behind firewalls) and there is basically an extra request, which means wasted time and bandwidth.

By using `Server.Redirect` instead, the server retrieves the new page and feeds it to the browser, which thinks it's still at the old URL. Unfortunately, this too can lead to problems if the user bookmarks the page, so basically it's a tradeoff.

> **Note**
>
> The `Server.Transfer` feature is new in ASP 3.0 and is not supported in older versions of IIS or PWS. If you receive an error saying
>
> `Object doesn't support this property or method: 'server.Transfer'`
>
> you can just use `Response.Redirect` instead.

If the customer chose the Complete Order button, we are going to display the credit card page for them. The first thing that we need to do in Listing 7.29 is display the final order, as it will be charged and shipped.

Listing 7.29—baz_order_review_action.asp: Confirming the final order

```
...
43:     if Request.form("p_button") = "Update Totals" then
44:
45:         prodSet.Close
46:         set prodSet = Nothing
47:
48:         outpostDB.Close
49:         set outpostDB = Nothing
50:
51:         Server.Transfer " /bazaar/baz_order_review.asp"
52:     else
53: %>
54:         <!--#include virtual="/pagetop.txt"-->
55:         <H2>Your Order</H2>
56:         Is something incorrect? Feel free to
57:         <A HREF="baz_order_review.asp">change your order</A>.
58:         <P>
59:
60:         <FORM ACTION="baz_order_complete_action.asp"
61:             METHOD="post">
62:
63:         <INPUT TYPE="hidden" NAME="p_order_id"
```

continues

Listing 7.29—continued

```
64:                VALUE="<%=p_order_id%>">
65:
66:         <TABLE border=1>
67:         <TR>
68:             <TH>Quantity</TH>
69:             <TH>Prod. #</TH>
70:             <TH>Description</TH>
71:             <TH>Unit Price</TH>
72:             <TH>Ext. Price</TH>
73:         </TR>
74: <%
75:         set prodInfoSet = Server.CreateObject("ADODB.RecordSet")
76:         prodInfoSet.Open "baz_products", outpostDB,
77:             adOpenStatic, adLockOptimistic, adCmdTable
78:
79:         p_total = 0
80:
81:         prodSet.MoveFirst
82:         while not prodSet.EOF
83:             prodInfoSet.MoveFirst
84:             prodInfoSet.Find "prod_id = " & prodSet("prod_id")
85:             p_prod_id = prodSet("prod_id")
86:             p_prod_name = prodInfoSet("prod_name")
87:             p_price = formatNumber(prodInfoSet("prod_price"), 2)
88:             p_quant = prodSet("quantity")
89:             p_extprice = formatNumber((p_price * p_quant), 2)
90:             p_total = p_total + p_extprice
91: %>
92:             <TR>
93:                 <TD><%= p_quant %></TD>
94:                 <TD><%= p_prod_id %></TD>
95:                 <TD><%= p_prod_name %></TD>
96:                 <TD ALIGN="right">$<%= p_price %></TD>
97:                 <TD ALIGN="right">$<%= p_extprice %></TD>
98:             </TR>
99:             <INPUT TYPE="hidden" NAME="p_orderitem"
100:                VALUE="<%=p_prod_id%>,<%=p_quant%>">
101:<%
102:            prodSet.MoveNext
103:         wend
104:%>
105:         <TR>
106:             <TD COLSPAN = 4> Subtotal:</TD>
107:             <TD ALIGN=right>
108:                 $<%= formatNumber(p_total, 2) %>
109:             </TD>
100:         </TR>
111:         <TR>
112:             <TD COLSPAN = 4> Shipping (5%):</TD>
113:             <TD ALIGN=right>
```

```
114:                         $<%= formatNumber((p_total*.05), 2) %>
115:                         <INPUT TYPE="hidden" NAME="p_shipping"
116:                             VALUE="<%=p_total*.05%>">
117:                 </TD>
118:             </TR>
119:             <TR>
120:                 <TD COLSPAN = 4> Total:</TD>
121:                 <TD ALIGN=right>
122:                     $<%= formatNumber((p_total*1.05), 2) %>
123:                     <INPUT TYPE="hidden" NAME="p_total"
124:                         VALUE="<%=p_total%>">
125:                 </TD>
126:             </TR>
127:
128:         </TABLE>
129:
130:         </FORM>
131:
132:         <!--#include virtual="/pagebottom.txt"-->
133:         </BODY>
134:          </HTML>
135:<%
136:         prodSet.Close
137:         set prodSet = Nothing
138:
139:         prodInfoSet.Close
140:         set prodInfoSet = Nothing
141:
142:     end if
143:
144:   end if
145:
146:   outpostDB.Close
147:   set outpostDB = Nothing
148:%>
```

Other than security, the most important thing here is making sure that the order the customers confirm is the order that they are actually charged for and the order that they actually get. To that end, we're displaying their items one more time, and if they want to change anything they need to go back to the review page.

We've already created a recordset of the items the customer ordered, so now we're creating a recordset of all product information and pulling out the relevant product details as we need them. On line 52 we're putting in a hidden form value that records the product ID and the quantity. When the credit card information is submitted, these are the only products that are going to be recorded, even if users have added other products in another window.

Finally, we give them a subtotal, their shipping total, and their grand total, which will be charged to their credit card. You can figure shipping however you like, but for simplicity's sake we're making it five percent of the total.

Now we're ready to actually take their payment information (see Listing 7.30).

Listing 7.30—baz_order_review_action.asp: Collecting Credit Card Information

```
...
120:            <TR>
121:                <TD COLSPAN = 4> Total:</TD>
122:                <TD ALIGN=right>
123:                    $<%= formatNumber((p_total*1.05), 2) %>
124:                <INPUT TYPE="hidden" NAME="p_total"
125:                    VALUE="<%=p_total%>">
126:                </TD>
127:            </TR>
128:            </TABLE>
129:            <P>
130:
131:            <H3>Payment Information</H3>
132:            <TABLE>
133:            <TR>
134:                <TD>Name:</TD>
135:                <TD>
136:                <INPUT TYPE="text" NAME="p_first" SIZE="10">
137:                <INPUT TYPE="text" NAME="p_last" SIZE="10">
138:                </TD>
139:            </TR>
140:             <TR>
141:                <TD>Address:</TD>
142:                <TD>
143:                <INPUT TYPE="text" NAME="p_address1" SIZE=21>
144:                </TD>
145:            </TR>
146:             <TR>
147:                <TD>Address:</TD>
148:                <TD>
149:                <INPUT TYPE="text" NAME="p_address2" SIZE=21>
150:                </TD>
151:            </TR>
152:             <TR>
153:                <TD>City, State, Postal Code: </TD>
154:                <TD>
155:                <INPUT TYPE="text" NAME="p_city" SIZE=10>
156:                <INPUT TYPE="text" NAME="p_state" SIZE=5>
157:                <INPUT TYPE="text" NAME="p_postalcode" SIZE=5>
158:                </TD>
159:            </TR>
160:             <TR>
161:                <TD>Country: </TD>
162:                <TD>
163:                <INPUT TYPE="text" NAME="p_country" SIZE=21>
164:                </TD>
165:            </TR>
166:             <TR>
```

```
167:          <TD>Telephone: </TD>
168:          <TD>
169:          <INPUT TYPE="text" NAME="p_phone" SIZE=21>
160:          </TD>
171:      </TR>
172:      <TR>
173:          <TD COLSPAN=2>
174:          <hr>
175:          <INPUT TYPE="radio" NAME="p_cc_type" VALUE="MC">
176:          MasterCard
177:          <INPUT TYPE="radio" NAME="p_cc_type" VALUE="V">
178:          Visa
179:          <INPUT TYPE="radio" NAME="p_cc_type" VALUE="AMEX">
170:          American Express
181:          </TD>
182:      </TR>
183:       <TR>
184:          <TD>Card Number: </TD>
185:          <TD>
186:          <INPUT TYPE="text" NAME="p_cc_number" SIZE=21>
187:          </TD>
188:       </TR>
189:       <TR>
190:          <TD>Name On Card: </TD>
191:          <TD>
192:          <INPUT TYPE="text" NAME="p_cc_nameoncard" SIZE=21>
193:          </TD>
194:      </TR>
195:
196:      <TR>
197:          <TD COLSPAN=2 ALIGN="center">
198:          <INPUT TYPE="submit" VALUE="Submit Order">
199:          </TD>
200:      </TR>
201:
202:      </TABLE>
203:      </FORM>
204:
205:      </CENTER>
206:
...
```

This is just a straightforward form to collect the customer's credit card information. The actual information that you collect will depend on what kind of validation you're doing, what your credit card processor requires, and whether you'll ship to an address other than the billing address.

OK, so now we have their credit card information, what do we do with it? Like their physical-world counterparts, online merchants have several options when it comes to accepting credit cards. The details vary depending on how things are set up. In all cases, though, there are several steps that must be accomplished:

- You must obtain a merchant account. This identifies you to the credit card companies as a valid merchant and allows you to accept charges, which they will then pay.

- You must make arrangements with a credit card processor. In almost all cases, you will be dealing with a bank or some other type of financial institution or company. This company will take the credit card information and tell you whether the card is valid and will also give you the money for your charges, less a percentage.

- When you accept a charge, you must submit it for processing.

You may have noticed that nowhere in this description do we talk about *how* this is all accomplished. This is because there are a myriad of options. You may get set up with a company such as CyberCash, which will process your charges online, or you may get an actual terminal that you will key the credit card information into.

If you choose to process your transactions on the spot over the Internet (a must for immediate delivery items like downloaded software) your provider will give you detailed instructions on how to set things up. In some cases, it involves installing software on your server; in others it involves making a call to a URL, which then sends you a result via another URL. Microsoft Site Server Commerce Edition includes real-time credit card authorization capabilities, but you will still need to provide your own merchant and processor accounts. For more information on credit card processing and merchant accounts, check any search engine. In fact, if you've ever posted to the Internet, you're probably already receiving spam from people trying to offer them to you.

In our case, we're going to assume that we've got a terminal in our office, and we're just going to accept the credit card information and process it later, by hand. Copy `template.asp` to `baz_order_complete_action.asp` in the bazaar directory (see Listing 7.31).

Listing 7.31—baz_order_complete_action.asp: Accepting payment information

```
0: <%@ LANGUAGE="VBSCRIPT" %>
1: <!--#include file="adovbs.inc"-->
2: <!--#include virtual="/pagetop.txt"-->
3: <%
4:     set outpostDB = Server.CreateObject("ADODB.Connection")
5:     outpostDB.Open "outpost"
6:
7:     p_order_id = Request.form("p_order_id")
8:
9:     set orderSet = Server.CreateObject("ADODB.RecordSet")
10:    orderSet.Open "select * from baz_orders where order_id = " _
11:       & p_order_id, outpostDB, adOpenStatic, adLockOptimistic, _
```

```
12:    adCmdText
13: if orderSet.EOF then
14:    Response.Write "There is a problem with your order. "
15:    Response.Write "Please contact customer service."
16: else
17:
18:    orderSet("shipping") = Request.form("p_shipping")
19:    orderSet("total") = Request.form("p_total")
20:    orderSet("first_name") = Request.form("p_first")
21:    orderSet("last_name") = Request.form("p_last")
22:    orderSet("address1") = Request.form("p_address1")
23:    orderSet("address2") = Request.form("p_address2")
24:    orderSet("city") = Request.form("p_city")
25:    orderSet("state") = Request.form("p_state")
26:    orderSet("postalcode") = Request.form("p_postal")
27:    orderSet("country") = Request.form("p_country")
28:    orderSet("phone") = Request.form("p_phone")
29:    orderSet("cc_type") = Request.form("p_cc_type")
30:    orderSet("cc_number") = Request.form("p_cc_number")
31:    orderSet("cc_nameoncard") = _
32:                               Request.form("p_cc_nameoncard")
33:    orderSet("status") = "COMPLETE"
34:    orderSet.Update
35:
36:    outpostDB.Execute("delete from baz_order_items where " _
37:        order_id = " & p_order_id)
38:
39:    set itemSet = Server.CreateObject("ADODB.RecordSet")
40:    itemSet.Open "baz_order_items", outpostDB,
41:        adOpenStatic, adLockOptimistic, adCmdTable
42:
43:    for each item in Request.form("p_orderitem")
44:
45:      p_orderitem = cstr(item)
46:      itemInfo = split(p_orderitem, ",")
47:
48:      itemSet.addNew
49:      itemSet("order_id") = p_order_id
50:      itemSet("prod_id") = itemInfo(0)
51:      itemSet("quantity") = itemInfo(1)
52:      itemSet.Update
53:
54:    next
55:    itemSet.Close
56:    set itemSet = Nothing
57:
58:    Session.abandon
59:
60: end if
61: orderSet.Close
62: set orderSet = Nothing
```

continues

Listing 7.31—continued

```
63:
64:  outpostDB.Close
65:  set outpostDB = Nothing
66:%>
67:
68:Your order has been received. Please allow 10 business
69:days for receipt.
70:<P>
71:Thank you for shopping with us!
72:
73:<!--#include virtual="/pagebottom.txt"-->
74:</BODY>
75:</HTML>
```

If our customers have gotten as far as completing their orders, we certainly don't want to discourage them by timing out their order, so instead of looking for the session variable, we're going to pull their order ID from the form on line 7. After we get that, we can check for an existing order on lines 10 through 12. If there isn't one, something fishy is going on because the order number should have been generated out of that table in the first place. If this error comes up in a live application, there's a good chance someone has been up to mischief, either in the request or the database. Either way, we need to pass it on to a real live person to deal with.

If the order does exist, the first thing that we're going to do is update the information for it on lines 18 through 34, including setting the status to complete, so we know that we need to process and ship it. (We'll take care of that in the next chapter.) Next we need to make sure that the items we're shipping match the items that the customer confirmed.

First, on lines 36 and 37, we are deleting all of their items from the baz_order_items table, and then we're going to replace them with the values we sent in from the form. Those items are in the array of elements in Request.form("p_orderitem"). Remember when we had check boxes with the same name way back when we did the user registration? This is the same principle. So for each item, we are actually pulling out both the item number and the quantity on lines 45 through 52. When we created the hidden value, it was in the form

`itemnumber,quantity`

On line 46, we are actually splitting this string into two values, separated by the comma. Because we are putting this into the variable iteminfo, iteminfo actually becomes an array of two items, numbered 0 and 1. For each p_orderitem, we do this split and then add the information to the database. Finally, we let the server know that this session is over so we can free up any resources that were being used. We're finished!

Next Steps

In this chapter, we created an entire online storefront from start to finish. We created a catalog with multiple categories and products that can belong to more than one category. We created a search engine that we can put anywhere on the site that uses dynamic SQL to get results. It also allows for wild cards and case-insensitivity. We talked about joining tables together in a single query and weeding out duplicates. We also talked about subroutines and how to use them, and scope, as it applies to subroutines, sessions, and the application itself. We talked about values tied to the session and application objects and how to initialize them when the application starts up using `Application_OnStart`.

In our next chapter, we'll talk about how to manage all of this information using our browser. Most database applictions have a client application specific to the database, through which changes like product updates are made. There's no reason we can't build a system that allows us to do this work through the browser. In Chapter 8, "System Administration via ASP," we'll look at maintaining all of the tables that we've created through the course of this project. We'll also look at security, database transactions, uploading files from the browser, creating and editing text files on the server, and importing data from a text file.

7

Chapter 8

In this chapter

- *Security*
- *Displaying a Table*
- *Storing myLinks Information in the Database*
- *Uploading myNews Files: From the Browser to the Server*
- *Creating Files on the Server: Formatting the News*
- *Reading a File: Importing Product Data*

System Adminstration via ASP

In the first seven chapters, we built—from scratch—a fully functional, dynamic, database-driven Web site using Active Server Pages. However, we haven't even considered how we're going to maintain the underlying database.

Sure, we could just have our administrator enter the information directly into the database. Access isn't too tough to use, after all. But you'll rarely be running a really major site using Access. In most cases, you'll be dealing with a much more powerful database (such as SQL Server or Oracle) and you'll need some way to update it. That means building screens for your users (even in Access) and training them on a new environment. Why go through all of that hassle when you have perfectly good Web skills that you can use?

Besides, if you build a Web interface for your administration, you (or whoever is maintaining the site) can administer it from anywhere! This kind of thin client architecture is becoming more and more common as people realize how much easier training and maintenance are. After all, if you have 500 people using a traditional client application, that means that they have a program on their computer that they have to fire up to use it. What happens if you want to change that program? Are you going to install the new software 500 times? Wouldn't it be better if you could just change the site once and be done with it?

Of course, the thin client architecture isn't without its problems. Security is much more of an issue when your database is being accessed over the web, and security features, as well as those dealing with concurrency in the database, are not necessarily as well developed as those in a traditional client-server application. That's not to say they're not sufficient, but if you're dealing with sensitive information, you'll need to keep this in mind. As we build our administration pages, we'll look at some of the issues that need to be considered.

That's what we're going to do in this chapter. Information in the database needs to be added, removed, and edited. We'll look at ways to accomplish this in the browser without compromising security or usability.

Security

In the last chapter, we talked about how to protect our customer's credit card number from being eavesdropped on as it traveled from their browser to our server. But what about protecting the information on the server itself?

After all, just because it's on our server doesn't mean we want to broadcast it to the world! I mean, you wouldn't want just anybody to pull up a list of credit card transactions you haven't processed yet. This process of identifying a user for access to specific information is called authentication, and there are several options we have for doing it.

The first option is actually something that we've already been doing: using a page that takes in a username and password. From there we can decide what content to give the user. The only problem with this is that we can only protect Active Server Pages. If we want to protect any straight HTML pages, we'll have to find another way.

Another option would be to set the authentication in the Web server software itself. In Windows NT, there are two kinds of authentication at the server level: Basic and Windows NT Challenge/Response.

Basic authentication is the standard in Web server authentication, and just about all browsers support it. In most cases, it's just fine, but there's one big problem with it. The username and password are sent in clear text; they're not encrypted at all, and can be snooped. Unfortunately, because this setting is at the Windows NT Server level, the usernames and passwords are the NT usernames and passwords, which opens the server up to a lot more than just unauthorized Web page access. What this means is that unless all of your password-protected requests come from secure (meaning SSL) pages, you'll run the risk of exposing your NT usernames and passwords to ill-intentioned hackers who can then wreak havoc on your server, and that's the last thing you need.

Integrated Windows Authentication (formerly Windows NT Challenge/Response) is a little better because the username and password are encrypted, but only Microsoft Internet Explorer supports it, and then only when the user is directly connected to the network (as opposed to dialing in to the Internet).

Another option would be to use one of the well written and tested third-party applications out there to manage your security. There are several good ones out there, such as Authentix, available at `http://www.flicks.com/flicks/authx.htm`. You could even write one yourself, but since this involves using a language like C++, you should probably stick to licensing one if you're not an experienced programmer. Security is one place I wouldn't fool around!

Whatever we use, the important thing is that we use it consistently and appropriately. Because we're concentrating on Active Server Pages and not Web server configuration, we're going to put our security check into a function that we can call from our pages, so that we can change the methodology at any time just by changing that function.

This means we're going to need a new template for our administration pages. It'll need to take into account the authentication issue, but also recognize the fact that we are not accessing the actual application here, just the administration pages; we don't need the bottom links.

Save a copy of `template.asp` as `admintemplate.asp` in the home directory and strip it down to the code shown in Listing 8.1.

Listing 8.1—admintemplate.asp: Modifying template.asp for the administration section

```
0: <%@ LANGUAGE="VBSCRIPT" %>
1: <!--#include file="adovbs.inc"-->
2: <!--#include file="pagetop.txt"-->
3: <!--#include file="isadmin.inc"-->
4: <%
5: if isAdmin then
6:
7:     set outpostDB = Server.CreateObject("ADODB.Connection")
8:     outpostDB.Open "outpost"
9:
10:
11:  outpostDB.Close
12:  set outpostDB = Nothing
13:else
14:
15:     Response.Write "You do not have access to this page."
16:
17:end if
18:%>
19:</BODY>
20:</HTML>
```

The value of `isAdmin` will be either `true` or `false`, and comes from a function. We're defining the function in the file `isadmin.inc`. That file looks like Listing 8.2:

Listing 8.2—isadmin.inc: Deciding if the user is an administrator

```
0:<%
1:   Function isAdmin
2:      if request.Cookies("IsLoggedOnAs")("username") = _
3:                        "admin" then
4:         isAdmin = true
5:      else
6:         isAdmin = false
7:      end if
8:   End Function
9:%>
```

Note Because this file is being included in another page, we don't need to declare the language, as we normally do on the first line. In fact, we can't; it can only be declared once per page.

This way, we can control our access using just this one function, which would simplify matters if we decided to change the way we decided whether a given user was an administrator. If we had Basic authentication enabled, we could have the Web server reject anyone who hadn't specifically been given permission to view that page. In that case, if someone gets the page, we know they're an administrator, so we could set the function as shown in Listing 8.3:

Listing 8.3—isadmin.inc: Allowing the Web server to decide

```
0:<%
1:   Function isAdmin
2:      isAdmin = true
3:   End Function
4:%>
```

The function would always return `true`, and our visitors, who had already been checked out by the Web server, would get their pages.

Or maybe we want to use Basic authentication, but we don't want to let the Web server decide who has access. Instead, we want to decide ourselves, using values in the database. This way we could administer the security remotely via ASP instead of having to log directly into the server and change permissions every time we wanted to add or remove someone. We could change our `isAdmin` function to read as shown in Listing 8.4.

Listing 8.4—isadmin.inc: Checking authenticated users against the database

```
1: <%
2:   Function isAdmin
3:       set outpostDB = Server.CreateObject("ADODB.Connection")
4:       outpostDB.Open "outpost"
5:
6:       p_currentuser = Request.ServerVariables("AUTH_USER")
7:
8:       set adminSet = outpostDB.Execute("select group from "_
9:           & " members where username='" & p_currentuser & "'" )
10:      if adminSet.EOF then
11:          isAdmin = false
12:      elseif adminSet("group") = "admin" then
13:          isAdmin = true
14:      else
15:          isAdmin = false
16:      end if
17:
18:      adminSet.Close
19:      set adminSet = Nothing
20:
21:      outpostDB.Close
22:      set outpostDB = Nothing
23:   end Function
24:%>
```

On line 6, we are reading the value of an environment variable. Environment variables are usually sent with the headers for the request and include information such as the site the user came from, their IP address, and the local date and time (of the server, that is).

If you don't have authentication enabled, AUTH_USER is going to be blank, because the Web server doesn't check to see who it is. In this case, everyone is accessing through the generic anonymous account. In this example, we're assuming that we've added a column to the members table for a group and that we've set the value equal to admin for those users we want to have access to these pages.

EXCURSION

Setting Permissions on Files and Directories

If you are using IIS, you can set the permissions using the Microsoft Management Console. Right-click the file or directory you want to protect and choose Properties. Click the Directory Security tab.

Uncheck Allow Anonymous Access and check either Basic Authentication or Integrated Windows Authentication. The Web server will use the normal Windows 2000 accounts, and if you use Integrated Windows Authentication and the user has already logged in to the Windows domain, he or she will not be asked to log in a second time. This is handy for intranet applications, where users are accessing the site over a local area network, or LAN.

At any rate, whatever we decide to use, the beauty of doing it this way is that we can implement it quickly by changing the isAdmin function in just one place. This also means we have the freedom to change methods at a moment's notice. For now, let's set the function so that it always returns true, so we can work on our Administrator pages (see Listing 8.3).

Displaying a Table

On my projects, it's an extremely rare occasion when I can work on the machine where the project is actually being built. After all, this is the Internet; I don't even have to be in the same country! One problem that I am constantly faced with is a security setup that blocks access directly to the database. This is, of course, how it should be, but it's awfully inconvenient when I'm trying to see what's in my tables.

So what I've done is build a generic page that will read and display the contents of any table that I specify. That way, when I need to know what's in a table, I just call up the proper URL, which includes the table name.

To do this, we're going to take advantage of the structure of a RecordSet. Copy admintemplate.asp to display_table.asp and add the code in Listing 8.5.

Listing 8.5—display_table.asp: Displaying the contents and structure of a table

```
 0: <%@ LANGUAGE="VBSCRIPT" %>
 1: <!--#include file="adovbs.inc"-->
 2: <!--#include file="pagetop.txt"-->
 3: <!--#include file="isadmin.inc"-->
 4: <%
 5: if isAdmin then
 6:     p_table_name = Request.querystring("p_table_name")
 7: %>
 8: <CENTER>
 9: <H2> Contents of table: <%=p_table_name%> </h2>
10:
11:<TABLE BORDER="1">
12:
13:<%
14:    set outpostDB = Server.CreateObject("ADODB.Connection")
15:    outpostDB.Open "outpost"
16:
17:    set tableSet = Server.CreateObject("ADODB.RecordSet")
18:    tableSet.Open p_table_name, outpostDB, adOpenForwardOnly, _
19:                         adLockOptimistic, adCmdTable
20:%>
21:    <TR>
22:<%    p_numberOfColumns = tableSet.fields.Count
23:      for x = 0 to (p_numberOfColumns - 1) %>
24:          <TH><%= tableSet.Fields(x).Name %></TH>
```

```
25:<%        next %>
26:     </TR>
27:
28:<%   while not tableSet.EOF  %>
29:         <TR>
30:<%          for each col in tableSet.Fields  %>
31:                <TD><%= col.Value %></TD>
32:<%          next          %>
33:         </TR>
34:<%        tableSet.MoveNext
35:       wend
36:       tableSet.Close
37:%>
38:
39:</TABLE>
40:</CENTER>
41:<%
42:     outpostDB.Close
43:     set outpostDB = Nothing
44:else
45:
46:    Response.Write "You do not have access to this page."
47:
48:end if
49:%>
50:</BODY>
51:</HTML>
```

Because we're pulling the name of the table out of the querystring one line 6—remember that shows up as part of the URL—we can get the listing of any table just by changing the name in the URL. For instance, to get a listing of the members, table, the URL would be

```
http://localhost/display_table.asp?p_table_NAME=members
```

After we get the table name, we can create a RecordSet from the table, which we're doing on lines 18 and 19. At this point we've got a collection of information that can tell us everything we need to know—if only we could get at it!

The main thing to realize is that a RecordSet is a collection of Fields. Remember, when we say

```
tableSet("username")
```

we really mean

```
tableSet.Fields.Item("username")
```

Every one of those fields has information associated with it—not just the value of the information, but also the name.

On lines 21 through 26, before we display any of the actual information, we want to get a row of headers so we know what the columns are called. One way to do this is to find out how many fields there are and count through them. We can find out using the Count property, which we're doing on line 22. One thing to keep in mind is that the first field is *not* number 1, it's number 0. So if we have 5 columns, the last one is number 4. If we try to call number 5, we're going to get an error. On lines 23 through 25, we'll go through and get the Name property for each column and then display it in a specially formatted table cell—a table header.

We're using a slightly different way to run through the actual data. Instead of counting through them, we'll use a for each loop to run through all of the fields on line 30. Every time it runs through the loop, col is set to be not a number, but an actual Field object in the collection. Because we are pointing to a specific field in the collection (as opposed to the whole collection itself), we don't need to tell the RecordSet which one—it already knows. All we have to do is ask for the Value property (see Figure 8.1).

Figure 8.1

With a little planning, we can see any table in the database.

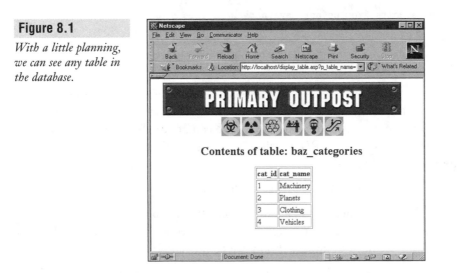

That's all there is to it! Of course, we're not actually affecting the data at all. Let's take a look at ways to maintain our data.

Storing myLinks Information in the Database

The links table is pretty simple, so let's take a look at it first. We're going to need the ability to do three things: insert, update, and delete records.

We're going to start by creating a form that will list all of the current records, along with a check box to mark them for deletion. We'll also have a link to a form where we can edit the record and a link that will give us to a blank form we can use to create a new one.

Copy `admintemplate.asp` to `edit_links.asp`. Add the code in Listing 8.6.

Listing 8.6—edit_links.asp: Deciding which records to edit or delete

```
0: <%@ LANGUAGE="VBSCRIPT" %>
1: <!--#include file="adovbs.inc"-->
2: <!--#include file="pagetop.txt"-->
3: <!--#include file="isadmin.inc"-->
4: <%
5: if isAdmin then
6: %>
7: <CENTER>
8: <H2> Edit Links</h2>
9:
10:<A HREF="edit_links_rec.asp">Create a New Record</A>
11:
12:<FORM ACTION="edit_links_action.asp" METHOD="post">
13:
14:<TABLE BORDER="1">
15:<%
16:    set outpostDB = Server.CreateObject("ADODB.Connection")
17:    outpostDB.Open "outpost"
18:
19:    set tableSet = Server.CreateObject("ADODB.RecordSet")
20:    tableSet.Open "select * from links order by link_id",
21:        outpostDB, adOpenForwardOnly, adLockOptimistic, adCmdText
22:
23:    while not tableSet.EOF
24:%>      <TR>
25:            <TD>
26:                <INPUT TYPE="checkbox" NAME="p_delete"
27:                            VALUE="<%=tableSet("link_id")%>">
28:            </TD>
29:<%          p_numberOfColumns = tableSet.Fields.Count
30:%>          <TD>
31:              <A HREF="edit_links_rec.asp?p_link_id=<%
32:                Response.Write tableSet("link_id")%>">
33:                <%= tableSet.Fields(0).Value %>
34:              </A>
35:            </TD>
36:
37:<%          for col = 1 to (p_numberofColumns-1)
38:%>              <TD>
39:                  <%= tableSet.fields(col).Value %>
40:              </TD>
41:<%          next %>
```

continues

Listing 8.6—continued

```
42:      </TR>
43:<%   tableSet.MoveNext
44:  wend
45:  tableSet.Close
46:  set tableSet = Nothing
47:%>
48:
49:</TABLE>
50:<INPUT TYPE="submit" VALUE="Delete Checked Rows">
51:</form>
52:
53:<A HREF="edit_links_rec.asp">Create a New Record</A>
54:
55:</CENTER>
56:<%
57:     outpostDB.Close
58:     set outpostDB = Nothing
59:else
60:
61:     Response.Write "You do not have access to this page."
62:
63:end if
64:%>
65:</BODY>
66:</HTML>
```

On line 10 we create a link to the new record form. We'll put it at the top and the bottom of the page, so it's less likely that our administrator will have to scroll for miles if there are a lot of records in our table. Obviously if there are *too* many records, we're going to have to manage this in a different way, but the basic idea is the same.

On line 12 we're creating a form that will note which records we want to delete. Displaying the table and the check boxes on lines 23 through 46 is very similar to what we did in display_table.asp. We could hard-code in the names of the fields, but if we change the table definition later, that'll come back to haunt us. The main difference between this and display_table.asp is that we've added a check box for every field on lines 26 and 27, and we've separated out the first column (number 0) on lines 30 through 35 so we can make it a link to an edit page (see Figure 8.2).

Let's look at that first column for a minute. It's link_id, the primary key for this table. That means that if we want to identify a specific record in the table, all we need is that value. We don't have to even know the actual link_name and link_desc. As long as we have the link_id, we can pinpoint which record it is. That's why it's important in your applications to make sure that every table has a primary key.

Figure 8.2

We can edit our tables directly from the Web.

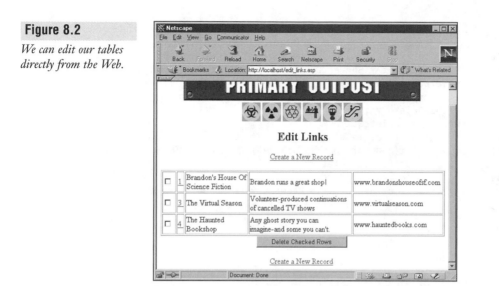

 Note

Even though we haven't been designating them as we've been building them, every table in our project has a primary key. Also, a primary key doesn't have to be just one column. For instance, in our order_items table, the primary key is actually a combination of the order_id and the prod_id.

Now we need a form action to take those check boxes and delete our records. Remember back in Chapter 4, "Database Access Using ASP," when we were comparing the links the user had chosen with the links that were in the table? We're doing the same thing here, only this time we're deleting the record when we find a match. When we're done deleting, we'll want to take the user back to the original form. Copy admintemplate.asp to edit_links_action.asp and add the code in Listing 8.7.

Listing 8.7—edit_links_action.asp: Deleting specific records

```
0: <%@ LANGUAGE="VBSCRIPT" %>
1: <%  Response.buffer = true   %>
2: <!--#include file="adovbs.inc"-->
3: <!--#include file="pagetop.txt"-->
4: <!--#include file="isadmin.inc"-->
5: <%
6: if isAdmin then
7:
8:     set outpostDB = Server.CreateObject("ADODB.Connection")
9:     outpostDB.Open "outpost"
```

continues

8

Listing 8.7—continued

```
10:
11:    set deleteSet = Server.CreateObject("ADODB.RecordSet")
12:    deleteSet.Open "select * from links order by link_id", _
13:        outpostDB, adOpenDynamic, adLockPessimistic, adCmdText
14:    p_thisDelete = 1
15:    while not deleteSet.EOF
16:        if cint(deleteSet("link_id")) = _
17:          cint(Request.form("p_delete").item(p_thisDelete)) then
18:            deleteSet.Delete
19:            deleteSetUpdate
20:            if p_thisDelete < Request.form("p_delete").Count then
21:                p_thisDelete = p_thisDelete + 1
22:            end if
23:        end if
24:        deleteSet.MoveNext
25:    wend
26:    deleteSet.Close
27:    set deleteSet = Nothing
28:
29:    outpostDB.Close
30:    set outpostDB = Nothing
31:
32:    Response.Clear
33:    Response.Redirect "http://localhost/edit_links.asp"
34:else
35:
36:    Response.Write "You do not have access to this page."
37:
38:end if
39:%>
40:</BODY>
41:</HTML>
```

In the past, when we were redirecting the user, we took great pains to make sure that we didn't send any text to the browser before we did it; we even went to the point of re-arranging the page. This time, instead of worrying about what we've already sent, we're going to tell the browser to hold all headers and text until the page is completely finished. To do this, on line 1 we tell the Response object to buffer it's output. Essentially, we're telling the Response object not to send anything at all until we tell it to, or until the page is completely finished. Then later, on line 32, just before we do the redirect, we tell it to throw away whatever else it was going to send and do the redirect instead.

 Note   This behavior is the default in IIS 5.0, but in previous versions it was not, requiring the developer to set it.

Lines 11 through 27 are similar to what we did in Chapter 4, when we were managing the user's chosen links. We're creating a list of all links and then comparing them, one by one, against those that we've marked for deletion. When we find a record that has been checked off, we delete it and move on.

We could also have looped through the links for deletion and let the RecordSet find each one. Again, there's more than one way to solve this problem.

Now let's look at creating a new record. Copy admintemplate.asp to edit_links_rec.asp and add the code in Listing 8.8.

Listing 8.8—edit_links_rec.asp: Adding a record

```
0: <%@ LANGUAGE="VBSCRIPT" %>
1: <!--#include file="adovbs.inc"-->
2: <!--#include file="pagetop.txt"-->
3: <!--#include file="isadmin.inc"-->
4: <%
5: if isAdmin then
6:
7:     set outpostDB = Server.CreateObject("ADODB.Connection")
8:     outpostDB.Open "outpost"
9:
10:    set maxSet = outpostDB.Execute("select * from links "_
11:        & "order by link_id desc")
12:    linkSet.MoveFirst
13:    if maxSet.EOF then
14:        p_link_id = 1
15:    else
16:        p_link_id = maxSet("link_id") + 1
17:    end if
18:    maxSet.Close
19:    set maxSet = Nothing
20:%>
21:    <CENTER>
22:    <FORM ACTION="edit_links_rec_action.asp" METHOD="post">
23:    <h2>Add a New Link</h2>
24:    <TABLE>
25:    <TR>
26:        <TD>Link ID</TD>
27:        <TD>
28:            <INPUT TYPE="hidden" NAME="p_link_id"
29:                VALUE="<%= p_link_id %>">
30:            <%= p_link_id %>
31:        </TD>
32:    </TR>
33:    <TR>
34:        <TD>Link Name</TD>
```

continues

Listing 8.8—continued

```
35:        <TD><INPUT TYPE="text" NAME="p_name" SIZE="25">
36:     </TR>
37:     <TR>
38:        <TD>Link Description</TD>
39:        <TD><INPUT TYPE="text" NAME="p_desc" SIZE="50"
40:              MAXLENGTH="255">
41:     </TR>
42:     <TR>
43:       <TD>Link URL: http://</TD>
44:       <TD><INPUT TYPE="text" NAME="p_url" SIZE="50"
45:              MAXLENGTH="100">
46:     </TR>
47:
48:     </TABLE>
49:
50:     <INPUT TYPE="submit">
51:
52:     </form>
53:     </CENTER>
54:<%
55:    outpostDB.Close
56:    set outpostDB = Nothing
57:else
58:
59:    Response.Write "You do not have access to this page."
60:
61:end if
62:%>
63:</BODY>
64:</HTML>
```

What we have here is just a form that lets us add a link name, description, and URL. The only tricky part is getting a unique link_id. To do that, we're selecting the maximum existing link_id and adding 1 to it on lines 10 through 19.

Adding the record itself is simple. Copy admintemplate.asp to edit_links_rec_action.asp and add the code in Listing 8.9.

Listing 8.9—edit_links_rec_action.asp: Creating the new record

```
0: <%@ LANGUAGE="VBSCRIPT" %>
1: <!--#include file="adovbs.inc"-->
2: <!--#include file="pagetop.txt"-->
3: <!--#include file="isadmin.inc"-->
4: <%
5: if isAdmin then
6:
7:     p_link_id = cint(Request.form("p_link_id"))
8:     p_link_name = cstr(Request.form("p_name"))
```

```
 9:    p_link_desc = cstr(Request.form("p_desc"))
10:    p_link_url = cstr(Request.form("p_url"))
11:
12:    set outpostDB = Server.CreateObject("ADODB.Connection")
13:    outpostDB.Open "outpost"
14:
15:    set insertSet = Server.CreateObject("ADODB.RecordSet")
16:    insertSet.Open "links", outpostdb, adOpenDynamic, _
17:      adLockOptimistic, adCmdTable
18:    insertSet.AddNew
19:    insertSet("link_id") = p_link_id
20:    insertSet("link_name") = p_link_name
21:    insertSet("link_desc") = p_link_desc
22:    insertSet("link_url") = p_link_url
23:    insertSetUpdate
24:    insertSet.Close
25:    set insertSet = Nothing
26:
27:    outpostDB.Close
28:    set outpostDB = Nothing
29:else
30:
31:    Response.Write "You do not have access to this page."
32:
33:end if
34:%>
35:</BODY>
36:</HTML>
```

On lines 7 through 10 we get the information from the form and convert it to the proper types because we're going to be putting it into the database. Then on lines 15 through 25 we create a RecordSet for the links table, add a new record, populate it, and close everything up. Nothing new there.

However, you may have noticed that when we created the edit_links.asp page, we were also sending the user to edit_links_rec.asp to *change* a record, as opposed to just adding a new one.

What we need is for the edit_links_rec.asp form to come up blank if we are creating a new record, but to be prepopulated if we're editing an existing one. Make the changes to edit_links_rec.asp shown in Listing 8.10.

Listing 8.10—edit_links_rec.asp: Editing an existing record

```
0: <%@ LANGUAGE="VBSCRIPT" %>
1: <!--#include file="adovbs.inc"-->
2: <!--#include file="pagetop.txt"-->
3: <!--#include file="isadmin.inc"-->
```

continues

Listing 8.10—continued

```
 4: <%
 5: if isAdmin then
 6:
 7:     set outpostDB = Server.CreateObject("ADODB.Connection")
 8:     outpostDB.Open "outpost"
 9:
10:     set linkSet = Server.CreateObject("ADODB.RecordSet")
11:     linkSet.Open "select * from links order by link_id desc", _
12:         outpostDB, adOpenStatic, adLockOptimistic, adCmdText
13:     linkSet.MoveFirst
14:     if linkSet.EOF then
15:         p_link_id = 1
16:     else
17:         p_link_id = linkSet("link_id") + 1
18:     end if
19:
20:     p_link_id_in = Request.querystring("p_link_id")
21:     if p_link_id_in <> "" then
22:         linkSet.Find "link_id = " & p_link_id_in
23:     end if
24:     if p_link_id_in = "" or linkSet.EOF then
25:         p_link_name = ""
26:         p_link_desc = ""
27:         p_link_url = ""
28:     else
29:         p_link_name = linkSet("link_name")
30:         p_link_desc = linkSet("link_desc")
31:         p_link_url = linkSet("link_url")
32:         p_link_id = p_link_id_in
33:         p_existing = p_link_id_in
34:     end if
35:
36:     linkSet.Close
36:     set linkSet = Nothing
37:%>
38:     <CENTER>
39:     <FORM ACTION="edit_links_rec_action.asp" METHOD="post">
40:     <INPUT TYPE="hidden" NAME="p_existing"
41:         VALUE="<%=p_existing%>">
42:     <h2>Edit Link</h2>
43:     <TABLE>
44:     <TR>
45:         <TD>Link ID</TD>
46:         <TD>
47:             <INPUT TYPE="hidden" NAME="p_link_id" VALUE="<%= p_link_id %>">
48:             <%= p_link_id %>
49:         </TD>
40:     </TR>
41:     <TR>
42:         <TD>Link Name</TD>
```

```
43:        <TD><INPUT TYPE="text" NAME="p_name" SIZE="25"
44                 VALUE="<%=p_link_name%>">
45:    </TR>
46:    <TR>
47:      <TD>Link Description</TD>
48:      <TD><INPUT TYPE="text" NAME="p_desc" SIZE="50"
49                 VALUE="<%=p_link_desc%>" MAXLENGTH="255">
50:    </TR>
51:    <TR>
52:      <TD>Link URL: http://</TD>
53:      <TD><INPUT TYPE="text" NAME="p_url" SIZE="50"
54                 VALUE="<%=p_link_url%>" MAXLENGTH="100">
55:    </TR>
56:
57:    </TABLE>
58:
59:    <INPUT TYPE="submit">
60:
61:    </form>
62:    </CENTER>
63:<%
64:    outpostDB.Close
65:    set outpostDB = Nothing
66:else
67:
68:    Response.Write "You do not have access to this page."
69:
70:end if
71:%>
72:</BODY>
73:</HTML>
```

What we're doing on lines 20 through 34 is checking to see whether we're supposed to be editing an existing record, and if we are, we're extracting the information from the RecordSet we've already created and populating the form with it. If there is no existing record, the fields will come up blank, just like they did before.

Because we're going to be searching the RecordSet on lines 21 through 23, we've changed it from the default Forward-only cursor you get with an Execute statement to a Static cursor so we can move up the list as well as down.

On line 21, we're checking to see whether there was an existing record submitted. Because we're coming from a link instead of a form, we're using Request. querystring instead of Request.form. Just in case there's no value coming in, we'll call it p_link_id_in so we don't inadvertently set p_link_id to an empty string.

If we did find a value for p_link_id_in, we're using it to find the appropriate record in the set. Then, whether we find it or not, we're populating variables that we're

8

going to use later. Also, if we did find a value for p_link_id_in, we're using it to replace p_link_id. We'll also set a flag to tell us that we're dealing with an existing record. That way, when we get to the form action, we know whether to update a record or create a new one.

Finally we'll use the new (or blank) values to populate the text boxes.

Now we have a form that will handle both new and existing records. All that's left is to modify the form action to handle the existing records. Go back to edit_links_rec_action.asp and make the changes in Listing 8.11.

Listing 8.11—edit_links_rec_action.asp: Saving changes to an existing record

```
0: <%@ LANGUAGE="VBSCRIPT" %>
1: <%  Response.buffer = true%>
2: <!--#include file="adovbs.inc"-->
3: <!--#include file="pagetop.txt"-->
4: <!--#include file="isadmin.inc"-->
5: <%
6: if isAdmin then
7:
8:     p_link_id = cint(Request.form("p_link_id"))
9:     p_link_name = cstr(Request.form("p_name"))
10:    p_link_desc = cstr(Request.form("p_desc"))
11:    p_link_url = cstr(Request.form("p_url"))
12:    p_existing = cstr(Request.form("p_existing"))
13:
14:    set outpostDB = Server.CreateObject("ADODB.Connection")
15:    outpostDB.Open "outpost"
16:
17:    set insertSet = Server.CreateObject("ADODB.RecordSet")
18: insertSet.Open "links", outpostdb, adOpenDynamic, _
19:     adLockOptimistic, adCmdTable
20:
21: if p_existing = "" then
22:     insertSet.AddNew
23: else
24:     insertSet.Find "link_id =" & p_existing
25: end if
26: insertSet("link_id") = p_link_id
27: insertSet("link_name") = p_link_name
28: insertSet("link_desc") = p_link_desc
29: insertSet("link_url") = p_link_url
30: insertSetUpdate
31: insertSet.Close
32: set insertSet = Nothing
33:
34: outpostDB.Close
35: set outpostDB = Nothing
36:
37: Response.Clear
```

```
38:    Response.Redirect "http://localhost/edit_links.asp"
39:else
40:
41:    Response.Write "You do not have access to this page."
42:
43:end if
44:%>
45:</BODY>
46:</HTML>
```

All we had to do differently with this page was to check and see whether there was an existing record, and if there was, find it instead of creating a new one. That's it! It certainly beats deciding whether to create an `insert` statement or an `update` statement and having to maintain them both!

Uploading myNews Files: From the Browser to the Server

So far, although we've used some new approaches, we really haven't seen anything new from a technical standpoint.

When we set up the News section of mySpace, we had planned to simply link to files that were on the server instead of storing entire news articles in the database. That's great for the database, but it means that to maintain this section, we're going to have to be able to upload files to the server and remove them when we're done with them.

Upload means to move something from your computer to another computer. This is the opposite of downloading, which is to take something from another computer and put it on your own.

Uploading files isn't something that's included in ASP as a matter of course, but there are numerous components out there that we can use to help us out. As you may remember, there was even a trial version of one installed with ASPEmail, ASPUpload. We're going to use that to take a look at some of the issues involved with uploading files to our site.

The basic process is the same as it was for editing the links table, so let's start by making a copy of those pages. Copy `edit_links.asp`, `edit_links_action.asp`, `edit_links_rec.asp`, and `edit_links_rec_action.asp` to `edit_news.asp`, `edit_news_action.asp`, `edit_news_rec.asp`, and `edit_links_rec_action.asp`, respectively.

Let's start with `edit_news.asp` (see Listing 8.12).

8

Listing 8.12—edit_news.asp: Selecting news items to delete

```
0: <%@ LANGUAGE="VBSCRIPT" %>
1: <!--#include file="adovbs.inc"-->
2: <!--#include file="pagetop.txt"-->
3: <!--#include file="isadmin.inc"-->
4: <%
5: if isAdmin then
6: %>
7: <CENTER>
8: <H2> Edit News</h2>
9:
10:<A HREF="edit_news_rec.asp">Create a New Record</A>
11:<FORM ACTION="edit_news_action.asp" METHOD="post">
12:
13:<TABLE BORDER="1">
14:<%
15:   set outpostDB = Server.CreateObject("ADODB.Connection")
16:   outpostDB.Open "outpost"
17:
18:   set catSet = Server.CreateObject("ADODB.RecordSet")
19:   catSet.Open "news_categories", outpostDB, adOpenStatic, _
20:       adLockReadOnly, adCmdTable
21:
22:   set tableSet = Server.CreateObject("ADODB.RecordSet")
23:   tableSet.Open "select * from news order by news_id", _
24:       outpostDB, adOpenForwardOnly, adLockReadOnly, adCmdText
25:
26:   while not tableSet.EOF
27:%>      <TR>
28:       <TD>
29:          <INPUT TYPE="checkbox" NAME="p_delete"
30:               VALUE="<%=tableSet("news_id")%>">
31:       </TD>
32:<%     p_numberOfColumns = tableSet.Fields.Count
33:%>      <TD>
34:          <A HREF="edit_news_rec.asp?p_news_id=<%
35:             Response.Write tableSet("news_id")%>">
36:             <%= tableSet("news_id")%>
37:          </A>
38:       </TD>
39:<%     catSet.MoveFirst
40:       catSet.Find "cat_id = " & tableSet("news_cat_id")
41:%>      <TD>
42:             <%= catSet("cat_name")%>
43:       </TD>
44:
45:<%     for col = 2 to (p_numberofColumns-1)
46:%>          <TD>
```

```
47:                    <%= tableSet.fields(col).Value %>
48:              </TD>
49:<%        next %>
50:          </TR>
51:<%         tableSet.MoveNext
52:    wend
53:    tableSet.Close
54:    set tableSet = Nothing
55:
56:    catSet.Close
57:    set catSet = Nothing
58:%>
59:
60:</TABLE>
61:<INPUT TYPE="submit" VALUE="Delete Checked Rows">
62:</form>
63:
64:<A HREF="edit_news_rec.asp">Create a New Record</A>
65:
66:</CENTER>
67:<%
68:    outpostDB.Close
69:    set outpostDB = Nothing
70:else
71:
72:    Response.Write "You do not have access to this page."
73:
74:end if
75:%>
76:</BODY>
77:</HTML>
```

For the most part, we just replaced the words link and links with news, but also we've added a slight enhancement (see Figure 8.3). Part of the news item is it's category, so we'll need a way for our administrator to set that. But rather than expect our administrator to remember every category ID, we're pulling the name from the news_categories table and displaying that. Additionaly, because we're not changing anything in the database—we're just reading it—we're setting the RecordSets to use Read Only locking. In other words, they don't have to lock anything at all.

Now you see part of the advantage of being as generic as we can. If we'd specifically listed the columns in the links table, we'd have to rewrite this whole page! Let's move on to edit_news_action.asp (see Listing 8.13).

8

Figure 8.3

With just a few simple modifications to `edit_links.asp`, we can display our edit page for news.

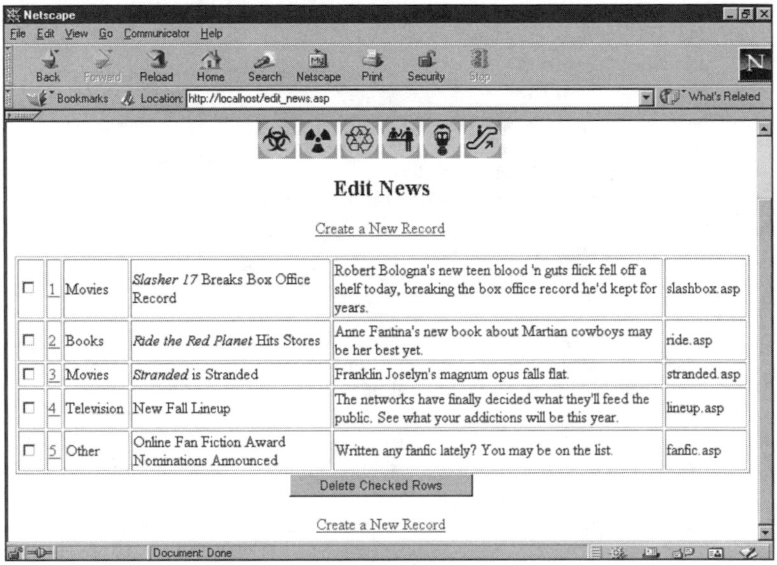

Listing 8.13—edit_news_action.asp: Changing/adding news items

```
0: <%@ LANGUAGE="VBSCRIPT" %>
1: <% Response.buffer = true  %>
2: <!--#include file="adovbs.inc"-->
3: <!--#include file="pagetop.txt"-->
4: <!--#include file="isadmin.inc"-->
5: <%
6: if isAdmin then
7:
8:     set outpostDB = Server.CreateObject("ADODB.Connection")
9:     outpostDB.Open "outpost"
10:
11:     set deleteSet = Server.CreateObject("ADODB.RecordSet")
12:     deleteSet.Open "select * from news order by news_id",
13:         outpostDB, adOpenDynamic, adLockPessimistic, adCmdText
14:     p_thisDelete = 1
15:     while not deleteSet.EOF
16:         if cint(deleteSet("news_id")) = _
17:             cint(Request.form("p_delete").item(p_thisDelete)) then
18:             deleteSet.Delete
19:             deleteSetUpdate
20:             if p_thisDelete < Request.form("p_delete").Count then
21:                 p_thisDelete = p_thisDelete + 1
22:             end if
23:         end if
24:         deleteSet.MoveNext
25:     wend
26:     deleteSet.Close
```

```
27:  set deleteSet = Nothing
28:
29:  outpostDB.Close
30:  set outpostDB = Nothing
31:
32:  Response.Clear
33:  Response.Redirect "http://localhost/edit_news.asp"
34:else
35:
36:  Response.Write "You do not have access to this page."
37:
38:end if
39:%>
40:</BODY>
41:</HTML>
```

In this case, literally all we did was change link and links to news. Again, being generic definitely has its advantages.

Now let's move on to edit_news_rec.asp (see Listing 8.14), where we start to get into the big changes.

Listing 8.14—edit_news_rec.asp: Adding the file upload box

```
0: <%@ LANGUAGE="VBSCRIPT" %>
1: <!--#include file="adovbs.inc"-->
2: <!--#include file="pagetop.txt"-->
3: <!--#include file="isadmin.inc"-->
4: <%
5: if isAdmin then
6:
7:     set outpostDB = Server.CreateObject("ADODB.Connection")
8:     outpostDB.Open "outpost"
9:
10:     set newsSet = Server.CreateObject("ADODB.RecordSet")
11:     newsSet.Open "select * from news order by news_id desc",_
12:         outpostDB, adOpenStatic, adLockOptimistic, adCmdText
13:     newsSet.MoveFirst
14:     if newsSet.EOF then
15:         p_news_id = 1
16:     else
17:         p_news_id = newsSet("news_id") + 1
18:     end if
19:
20:     p_news_id_in = Request.querystring("p_news_id")
21:     if p_news_id_in <> "" then
22:       newsSet.Find "news_id = " & p_news_id_in
23:     end if
24:     if p_news_id_in = "" or newsSet.EOF then
25:         p_news_cat_id = "0"
26:         p_news_name = ""
```

continues

Listing 8.14—continued

```
27:          p_news_desc = ""
28:          p_news_url = ""
29:     else
30:         p_news_cat_id = newsSet("news_cat_id")
31:         p_news_headline = newsSet("news_headline")
32:         p_news_blurb = newsSet("news_blurb")
33:         p_news_url = newsSet("news_url")
34:         p_news_id = p_news_id_in
35:         p_existing = p_news_id_in
36:     end if
37:
38:     newsSet.Close
39:     set newsSet = Nothing
40: %>
41:     <CENTER>
42:     <FORM ACTION="edit_news_rec_action.asp"
43:             METHOD="post" enctype="multipart/form-data">
44:     <INPUT TYPE="hidden" NAME="p_existing" VALUE="<%=p_existing%>">
45:     <h2>Edit News</h2>
46:     <TABLE>
47:     <TR>
48:        <TD>News ID </TD>
49:        <TD>
50:            <INPUT TYPE="hidden" NAME="p_news_id"
51:                VALUE="<%= p_news_id %>">
52:            <%= p_news_id %>
53:        </TD>
54:     </TR>
55:     <TR>
56:        <TD>Category </TD>
57:        <TD><select NAME="p_news_cat_id">
58: <%        set catSet = outpostDB.Execute("select * from "_
59:                              & "news_categories")
60:           while not catSet.EOF
61:               Response.Write "<option VALUE="&chr(34)&_
62:                                   catSet("cat_id")&chr(34)
63:               if cint(catSet("cat_id"))=cint(p_news_cat_id) then
64:                   Response.Write " SELECTED"
65:               end if
66:               Response.Write ">" & catSet("cat_name")
67:               catSet.MoveNext
68:           wend
69: %>        </select>
70:        </TD>
71:     </TR>
72:     <TR>
73:        <TD>News Headline</TD>
74:        <TD><INPUT TYPE="text" NAME="p_headline" SIZE="50"
75:                    VALUE="<%=p_news_headline%>">
76:     </TR>
```

```
77:    <TR>
78:      <TD>News Blurb</TD>
79:      <TD><INPUT TYPE="text" NAME="p_blurb" SIZE="50"
80:                    VALUE="<%=p_news_blurb%>" MAXLENGTH="255">
81:    </TR>
82:    <TR>
83:        <TD>News filename </TD>
84:        <TD><INPUT TYPE="text" NAME="p_url" SIZE="50"
85:                     VALUE="<%=p_news_url%>" MAXLENGTH="100">
86:    </TR>
87:    <TR>
88:        <TD>News File to Upload: </TD>
89:        <TD><INPUT TYPE="file" NAME="p_file"></TD>
90:    </TR>
91:
92:    </TABLE>
93:
94:    <INPUT TYPE="submit">
95:
96:    </form>
97:    </CENTER>
98: <%
99:    outpostDB.Close
100:   set outpostDB = Nothing
101:else
102:
103:    Response.Write "You do not have access to this page."
104:
105:end if
106:%>
107:</BODY>
108:</HTML>
```

In this case, we did hard-code the field names, so we'll have to change the names to match the news table. We also needed to add a field for the category ID, which didn't exist in the links table. We're doing all of that on lines 25 through 36.

On lines 56 through 71 we added a line to the form for our news category, checking to make sure that the current category for the item is marked as selected. Again, we didn't want to just display a category ID—or even worse, expect our administrator to type it in—so we're creating a pull-down menu.

The only thing new here is the way that we've implemented this. Normally, when we've been putting dynamic data into form elements, we've been doing it with the <%= %> syntax. This was because we wouldn't have to worry about how to print a double quote to the page. After all, if we tried

```
Response.Write ""Hello!""
```

ASP wouldn't know what to do with it. It would hit the second quote and think the line was finished, so it would consider everything from the "H" to the last quote an error. When we had single quotes in SQL, we could put two of them together and the database knew what to do with it. Not so for double quotes and VBScript.

Instead, what we did this time on line 62 was to use `Response.Write`, but for each double quote we've told ASP to print out character number 34. Every character you can type (and lots that you can't) has a number, called an ASCII code. It just so happens that the ASCII code for a double quote is 34. So if `catSet(cat_id)` was 5, the code

```
Response.Write "<option VALUE="&chr(34)&catSet("cat_id")&chr(34)&>
```

is going to print out

```
<option VALUE="5">
```

None of this has been too much of a change from editing the links table, but now we're getting into something new. On line 89, we've put in a new kind of form element, a file element. This tells the browser to display not only a box for the name of the file, but a Browse button that will let us designate a file to upload (see Figure 8.4).

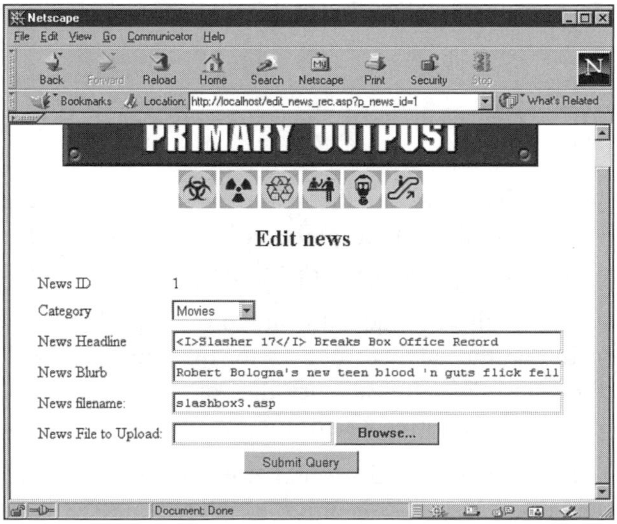

Figure 8.4

The file element tells the browser to let us browse our computer for a file to upload.

But the file element won't do us any good unless the browser also knows it should send the whole file, and not just the name. We tell it to do so by adding an encoding type to the form tag on lines 42 and 43.

```
enctype="multipart/form-data"
```

is required if we're going to be uploading files.

Those were substantial changes, but they're nothing compared to what we're going to do with `edit_news_rec_action.asp`. That's where we're actually going to take in that file and do something with it. Open `edit_news_rec_action.asp` and add the changes in Listing 8.15.

 Note   If you didn't register and install the ASPUpload component back in Chapter 6, "Adding Person-To-Person Auction Capabilities," go back and do it now.

Listing 8.15—edit_news_rec_action.asp: Saving the uploaded file

```
0: <%@ LANGUAGE="VBSCRIPT" %>
1: <% Response.buffer = true    %>
2: <!--#include file="adovbs.inc"-->
3: <!--#include file="pagetop.txt"-->
4: <!--#include file="isadmin.inc"-->
5: <%
6: if isAdmin then
7:
8:     set Upload = Server.CreateObject("PersitsUpload.1")
9:     count = Upload.Save("c:\inetpub\wwwroot")
10:
11:    p_news_id = cint(Upload.form("p_news_id"))
12:    p_news_cat_id = cint(Upload.form("p_news_cat_id"))
13:    p_news_headline = cstr(Upload.form("p_headline"))
14:    p_news_blurb = cstr(Upload.form("p_blurb"))
15:    p_news_url = cstr(Upload.form("p_url"))
16:    p_existing = cstr(Upload.form("p_existing"))
17:
18:    set Upload = Nothing
19:
20:    set outpostDB = Server.CreateObject("ADODB.Connection")
21:    outpostDB.Open "outpost"
22:
23:    set insertSet = Server.CreateObject("ADODB.RecordSet")
24:    insertSet.Open "news", outpostdb, adOpenDynamic, _
25:        adLockOptimistic, adCmdTable
26:
27:    if p_existing = "" then
28:      insertSet.AddNew
29:    else
30:        insertSet.Find "news_id =" & p_existing
31:    end if
32:    insertSet("news_id") = p_news_id
```

continues

Listing 8.15—continued

```
33:    insertSet("news_cat_id") = p_news_cat_id
34:    insertSet("news_headline") = p_news_headline
35:    insertSet("news_blurb") = p_news_blurb
36:    insertSet("news_url") = p_news_url
37:    insertSetUpdate
38:    insertSet.Close
39:    set insertSet = Nothing
40:
41:    outpostDB.Close
42:    set outpostDB = Nothing
43:
44:    Response.Clear
45:    Response.Redirect "http://localhost/edit_news.asp"
46:else
47:
48:    Response.Write "You do not have access to this page."
49:
50:end if
51:%>
52:</BODY>
53:</HTML>
```

Except for changing the names and accommodating the news_cat_id field, we really only added three lines to this page, but they make all the difference in the world.

On line 8, we're creating an instance of the Upload object, the third-party component that will handle the information we've told the browser to send. Line 9 is where we're actually doing the work, asking it to Save. Until we do that, we won't be able to get at any of the information, including the file.

When we tell the Upload object to Save, it looks through all of the content and headers that were sent to the server and picks out the files and the rest of the form data. We could even, if we wanted, send multiple files at one time by creating more than one file element to our form. The Upload object will then save them in whatever directory we've specified on line 9.

It would seem that that was all we had to do, but that's not quite true. Because of the encoding we used—multipart-formdata—the rest of our form elements aren't available to the normal Request.form object. Fortunately, the Upload object takes care of that, basically replacing Request.form with Upload.form, so we can still get at our data.

Finally, on line 18, we destroy the Upload object. We've saved the data from it, so we can destroy it and and save our data to the database as usual.

Here's a question, though: If Upload saves the file with it's original name (which it will) and also enables us to retrieve that name (which it does, using Upload.files().path), why did we bother to include a field for our administrator to enter a filename? Wouldn't it just make more sense for them to upload it directly to it's final location and be done with it?

The answer is a definite sometimes. If we were to go that route, the file would have to be completely prepared, including headers and footers, before it was uploaded. There's nothing wrong with that if we have a low volume of material and an administrator with time to spare. Of course, we'd never be able to use that file in any other way, say, as a compilation of some sort.

But what if we could upload a plain text file and have the server do the rest of the work for us? That's what we'll talk about next.

Creating Files on the Server: Formatting the News

So far, except for the file we just uploaded, any information we've been storing has been in the database. Now we're going to look at actually writing to the hard drive on the server.

The task at hand is to take the raw file that we uploaded in the last section and use it to create a formatted news file. The best way to do this—and the way requiring the least hassle for maintenance—would be to create a file that has our header and footer and a Server Side Include for the raw file in the middle.

To do this, we're going to use the fileSystemObject object. Yes, that's really what it's called. The fileSystemObject is part of the Scripting object we saw when we were creating a dictionary. The fileSystemObject has everything we need to manipulate, read, and write files, directories, and pretty much anything else we need to do on the disk.

That's lot of complexity, though, so let's start small. All we want to do is create a text file, write to it, and close it.

Add the code in Listing 8.16 to edit_news_rec_action.asp.

Listing 8.16—edit_news_rec_action.asp: Writing a text file

```
0: <%@ LANGUAGE="VBSCRIPT" %>
1: <% Response.buffer = true  %>
2: <!--#include file="adovbs.inc"-->
3: <!--#include file="pagetop.txt"-->
4: <!--#include file="isadmin.inc"-->
5: <%
6: if isAdmin then
```

continues

Listing 8.16—continued

```
7:
8:      set Upload = Server.CreateObject("PersitsUpload.1")
9:      Upload.Save("c:\inetpub\wwwroot")
10:
11:     p_news_id = cint(Upload.form("p_news_id"))
12:     p_news_cat_id = cint(Upload.form("p_news_cat_id"))
13:     p_news_headline = cstr(Upload.form("p_headline"))
14:     p_news_blurb = cstr(Upload.form("p_blurb"))
15:     p_news_url = cstr(Upload.form("p_url"))
16:     p_existing = cstr(Upload.form("p_existing"))
17:
18:     p_subfile_name = Upload.Files(1).Path
19:     p_subfile_name = replace(p_subfile_name, _
20:                                   "c:\inetpub\wwwroot\", "")
21:
22:     set newFileObject = _
23:             Server.CreateObject("Scripting.FileSystemObject")
24:     set newFile = _
25:             newFileObject.CreateTextFile("c:\inetpub\wwwroot\" _
26:                                            & p_news_url)
27:
28:     newFile.WriteLine("<!--#include file=" &chr(34)& _
29:                               "pagetop.txt" &chr(34)& "-->")
30:     newFile.WriteLine("<!--#include file=" &chr(34)& _
31:                               p_subfile_name &chr(34)& "-->")
32:     newFile.WriteLine("<!--#include file=" &chr(34)& _
33:                               "pagebottom.txt" &chr(34)& "-->")
34:     newFile.Close
35:
36:     set newFile = Nothing
37:     set newFileObject = Nothing
38:
39:     set Upload = Nothing
40:
41:     set outpostDB = Server.CreateObject("ADODB.Connection")
42:     outpostDB.Open "outpost"
43:
44:     set insertSet = Server.CreateObject("ADODB.RecordSet")
45:     insertSet.Open "news", outpostdb, adOpenDynamic, _
46:         adLockOptimistic, adCmdTable
47:
48:     if p_existing = "" then
49:         insertSet.AddNew
50:     else
51:         insertSet.Find "news_id =" & p_existing
52:     end if
53:     insertSet("news_id") = p_news_id
54:     insertSet("news_cat_id") = p_news_cat_id
55:     insertSet("news_headline") = p_news_headline
56:     insertSet("news_blurb") = p_news_blurb
57:     insertSet("news_url") = p_news_url
58:     insertSetUpdate
```

```
59:    insertSet.Close
60:    set insertSet = Nothing
61:
62:    outpostDB.Close
63:    set outpostDB = Nothing
64:
65:    Response.Clear
66:    Response.Redirect "http://localhost/edit_news.asp"
67:else
68:
69:    Response.Write "You do not have access to this page."
70:
71:end if
72:%>
73:</BODY>
74:</HTML>
```

On line 18, we're recording the complete path of the first file uploaded, including the drive and directory information. It's also the only file we uploaded, but we still need to specify a number. On line 19, we're stripping out the path information by replacing it with an empty string, so that all we are left with is the name.

On line 22, we're actually creating the fileSystemObject. Even though we're not using it directly, we still need to create it so we can create other things, such as the new file, from it.

After we've got the fileSystemObject, on line 23 we're using it to create a new file. We've specified the path, including the name that we pulled from the form. This gives us the location where the browser will be expecting to find the file.

> **Note**
>
> Remember that c:\inetpub\wwwroot\ is our home directory. If you've got your home directory somewhere else, make the changes accordingly.

After we've created the file, it's a simple matter of writing to it, which we do on lines 28 through 33. All we really need are three lines: the top, the content, and the bottom. So for a new filename of fanfic.asp and an old filename of fannominations.txt, the new file would be at

C:\inetpub\wwwroot\fanfic.asp

and would read like this:

```
<!--#include file="pagetop.txt"-->
<!--#include file="fannominations.txt" -->
<!--#include file="pagebottom.txt"-->
```

After we've written those lines, we can close the text file on line 34, and then close and destroy the fileSystemObject objects and the Upload object.

8

This is great, but what if all the administrator wants to do is change the database information and not re-upload the file? We wouldn't want to replace a perfectly good file with an empty one. To get around this, we can check to see whether there was a file uploaded and only write out the new news file if there was. Add the changes in Listing 8.17 to edit_news_rec_action.asp.

Listing 8.17—edit_news_rec_action.asp: Checking for an uploaded file

```
 …
 8:   set Upload = Server.CreateObject("PersitsUpload.1")
 9:   p_count = Upload.Save("c:\inetpub\wwwroot")
10:
11:   p_news_id = cint(Upload.form("p_news_id"))
12:   p_news_cat_id = cint(Upload.form("p_news_cat_id"))
13:   p_news_headline = cstr(Upload.form("p_headline"))
14:   p_news_blurb = cstr(Upload.form("p_blurb"))
15:   p_news_url = cstr(Upload.form("p_url"))
16:   p_existing = cstr(Upload.form("p_existing"))
17:
18:   if p_count = 1 then
19:       p_subfile_name = Upload.Files(1).Path
20:       p_subfile_name = replace(p_subfile_name, "c:\inetpub\wwwroot\", "")
21:       fileUploaded = true
22:   else
23:       fileUploaded = false
24:   end if
25:
26:   if fileUploaded then
27:       set newFileObject = _
28:           Server.CreateObject("Scripting.FileSystemObject")
29:       set newFile = _
30:           newFileObject.CreateTextFile("c:\inetpub\wwwroot\" _
31:                                                 & p_news_url)
32:
33:       newFile.WriteLine("<!--#include file=" &chr(34)& _
34:                               "pagetop.txt" &chr(34)& "-->")
35:       newFile.WriteLine("<!--#include file=" &chr(34)& _
36:                               p_subfile_name &chr(34)& "-->")
37:       newFile.WriteLine("<!--#include file=" &chr(34)& _
38:                               "pagebottom.txt" &chr(34)& "-->")
39:       newFile.Close
40:
41:       set newFile = Nothing
42:       set newFileObject = Nothing
43:   end if
44:
45:   set Upload = Nothing
46:
 …
```

Whether we collect it, as we're doing on line 9, `Upload.Save` will return the number of files that were uploaded. This way, we can check and create the new file or not accordingly.

Before we move on to reading files, we do have two loose ends to clean up with regards to the news. We can add a file, and we can change and delete the database entries for the file, but we haven't considered how to remove or change the names of the files that we have on the filesystem already.

 The *filesystem* is made up of the local and remote disk drives attached to a computer.

Let's take a look at the logic first, and then we'll worry about how to do it. Add the code in Listing 8.18 to `edit_news_rec_action.asp`.

Listing 8.18—edit_news_rec_action.asp: Preparing to delete or rename files

```
...
44:  set insertSet = Server.CreateObject("ADODB.RecordSet")
45:  insertSet.Open "news", outpostdb, adOpenDynamic, _
46:      adLockOptimistic, adCmdTable
47:
48:  if p_existing = "" then
49:      insertSet.AddNew
50:  else
51:      insertSet.Find "news_id =" & p_existing
52:      if insertSet("news_url") <> p_news_url then
53:          if fileUploaded then
54:              'DELETE OLD FILE
55:          else
55:              'RENAME OLD FILE
57:          end if
58:      end if
59:  end if
60:  insertSet("news_id") = p_news_id
61:  insertSet("news_cat_id") = p_news_cat_id
62:  insertSet("news_headline") = p_news_headline
63:  insertSet("news_blurb") = p_news_blurb
64:  insertSet("news_url") = p_news_url
65:  insertSetUpdate
66:  insertSet.Close
67:  set insertSet = Nothing
...
```

There is only one time when this is going to matter: when we're editing an existing record, *and* we've changed the name of the final file. Otherwise, there's no old file to change or delete.

So let's say that we are updating an existing record, and we've changed the name. This leads us to another fork in the road. Either we've uploaded a new file, in which case we need to delete the old one, or we haven't, in which case we just want to change the name on the old one. Add the changes in Listing 8.19 to `edit_news_rec_action.asp`.

Listing 8.19—edit_news_rec_action.asp: Deleting or changing files

```
...
48:  if p_existing = "" then
49:     insertSet.AddNew
50:  else
51:     insertSet.Find "news_id =" & p_existing
52:     if insertSet("news_url") <> p_news_url then
53:
54:         p_oldFilePath = "c:\inetpub\wwwroot\"& insertSet("news_url")
55:         p_newFilePath = "c:\inetpub\wwwroot\"& p_news_url
56:
57:         set oldFileObject = Server.CreateObject("Scripting.FileSystemObject")
58:         if oldFileObject.fileExists(p_oldFilePath) then
59:             if fileUploaded then
60:                 oldFileObject.DeleteFile(p_oldFilePath)
61:             else
62:                 oldFileObject.MoveFile p_oldFilePath, p_newFilePath
63:             end if
64:         end if
65:         set oldFileObject = Nothing
66:     end if
67:  end if
...
```

So if we are going to have to do anything, we're going to need to know what we're moving (or deleting) and to where (if anywhere). On lines 54 and 55, we're setting the old and new path information, from the database and the form respectively. On line 57, we're creating the actual `fileSystemObject` that's going to do the work.

Before we try and do anything, we need to account for the possibility that the old file has already been cleaned up, so on line 58, we'll check to see if it still exists. If it doesn't, we won't do anything.

If it does exist, we need to handle it. If it's already been replaced, we need to delete it, and we'll do that on line 60. If we're just renaming, we'll do that on line 62 by "moving" the file. Even though they're both in the same place, it's still referred to as moving the file, only it's from one name to the other instead of one directory to the other.

That takes care of our loose ends in `edit_news_rec_action.asp`. No matter what happens, our file should be right. Now we just have to delete a file when we remove the reference to it in `edit_news_action.asp` (see Listing 8.20).

Listing 8.20—edit_news_action.asp: Deleting a file that's no longer in use

```
 0: <%@ LANGUAGE="VBSCRIPT" %>
 1: <% Response.buffer = true  %>
 2: <!--#include file="adovbs.inc"-->
 3: <!--#include file="pagetop.txt"-->
 4: <!--include file="isadmin.inc"-->
 5: <%
 6: if isAdmin then
 7:
 8:     set outpostDB = Server.CreateObject("ADODB.Connection")
 9:     outpostDB.Open "outpost"
10:
11:     set deleteSet = Server.CreateObject("ADODB.RecordSet")
12:     deleteSet.Open "select * from news order by news_id", _
13:         outpostDB, adOpenDynamic, adLockPessimistic, adCmdText
14:     p_thisDelete = 1
15:     while not deleteSet.EOF
16:         if cint(deleteSet("news_id")) = _
17:           cint(Request.form("p_delete").item(p_thisDelete)) then
18:
19:             set oldFileObject = _
20:               Server.CreateObject("Scripting.FileSystemObject")
21:             p_oldFilePath = _
22:               "c:\inetpub\wwwroot\"& deleteSet("news_url")
23:             if oldFileObject.fileExists(p_oldFilePath) then
24:                 oldFileObject.DeleteFile(p_oldFilePath)
25:             end if
26:             set oldFileObject = Nothing
27:
28:             deleteSet.Delete
29:             deleteSet.Update
30:             if p_thisDelete < Request.form("p_delete").Count then
31:                 p_thisDelete = p_thisDelete + 1
32:             end if
33:         end if
34:         deleteSet.MoveNext
35:     wend
36:     deleteSet.Close
37:     set deleteSet = Nothing
38:
39:     outpostDB.Close
40:     set outpostDB = Nothing
41:
42:     Response..Clear
43:     Response.Redirect "http://localhost/edit_news.asp"
44:else
45:
46:     Response.Write "You do not have access to this page."
47:
48:end if
49:%>
50:</BODY>
51:</HTML>
```

This is exactly the same code we used in the previous example, except that we've changed `insertSet` to `deleteSet` and we don't need to worry about renaming the file.

So we can now add, update, and delete information not only in the database but on the filesystem itself.

Reading a File: Importing Product Data

Strictly speaking, the file we created earlier wasn't really a file at all. It was actually a `TextStream` object that created a file. Now we are going to look at how to create a file object that will enable us to read in data from a file and insert that data into the database.

The first thing that we are going to do is actually create the file. We're going to start in Excel or another spreadsheet application, but our ultimate goal is a tab-delimited text file, so don't worry if you don't have one.

It's very common to find that the data you either have or want to have in your database started life as a spreadsheet. Because they're easy to use and nontechnical people can update them themselves, this is often the chosen means of maintenance for small to moderate amounts of data. (Not to say that it's the best way, just that its how life currently works.)

Start up your spreadsheet and create a file that lists our products. The format is like this (see Figure 8.5):

Prod_id	Prod_name	Prod_desc	Price	Image	Category1	Category2

Figure 8.5

Our sample product import file.

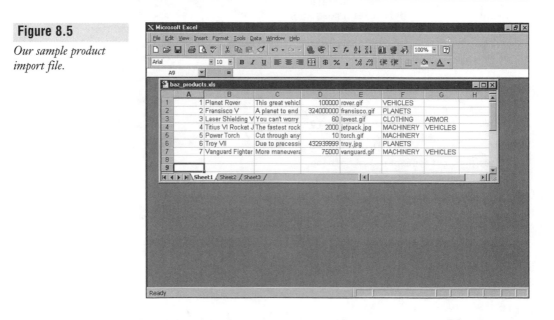

First comes the product information, and then any number of categories, listed by name.

After the spreadsheet is finished, go to File, Save As and save it as a tab-delimited text file. If it tells you that you can't save multiple sheets in this format, tell it you only want the current sheet.

Folders and Subfolders: Moving around in the Filesystem

Now that we have our import file, we're ready to start building our utility. We're going to start by assuming that the import file can be anywhere on any local or remote drive. We're going to build a utility that will allow us to drill down through drives and directories until we find the proper file. At that point we will click the file and it will be imported. The first thing we need to do is find out what drive it's on, so copy `admintemplate.asp` to `importstart.asp` and add the code in Listing 8.21.

Listing 8.21—importstart.asp: Listing available drives

```
0: <%@ LANGUAGE="VBSCRIPT" %>
1: <!--#include file="adovbs.inc"-->
2: <!--#include file="pagetop.txt"-->
3: <!--#include file="isadmin.inc"-->
4: <%
5: if isAdmin then
6: %>
7: <H1>Choose a Drive</H1>
8:
9: <% set fsObject = Server.CreateObject("Scripting.FileSystemObject")
10:
11:   for each driveObj in fsObject.Drives
12:%>    <A HREF="importstart.asp?p_drive=<%=driveObj.driveLetter%>">
13:      <%=driveObj.driveLetter%>
14:    </A><BR>
15:<% next
16:
17:   set fsObject = Nothing
18:else
19:
20:   Response.Write "You do not have access to this page."
21:
22:end if
23:%>
24:</BODY>
25:</HTML>
```

On line 9, we're creating a new `fileSystemObject`, `fsObject`. The same way that a RecordSet has a collection of fields, this object has a collection of drives that includes all of the drives that are available to us. On lines 11 through 15, we are looping through each of these drive objects. This object is actually a wealth of information, including not just the drive letter but the path, type of drive, even how much space is left. We're going to pull the `DriveLetter` property and display it on the page. We're also going to use it to create a link. When we click the link, we want to see all of the folders for the drive in question. Add the new code in Listing 8.22 to `importstart.asp` (see Figure 8.6).

Figure 8.6

Using the `FileSystemObject`, *we can create a page that enables us to navigate through our hard drive via the browser.*

> **Note**
>
> Obviously this is not something that we would want to make available to the general public! Make sure that you protect these pages using at least one of the security methods we discussed earlier.

Listing 8.22—importstart.asp: Choose a directory

```
0: <%@ LANGUAGE="VBSCRIPT" %>
1: <!--#include file="adovbs.inc"-->
2: <!--#include file="pagetop.txt"-->
3: <!--#include file="isadmin.inc"-->
4: <%
5: if isAdmin then
6:
7:     set fsObject=Server.CreateObject("Scripting.FileSystemObject")
8:
9:     p_drive = Request.querystring("p_drive")
0:
11:    if p_drive = "" then
12:%>
13:        <H1>Choose a Drive</H1>
```

```
14:
15:<%        for each driveObj in fsObject.Drives
16:%>            <A HREF="importstart.asp?p_drive=<%
16a:                    Response.Write driveObj.driveLetter%>">
17:             <%=driveObj.driveLetter%>
18:             </A><BR>
19:<%        next
20:        else
21:%>
22:            <H1>Choose a Directory</H1>
23:            <A HREF="importstart.asp">Top Level</A><P>
24:
25:<%        set driveObj = fsObject.getDrive(p_drive)
26:
27:            set folderObj = driveObj.RootFolder
28:
29:            for each subFolderObj in folderObj.subFolders
30:                p_subFolder = Server.URLEncode(subFolderObj.path)
31:%>                <A HREF="importstart.asp?p_drive=<%
32:                    Response.Write p_drive%>&p_folder=<%
33:                    Response.Write p_subFolder%>">
34:                    <%=subFolderObj.path%>
35:                </A><BR>
36:<%        next
37:            set folderObj = Nothing
38:            set driveObj = Nothing
39:
40:        end if
41:
42:        set fsObject = Nothing
43:else
44:
45:        Response.Write "You do not have access to this page."
46:
47:end if
48:%>
49:</BODY>
50:</HTML>
```

On line 11, we're checking to see if we've arrived at this page because our administrator has picked a drive. If we have, we certainly don't need to list them all over again. Instead, we can use that drive letter to create a drive object on line 25. That drive object has a root folder—the top level for that drive. This is a Folder object.

A Folder object has lots of properties that we can access, such as the size, parent folder, and date of last access. We're going to make use of the subFolders property, which is actually a collection of more Folder objects.

On lines 29 through 36, we're looping through all of the subfolders in the root folder, creating links that will drill down for us. The idea is that after we've specified a drive, we need to specify a directory. Because we're going to include the path in the URL on lines 31 through 35, we need to URLEncode it.

This will give us a list of the folders at the top level of the drive, but what we really want to do is drill down into the folders to find our file. Add the new code in Listing 8.23 to importstart.asp.

Listing 8.23—importstart.asp: Drilling down through subfolders

```
...
22:    <H1>Choose a Directory</H1>
23:    <A HREF="importstart.asp">Top Level</A><P>
24:
25:<%    set driveObj = fsObject.getDrive(p_drive)
26:
27:    p_folder = Request.querystring("p_folder")
28:    if p_folder = "" then
29:      set FolderObj = driveObj.RootFolder
30:    else
31:        set FolderObj = fsObject.getFolder(p_folder)
32:    end if
33:
34:    for each subFolderObj in FolderObj.subFolders
35:        p_subFolder = Server.URLEncode(subFolderObj.Path)
36:%>        <A HREF="importstart.asp?p_drive=<%
37:            Response.Write p_drive%>&p_folder=<%
38:            Response.Write p_subFolder%>">
39:            <%=subFolderObj.path%>
40:        </A><BR>
41:<%    next
42:    set FolderObj = Nothing
43:    set driveObj = Nothing
...
```

On lines 27 and 28, we're checking for a folder the same way we checked for a drive. If p_folder is empty, it means that we've just come from choosing a drive, so we need the root folder. If not, we can have the fsObject create a folder object out of our path on line 31.

This is great, and will drill down as far as we want, but it doesn't show us any files. Let's go ahead and add the logic, in Listing 8.24, to show us the actual files in importstart.asp.

Listing 8.24—importstart.asp: Listing files in the target directory

```
...
31:    p_folder = Request.querystring("p_folder")
32:    if p_folder = "" then
33:        set FolderObj = driveObj.RootFolder
34:    else
35:        set FolderObj = fsObject.getFolder(p_folder)
36:    end if
37:
```

```
38:%>    <h3>Folders</h3>
39:
40:<%    for each subFolderObj in FolderObj.subFolders
41:        p_subFolder = Server.URLEncode(subFolderObj.Path)
42:%>      <A HREF="importstart.asp?p_drive=<%
43:            Response.Write p_drive%>&p_folder=<%
44:            Response.Write p_subFolder%>">
45:            <%=subFolderObj.path%>
46:        </A><BR>
47:<%    next
48:
49:%>    <h3>Files</h3>
50:
51:<%    for each fileObj in FolderObj.files
52:        p_file = fileObj.name
53:        p_full_path = Server.URLEncode(p_folder & "\" & p_file)
54:%>      <A HREF="importfile.asp?p_full_path=<%=p_full_path%>">
55:            <%=FileObj.name%>
56:        </A><BR>
57:<%    next
58:
59:    set FolderObj = Nothing
60:    set driveObj = Nothing
61:
62:  end if
63:
64:  set fsObject = Nothing
...
```

The same way that we could loop through the subfolders in a folder, on lines 51 through 57 we can loop through the files collection and pull out the names. If we do find the file we want, we want to go to `importfile.asp` and pass it the file's complete path.

We could add some enhancements to this to allow us to move up and down in the hierarchy, and we could use this for anything that requires us to move around looking for files, but for now we'll leave it as-is and work on reading the file now that we've found it.

Reading a File from the Filesystem

Now that we can find the file that we want, we can go ahead and start importing. Copy `admintemplate.asp` to `importfile.asp` and make the modifications shown in Listing 8.25.

Listing 8.25—importfile.asp: Reading the text file

```
0: <%@ LANGUAGE="VBSCRIPT" %>
1: <!--#include file="adovbs.inc"-->
2: <!--#include file="pagetop.txt"-->
3: <!--#include file="isadmin.inc"-->
4: <%
5: if isAdmin then
6:
7:     p_full_path = cstr(Request.querystring("p_full_path"))
8:
9:     set fsObject = Server.CreateObject("Scripting.FileSystemObject")
10:    set importFileObj = fsObject.OpenTextFile(p_full_path)
11:
12:    while not importFileObj.AtEndOfStream
13:
14:        p_product = importFileObj.readLine
15:        Response.Write p_product
16:        Response.Write "<BR>"
17:
18:    wend
19:
20:    set importFile = Nothing
21:    set fsObject = Nothing
22:
23:    set outpostDB = Server.CreateObject("ADODB.Connection")
24:    outpostDB.Open "outpost"
25:
26:
27:    outpostDB.Close
28:    set outpostDB = Nothing
29:else
30:
31:    Response.Write "You do not have access to this page."
32:
33:end if
34:%>
35:</BODY>
36:</HTML>
```

Before we worry about what to do with the data, let's make sure that we can read it.

On line 7, we're extracting the full path of the file from the URL so that we know where to find the file we want to open. On line 10, we're opening the file, or rather a TextStream from the file.

When we were dealing with database tables and RecordSets, we knew we were at the end of the table when we reached the End Of File. So naturally now, when we're dealing with files, it's called something else. This is because again, this is not really a file, it's a stream of text that is coming from a file.

So in the same way that we looped through the database tables, on lines 12 through 18 we're going to loop through the TextStream until we get to the end. What we want to do is literally read each line of the file, and we're doing that on line 14. As we do that, we're storing the value in p_product, which we'll use later.

We're not limited to reading files in order. In fact, we can skip around, read a specific number of characters, even read in the whole file at once. But remember when we created the file, all of the information for a single product was on one line, so we're going to deal with the file one line at a time. When we read the line, the pointer moves to the next line, so we don't have to move it manually like we did with RecordSets.

Now that we've got the information out of the file, let's put it into some sort of useful form. Add the changes in Listing 8.26 to importfile.asp.

Listing 8.26—importfile.asp: Parsing the data

```
0: <%@ LANGUAGE="VBSCRIPT" %>
1: <!--#include file="adovbs.inc"-->
2: <!--#include file="pagetop.txt"-->
3: <!--#include file="isadmin.inc"-->
4: <%
5: if isAdmin then
6:
7:     set outpostDB = Server.CreateObject("ADODB.Connection")
8:     outpostDB.Open "outpost"
9:
10:    p_full_path = cstr(Request.querystring("p_full_path"))
11:
12:    set fsObject=Server.CreateObject("Scripting.FileSystemObject")
13:    set importFileObj = fsObject.OpenTextFile(p_full_path)
14:%>
15:<TABLE>
16:<%
17:    dim p_product_array(10)
18:
19:    while not importFileObj.AtEndOfStream
20:        p_product = importFileObj.readLine
21:
22:        Response.Write "<TR>"
23:
24:        p_count = 1
25:        p_tabPos = instr(p_product, chr(9))
26:
27:        while not p_tabPos = 0
28:
29:            p_product_array(p_count)=left(p_product, p_tabPos-1)
30:            p_product=right(p_product, (len(p_product)-p_tabpos))
31:
32:            Response.Write "<TD>"&p_product_array(p_count)&"</TD>"
```

continues

Listing 8.26—continued

```
33:
34:             p_count = p_count + 1
35:             p_tabPos = instr(p_product, chr(9))
36:         wend
37:
38:         p_product_array(p_count) = p_product
39:         Response.Write "<TD>"&p_product_array(p_count)&"</TD>"
40:
41:         Response.Write "</TR>"
42:     wend
43:%>
44:</TABLE>
45:
46:<%  set importFile = Nothing
47:     set fsObject = Nothing
48:
49:     outpostDB.Close
50:     set outpostDB = Nothing
51:else
52:
53:     Response.Write "You do not have access to this page."
54:
55:end if
56:%>
57:</BODY>
58:</HTML>
```

Taking things in steps, our next goal is going to be just printing the information so we can be sure we're parsing it correctly. To make things easier to see, let's put it into an HTML table.

For each line in the file, we're going to go through and pull out the individual tab-delimited elements and place them into an array. In a little while, we'll put them in the database, but for now we'll just print them.

Because we're eventually going to need to deal with each of the elements on the line, on line 17, we've created the array to hold the individual pieces of data. Because we've created it with a dimension of 10, we can only put 11 elements in it (0 through 10).

To keep track of which array element we're up to, we've got the variable p_count. As we process each element, we'll increment p_count, so before we start processing each line of the file, we re-initialize p_count to 1. We do that on line 24.

Line 25 is where we start parsing the information. The ASCII code for a tab is 9, so chr(9) represents a tab. So the function instr (or in string) is going to return us the position of the first tab in the string, and a 0 if there aren't any tabs.

If we find a tab on line 25, we know we need to go through the entire line. We're going to keep looping as long as we keep finding tabs.

Each time we find one, we need to take all the characters up to that tab and put them into the current element of the array. We do that on line 29. For instance, if we found a tab as the tenth character in the string, the `left()` function will give us, in this case, the first 9 characters—everything up to but not including the tab.

Of course, after we've done that, we need to strip that information off so we don't read it again. We do that using the `right()` function to pull off only the characters after the tab. We do that on line 30.

On line 32, we're just printing out our current element; then on 34 and 35 we're getting ready for the next loop, checking to see if there are any more tabs.

After the last tab has been removed, there is a possibility of having one last element that wasn't followed by a tab. So the last thing that we're doing, on line 38 after we've finished the loop, is to save that last piece of information.

So if we have five fields of information and two categories, we will be looking at an array with seven elements in it, each containing a piece of information we need to put into the database.

But what if we have more than 11 elements? We can't add them all to the array as-is, and because of the way that we declared the array, we can't extend it. But we still have options in `importfile.asp` (see Listing 8.27).

Listing 8.27—importfile.asp: Extending the array

```
...
15:<TABLE>
16:<%
17:   dim p_product_array()
18:   p_max = 10
19:   redim preserve p_product_array(p_max)
20:
21:   while not importFileObj.AtEndOfStream
22:     Response.Write "<TR>"
23:     p_product = importFileObj.readLine
24:
25:     p_count = 1
26:     p_tabPos = instr(p_product, chr(9))
27:     while not p_tabPos = 0
28:
29:       if p_count > p_max then
30:         p_max = p_max + 10
31:         redim preserve p_product_array(p_max)
32:       end if
33:
34:       p_product_array(p_count)=left(p_product, p_tabPos-1)
```

continues

Listing 8.27—continued

```
35:        p_product=right(p_product, (len(p_product)-p_tabpos))
36:
37:        Response.Write "<TD>"&p_product_array(p_count)&"</TD>"
38:
39:        p_count = p_count + 1
40:        p_tabPos = instr(p_product, chr(9))
41:    wend
42:
43:    p_product_array(p_count) = p_product
44:    Response.Write "<TD>"&p_product_array(p_count)&"</TD>"
45:
46:    Response.Write "</TR>"
47: wend
48:%>
49:</TABLE>
...
```

If we assign a size to an array when we first declare it, we're stuck with it. This is called a static array. But we can declare an open-ended, or dynamic array, which will enable us to set the size as we see fit. In this case, we've set a variable to help us keep track of the longest line, p_max. We start it at 10, but in lines 29 through 32, we bump it up as necessary, redimensioning the array as we go. So no matter how long a line is, the array will accommodate it. We do have to tell ASP that we want to preserve the current contents of the array on line 31, though, or it'll get wiped out each time.

So now we have an array of data, and it doesn't matter how big it gets, it will just adjust itself. Now we're ready to put it into the database. Add the new code in Listing 8.28 to importfile.asp.

Listing 8.28—importfile.asp: Adding the database to the database

```
...
12:   set fsObject=Server.CreateObject("Scripting.FileSystemObject")
13:   set importFileObj = fsObject.OpenTextFile(p_full_path)
14:
15:   outpostDB.Execute("delete * from baz_products")
16:   outpostDB.Execute("delete * from baz_product_categories")
17:
18:   set insertSet = Server.CreateObject("ADODB.RecordSet")
19:   insertSet.Open "baz_products", outpostDB, adOpenDymamic, _
20:       adLockPessimistic, adCmdTable
21:
22:   set catSet = Server.CreateObject("ADODB.RecordSet")
23:   catSet.Open "baz_categories", outpostDB, adOpenStatic, _
24:       adLockReadOnly, adCmdTable
25:
```

```
26:    set prodCatSet = Server.CreateObject("ADODB.RecordSet")
27:    prodCatSet.Open "baz_product_categories", outpostDB, _
28:        adOpenDynamic, adLockPessimistic, adCmdTable
29:
30:    dim p_product_array()
31:    p_max = 10
32:    Redim p_product_array(p_max)
33:
34:    while not importFileObj.AtEndOfStream
35:        p_product = importFileObj.readLine
36:
37:        p_count = 1
38:        p_tabPos = instr(p_product, chr(9))
39:        while not p_tabPos = 0
40:
41:            if p_count > p_max then
42:                p_max = p_max + 10
43:                redim preserve p_product_array(p_max)
44:        end if
45:
46:        p_product_array(p_count)=left(p_product,p_tabPos-1)
47:        p_product=right(p_product, (len(p_product)-p_tabpos))
48:
49:        p_count = p_count + 1
50:        p_tabPos = instr(p_product, chr(9))
51:    wend
52:    p_product_array(p_count) = p_product
53:
54:    insertSet.AddNew
55:    insertSet("prod_id") = p_product_array(1)
56:    insertSet("prod_name") = p_product_array(2)
57:    insertSet("prod_desc") = p_product_array(3)
58:    insertSet("prod_price") = p_product_array(4)
59:    insertSet("prod_image") = p_product_array(5)
60:    insertSetUpdate
61:
62:    for p_catNum = 6 to p_count
63:        if p_product_array(p_catNum) <> "" then
64:          catSet.MoveFirst
65:          catSet.Find "cat_name= '" & _
66:              p_product_array(p_catNum)&"'"
67:
68:          if catSet.EOF then
69:              'This record is a reject
70:          else
71:              prodCatSet.AddNew
72:              prodCatSet("prod_id") = p_product_array(1)
73:              prodCatSet("cat_id") = catSet("cat_id")
74:              prodCatSet.Update
75:          end if
```

8

continues

Listing 8.28—continued

```
76:      end if
77:  next
78:
79:    wend
80:
81:    prodCatSet.Close
82:    set prodCatSet = Nothing
83:
84:    catSet.Close
85:    set catSet = Nothing
86:
87:    insertSet.Close
88:    set insertSet = Nothing
89:
90:    set importFile = Nothing
91:    set fsObject = Nothing
92:
93:    outpostDB.Close
94:    set outpostDB = Nothing
95:  else
96:
97:    Response.Write "You do not have access to this page."
98:
99:  end if
100:%>
101:</BODY>
102:</HTML>
```

We're assuming that all maintenance of products is going to be done through the spreadsheet, so we don't need to save any of the old information in the database. In fact, we need to get rid of it, which we do on lines 15 and 16.

> **Note**
> Obviously this could be a huge problem if the delete succeeds and for some reason the load doesn't. We'll deal with that kind of issue in the next section. Also, in a real world application, we would probably delete records as we replaced them, so we wouldn't wind up with orphaned products in orders.

After we've cleared the old data, on lines 18 through 28 we create three RecordSets. Two of them, insertSet and prodCatSet, are for inserting data, and the third, catSet, is there just for looking up category IDs because the spreadsheet uses category names.

On lines 54 through 60, we're inserting the product data. This is pretty straightforward because we know what the fields are and where they are in the array.

Creating the product-category associations is a little tougher, however.

Fortunately for us, we know exactly how many elements are in the array because we still have p_count. Unfortunately for us, the last element could just as easily be an empty string, which can cause us problems if we're not careful. On line 63 we're accounting for empty strings by simply not processing them. Lines 64 through 66 find the category that corresponds to the name in the spreadsheet.

Finally, if the category does exist, we know that everything is all right, and we add the association between the product and the category on lines 71 through 74. But because we're not doing any sort of validation in the spreadsheet, there's always the possibility that someone has mistyped the name of a category, or tried to put in a category that just doesn't exist. We're going to have to handle those rejects. We take care of that with the new code in Listing 8.29. Add it to `importfile.asp`.

Listing 8.29—importfile.asp: Handling non-existent categories

```
...
62:    for p_catNum = 6 to p_count
63:       if p_product_array(p_catNum) <> "" then
64:          catSet.MoveFirst
65:          catSet.Find "cat_name = '" & _
66:             p_product_array(p_catNum)&"'"
67:
68:          if catSet.EOF then
69:             errorMsg = errorMsg & "Import Error: <BR>"
70:             errorMsg = errorMsg & "Product ID = "
71:             errorMsg = errorMsg & _
72:                p_product_array(1) & "<BR>"
73:             errorMsg = errorMsg & "Proposed Category = "
74:             errorMsg = errorMsg & _
75:                p_product_array(p_catNum)&"<P>"
76:             errorsEncountered= true
77:          else
78:             prodCatSet.AddNew
79:             prodCatSet("prod_id") = p_product_array(1)
80:             prodCatSet("cat_id") = catSet("cat_id")
81:             prodCatSetUpdate
82:          end if
83:       end if
84:    next
85:
86:  wend
87:
88: %>
89:    <H1>Products Imported</H1>
90:
91:    The product file has been loaded.<P>
92:
93: <%
```

continues

Listing 8.29—continued

```
94:    if errorsEncountered then
95: %>
96:        Some errors were encountered. Please correct the
97:        spreadsheet and re-import.<P>
98:        <%= errorMsg %>
99: <%
100:  end if
101:
102:  prodCatSet.Close
103:  set prodCatSet = Nothing
104:
105:  catSet.Close
106:  set catSet = Nothing
...
```

Instead of printing out the problems right away when we can't find a category on line 68, we're saving the message on lines 69 through 76 to run later, when we give a final status report, which lists the products that were a problem and their respective categories. The final status report on lines 96 through 98 could also show how many records were imported or give other information as well, but the important thing is that it's useful to the person who's doing the importing. If there are errors, tell the user how to correct them!

Obviously there's much more that can go wrong in an import like this than just not being able to find a category. We could have duplicate product numbers, or text where only numbers should go, and so on. Lots of things can go wrong. Fortunately ASP provides us with a fairly elegant way of detecting and dealing with errors.

In real life, we would need to add error checking to this page and deal with the fact that if the delete succeeds and the import doesn't, we now have a blank product table. We're going to deal with these issues in the context of our credit card transactions, where there's money involved, and not just elbow grease.

Before we deal with that, however, let's look at one more way to pass data into and out of the database.

The Next Big Thing: eXtensible Markup Language

Earlier we discussed Custom Style Sheets and how they enabled the developer set the appearance of specific tags, freeing us up to use the proper structural HTML instead of jury-rigging for appearance's sake.

Extensible Markup Language (XML) takes this one step farther. In XML, everything is described by generic structure tags, and the browser uses an eXtensible Style Sheet

(XSL) to determine their appearance. This is still an emerging standard, however, and the existence and level of sophistication of this XML parser varies wildly from browser to browser.

If XML were only being used for displaying text, we might not even mention it here. Instead, it has a more important use as a way of storing data that can then be accessed by any system.

If we wanted to format our product information as XML, for example, it would look something like Listing 8.29b.

Listing 8.29b—products.xml: The product structure in XML

```
<PRODUCTS>
    <PRODUCT>
        <PRODUCT_ID>1</PRODUCT_ID>
        <NAME>Planet Rover</NAME>
        <DESCRIPTION>Simply the best, most reliable vehicle on the
            market.</DESCRIPTION>
        <PRICE>100000</PRICE>
        <IMAGE>rover.gif</IMAGE>
    </PRODUCT>
    <PRODUCT>
        <PRODUCT_ID>2</PRODUCT_ID>
        <NAME>Fransisco V</NAME>
        <DESCRIPTION>This planet has perfect weather everywhere, at
            all times.</DESCRIPTION>
        <PRICE>324000000</PRICE>
        <IMAGE> fransisco.gif</IMAGE>
    </PRODUCT>
     <PRODUCT>
        <PRODUCT_ID>3</PRODUCT_ID>
        <NAME>Laser Shielding Vest</NAME>
        <DESCRIPTION>Take the worry out of intergalactic trade with this
            premium laser sheilding vest.</DESCRIPTION>
        <PRICE>324000000</PRICE>
        <IMAGE> fransisco.gif</IMAGE>
    </PRODUCT>
</PRODUCTS>
```

In this case the entity that we're looking at is products. Each item is a product, and each product has attributes, such as the product_id or price.

If we knew that the user's browser supported it, we could allow the browser to handle formatting the XML, as in Listing 8.29c.

8

Listing 8.29c—simplexml.htm

```
0: <HTML>
1: <HEAD><TITLE>Outpost Product Catalog</TITLE></HEAD>
2: <BODY>
3: <XML ID="Products">
4: <?xml version="1.0" ?>
5: <PRODUCTS>
6:     <PRODUCT>
7:         <PRODUCT_ID>1</PRODUCT_ID>
8:         <NAME>Planet Rover</NAME>
9:         <DESCRIPTION>Simply the best, most reliable vehicle on
10:             the market.</DESCRIPTION>
11:         <PRICE>100000</PRICE>
12:         <IMAGE>rover.gif</IMAGE>
13:     </PRODUCT>
14:     <PRODUCT>
15:         <PRODUCT_ID>2</PRODUCT_ID>
16:         <NAME>Fransisco V</NAME>
17:         <DESCRIPTION>This planet has perfect weather everywhere,
18:             at all times.</DESCRIPTION>
19:         <PRICE>324000000</PRICE>
20:         <IMAGE> fransisco.gif</IMAGE>
21:     </PRODUCT>
22:     <PRODUCT>
23:         <PRODUCT_ID>3</PRODUCT_ID>
24:         <NAME>Laser Shielding Vest</NAME>
25:         <DESCRIPTION>Take the worry out of intergalactic trade with
26:             this premium laser sheilding vest.</DESCRIPTION>
27:         <PRICE>324000000</PRICE>
28:         <IMAGE> fransisco.gif</IMAGE>
29:     </PRODUCT>
30:</PRODUCTS>
31:</XML>
32:<H1>Outpost Products</H1>
33:<TABLE DATASRC="#Products">
34:   <TR>
35:      <TD><DIV DATAFLD="PRODUCT"></DIV></TD>
36:      <TD><DIV DATAFLD="NAME"></DIV></TD>
37:      <TD><DIV DATAFLD="DESCRIPTION"></DIV></TD>
38:      <TD><DIV DATAFLD="PRICE"></DIV></TD>
39:      <TD><DIV DATAFLD="IMAGE"></DIV></TD>
40:   </TR>
41:</TABLE>
42:</BODY>
43:</HTML>
```

Lines 3 through 31 are the XML, which has been assigned an ID of Product. This allows us to set this section as the data source for the table on line 33. On lines 35 through 39, the table populates each cell with the appropriate attribute of the product element.

This is fairly straightforward, but unless we are in a controlled environment such as an Intranet, we can't guarantee that the browser will support this. Another option would be to transform the XML into HTML on the server side and simply pass the HTML back to the browser. We can do that with an Active Server Page such as `product_table.asp`, shown in Listing 8.29d.

Listing 8.29d—product_table.asp: Transforming XML on the server

```
0: <%@ LANGUAGE="VBSCRIPT" %>
1: <!--#include file="adovbs.inc"-->
2: <!--#include virtual="/pagetop.txt"-->
3: <%
4:     p_product_file = Server.Mappath("products.xml")
5:     p_product_style = Server.Mappath("products.xsl")
6:
7:     set xmlPage = Server.CreateObject("Microsoft.XMLDOM")
8:     xmlPage.load(p_product_file)
9:
10:    set xmlStyle = Server.CreateObject("Microsoft.XMLDOM")
11:    xmlStyle = load(p_product_style)
12:
13:    Response.Write xmlPage.transformNode(xmlStyle)
14:
15:<!--#include virtual="/pagebottom.txt"-->
16:</BODY>
17:</HTML>
```

On lines 4 and 5 we're creating variables that hold the full paths to our files. Server.Mappath takes a virtual path such as "products.xml" and translates it into a physical path, such as "`C:\inetpub\wwwroot\products.xml`". On lines 7 through 11 we're loading each file into an eXtensible Markup Language Document Object Model (XMLDOM). The transformation happens on line 13, when the `xmlPage` is transformed using the `xmlStyle`.

Note

The Microsoft.XMLDOM object is part of the Microsoft Internet Explorer 5.0 XML implementation. Since Windows 2000 comes with IE5 pre-installed, it is available to you in IIS5.0 without further efforts, but if you are using an earlier operating system or server you will need to install IE5.

To use this method, we will need the .xml and .xsl files, however. We created `products.xml` in Listing 8.29b. Listing 8.29e shows `products.xsl`.

8

Listing 8.29e—products.xsl: Formatting products

```
0: <?xml version="1.0"?>
1: <xsl:stylesheet xmlns:xsl="http://www.w3.org/TR/WD-xsl">
2:     <xsl:template match="/">
3:       <xsl:for-each select="PRODUCTS/PRODUCT">
4:         <DIV><xsl:value-of select="PRODUCT_ID"/>:
5:         <xsl:value-of select="NAME"/></DIV>
6:         <DIV><xsl:value-of select="DESCRIPTION"/></DIV>
7:         <DIV>Price: $<xsl:value-of select="PRICE"/>US</DIV>
8:       </xsl:for-each>
9:     </xsl:template>
10:</xsl:stylesheet>
```

On line 0 we're defining the version of XML, and on line 1 we're defining this as a style, referring back to the standard. This is a template, as indicated on line 2, where we're looping through each product in products, as indicated on line 3. For each of those products, we are going to pull out the appropriate attribute and display it.

Notice that we have some normal text in this stylesheet as well, such as the price designation on line 7. The parser will insert the appropriate information in these slots.

While this gives us some idea of how XML works, we need to take a look at two important issues: creating XML out of our database, and reading it back in.

Creating XML

Because XML is simply text, creating XML from a database source is easy. All we need to do is open a text file and stream the data into it. We do this with product_export.asp, as shown in Listing 8.29f.

Listing 8.29f—product_export.asp: Creating an XML file

```
0: <%@ LANGUAGE="VBSCRIPT" %>
1: <%
2:     set outpostDB = Server.CreateObject("ADODB.Connection")
3:     outpostDB.Open "outpost"
4:
5:     set newFileObject = _
6:       Server.CreateObject("Scripting.FileSystemObject")
7:     set newFile = _
8:       newFileObject.CreateTextFile("c:\inetpub\wwwroot\" _
9:       & "products.xml")
10:
11:    newFile.WriteLine("<PRODUCTS>")
12:
13:    set productSet = _
14:      outpostDB.execute("select * from baz_products")
15:    while not productSet.EOF
16:      newFile.WriteLine("<PRODUCT>")
```

```
17:      newFile.WriteLine("<PRODUCT_ID>" & _
18:        productSet("prod_id") & "</PRODUCT_ID>")
19:      newFile.WriteLine("<NAME>" & _
20:        productSet("prod_name") & "</NAME>")
21:      newFile.WriteLine("<DESCRIPTION>" & _
22:        productSet("prod_desc") & "</DESCRIPTION >")
23:      newFile.WriteLine("<PRICE>" & _
24:        productSet("prod_price") & "</PRICE >")
25:      newFile.WriteLine("<IMAGE>" & _
26:        productSet("prod_image") & "</IMAGE >")
27:      newFile.WriteLine("</PRODUCT>")
28:      productSet.MoveNext
29:  wend
30:
31:  newFile.WriteLine("</PRODUCTS>")
32:
33:  productSet.close
34:  set productSet = Nothing
35:
36:  newFile.Close
37:
38:  set newFile = Nothing
39:  set newFileObject = Nothing
40:
41:
42:
43:  outpostDB.Close
44:  set outpostDB = Nothing
45:%>
```

Absolutely none of this is new. On lines 5 through 9 we're creating the text file. On lines 13 and 14 we're selecting all the products in baz_products, and then on lines 15 through 29 we're writing them out to the file surrounded by the proper XML tags.

Importing XML

While this is all useful, it would be even more useful if we could pull XML back into the database. Fortunately, the XMLDOM object provides everything we need to do this. Copy admintemplate.asp to product_import.asp and add the changes in Listing 8.29g.

Listing 8.29g—product_import.asp: Importing from an XML file

```
0: <%@ LANGUAGE="VBSCRIPT" %>
1: <%
2:     set outpostDB = Server.CreateObject("ADODB.Connection")
3:     outpostDB.Open "outpost"
4:     set productSet = Server.CreateObject("ADODB.RecordSet")
5:     productSet.open "baz_products", outpostDB, adOpenDynamic, _
```

continues

Listing 8.29g—continued

```
6:        adLockPessimistic, adCmdTable
7:
8:    set products = server.createobject("Microsoft.XMLDOM")
9:    xmlFile = server.mappath("products.xml")
10:   products.load(xmlFile)
11:
12:   set allProducts = products.documentElement
13:   num_products = allProducts.childNodes.length
14:
15:   for this_product_num = 0 to num_products - 1
16:     set this_product = _
17:         allProducts.childnodes.item(this_product_num)
18:
19:     productSet.AddNew
20:     productSet("product_id") = _
21:       this_product.childnodes.item(0).text
22:     productSet("prod_name") = _
23:       this_product.childnodes.item(1).text
24:     productSet("prod_desc") = _
25:       this_product.childnodes.item(2).text
26:     productSet("prod_price") = _
27:       this_product.childnodes.item(3).text
28:     productSet("prod_image") = _
29:       this_product.childnodes.item(4).text
30:     productSet.Update
31:   next
32:
33:   productSet.close
34:   set productSet = Nothing
35:
36:   outpostDB.Close
37:   set outpostDB = Nothing
38:%>
```

On lines 2 through 6 we're doing the normal job of creating a recordset so we can add products. Then on lines 8 through 10, we're creating an XLM document object and populating it with the contents of the products.xml file we created earlier. On line 12, we are reading the contents of the DocumentElement, which is to say, all of the products and their information, into the allProducts object.

At this point allProducts has all of the information we need, we just need to get at it. Each product is a child of the overall object, so on line 13 we can get the number of products by checking the length of the childNodes collection.

Now, this collection is zero-based. That means that the first item is number 0, so if there are 5 products they'll be numbered 0 through 4. On lines 15 through 31, we're looping through each product.

Each product is an object that has its own children, which are the attributes such as the name, description, and so on. So once we set `this_product` on lines 16 and 17, we can extract the attributes by checking its own `childNodes` collection.

Finally, on lines 33 through 37, we clean up the database connections.

XML is a tremendously powerful concept, and in the coming months it will become more and more entrenched, both on the front end in the browser, and on the back end in the server. Microsoft, HP, and several other companies are currently working on interoperability products to let different XML-based systems speak to each other.

For more information on XML, see `http://msdn.microsoft.com/xml/`.

Transactions and Errors

In Chapter 7, "Creating Electronic Storefronts and Implementing Shopping Carts," we built an electronic storefront and took orders for various pieces of merchandise, keeping the information in the `baz_orders` and `baz_order_items` tables. Now we need to take care of fulfillment. How do we know when an order has been shipped? We certainly don't want to lose orders or (almost as bad) ship duplicate orders.

The first thing that we need is a form on which to mark up the orders. Copy `admintemplate.asp` to `order_complete.asp` to produce the code shown in Listing 8.30.

Listing 8.30—order_complete.asp: Marking completed orders for processing

```
0: <%@ LANGUAGE="VBSCRIPT" %>
1: <!--#include file="adovbs.inc"-->
2: <!--#include file="pagetop.txt"-->
3: <!--#include file="isadmin.inc"-->
4: <%
5: if isAdmin then
6: %>
7: <H1>Completed Orders Ready for Charging and Shipment</H1>
8:
9: <FORM ACTION="order_complete_action.asp" METHOD="post">
10:
11: <TABLE BORDER="1">
12: <%
13:     set outpostDB = Server.CreateObject("ADODB.Connection")
14:     outpostDB.Open "outpost"
15:
16:     set orderSet = outpostDB.Execute("select * from " & _
17:         " baz_orders where status = 'COMPLETE'")
18:
19:     set orderItemSet = Server.CreateObject("ADODB.RecordSet")
```

continues

Listing 8.30—continued

```
20:        orderItemSet.Open "baz_order_items", outpostDB, _
21:            adOpenStatic, adLockReadOnly, adCmdTable
22:
23:        set prodSet = Server.CreateObject("ADODB.RecordSet")
24:        prodSet.Open "baz_products", outpostDB, adOpenStatic, _
25:            adLockReadOnly, adCmdTable
26:
27:        while not orderSet.EOF
28:            'FOR EACH ORDER
29:            p_order_id = orderSet("order_id")
30: %>          <TR>
31:               <td valign="top">
32:                  <% 'INFORMATION FOR PROCESSING THE ORDER %>
33:                  Order ID: <%= p_order_id %><P>
34:                  <INPUT TYPE="hidden" NAME="p_order_id"
35:                      VALUE="<%=p_order_id%>">
36:
37:                  Status:<BR>
38:                  <select NAME="p_status<%= p_order_id %>">
39:                  <option VALUE="COMPLETE" SELECTED>COMPLETE
40:                  <option VALUE="Shipped" >Shipped
41:                  <option VALUE="Cancelled" >Cancelled
42:                  <option VALUE="Declined" >Declined
43:                  <option VALUE="Backorder" >Backorder
44:                  <option VALUE="Other" >Other
45:                  </select>
46:                  <P>
47:
48:                  Date:<BR>
49:                 <input NAME="p_date<%= p_order_id%>"
50:                     VALUE="<%=Date%>" type="text" SIZE=10">
51:          </TD>
52:          <td valign="top">
53:             <% 'CHARGE INFORMATION %>
54:             <b>Credit Card:</b> <%= orderSet("cc_type") %>
55:                <%= orderSet("cc_number") %> <BR>
56:             <b>Expiration:</b> <%= orderSet("cc_exp") %><BR>
57:             <b>Name on Card:</b>
58:                <%= orderSet("cc_nameoncard") %><BR>
59:             <b>Customer Information:</b> <P>
60:             <%= orderSet("first_name") %> 
61:                <%=orderSet("last_name")%><BR>
62:             <%= orderSet("address1") %><BR>
63:             <%= orderSet("address2") %><BR>
64:             <%= orderSet("city") %>, <%= orderSet("state") %>
65:                <%= orderSet("postalcode") %><BR>
66:             <%= orderSet("country") %><P>
67:             <b>Phone:</b> <%= orderSet("phone") %><P>
68:
69:                'COST — put into a table only for formatting $$
```

```
70:                 'to the right
71:                 <TABLE width=100%>
72:                     <TR>
73:                         <TD><b>Shipping:</b></TD>
74:                         <td align="right">
75:                           $<%=formatNumber(orderSet("shipping"),2)%>
76:                         </TD>
77:                     </TR>
78:                     <TR>
79:                         <TD><b>Total charge:</b></TD>
80:                         <td align="right">
81:                           $<%=formatNumber(orderSet("total"),2)%>
82:                         </TD>
83:                     </TR>
84:                 </TABLE>
85:           </TD>
86:         <td valign="top">
87: <%          'ACTUAL PRODUCTS to be shipped --
88:             'again in a table just for formatting %>
89:             <TABLE width=100%>
90:                 <TR>
91:                     <TH>Quantity</TH>
92:                     <TH>Product ID</TH>
93:                     <TH>Product Name</TH>
94:                     <TH>Unit Price</TH>
95:                 </TR>
96: <%          'Find just the items on this particular order
97:             orderItemSet.Filter = "order_id = " & p_order_id
98:             orderItemSet.MoveFirst
99:             while not orderItemSet.EOF
100:                'FOR EACH ITEM on the order
101:
102:             'Get specific product information
103:             prodSet.MoveFirst
104:             prodSet.Find "prod_id = " & _
105:                 orderItemSet("prod_id")
106:
107:             'Product may have been removed from the database
108:             'since it was ordered
109:             if prodSet.EOF then
110:                 p_prod_name = "NO LONGER CARRIED"
111:                 p_prod_price = "See archives"
112:             else
113:                 p_prod_name = prodSet("prod_name")
114:                 p_prod_price = "$" & _
115:                   formatNumber(prodSet("prod_price"), 2)
116:             end if
117:
118:%>              <TR>
119:                 <TD><%=orderItemSet("quantity")%></TD>
120:                 <TD><%=orderItemSet("prod_id")%></TD>
121:                 <TD><%=p_prod_name%></TD>
```

continues

Listing 8.30—continued

```
122:              <td align="right"><%=p_prod_price%></TD>
123:         </TR>
124:<%        orderItemSet.MoveNext
125:      wend
126:
127:      'Restore the set or order items for the next order
128:      orderItemSet.Filter = 0
129:%>        </TABLE>
130:      </TD>
131:    </TR>
132:<%   orderSet.MoveNext
133:  wend
134:%>
135:</TABLE>
136:
137:<%
138:   prodSet.Close
139:   set prodSet = Nothing
140:
141:   orderItemSet.Close
142:   set orderItemSet = Nothing
143:
144:   orderSet.Close
145:   set orderSet = Nothing
146:
147:   outpostDB.Close
148:   set outpostDB = Nothing
149:%>
150:</TABLE>
151:<INPUT TYPE="submit" VALUE="Save Changes">
152:</form>
153:<%
154:else
155:
156:  Response.Write "You do not have access to this page."
157:
158:end if
159:%>
160:</BODY>
161:</HTML>
```

From a technical standpoint, this is nothing new, just a combination of things that we have already done. The idea is to display all of the information that we need to charge the credit card, verify any information that needs to be verified, and send it off to fulfillment (see Figure 8.7).

Figure 8.7

Our order fulfillment form.

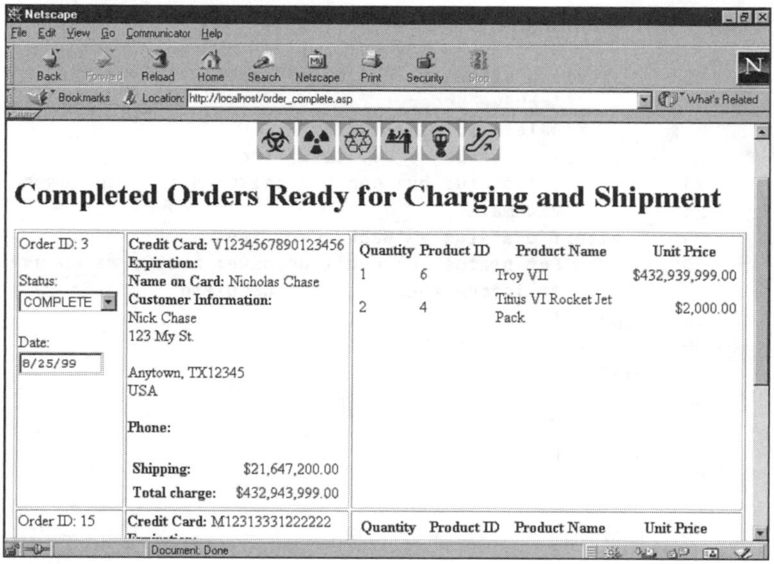

So now that we can get a report that enables us to key in our charges and get paid (or to simply mark orders for shipping, if they've already been submitted for payment), we need to be able to process the records after we're done with them. Copy `admintemplate.asp` to `order_complete_action.asp` and add the logic shown in Listing 8.31.

Listing 8.31—order_complete_action.asp: Preparing to process orders

```
0: <%@ LANGUAGE="VBSCRIPT" %>
1: <!--#include file="adovbs.inc"-->
2: <!--#include file="pagetop.txt"-->
3: <!--#include file="isadmin.inc"-->
4: <%
5: if isAdmin then
6:
7:    set outpostDB = Server.CreateObject("ADODB.Connection")
8:    outpostDB.Open "outpost"
9:
10:   for each p_order_id in Request.form("p_order_id")
11:
12:      p_status = Request.form("p_status"&p_order_id)
13:      if p_status = "COMPLETE" then
14:        'We don't need to do anything, this is where we
15:        'started
16:      elseif p_status = "Shipped" then
17:        'Need to notify warehouse and archive order
18:        'Delete original order
```

continues

Listing 8.31—continued

```
19:    elseif p_status = "Cancelled" then
20:        'Archive order
21:        'Delete original order
22:    elseif p_status = "Declined" then
23:        'Set status but don't archive: notify customer
24:        'via mail
25:    elseif p_status = "Backorder" then
26:        'Set status but don't archive: notify warehouse
27:        'to inform when order is complete
28:    end if
29:
30: next
31:
32: outpostDB.Close
33: set outpostDB = Nothing
34:else
35:
36: Response.Write "You do not have access to this page."
37:
38:end if
39:%>
40:</BODY>
41:</HTML>
```

As usual, we take the small step and look at what we're going to do before we worry about how to do it. For each order, we need to check the status and handle it appropriately.

You have to realize, though, that this is only a small part of our overall system. We will also need some way for the warehouse to track shipped orders, inventory control for backordered products, and so on. The concept is the same as what we've been doing, however, so we're just going to concentrate on making this one piece work.

We don't want to keep orders in the live system after they've been shipped, so we need a way to archive them. Specifically, we need to have somewhere to put them.

The information we're archiving is a combination of baz_orders and baz_order_items, with the actual product information as well, because this is a historical system. (Six months down the line when a customer wants to chargeback their order, it helps to know what it is they actually bought. You don't want to get into a spot where you don't know because you don't carry it anymore!)

We're going to create two new tables to hold this archived information. See Listing 8.32 for the SQL create table statements.

Listing 8.32—Archive tables: create scripts

```
1: create table archive_orders (
2:      order_id integer,
3:      first_name char(100),
4:      last_name char(100),
5:      address1 char(255),
6:      address2 char(255),
7:      city  char(255),
8:      state char(100),
9:      postalcode char(50),
10:     country  char(100),
11:     phone  char(50),
12:     shipping numeric(18,2),
13:     total numeric(18,2)
14:     cc_type  char(50),
15:     cc_number char(20),
16:     cc_exp  char(10),
17:     cc_nameoncard char(100),
18:     status  char(25),
19:     statusdate  date
20:)
21:
22:create table archive_order_items (
23:     order_id  integer,
24:     prod_id integer,
25:     prod_name  char(100),
26:     prod_price  char(50),
27:     quantity integer
28:)
```

To the `baz_orders` table we've added a status date on line 19 so that we know not only what's happened to an order, but when it happened. If we were being really rigorous, we could include the name or userid of the person who made the change.

To the `baz_order_items` table, we've added the product name and price on lines 25 and 26. Note that the price is not a numeric field. This way we can note whether something is a replacement, promotional, or anything that's text based.

So let's go ahead and add the archiving functionality to `order_complete_action.asp` (see Listing 8.33).

Listing 8.33—order_complete_action.asp: archiving orders

```
0: <%@ LANGUAGE="VBSCRIPT" %>
1: <!--#include file="adovbs.inc"-->
2: <!--#include file="pagetop.txt"-->
3: <!--#include file="isadmin.inc"-->
4: <%
```

continues

Listing 8.33—continued

```
 5:    sub sub_ArchiveOrder (s_order_id)
 6:        orderSet.MoveFirst
 7:        orderSet.Find "order_id = " & s_order_id
 8:
 9:        archOrderSet.AddNew
10:        archOrderSet("order_id") = OrderSet("order_id")
11:        archOrderSet("first_name") = OrderSet("first_name")
12:        archOrderSet("last_name") = OrderSet("last_name")
13:        archOrderSet("address1") = OrderSet("address1")
14:        archOrderSet("address2") = OrderSet("address2")
15:        archOrderSet("city") = OrderSet("city")
16:        archOrderSet("state") = OrderSet("state")
17:        archOrderSet("postalcode") = OrderSet("postalcode")
18:        archOrderSet("country") = OrderSet("country")
19:        archOrderSet("phone") = OrderSet("phone")
20:        archOrderSet("shipping") = OrderSet("shipping")
21:        archOrderSet("total") = OrderSet("total")
22:        archOrderSet("cc_type") = OrderSet("cc_type")
23:        archOrderSet("cc_number") = OrderSet("cc_number")
24:        archOrderSet("cc_exp") = OrderSet("cc_exp")
25:        archOrderSet("cc_nameoncard") = OrderSet("cc_nameoncard")
26:        archOrderSet("status") = OrderSet("status")
27:        archOrderSet("statusdate") = _
28:            Request.form("p_date" & s_order_id)
29:        archOrderSetUpdate
30:
31:        orderSet.Delete
32:
33:        orderItemSet.filter = "order_id = " & s_order_id
34:        while not orderItemSet.EOF
35:            prodInfoSet.MoveFirst
36:            prodInfoSet.Find "prod_id="&orderItemSet("prod_id")
37:            archOrderItemSet.AddNew
38:            archOrderItemSet("order_id") = _
39:                orderItemSet("order_id")
40:            archOrderItemSet("prod_id") = _
41:                orderItemSet("prod_id")
42:            archOrderItemSet("prod_name") = _
43:                prodInfoSet("prod_name")
44:            archOrderItemSet("prod_price") = _
45:                prodInfoSet("prod_price")
46:            archOrderItemSet("quantity") = _
47:                orderItemSet("quantity")
48:            archOrderItemSetUpdate
49:
50:            orderItemSet.Delete
51:
52:            orderItemSet.MoveNext
53:        wend
54:
55:        orderItemSet.filter = 0
```

```
56:
57:    end Sub
58:
59:    sub sub_notifyWarehouse (s_order_id, s_status)
60:
61:        'This notification can be whatever the business process
62:        'calls for, be it phone call, bulletin board, email,
63:        'data transfer, whatever. We don't need to specify it
64:        'here.
65:
66:    end sub
67:
68: %>
69: <% '------- MAIN PROGRAM STARTS HERE --------
70: if isAdmin then
71:
72:    set outpostDB = Server.CreateObject("ADODB.Connection")
73:    outpostDB.Open "outpost"
74:
75:    set orderSet = Server.CreateObject("ADODB.RecordSet")
76:    orderSet.Open "baz_orders", outpostDB, adOpenDynamic, _
77:      adLockPessimistic, adCmdTable
78:
79:    set orderItemSet = Server.CreateObject("ADODB.RecordSet")
80:    orderItemSet.Open "baz_order_items", outpostDB, adOpenDynamic, _
81:      adLockPessimistic, adCmdTable
82:
83:    set prodInfoSet = Server.CreateObject("ADODB.RecordSet")
84:    prodInfoSet.Open "baz_products", outpostDB, adOpenStatic, _
85:      adLockReadOnly, adCmdTable
86:
87:    set archOrderSet = Server.CreateObject("ADODB.RecordSet")
88:    archOrderSet.Open "archive_orders", outpostDB, adOpenDynamic, _
89:      adLockPessimistic, adCmdTable
90:
91:    set archOrderItemSet = Server.CreateObject("ADODB.RecordSet")
92:    archOrderItemSet.Open "archive_order_items", outpostDB, _
93:      adOpenDynamic, adLockPessimistic, adCmdTable
94:
95:
96:    for each p_order_id in Request.form("p_order_id")
97:
98:      p_status = Request.form("p_status"&p_order_id)
99:      if p_status = "COMPLETE" then
100:        'We don't need to do anything, this is
101:        'where we started
102:      elseif p_status = "Shipped" then
103:
104:        sub_archiveOrder p_order_id, "Shipped"
105:
106:        'Need to notify warehouse
```

continues

Listing 8.33—continued

```
107:          sub_notifyWarehouse p_order_id
108:
109:     elseif p_status = "Cancelled" then
110:
111:          sub_archiveOrder p_order_id, "Cancelled"
112:
113:     elseif p_status = "Declined" then
114:          'Set status but don't archive: notify customer
115:          'via mail
116:
117:          orderSet.MoveFirst
118:          orderSet.Find "order_id = " & p_order_id
119:          orderSet("status") = "Declined"
120:          orderSetUpdate
121:
122:     elseif p_status = "Backorder" then
123:          'Set status but don't archive: notify
124:          'warehouse to inform when order is complete
125:
126:          orderSet.MoveFirst
127:          orderSet.Find "order_id = " & p_order_id
128:          orderSet("status") = "Backorder"
129:          orderSetUpdate
130:
131:          sub_notifyWarehouse p_order_id, "BACKORDER"
132:
133:     end if
134:
135: next
136:
137: archOrderItemSet.Close
138: set archOrderItemSet = Nothing
139:
140: archOrderSet.Close
141: set archOrderSet = Nothing
142:
143: prodInfoSet.Close
144: set prodInfoSet = Nothing
145:
145: orderItemSet.Close
146: set orderItemSet = Nothing
147:
148: orderSet.Close
149: set orderSet = Nothing
150:
151: outpostDB.Close
152: set outpostDB = Nothing
153:else
```

```
154:
155:    Response.Write "You do not have access to this page."
156:
157:end if
158:%>
159:</BODY>
160:</HTML>
```

We're really working the ADO here! The main program begins on line 70. On lines 75 through 93, we're creating all of the RecordSets we're going to need to do this. We need order information, order item information, product information, and RecordSets to archive all that information.

Note We're going to be searching and filtering these RecordSets extensively. You may find that you're better off letting the database handle it on a case-by-case basis. It's a matter of knowing which machines are better able to handle the load.

Moving down to line 102, we have an order that's been shipped, so we want to archive it. We could have put the archive routine right here, but that wouldn't be the best move. We're also going to archive cancelled orders, so it makes sense to pull the archive functionality out into a subroutine, which starts on line 5. This will also make our lives a whole lot easier from a maintenance standpoint.

Taking a look at that subroutine, we've got several things to do here. First we need to find the proper order, which we're doing on lines 6 and 7. After we have the order information, we need to add a new record to archOrderSet and populate it, which we do on lines 9 through 29. All of the information is coming from orderSet except for the status, which we're setting directly, and the statusdate, which is coming in on the form. The handy thing about the s_status variable is that we can call this subroutine to archive any kind of order, as long as we specify the status when we call it.

After we've made a copy of that record in archive_orders, we can delete it from orderSet on line 31, and thus from the baz_orders table itself.

We also need to move over the actual order items. First, on line 33, we filter out everything that doesn't belong to this order. Then for each item that's left, we'll also need to find the product information on lines 35 and 36.

Between the two RecordSets (orderItemSet and prodInfoSet) we now have all of the information we need for archOrderItemSet, and on lines 37 through 48 we add and populate the new record. As we move each record over, we're deleting it from orderItemSet, and the baz_order_items table on line 50. When we're finished with the order, we remove the filter on line 55, so we'll be ready for the next one.

When the subroutine finishes, control drops back down to line 107, where we encounter the subroutine sub_notifyWarehouse. If you look at the definition of sub_notifyWarehouse on lines 59 through 66, you'll see that we're not actually doing anything. This is the beauty of modularity. We've got it set, we've got the process in place, and the page doesn't care what the actual process is to notify the warehouse. What's more, even if we did want it to, say, send an email to the shipping manager, we could change it whenever we wanted by just altering the subroutine. We wouldn't have to find every single place where we send a notification and rewrite it and retest it, and so on.

When sub_notifyWarehouse finishes, control drops back down to the main program.

That's what happens if the order is set to be shipped. If the order is cancelled, we'll archive it just as we archived a shipped order, but there's nobody to notify. Again, because it's a subroutine, all of our work is already done.

If we process the credit card and it's declined, we will find the right order in the RecordSet on lines 117 and 118, and update the status on line 119, but not archive it. We'll need to contact the customer and see if we can't resolve the issue, rather than lose an order.

Finally, if some of the items are on backorder, we will set the status on lines 126 through 129 and notify the warehouse to let us know when the order is available on line 131. Again, how we do this isn't important right now.

Finally, we'll close and destroy all of those RecordSets on lines 137 through 149 before we swamp the machine!

This is all great except for the fact that we haven't considered the possibility of errors. What happens if something goes wrong? What if we delete the order but we can't notify the warehouse? What if we delete the order information but not the order items? This is an all-or-nothing proposition.

That's where transactions come in. What we need to do is set this page up as a transaction and only commit it if everything works out.

But how do we know if everything works out? After all, we know if we get an error because everything stops processing and we see the error message on the page. But if that happens, we don't have a chance to roll the transaction back, so that's not going to do us any good.

To get around this, we're going to use the On Error Resume Next statement to keep from crashing if there's an error, and we're going to use the Err object to let us know whether everything went according to plan.

Handling Errors in ASP

The Err object is extremely handy because even if we tell the script to keep executing after an error, the Err object will keep track of the fact that the error occurred. It will also provide us with information about the error. In Listing 8.34, we add error checking to order_complete_action.asp.

Listing 8.34—order_complete_action.asp: Adding error checking

```
0: <%@ LANGUAGE="VBSCRIPT" %>
1: <!--#include file="adovbs.inc"-->
2: <!--#include file="pagetop.txt"-->
3: <!--#include file="isadmin.inc"-->
4: <%
5:    sub sub_ArchiveOrder (s_order_id, s_status)
...
52:             orderItemSet.MoveNext
53:         wend
54:
55:         orderItemSet.filter = 0
56:
57:         if Err.Number = 0 then
58:             'There were no errors
59:             Response.Write "Order number " & p_order_id
60:             Response.Write " was processed successfully.<BR>"
61:         else
62:             Response.Write "<P>Error in processing order number " & p_order_id
63:             Response.Write "<BR>Error Number: " & Err.Number
64:             Response.Write "<BR>Error Source: " & Err.Source
65:             Response.Write Err.Description
66:         End If
67:
68:
69:    end Sub
70:
71:
72:    sub sub_notifyWarehouse (s_order_id, s_status)
73:
74:         'This notification can be whatever the business process
75:         'calls for, be it phone call, bulletin board, email,
76:         'data transfer, whatever. We don't need to specify it
77:         'here.
78:
79:    end sub
80:
81: %>
82: <%
83: if isAdmin then
84:
```

8

continues

Listing 8.34—continued

```
85:    set outpostDB = Server.CreateObject("ADODB.Connection")
86:    outpostDB.Open "outpost"
87:
88:    On Error Resume Next
89:    outpostDB.BeginTrans
90:
91:    set orderSet = Server.CreateObject("ADODB.RecordSet")
92:    orderSet.Open "baz_orders", outpostDB, adOpenDynamic, _
93:      adLockPessimistic, adCmdTable
...
165:
164:   orderSet.Close
165:   set orderSet = Nothing
166:
167:
168:   if Err.Number = 0 then
169:     'There were no errors
170:     outpostDB.CommitTrans
171:     Response.Write "<P>All orders processed " _
172:       successfully.<BR>"
173:   else
174:     outpostDB.RollbackTrans
175:     Response.Write "<P>Error in processing orders. "_
176:       & "Please re-submit successful orders."
177:   End If
178:
179:   outpostDB.Close
180:   set outpostDB = Nothing
181:else
182:
183:   Response.Write "You do not have access to this page."
184:
185:end if
186:
187:%>
188:</BODY>
189:</HTML>
```

There are a few things to keep in mind about transactions. First, they have to take place over the course of only one page. Even with Microsoft Transaction Server, transactions can't span more than one ASP page.

Second, we have to create and destroy our RecordSets within the transaction, so unfortunately we can't make each order its own transaction without destroying and re-creating the RecordSets each time.

When we set On Error Resume Next on line 88, we did two things. We told the page to keep going after an error, and we gave ourselves the opportunity to examine the Err object to detect it.

Next, on line 89, we explicitly created a new transaction. If we don't do that, we can't roll back any changes. Then we process as usual, but on lines 168 through 177 we're checking as each order is processed to see if there were any problems with it, and to display the status as it's processed.

Finally, when all our orders have been processed, whether successfully or unsuccessfully, we take a last look at the Err object on line 168 to see whether the changes were all successful. If they were, we commit the changes on line 170. If they weren't, we roll them back on line 174 and give the user an error message.

Summary

In this chapter, we've discussed methods of maintaining database-driven data via the Web. We've also talked about uploading files and used the fileSystemObject object to navigate around our server and to read and write files on the filesystem. We've imported a tab-delimited text file into the database and processed our orders while taking into account error handling and transactions.

Next Steps

In the next chapter we'll talk about how to tie it all together. Now that we've built our site, how do we make it a success? We'll take a look at some of the issues that arise once your site is complete, such as monitoring your users, adding new features such as discussion groups, and site promotion.

8

Chapter 9

In this chapter

- *Know Your Audience*
- *Bells and Whistles*
- *Letting the World Know You're Out There*
- *Search Engines*
- *Where Do We Go From Here?*

Adding Professional Site Features

We did it! We built a complete site, start to finish. We're done now, right?

Wrong.

Yes, you can go get some well-deserved sleep, reconnect with the family that loves you, take some time away from the virtual world. But just when you think you're done, there's a lot more to think about.

There's only one constant in the world of the Internet, and that's change. Our site's got to keep up, or it's going to be history very, very quickly. So what do we do to keep ahead of things?

Know Your Audience

In the real world, we will have done some research about who our audience was and what they wanted before we built our site, much less launched it. Regardless, though, we'll need to keep a careful eye on our users. Is there something new that caught their fancy? Have they lost interest in some of our key content? Have we attracted a whole new user base that we weren't expecting?

The best source for this kind of information is right at our fingertips. Our web server logs can provide a wealth of information about what our users want and don't want. Just looking at them will give us a sense of which areas are most popular and which are rarely seen by human eyes.

We can get even more information with log analysis tools such as WebTrends and other tools like it. These tools will show us information such as how long users are staying on our site, what pages are most and least popular, typical paths through the site, and how many unique visitors we've had, which is a much better indicator of success than the old hit count. After all, a page with six images on it is technically seven hits, but it's still only one person.

Looking at our logs can also give us valuable information not only on how people are finding our site, but what they're interested in. This referrer log will show all of the pages where users clicked links that brought them to us. We can go and visit these sites to find out what they feature and what kind of audience they seem to cater to. The referrer log can also tell us what banners or other ads are pulling in the most traffic.

The `referrer log` records pages where users have clicked a link to your site.

A nice thing that the referrer logs will give us is an idea of how people are finding us in the search engines. This means that we'll know not only which search engines, but also what users have searched on! For instance, if I found the following URL in my referrer log,

```
http://www.altavista.com/cgi-bin/query?pg=q&kl=
XX&stype=stext&q=science+fiction
```

I know not only that this user came from the Google search engine, but also that they had searched on the term science fiction. What are the most popular search terms people are using to find us? Are they using terms we may not have expected? For instance, if we were catering only to science fiction and we noticed that we were getting a lot of visitors based on the search term outer space, we should give some thought to adding more space science and news content.

Another source of information about our users is our own search engine. For instance, we built a search engine for our storefront's products. By adding one line to that search engine, we could log all searches and whether or not they were successful. This log would tell us not only what was most popular, but also what people want that we're not providing for them. And this log doesn't need to be limited to products. If our site is a decent size, we will probably want to provide a site search engine that will enable users to find content more quickly. This is a wealth of information on what our users want to see.

In some cases building and keeping an audience comes down to one-to-one marketing, where the message is tailored for each individual. Ok, some of you, especially the more technical, might not like the m-word, but if a site lives on the Internet and nobody's around to see it, does it serve any purpose? One-to-one marketing is just the science of giving people what they want. We talked about some examples in our chapter on storefronts, when we discussed how Amazon suggests other items based on what you've selected. How can we put this to work on our site? Every piece of information we collect from our users, directly or indirectly, can be used to customize their experience.

We've already gone to some lengths to customize the experience of our sample Primary Outpost site with `mySpace`, where users can pick and choose their own content. We can also use these preferences to show them related content in other areas. For instance, let's say that our user has listed a preference for news about the world of books. What if we had a randomly generated item highlighted on the first page of our catalog? We could easily skew this page to point to books we're selling, making the featured item more likely to be of interest to our user.

The main idea of all this is to make the user feel like he or she has a reason to come back. Their time is valuable, and if we're not providing something of value, the best we're going to get out of a killer marketing campaign is a string of one-time visitors. Just remember, it's a lot cheaper to keep a customer than get a new one.

Providing something of value can mean many different things. Probably the most important is fresh, compelling, ever-changing content. We should also consider providing a rare or even unique resource. To use Primary Outpost as an example, we could provide a directory of memorabilia dealers and independent traders. Not only would we be providing a service to our users, but many of those sites we're listing will be more than happy to link back to us. The key is finding something you can provide that nobody else is providing.

Our users can be very helpful in providing a resource that nobody else has: themselves. Community as a buzzword is starting to fade—another example of how things change!—but getting together with virtual friends can still be an important part of our site's appeal, especially if we cover something that people are passionate about.

Part of this idea of virtual community is the paradoxical nature of the Internet. It can put you in touch with resources all over the world if you shut out the world where you physically are. The Internet leaves people longing for that human touch in a whole new way.

The main idea of community is to put people in touch with each other. Two ways to do that are by using discussion groups, where messages can be left for people to read later, and chat rooms, where users have real-time conversations.

Setting up these services takes some thought. For one thing, we need to have at least a small community to start with or a lot of determination. There are few things that kill a community as fast as an empty chat room, so unless we've got at least a reasonable number of simultaneous users, we'll want to put that on hold for a little while.

9

A discussion group is a little easier to get started because users don't have to be on the site at the same time to take advantage of it.

Either way, before seriously plunging into the work of putting together an online community, we need to decide on a few things, such as its focus, and how we're going to handle troublemakers. Yes, this is the Internet, bastion of free speech. But very few people (except maybe for a club of masochists) will spend very long in an environment where they're uncomfortable, and a problem user can make people uncomfortable very quickly.

The main thing is to have clear rules, and a clear understanding of how they will be enforced. Some common guidelines include rules against personal attacks (also known as flaming) and unsolicited advertising. We should have at least one person responsible for monitoring our community, even if that just means watching out for that sort of thing.

So after we have thought about all of this, how do we actually implement it?

In addition to sites that will provide these services for you, our Web-hosting provider may provide some of this software for us to use. But what if we are our own hosting provider?

Discussion Groups

One option for hosting online discussion groups is Usenet Newsgroups. Pre-dating the Web, the Network News Transfer Protocol (NNTP) allows various client programs to read and respond to threaded discussion groups, where one topic can easily be followed through a series of messages left by other users.

> **Note**   The NNTP service is only available in IIS 5.0 on Windows 2000 Server. It is also available in IIS 4.0.

To set up a newsgroup, choose Start/Programs/Administrative Tools/Internet Services Manager and right-click Default NNTP Virtual Server, then choose `Properties`. Click the Groups tag to show the existing groups for this server (see Figure 9.1).

Figure 9.1

The NNTP Virtual Server hosts our newsgroups.

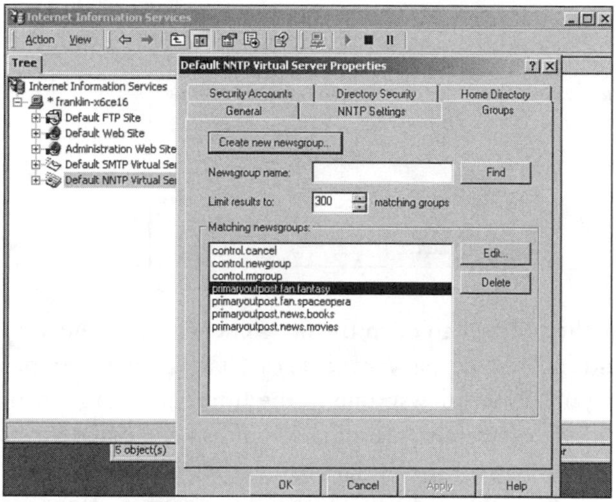

Click Create new newsgroup to bring up the Newsgroup Properties box (see Figure 9.2). There are a few properties we can set for each newsgroup. First we'll have to pick a name. If we were going to create some newsgroups for Primary Outpost, we might choose

```
primaryoutpost.news.books
primaryoutpost.news.movies
primaryoutpost.fan.spaceopera
primaryoutpost.fan.fantasy
primaryoutpost.fan.fantasy.swordandfur
primaryoutpost.fan.hardsf
```

The naming convention is that names get more specific as they get longer. This is the address for the newsgroup, the way www.primaryoutpost.com would be the address for our site.

We will also set a Description and a Display Name, which will be picked up by newsgroup clients.

A newsgroup client is software that actually reads the newsgroup like a browser reads a Web site. Unfortunately, unless we have some sort of Web-enabling software installed, users will need a separate client for reading them. Fortunately, both Netscape Communicator and Microsoft Internet Explorer have a client in them, so all we need to do is make sure that we put the proper link in our site. To create a link that would automatically open up the client for our hardsf newsgroup, for example, we could use

```
Join our
<a href="news://www.primaryoutpost.com/primaryoutpost.fan.hardsf">
hard science fiction newsgroup</a>!
```

Figure 9.2

*The Newsgroup
Properties dialogue box
allows us to set up a new
newsgroup.*

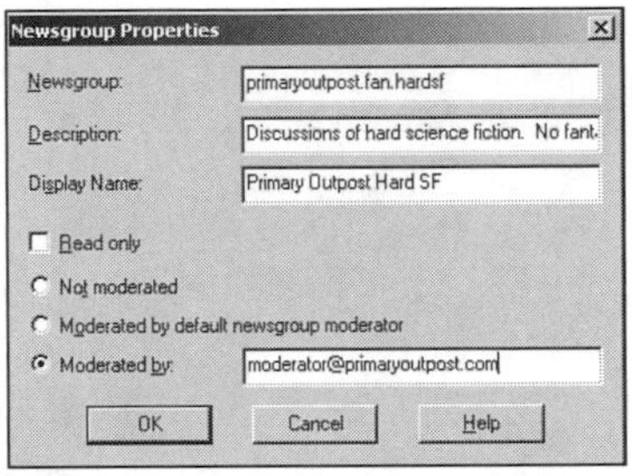

This tells the browser to open the news client, access the www.primaryoutpost.com server, and read the primaryoutpost.fan.hardsf newsgroup. We also have the option to publish this newsgroup to the Internet at large, which is why we have such long names. If we weren't planning to publish, we could get away with shorter names that don't necessarily differentiate from other groups out there. Newsgroups are generally set up to facilitate discussions, and the conversations can get quite lively. We can increase the signal-to-noise ratio of a group by setting it to be moderated. In this case, no messages are posted unless they are first approved by a moderator. To simply display information, we can set the newsgroup up as Read only, preventing conversation altogether.

Chat Rooms

If we decide to implement a chat room (or chat rooms) on our site, we would have to either build it ourselves or buy separate software, as this doesn't come with IIS. It does come with Microsoft's messaging server, Microsoft Exchange Server, and with Microsoft Commercial Internet System Chat Server. There are also a host of third-party products that will provide chat services. Follow the installation and administration instructions for whichever solution you choose.

Upsizing the Database

We've built our site on Microsoft Access, but if our site is a success it won't be long before we need to start thinking about moving to a more powerful database such as Oracle or Microsoft SQL Server. A successful site can have dozens, hundreds, or even thousands of database hits occurring simultaneously, so we'll need a database that can handle this much traffic.

If we've planned our naming conventions with upsizing the database in mind, it shouldn't be very difficult. In fact, many databases help you through the process, such as SQL Server and its Upsizing Wizard, or Oracle and its Access Migration Assistant. If not, we'll need to export our data and re-import it into the new database.

After we've done that, we'll need to create a new DSN, preferably with the same name, pointing at the new database. The basic process is the same as the one we used to create the Access DSN in chapter 4.

We also need to look at tuning issues. Do our frequently searched tables have indexes on them that will make the searches more efficient? There are a lot of things that can affect the performance of our database, so it's probably best to work with our DBA, or database administrator, to get the most out of it.

Bells and Whistles

If you're a designer, you've probably been cringing at the simplicity of what we've been doing here. Where are the animations, the interactive buttons, and the sound and video?

We can certainly incorporate all of these into our site, but we'll have to use other technologies in addition to Active Server Pages. The key is to do it intelligently.

As we mentioned earlier, not all browsers are created equal. Not every browser is going to be able to handle all the latest and greatest features. We have three potential problem areas: built-in capabilities, Java applets, and plug-ins.

Let's take plug-ins first. A plug-in is a program that you can download and install to give your browser new capabilities, such as embedded sound or video like RealAudio or QuickTime, or interactive animations, such as Shockwave or Flash. If we're going to design a site that uses them extensively, we're going to need to take into account that they have to be downloaded, and this may discourage some users. In many cases we'll want to provide an alternative for those who don't have it and don't want to get it. We'll also need to think about what kinds of plug-ins we want to support. If we're going to support streaming audio or video, where the user sees or hears results right away instead of waiting for a whole file to download, we'd better make sure that we've got enough bandwidth.

Streaming media is audio or video that doesn't have to be downloaded in its entirety to begin playing. This can be extremely handy because these files can be very, very large, and also because it enables us to do live broadcasts, or webcasts.

Bandwidth refers to the size of the pipe that we're serving our content through. Just as we can get a whole lot more water through a fire hose than a straw, we can get more content through a T3 line than, say, a 128K ISDN connection.

MIME-type tells the browser what kind of information, such as HTML text or an image, the current stream of data is, so it knows what to do with it. Every type of media has its own standard MIME-type, such as text/html or audio/x-pn-realaudio.

In some cases, we can use client-side scripting to take care of the problem of whether a plug-in is supported by checking for the acceptability of the MIME-type. Client-side scripting is similar to the scripting we've been doing, except that it is executed by the browser instead of the server. We can do client-side scripting in JavaScript or in VBScript, but only Internet Explorer supports VBScript. So unless we're working in a IE-only environment, it's better to use JavaScript.

While we're on the subject, let's talk about how we can tell what a browser does or doesn't support. There is a variable in `request.ServerVariables`, called `HTTP_USER_AGENT`, that will tell us what kind of browser our user has, and from there we could decide what is and is not supported.

It'd be a tremendous hassle to try and keep track of it, though. Instead, we can use a component that comes with ASP called Browser Capabilities.

Browser Capabilities

The Browser Capabilities component tells us whether the browser supports a particular feature, such as VBScript. For instance, take Listing 9.1:

Listing 9.1—scriptlang.asp: Using the Browser Capabilites component

```
1: <%@ Language=VBSCRIPT %>
2: <HTML>
3: <HEAD><TITLE>Our Scripting Language</TITLE></HEAD>
4: <BODY>
5: <%
6:     set userBrowser = Server.CreateObject("MSWC.BrowserType")
7:     if userBrowser.vbScript then
8:         Response.write "We could use VBScript with this browser."
9:     else
10:        Response.write "No VBScript.  Use JavaScript instead."
11:    end if
12:    set userBrowser = Nothing
13:%>
14:</BODY>
15:</HTML>
```

On line 6 we're creating a `BrowserType` object, and on line 7 we're looking at the `vbscript` property to tell us about the browser. If we run this in IE, it will give us

```
We could use VBScript with this browser.
```

because `userBrowser.vbscript` returns `true`. If we run it in Netscape, however, it will give us

```
No VBScript. Use JavaScript instead.
```

because Netscape doesn't support VBScript *in the browser*. We can use whatever we want for our ASPs because all the browser ever sees is the final HTML.

The component gets this information from a file called `browscap.ini`, which lists all of the properties for various browsers. This file comes with the component (which comes with ASP) but we can get updated versions from `http://www.cyscape.com/browscap/`.

There are also third-party components, such as BrowserHawk (also available at the previous address) to help us detect various capabilities of the user's browser.

IIS5.0 also introduces a new way of determining browser capabilities, but it currently works only with IE 5.0. By generating a cookie called `BrowsCap`, we can add any property that we want. Not only can this solve the problem of out of date `browscap.ini` files, but we now can track information that the user may have changed, such as the height and width of the browser window itself.

This is accomplished by using two files. The page itself has a METADATA command (see listing 9.2), which instructs the server to call a second file. The second file creates a cookie with the information we want (see listing 9.3).

Listing 9.2—decideChat.asp: Calling a METADATA file for a browser capabilities cookie

```
<%@Language=VBSCRIPT%>
<%  Response.buffer=TRUE
    Response.Expires=-1 %>
<!--METADATA TYPE="Cookie" NAME="BrowsCap" SRC="capCookie.htm"-->
<HTML>
    <HEAD>
        <TITLE>Primary Outpost Real-Time Chat</TITLE>
    </HEAD>
    <BODY>
    <%
    set browsCap = Server.CreateObject("MSWC.BrowserType")
    if browsCap.javaEnabled then
        h = .75 * browsCap.availHeight
        w = .50 * browsCap.availWidth
        Response.redirect "chat.asp?useJava=yes&javaH="&h&"&javaW="&w
    else
        Response.write "Your browser must support Java to take part "
        Response.write "in Primary Outpost Real-Time Chats."
    end if %>
    </BODY>
</HTML>
```

9

This file will call the METADATA file, `capCookie.htm`.

Listing 9.3—capCookie.htm: Generating the cookie used by decideChat.asp

```
<HTML xmlns:MSIE="http://www.microsoft.com/ie">
<HEAD>
<STY
@media all
{
MSIE\:CLIENTCAPS {behavior:url(#default#clientcaps)}
}
</STYLE>
</HEAD>

<BODY onload="GetBrowserProp()">
<MSIE:CLIENTCAPS ID="outpostWindow" />

<SCRIPT language="JavaScript">
<!--
function GetBrowserProp()
{
cookieText += "availHeight=" + outpostWindow.availHeight;
cookieText += "&availWidth=" + outpostWindow.availWidth;
cookieText += "&javaEnabled=" + outpostWindow.javaEnabled;
document.cookie = "BrowsCap=" + cookieText
}
-->
</SCRIPT>
</BODY></HTML>
```

Dynamic HTML (DHTML)

One area where caution is definitely warranted is Dynamic HTML, or DHTML. A combination of traditional scripting and Cascading Style Sheets (CSS), DHTML gives us more control than was ever possible without having to resort to plug-ins or Java applets (small programs that are downloaded and run in the browser window).

For instance, in addition to just being able to control the color and size of our text, we could set the font, the style (such as bold or italic), or even make the text draggable. More than that, though, we can create items that appear when the user rolls over a button.

DHTML is one of the most powerful technologies to come around in a while, and it's easy to go overboard. There isn't necessarily anything wrong with that. We just need to make sure we're not leaving people out in the cold if they're not using our browser of choice.

We can do this two ways. One way would be to actually go ahead and double-publish our site, providing a high-octane and a watered-down version. We might consider this if our site is heavily graphical because even a user with a high-powered browser might be on a slow connection. Of course, we could still start them out on the high-powered version based on what the Browser Capabilities component tells us, but offering the choice will earn us points.

A second way would be to design the site in such a way that even if the DHTML doesn't work, the site is still usable. For instance, just the other day, I was having a conversation with a designer who wanted to use DHTML to trigger a submenu when the user rolled over the button. Then the user could pick the subtopic off that menu. The trouble was that the site needed to be usable in all browsers, and the engineer wasn't too keen on creating two different versions.

The answer was to design the site so that if you roll over the button and your browser does support it, you get the submenu. Either way, though, if you simply click the button, you get a submenu page. The high-powered browser gets there faster, but the low-powered browser still gets there and without even knowing that they're missing something.

Java Applets

A Java applet is a small program that is downloaded and run in your browser window. As developers, we'll find that this does solve some problems for us, in that we don't have to worry about sending our users off to download a plugin, but it's not perfect. Some corporate sites won't allow applets to be downloaded through their firewall, and there can be problems in compatibility with older browsers if we use the latest features. Implemented properly, however, Java is an excellent way to add advanced features to our site.

You can find more information on building Java programs and applets at `http://java.sun.com`. There are also a great number of books on the subject.

Letting the World Know You're Out There

At the time of this writing, there are something like 360 million Web sites out there, and they're all vying for those precious moments that we want to spend with our users. We used to say that one of the great things about the Web was that a little mom and pop shop could have the same impact as a multibillion dollar corporation on the Web.

Then we said that the great thing about the Web was that anybody could have a Web page. The bad thing about the Web was that anybody could have a Web page.

Eventually, the potential complexity for sites grew so much and there was so much competition in terms of getting noticed that it seemed like the only way that a mom and pop shop could compete was by spending tremendous amounts of cash.

So how do we get ourselves noticed in the great throng? Well, fortunately, it's not all about money and power. It's about smarts. After all, even some of the biggest corporations jumped onto the Web in a panic when they realized they were being left behind, and they did it badly—very badly.

The amount of money that's been wasted on poorly thought out attempts is phenomenal. Which brings us back to where we started, all those chapters ago: planning.

If we've analyzed our audience correctly and designed a site that's both usable and valuable to them (which is half the battle), we will be able to get people to use it. We'll just have to move beyond the scattershot approach.

Search Engines

Let's say right off the bat that search engines are not the only way to get traffic to our site. There are many other ways, some of which are even more effective.

But the fact is that the vast majority of Web traffic does come from search engines. I've seen surveys quote anywhere from 76 percent to 90 percent. The fact is also that the vast majority of users using a search engine never look beyond the thirtieth listing for any given search term, and many of them never look beyond the first ten. That doesn't mean they're necessarily finding what they want in those first 10 or 30 results, it just means that if they don't, they're not looking any further, usually trying a different search term.

What does that mean to us? It means that if we're going to count on search engines, we need to get ourselves towards the top of the list for the search terms that are important to us.

Of course, figuring out how to do this has spawned an industry in and of itself, the search engine positioning business. There are companies that will get us close to the top of the list, and there are companies that will claim to get us to the top of the list. The words here are definitely buyer beware.

Fortunately, this is something that we can, to some extent, do for ourselves.

The Basics of Search Engines

The very first Internet search engine wasn't really a search engine at all. It was just a collection of links that the college students who put it together thought were cool. Eventually it became so popular that Yahoo! began to swamp the network over at Stanford, and it was moved to servers over at Netscape.

These days Yahoo! is so large that it's considered next to impossible to get listed. It's actually not impossible, but make sure that your site is completely finished before you try, and only submit to appropriate categories. Yahoo! is administered by real live people, and they'll notice if you try and fudge it.

But as we said, Yahoo! isn't really a search engine, it's a directory. When you do a search, you're searching the categories, names, and descriptions of sites, not the actual pages.

But don't discount it as a resource for traffic! Yahoo! still has the majority of the market, so to speak, when people are looking for something. The hierarchical nature of it is useful for people who want to drill down through categories, to avoid gibberish sites.

Gibberish sites are pages that show up on search engines that probably weren't intended to be there, even by their authors. So how does this happen?

Most pages that a search engine knows about were not put in by a human being. Instead they were spidered. A spider is a program that starts on one page and records what's on it, then records what's on all of the pages it links to, and all of the pages they link to, and so on and so on. The result is that the search engine has a tremendous amount of data to go by, but not all of it is even faintly useful.

So how do we rise to the top of this milky mass? We do it by understanding how search engines work and think. A search engine takes notice of various pieces of information about our page:

- The URL itself
- The title
- The content
- The keywords
- The description

The first three are fairly self-explanatory, but what's this about keywords and description? Keywords and descriptions are information that we put into metatags. Metatags describe our document. Some sample metatags for our site might be

```
<META NAME="description" content="Science fiction and fantasy news updated
daily.  We cover books, movies, television, fanzines, and the online scene.">
```

```
<META NAME="keywords" content="science fiction, scifi, sci fi, sf, science,
fiction, space, outer space, movies, books, tv, television">
```

This is the information that's going to get picked up by search engines. The keywords will be used to help find us, and the description will be displayed when they do.

Sounds simple, right? Of course it's not that simple. How a search engine ranks a site depends on many factors, such as the number of keywords, what the keywords are,

9

where the search term is located in the body of the page, and so on. To make things worse, every search engine is different. And if that isn't bad enough, they all change constantly. A page that ranks up at the top today might not be on the first page tomorrow. Why?

The people who run the search engines realized early on that unscrupulous people were spamming the indexes, or artificially altering their pages so they scored well for popular searches that might not have had anything to do with their content.

The current line of thought on improving a sites position involves creating multiple doorway pages, optimizing each doorway for a single targeted search engine. There was initial resistance to this idea, but it seems to be gaining acceptance as a mainstream technique.

I could do a whole book on search engine positioning (if it wouldn't be hopelessly out-of-date by the time it was published) but here are some tips.

- Choose your keywords carefully. That's not to say that you shouldn't have a lot of them. In fact, you should try to include every keyword you think people might search on to find you, including common misspellings. But some search engines will penalize sites that include the same keyword more than a few times.
- Include keywords in the title, and (even better) the domain name.
- Try to include keywords early in the text on your pages.
- Include text equivalents for your graphics, especially if they contain keywords. Really, you should be doing that anyway for text-based browsers and users surfing without images.
- Look at the page that grabs the top spot for the search you want. What are they doing that you're not doing? (This doesn't mean that you should copy their page, of course. That would be a probable copyright infringement, and in any case is just plain wrong.)

There are resources out there to help put us on the right track with the search engines, from automatically submitting our page to as many as 1550 search engines and specialized directories to informational sites. Perhaps the best source of information is Danny Sullivan's Search Engine Watch, at

`http://www.searchenginewatch.com.`

If all else fails, we can also pay for placement. A fairly recent entry into the search engine market, GoTo, allows us to bid on a search term, and pay for performance. In other words, let's say we want the top spot for science fiction. As of this writing, we could get it by bidding 21 cents per user. That means that every time someone searches on science fiction and clicks our site, we pay 21 cents. If someone else wants the top spot, they'd have to bid 22 cents. GoTo is very honest about all this. The prices are included right in the listing. What's interesting is the diversity of results. Some of the sites (in this case) are not really about science fiction. They're just trying to get science fiction fans to their site. But the top 10 also shows smaller sites that wouldn't be able to purchase large advertising campaigns.

Stealth Advertising

Sending unsolicited advertising to a newsgroup or (worse) mailing list is likely to get us a bad reputation in a hurry, but there are other ways to advertise there. Every email and newsgroup message can have a signature—four or five lines of text that identify us and can carry a short message and our URL. One means of advertising is to make that short message as effective as possible and to participate in relevant newsgroups. Not only will this put our URL in front of potential visitors, but if we include keywords, our archived messages will continue to pull people in long after we've posted the message.

Note

Newsgroups are one of the primary places spammers obtain email addresses, so if you post a message from your primary address, you will start to receive unwanted and potentially unsettling emails. One solution is to have an alternative address for posting, which you check periodically and clean out, rather than having to wade through it for your personal mail. You can get free email addresses at sites like Yahoo! and Netscape.

If you do get spam at your personal address, *don't* reply with a *Remove* request, as the mail instructs you to do. This instruction was made mandatory by new laws regarding unsolicited email, but spammers are using these requests to confirm that an account is active.

Link Exchanges and Partnerships

A link exchange can actually mean two different things. The original link exchanges were agreements between two sites: you link to my site, and I'll link to yours. This is still an extremely effective means for generating traffic.

One variation on that is the Web ring, where a group of sites get together and agree to link to each other in a giant circle. A user can hop forwards or backwards among the sites.

These days a link exchange has come to mean a much more formalized version of that friendly process. For instance, if you and I agree to link to each other, how would I know if you took off the link and didn't tell me, or if I simply wasn't getting as much traffic as you were, so you were essentially getting a bad deal?

In a link exchange, we put a single piece of code on our page, and it dynamically pulls a banner ad from one of the other members when a user comes to the page. Each time that happens, we get a credit. The more credits we get, the more times our ad shows up on other people's sites.

This way, everyone gets benefits in proportion to the traffic they provide everyone else. Microsoft has purchased the original Link Exchange, but you can still find it at

```
http://www.linkexchange.com.
```

Paid Banners, Sponsorships, and Affiliate Programs

Having long been a staple of online marketing, the paid banner is undergoing somewhat of a transformation. You can still arrange to buy a certain number of impressions, or times your banner will be displayed on a certain site, but with the information overload out there, advertisers are starting to wonder if they're really getting their money's worth because the click-through rate is falling.

Another way is to simply pay by the click through. If the user doesn't click your ad, you don't pay.

A variation on this is the affiliate program. Some of the major commerce sites, such as Amazon and eToys, offer programs where we can display their ad on our site, and if someone clicks it and then buys something, we get a percentage. Seeing the success of this, many smaller sites are starting to do something similar. You can find a list of resources for starting your own program at

```
http://www.refer-it.com.
```

Press Releases and Testimonials

Like any other field, mentions in magazines and books can draw lots of traffic to our site. Another way is to talk to people influential in their field about recommending our site. This doesn't necessarily mean celebrities, either. For our science fiction site, we might talk to well-respected users of science fiction-based email lists about a recommendation.

The Real World

There is one particularly effective means of advertising that's just starting to be widely used: real-world advertising. That's right, actually buying advertising in magazines, and so on. I saw billboards and heard radio spots for Priceline long before I ever saw an ad for them online. (Come to think of it, I still don't think I've ever seen one.) At the very least, if your Web site supports an offline business, your URL should be on every single piece of letterhead, business card, and advertising.

Where Do We Go From Here?

We started out with the assumption that you didn't know anything at all about how to put together an Active Server based Web site. By now you should be able to at least build a fairly functional site, but there's lots more to learn!

Now would be a good time for you to pick up a more advanced book on ASP programming and take a look at some of the more complex features, especially the ActiveX Data Objects.

A couple of good ones are *Active Server Pages Developer's Guide*, by Anthony Tanner and Sams *Teach Yourself Web Development with ASP in 24 Hours* (Complete Development Edition) by Sanjaya Hettihewa. Don't let the title on this last one fool you; it's 800 pages long and concentrates on real-world examples way beyond what we've covered here.

There are also excellent online resources starting with

`http://www.activeserverpages.com`.

This is a great collection of resources, including more than 200 minilessons. It's maintained by Charles Carroll, who also takes care of `www.asplists.com`, where you can find an email list/newsgroup for just about every ASP-related topic imaginable.

Keeping in Touch

I'd love to hear how you're doing, and any problems you may have. You can reach me at `nick@nicholaschase.com`. I'll also be keeping errata, source code, and other information on my Web site at

`http://www.nicholaschase.com`.

The important thing is to enjoy yourself!

9

Index

A

absolute links, 75
accepting credit cards, 284
Access. *See also* **databases**
  creating connections (ADOs), 102-103
  inserting records, 100-102
  ODBC DSN, 98, 100
ActiveConnection recordsets, 198
ActiveX Data Object. *See* **ADO**
adding. *See also* **inserting**
  audio, 369-370
  category listings (storefronts), 234-240
  content, 69-74
  cookies, 133-139, 149-153
    properties, 152-153
  databases, 336

  graphics to HTML documents, 50-56
  hit counters, 95
  HTML structure tags, 47-49
  include files, 254
  interactivity to Web forms, 106-115
  interface, 66
  items, 204-216
    constants, 201
    email, 225-229
    inserting data, 201-203
    personalizing (myAuctions), 216-225
    recordsets, 197-200
    third party components, 225-229
  lines, 72
  links, 69
  myNews, 166, 169
  news items, 312
  orders, 255-288
  radio buttons, 113
  records, 303
    databases, 100-102

  search forms, 241-255
  sound, 369-370
  text
    ASP, 58
    HTML documents, 52-56
  titles, 81
  video, 369-370
  wildcards, 251
administration, security, 293-295
ADO(ActiveX Data Object), 98, 139-149
  creating database connections, 102-103
AdRotator, 90, 92-94
advertising, 378. *See also* **generating traffic**
affiliate programs, 378
analyzing logs, 363-369
API (Application Programming Interface), 97
Application Programming Interface. *See* **API**

applications
FT clients, 44-45
initializing, 267
spreadsheets, 326-340
variables, 265
Visual InterDev, 43
applying
AdRotator, 92-94
application variable, 265
DHTML, 372
functions, 195
if-then-else statements, 60
HTML, 61
preformatted text, 71
Response Write, 60
Script Debugger, 62
Visual InterDev, 41-43
architecture (Web projects), 16-19
archives, 83-90
Content Rotator, 89-90
data, 352, 354-358
lists, 84
navigating, 87-88
objects, 84-86
data, 352, 354-358
arrays, 115
extending, 335
ASP (Active Server Pages)
ADO, 139-149
AdRotator, 90-94
archives, 83-90
audience, 363-369
banner ads, 90-94
commands, 57-63

content, 69-74
Content Rotator, 89-90
cookies
adding, 134-139
expiration dates, 149-153
properties, 152-153
interface design, 36-38
languages, 57-59
mySpace
customizing, 154-170
finalizing, 170-177
objects, 59-61
Page Counter component, 95
PWM, 24-28
SSI, 75-77
subpages, 34-35
text, 58
troubleshooting, 359-361
user interface, 65-69
Visual InterDev, 41-43
Web sites
browser capabilities, 370-372
customizing, 369-372
Windows 2000, 20-23
Windows 95/98/NT, 23
auction data models, 179-196
audience, 363-369
target, 14
audio, 369-370

B

backgrounds, configuring, 54
bandwidth, 14
banner ads, 90-94
Page Counter component, 95
paid, 378
borders, hiding, 55-56
browsers
capabilities, 370-372
tags (HTML), 48
building shells, 29-34
built-in objects, 59-61.
See also **objects**

C

CA (certifying authority0, 272
capabilities of storefronts, 232-234
Cascading Style Sheets. *See* **CSS**
catalogs. *See* **storefronts**
categories, 234-240
certifying authority. *See* **CA**
chat rooms, implementing, 368
check boxes, 114
ChiliASP!, 23
clients (FTP), 24, 44-45
closing objects, 148

code
debugging, 62
modular, 261
Personal Web Server,
62-63
**collections (cookies),
136-139**
**colors, configuring
backgrounds, 54**
**columns, spanning,
130**
commands, 57-63
File menu, New
Project, 41
Project menu, Add
Web Item, 43
SQL, Insert state-
ment, 104-106
commerce. *See* **shopping carts; storefronts**
components
browser capabilities,
370-372
counters, 268-271
Page Counter, 95
third party (auction
data model),
225-229
configuring
background colors, 54
languages, 57-59
newsgroups, 366
permissions in direc-
tories/files, 295
search forms, 242
**connections, creating
(ADOs), 102-103**
**consistency (Web site
design), 77-80**
constants, 201

content
adding, 69-74
archives, 83-90
Content Rotator,
89-90
cookies
*expiration dates,
149-153*
properties, 152-153
links, 73
mySpace
*customizing,
154-170*
finalizing, 170-177
personalizing,
133-139
Web projects, 15-16
**Content Rotator,
89-90**
**conventions, naming,
140-149**
**converting icons into
links, 53-56**
cookies, 260
adding, 134-139
collections, 136-139
expiration dates,
149-153
privacy, 135-136
properties, 152-153
copying graphics, 50
counters
adding, 268-271
hit, 95
**credit cards, accepting,
284**
**CSS (Cascading Style
Sheets), 372**
**CursorType record-
sets, 198-199**

customers. *See also*
counters
tracking, 268-271
customizing
myNews, 166
mySpace, 154-170
finalizing, 170-177
page layout, 127
preferences, 128
search forms, 242
Web sites, 369-372
*browser capabilities,
370-372*
content, 133-139
*expiration dates
(cookies), 149-153*
*properties (cookies),
152-153*

D

data
archiving, 352,
354-358
integrity, 180-181
modeling, 115-120
parsing, 333
Data Source Name. *See*
DSN
databases
Access
*creating connections
(ADOs), 102-103*
*inserting records,
100-102*
*ODBC DSN, 98,
100*
adding, 336

auction data models,
179-196
*adding items,
204-216*
constants, 201
email, 225-229
*inserting data, 201,
203*
*personalizing
(myAuctions),
216-225*
recordsets, 197-200
*third party compo-
nents, 225-229*
cookies
adding, 133-139
*expiration dates,
149-153*
properties, 152-153
data modeling,
115-120
entities, 116-118
*inserting data,
119-120*
tables, 118-119
myLinks, 298-309
mySpace
*customizing,
154-170*
finalizing, 170-177
ODBC DSN
*creating connections
(ADOs), 102-103*
*inserting records,
100-102*
querying, 139-149
SQL commands
(Insert), 104-106
tables, 101
troubleshooting,
120-123

upsizing, 368
XML
creating, 344-345
importing, 345-347
dates, printing, 59
debugging code, 62
Personal Web Server,
62-63
**defining Web projects,
12-19**
deleting
files, 323
records, 298-309
user choices, 163
design
interface, 36-38
Web sites, 77-80
plug-ins, 369-370
Design Time Controls.
See **DTCs**
**DHTML (Dynamic
HTML), 14, 372**
directories
permissions, 295
PWM, 27-28
discussion groups. *See
also* **newsgroups**
hosting, 366-367
**displaying user
choices, 163**
documents
HTML, 45-49
graphics, 50-56
text, 52-56
Web forms
*adding interactivity,
106-115*
*registration,
127-130*
servers, 123-126

downloading files, 24
drives, hard, 319-326
**DSN (Data Source
Name), 99**
databases
creating, 98, 100
*creating connections
(ADOs), 102-103*
*inserting records,
100-102*
viewing, 99
**DTCs (Design Time
Controls), 41**
Dynamic HTML. *See*
DHTML
**dynamic SQL state-
ments, creating, 248**

E

e-commerce. *See* **shopping carts; storefronts**
editing
files, 43
tables, 301
**electronic signatures,
272.** *See also* **security**
**email, auction data
models, 225-229**
**enabling Server Side
debugging, 62**
encoding URLs, 189
entities
auction data model,
179-196
*adding items,
204-216*
constants, 201
email, 225-229
*inserting data,
201-203*

personalizing (myAuctions), 216-225
recordsets, 197-200
third party components, 225-229
data modeling, 116-118
entity relationship diagram. *See* **ERD**
ERD (entity relationship diagram), 180
Err object, 359-361
errors, 347-358. *See also* **troubleshooting**
ASP, 359-361
handling, 120-123
messages, 143
Excel. *See also* **spreadsheets**
file objects, 326-340
executing PWM, 24-27
expiration dates, cookies, 149-153
exporting files (FTP), 44-45
extending arrays, 335
eXtensible Markup Language. *See* **XML**
eXtensible Style Sheet. *See* **XSL**

F

File menu commands, New Project, 41
File Transfer Protocol. *See* **FTP**

files
archives, 87-90
cookies. *See* cookies
deleting, 323
directories
creating, 27-28
downloading, 24
editing, 43
FTP clients, 44-45
HTML
creating, 30
formatting text, 30-32
images, 33-34
links, 32-33
importing, 331-340
include, 254
myNews, 309-319
objects, 326-340
permissions, 295
reading, 326-340
renaming, 323
servers, 319-326
SSI, 75-77
commands, 80-83
text, 319
uploading, 24
saving, 317
XML
creating, 344-345
importing, 345-347
filesystems
navigating, 327-331
reading, 331-340
finding products (storefronts), 241-255
Flash, 369-370
folders, navigating, 327-331
foreign keys, 180-181

formatting
news, 319-326
search forms, 242
text, 30-32
VBScript, 59-61
forms
auction data model, 184
multi-purpose, 125-126
orders, 255-288
adding, 255-268
counters, 268-271
reviewing, 273-288
security, 271-273
printing, 158
search, 241-255
transactions/errors, 347-358
Web
adding interactivity, 106-115
registration, 127-130
servers, 123-126
FTP (File Transfer Protocol), 24, 44-45
functionality (Web projects), 15-16
functions, 195

G

generating traffic, 373-378
affiliate programs, 378
link exchanges, 377-378

paid banners, 378
partnerships, 377-378
search engines,
   374-377
spam, 377
sponsorships, 378
**get method, modifying,
123-126**
global variables, 264
goals
   user, 15
   Web projects, 13
graphics
   borders, 55-56
   copying, 50
   tags (HTML), 51

H

**hard drives, writing to,
319-326**
hard-coding
link locations, 74
hiding borders, 55-56
**hit counters, adding,
95**
home pages. *See*
   HTML documents
**horizontal lines,
adding, 72**
**hosting, discussion
groups, 366-367**
**HTML (HyperText
markup language),
29, 47**
   documents
      graphics, 50-56
      *starting interface,
      45-49*
      text, 52-56

files
   creating, 30
   *formatting text,
   30-32*
   images, 33-34
   links, 32-33
   if-then-else state-
      ments, 61
   structure tags, 47-49
   tables (Web forms),
      127-130
hyperlinks. *See also*
   links
   categories (store-
      fronts), 236-240
   icons, 53-54
   lists, 156
**HyperText Markup
Language.** *See* **HTML**

I

**icons, converting,
53-56**
**if-then-else state-
ments, 60**
   HTML, 61
IIS, 295
images, 50. *See also*
   graphics
   shells, 33-34
**implementing chat
rooms, 368**
importing
   files, 331-340
      FTP, 44-45
   product data, 326-340
   XML, 345-347
**include files, adding,
254**

**information architec-
ture, Web projects,
16-17, 19**
initializing
   applications, 267
   statements, 249
**Insert statement,
104-106**
inserting
   graphics into HTML
      documents, 50-56
   HTML structure tags,
      47-49
   interactivity into Web
      forms, 106-115
   links, 32-33
   records, 298-309
      databases, 100-102
   text into HTML doc-
      uments, 52-56
   data into auction data
      model, 201, 203
**installing Visual
InterDev Script
Library, 42**
InstantASP!, 23
integrity
   data, 180-181
**interactivity, adding to
Web forms, 106-115**
interface, 17
   design, 36-38
   SSI, 75-77
      commands, 80-83
   starting, 45-49
   user, 65-69
Internet. *See also* **Web**
   overview, 19-24
   Web sites
      *data modeling,
      115-120*
      *entities (data model-
      ing), 116-118*

inserting data (data modeling), 119-120
tables (data modeling), 118-119
items
adding, 312
modifying, 312
saving, 196

J-K

joining tables, 247
JScript, 58

keys, foreign, 180-181
keywords, search engines, 376

L

languages, configuring, 57-59
lines, adding, 72
links. *See also* **hyperlinks**
absolute links, 75
categories (storefronts), 236-240
content, 73
creating, 32-33
generating traffic, 377-378
icons, 53-56
lists, 156
selecting, 155
tags, 53-56

lists
archives, 84
categories (storefronts), 234-240
Content Rotator, 89-90
links, 156
orders (storefronts), 255-288
adding, 255-268
counters, 268-271
reviewing, 273-288
security, 271-273
products (storefronts), 241-255
local variables, 264
LockerType recordsets, 199-200
login
pages, 140
saving, 152
logos. *See also* **graphics; images**
adding, 50-56
logs
analyzing, 363-369
referrer, 364

M

Macintosh, 24
managing
security, 292-295
tables, 296-298
methods
get (Web forms), 123-126
post (Web forms), 123-126

Microsoft
Windows 2000, 20, 22-23
Windows 95/98/NT, 23
Script Debugger, 62
MIME-type, 369
models. *See* **auction data models**
modifying
forms (get/post methods), 123-126
news items, 312
modular codes, 261
multimedia plug-ins, 369-370
multi-purpose forms, 125-126
myAuctions, 216-225
myLinks, 298-309
preferences, 159
myNews
adding, 169
customizing, 166
myNews files, 309-319
mySpace, 365
customizing, 133-170
finalizing, 170-177

N

naming conventions, 140-149
navigating
archives, 87-88
folders/subfolders, 327-331
Network News Transfer Protocol. *See* **NNTP**

New Project command (File menu), 41
news, formatting, 319-326
Newsgroup Properties box, 367
newsgroups
configuring, 366
discussion groups, 366-367
spam, 377
NNTP (Network News Transfer Protocol), 366

O

objects, 59-61
ADO, 139-149
archives, 84-86
closing, 148
Err, 359-361
error handling, 120-123
files, 326-340
ODBC databases
creating, 98-100
creating connections (ADOs), 102-103
inserting records, 100-102
online catalogs. *See* **storefronts**
opening interfaces, 45-49
options, recordsets, 200
orders, 255-288

adding, 255-268
archiving, 354
counters, 268-271
reviewing, 273-288
security, 271-273
transactions/errors, 347-358
overview, Web, 19-24

P

Page Counter component, 95
page layout, customizing, 127
paid banners, generating traffic, 378
parsing data, 333
partnerships, generating traffic, 377-378
passwords, 139-149.
See also **security**
retrieving, 141
troubleshooting, 122
paths, creating, 27
payments, accepting, 284
permissions, configuring directories/files, 295
Personal Web Manager. *See* **PWM**
Personal Web Server, 62-63
personalizing
auction data model (myAuctions), 216-225

Web sites, 133-139
cookie expiration dates, 149-153
customizing mySpace, 154-170
finalizing mySpace, 170-177
planning Web projects, 12-19
plug-ins, 369-370
post method, modifying, 123-126
preferences
adding, 133-139
cookies
expiration dates, 149-153
properties, 152-153
customizing, 128
myLinks, 159
mySpace, 154-170
finalizing, 170-177
preformatted text, 71
press releases, 378
Primary Outpost, creating, 367
printing
dates, 59
forms, 158
privacy, cookies, 135-136
processing
orders, 348
storefronts, 255-288
search forms, 245
products
category listings, 234-240
orders, 255-288
adding, 255-268
counters, 268-271

reviewing, 273-288
security, 271-273
searching, 241-255
storefront capabilities,
232-234
programs. *See* **applications**
**Project menu com-
mands, Add Web
Item, 43**
projects
Visual InterDev,
41-43
Web
content, 15-16
defining, 12-19
goals, 13
*information architec-
ture, 16-17*
target audiences, 14
user goals, 15
**properties, cookies,
152-153**
protocols
FTP, 44-45
NNTP, 366
**publicizing Web sites,
373-378**
affiliate programs, 378
links exchanges,
377-378
paid banners, *378*
partnerships, 377-378
search engines,
374-377
spam, *377*
sponsorships, 378
**PWM (Personal Web
Manager), 24-27**
directories, 27-28

Q-R

**querying databases,
139-149**
QuickTime, 369-370

**radio buttons, adding,
113**
reading files, 326-340
real estate. *See* **interface**
RealAudio, 369-370.
See also **plug-ins**
records
adding, 303
creating, 304
databases, 100-102
modifying, 298-309
recordsets, 197
ActiveConnection,
198
CursorType, 198-199
LockType, 199-200
options, 200
passwords/usernames,
139-149
sources, 197-198
referrer log, 364
**registration forms,
127-130**
relative links, 75
relative references, 34
renaming files, 323
**researching audiences,
363-369**
**Response Write,
applying, 60**
**retrieving
passwords/usernames,
141**
**reviewing orders,
273-288**

S

saving
cookie collections,
136-139
data 9XML), 340-343
items, 196
login data, 152
myLinks
*in databases,
298-309*
preferences, 159
uploaded files, 317
Script Debugger, 62
scripts, 154
**search engines,
374-377**
searching
dynamic SQL state-
ments, 248
forms, 241-255
products, 241-255
wildcards, 251
**sections, customizing,
133-139**
security
servers, 292-295
tables, 296-298
storefronts, 271-273
session values, 260
selecting links, 155
Server Side Include.
See **SSI**
servers
files, 319-326
myNews files,
309-319
security, 292-295
tables, 296-298
Server Side
Debugging, 62
Web forms, 123-126
XML, 343

shells
building, 29-34
HTML, 29
creating files, 30
formatting text,
30-32
images, 33-34
links, 32-33
ShockWave, 369-370.
See also **plug-ins**
shopping carts
capabilities, 232-234
category listings,
234-240
orders, 255-288
adding, 255-268
counters, 268-271
reviewing, 273-288
security, 271-273
products, 241-255
signatures, electronic,
272. *See also* **security**
sound, 369-370
sources
recordsets, 197-198
space, customizing,
154-164. *See also*
mySpace
spam, 377
spanning columns, 130
sponsorships, generat-
ing traffic, 378
spreadsheets, 326-340
SQL
databases, 104-106
dynamic statements,
248
SSI (Server Side
Include), 75, 75-77
ASP commands
translating, 82
commands, 80-83

starting
applications, 267
interface, 45-49
Visual InterDev,
41-43
statements
dynamic SQL, 248
error, 120-123
if-then-else, 60
HTML, 61
initializing, 249
SQL databases,
104-106
storefronts
capabilities, 232-234
category listings,
234-240
orders, 255-288
adding, 255-268
counters, 268-271
reviewing, 273-288
security, 271-273
products, 241-255
storing
data (XML), 340-343
myLinks in databases,
298-309
streaming media, 369
structure tags
(HTML), adding,
47-49
subfolders, navigating,
327, 329-331
submitting
forms (auction data
model), 184
passwords/usernames,
139-149
subpages, creating,
34-35
support, browsers,
370-372

T

tables
data modeling,
118-119
inserting, 119-120
databases, 101
data modeling,
118-119
editing, 301
HTML (Web forms),
127-130
joining, 247
viewing, 296-298
tags (HTML)
browsers
troubleshooting, 48
graphics, 51
links, 53-56
structure, 47-49
target audiences, Web
projects, 14
templates, security,
293-295
text
ASP, 58
cookies. *See* cookies
files, 319
formatting, 30-32
preformatted, 71
third party compo-
nents (auction data
model), 225-229
titles, adding, 81
tools
logs, 363-369
Visual InterDev,
41-43
tracking. *See also* **coun-**
ters

content, 133-139
  *cookie expiration
    dates, 149-153*
  *cookie properties,
    152-153*
customers, 268-271
data, 116-118
  inserting, 119-120
  tables, 118-119
traffic
  affiliate programs, 378
  generating, 373-378
  link exchanges,
    377-378
  paid banners, 378
  partnerships, 377-378
  search engines,
    374-377
  spam, 377
  sponsorships, 378
transactions, 347-358
transforming XML,
  343
translating ASP com-
  mands (SSI), 82
troubleshooting
  code, 62
  passwords, 122
    usernames, 143
  tags (HTML)
    browsers, 48
  transactions, 347-358
  Web pages, 120-123

U

Uniform Resource
  Locators. *See* URLs
updating records,
  298-309

uploading
  files, 24
    saving, 317
  myNews files,
    309-319
upsizing databases, 368
Upsizing Wizard, 368
URLs (Uniform
  Resource Locators),
  46
  encoding, 189
usability testing, 17
Usenet newsgroups.
  See newsgroups
usernames, 139-149
  retrieving, 141
users
  choices
  deleting, 163
  goals, Web projects,
    15
  interface, 65-69
  links, 155

V

values, sessions, 260
variables
  applications, 265
  global, 264
VBScript, 57-59
  browser capabilities,
    370-372
  formatting, 59-61
Verisign, Web site, 272
video, 369-370
viewing
  DSNs, 99
  tables, 296-298
virtual paths, creating,
  27

Virtual Server
  (NNTP), 366
Visual InterDev, 41-43

W-Z

Web. *See also* Internet
  forms, 106-114
    *adding interactivity,
      115*
    *registration,
      127-130*
    servers, 123-126
  overview, 19-24
  pages
    *adding content,
      69-74*
    adding links, 69
    SSI, 75-83
    user interface, 65-69
  projects
    content, 15-16
    defining, 12-19
    goals, 13
    *information architec-
      ture, 16-19*
  target audiences, 14
    user goals, 15
  sites. *See* Web sites
Web forms, HTML
  tables, 127-130
Web pages, trou-
  bleshooting, 120-123
Web sites
  ADO, 139-149
  AdRotator, 90-94
  affiliate programs, 378
  archives, 83-90
  audience, 363-367,
    369

banner ads, 90-94
browser capabilities,
  370-372
chat rooms, 368
Content Rotator,
  89-90
cookies
  adding, 133-139
  expiration dates,
    149-153
  properties, 152-153
customizing, 369-372
data modeling,
  115-120
  entities, 116-118
  inserting data,
    119-120
  tables, 118-119
design, 77-80
interface design,
  36-38
link exchanges,
  377-378
mySpace
  customizing,
    154-170
  finalizing, 170-177
newsgroups, 367
Page Counter compo-
  nent, 95
paid banners, 378
partnerships, 377-378
personalizing,
  133-139
publicizing, 373-378
search engines,
  374-377
spam, 377
sponsorships, 378
subpages, 34-35
Verisign, 272

WebTrends, 363
wildcards, adding, 251
Windows 2000, 20,
  22-23
Windows 95/98/NT,
  23
wizards, Upsizing, 368
writing
  text files, 319
  to hard drives,
    319-326

XML (eXtensible
  Markup Language),
  340-343
  creating, 344-345
  importing, 345-347
XSL (eXtensible Style
  Sheet), 341

Yahoo!, 374. *See also*
  search engines

CD-ROM Installation

Windows 95/NT Installation Instructions

1. Insert the CD-ROM disc into your CD-ROM drive.
2. From the Windows 95/NT desktop, double-click on the My Computer icon.
3. Double-click on the icon representing your CD-ROM drive.
4. Double-click on the icon titled START.EXE to run the CD-ROM interface.

 Note If Windows 95/NT is installed on your computer and you have the AutoPlay feature enabled, the START.EXE program starts automatically whenever you insert the disc into your CD-ROM drive.

Macintosh Installation Instructions

1. Insert the CD-ROM disc into your CD-ROM drive.
2. Open the ReadMe file which contains a list of the CD-ROM contents.